ARCANA

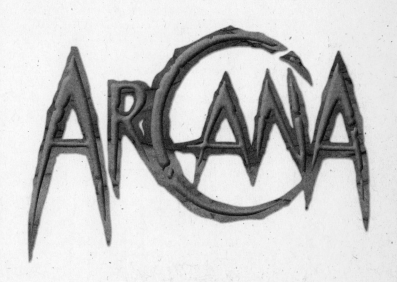

Arcana Vol. 5
Created by So-Young Lee

Translation - Ellen Choi
English Adaption - Barbara Randall Kesel
Copy Editor - Stephanie Duchin
Retouch and Lettering - Star Print Brokers
Production Artist - Lucas Rivera
Cover Design - James Lee

Editor - Bryce P. Coleman
Digital Imaging Manager - Chris Buford
Pre-Production Supervisor - Erika Terriquez
Art Director - Anne Marie Horne
Production Manager - Elisabeth Brizzi
Managing Editor - Vy Nguyen
VP of Production - Ron Klamert
Editor-in-Chief - Rob Tokar
Publisher - Mike Kiley
President and C.O.O. - John Parker
C.E.O. and Chief Creative Officer - Stuart Levy

A  Manga

TOKYOPOP and  are trademarks or registered trademarks of TOKYOPOP Inc.

TOKYOPOP Inc.
5900 Wilshire Blvd. Suite 2000
Los Angeles, CA 90036

E-mail: info@TOKYOPOP.com
Come visit us online at www.TOKYOPOP.com

ISBN: 978-1-59816-902-7

First TOKYOPOP printing: January 2007
10 9 8 7 6 5 4 3 2 1
Printed in the USA

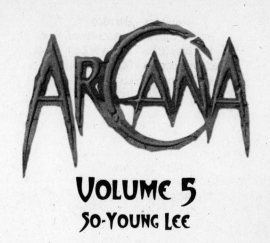

VOLUME 5
SO-YOUNG LEE

HAMBURG // LONDON // LOS ANGELES // TOKYO

The Journey Thus Far...

As the group continues their dangerous mission to locate the guardian dragon that will protect Inez's homeland, even more secrets are uncovered. It seems that Yulan has a history with the being residing within Inez, known as "The One," and it is a conflicted history at that. The mysterious Kyrette desires the dragon essence Inez carries for his own, as of yet undisclosed, purposes. And Inez begins to question whether or not she should be entrusted with such a crucial assignment...

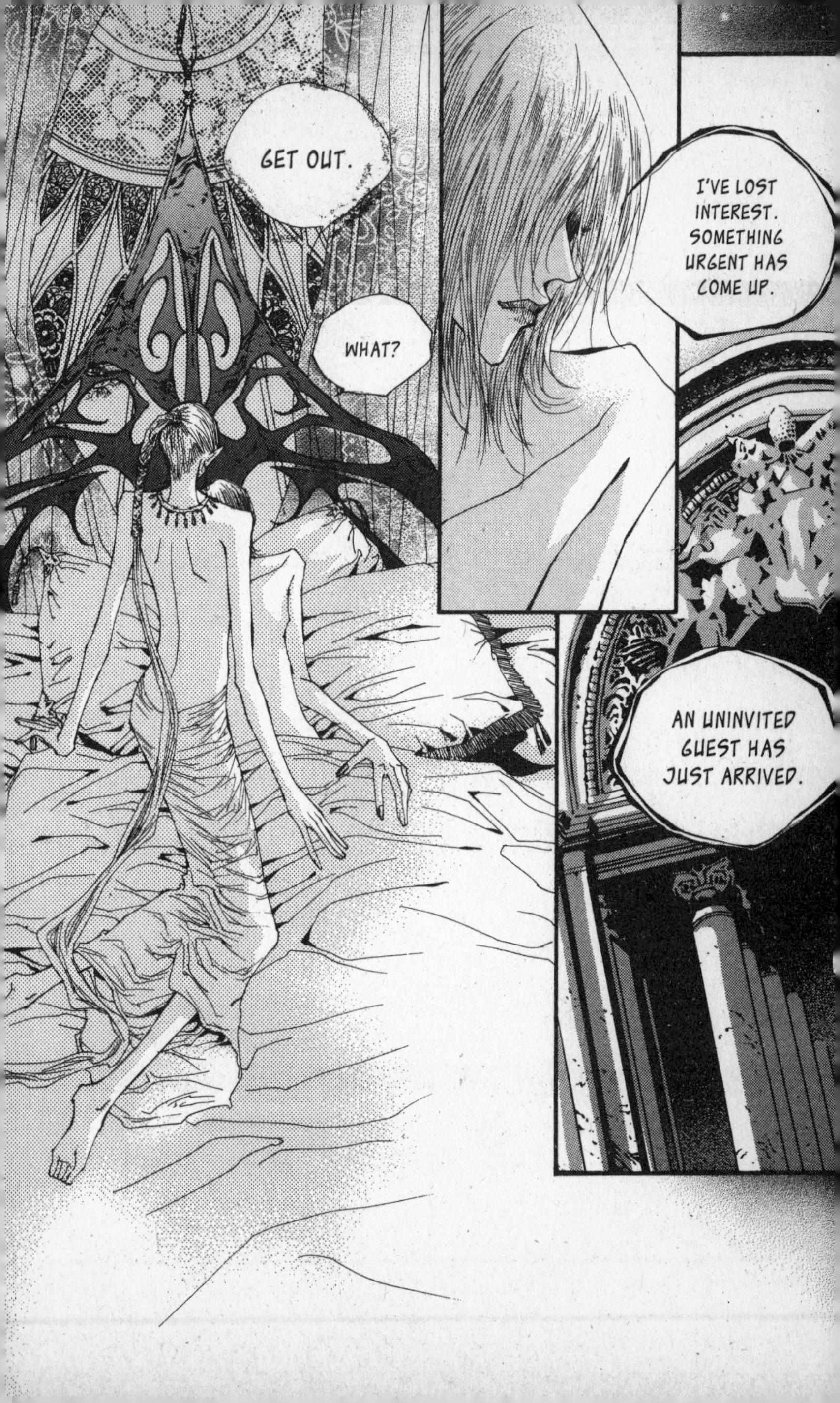
GET OUT.
WHAT?
I'VE LOST INTEREST. SOMETHING URGENT HAS COME UP.
AN UNINVITED GUEST HAS JUST ARRIVED.

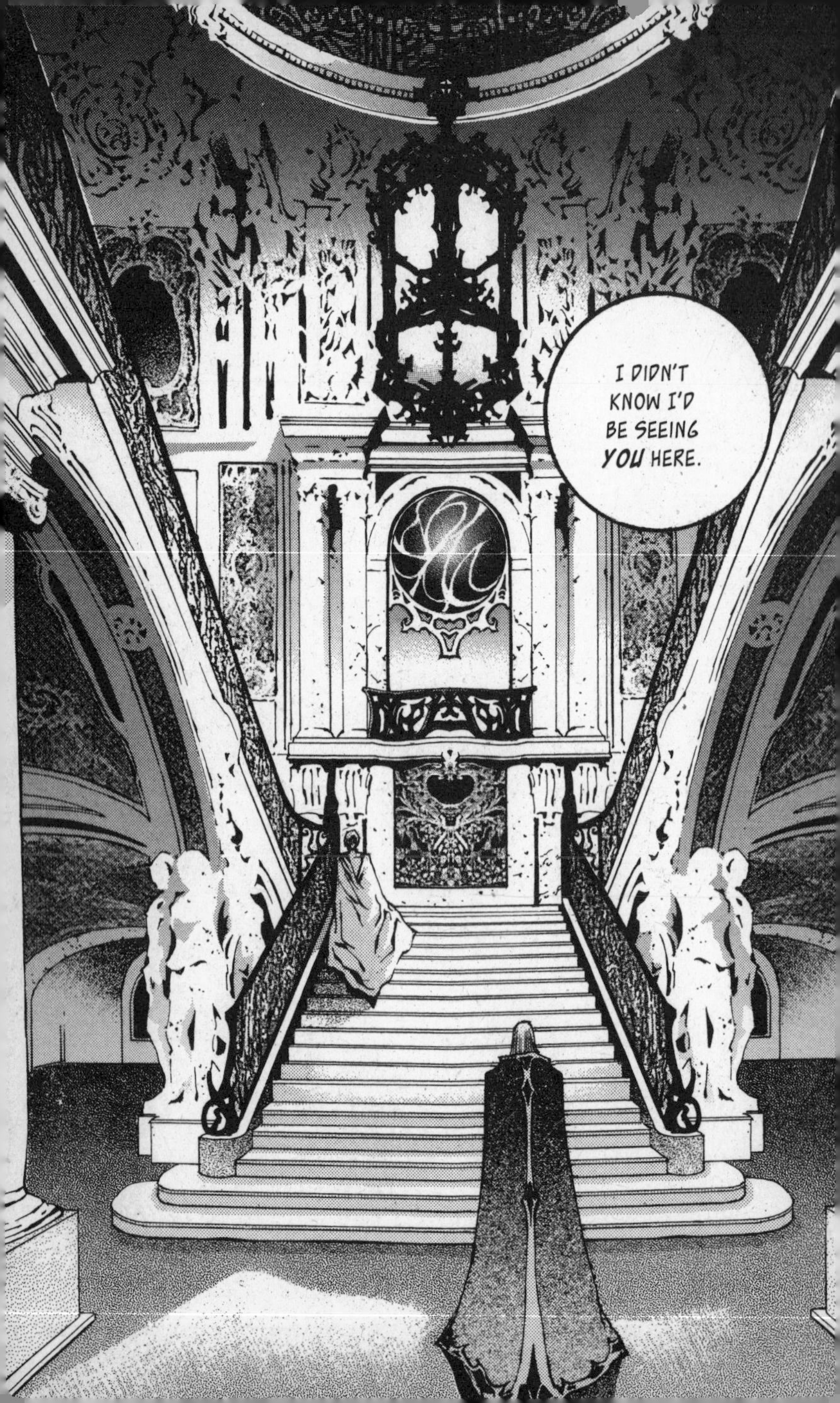
I DIDN'T KNOW I'D BE SEEING YOU HERE.

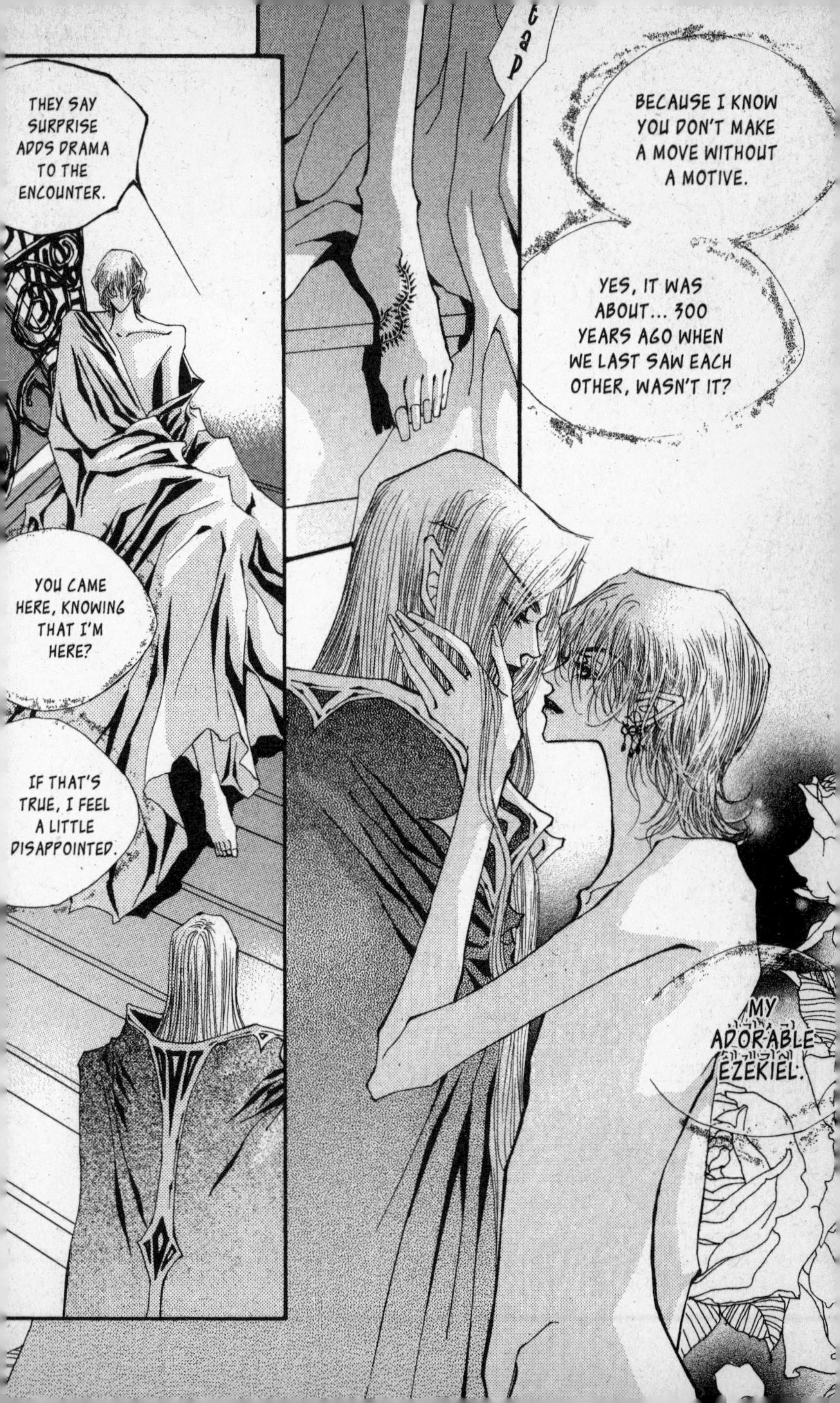
THEY SAY SURPRISE ADDS DRAMA TO THE ENCOUNTER.
YOU CAME HERE, KNOWING THAT I'M HERE?
IF THAT'S TRUE, I FEEL A LITTLE DISAPPOINTED.
tap
BECAUSE I KNOW YOU DON'T MAKE A MOVE WITHOUT A MOTIVE.
YES, IT WAS ABOUT... 300 YEARS AGO WHEN WE LAST SAW EACH OTHER, WASN'T IT?
MY ADORABLE EZEKIEL.

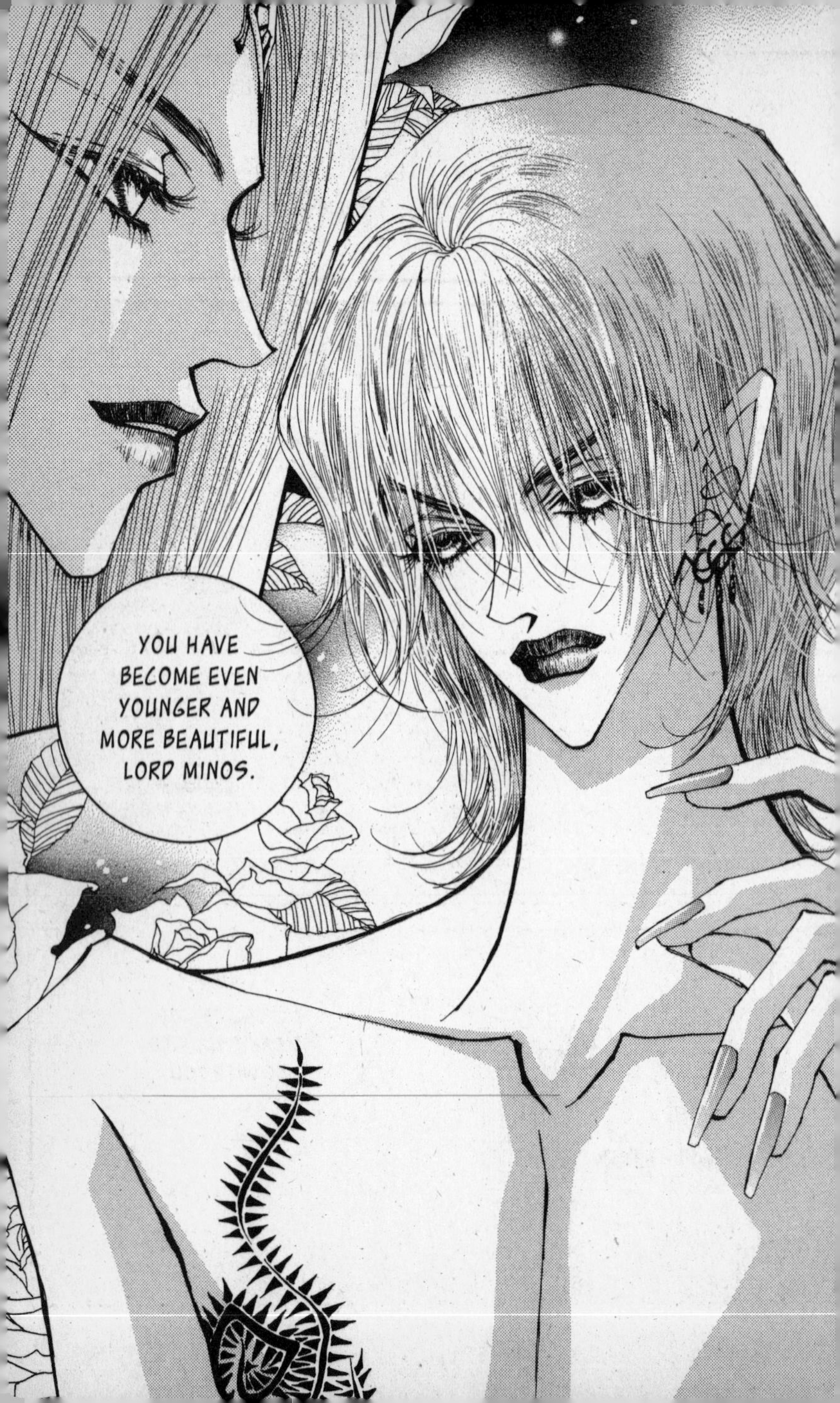
YOU HAVE BECOME EVEN YOUNGER AND MORE BEAUTIFUL, LORD MINOS.

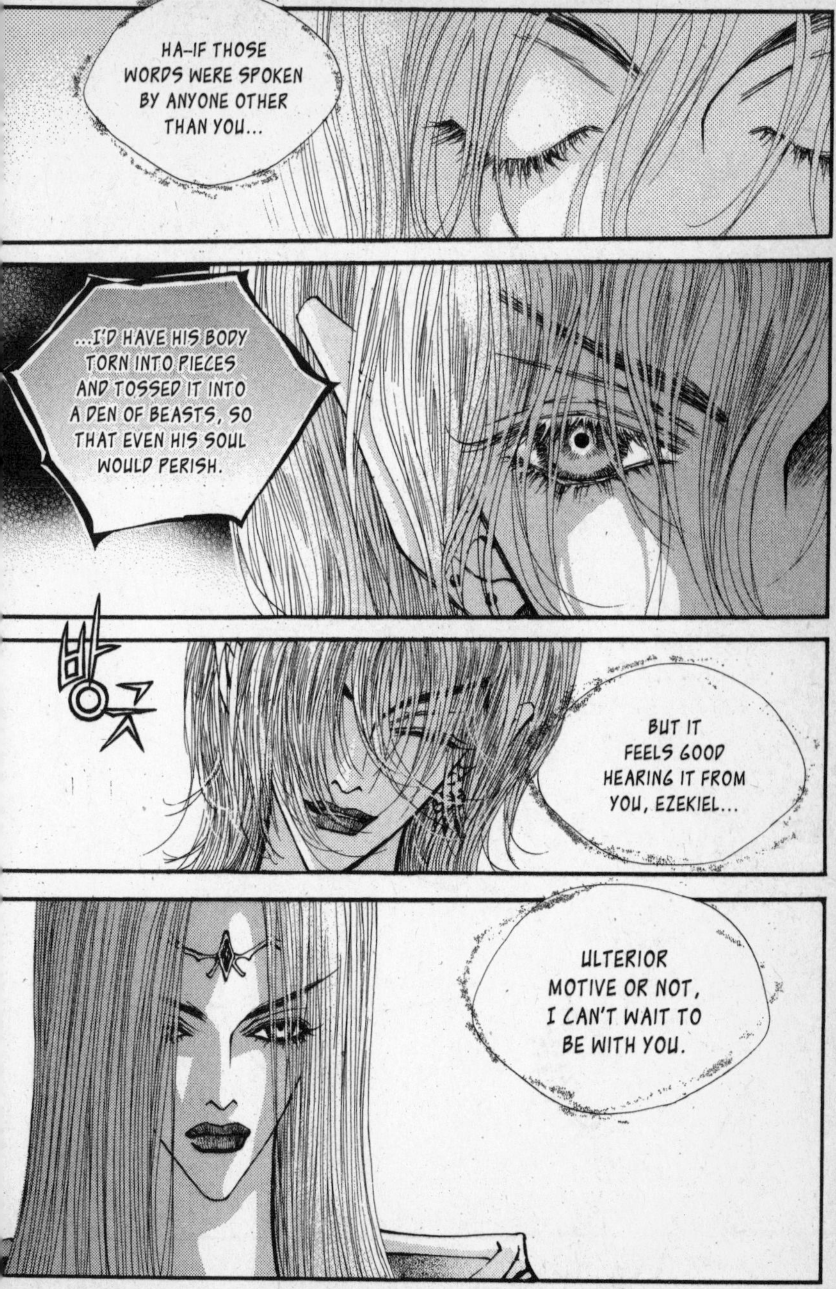
HA–IF THOSE WORDS WERE SPOKEN BY ANYONE OTHER THAN YOU...
...I'D HAVE HIS BODY TORN INTO PIECES AND TOSSED IT INTO A DEN OF BEASTS, SO THAT EVEN HIS SOUL WOULD PERISH.
BUT IT FEELS GOOD HEARING IT FROM YOU, EZEKIEL...
ULTERIOR MOTIVE OR NOT, I CAN'T WAIT TO BE WITH YOU.

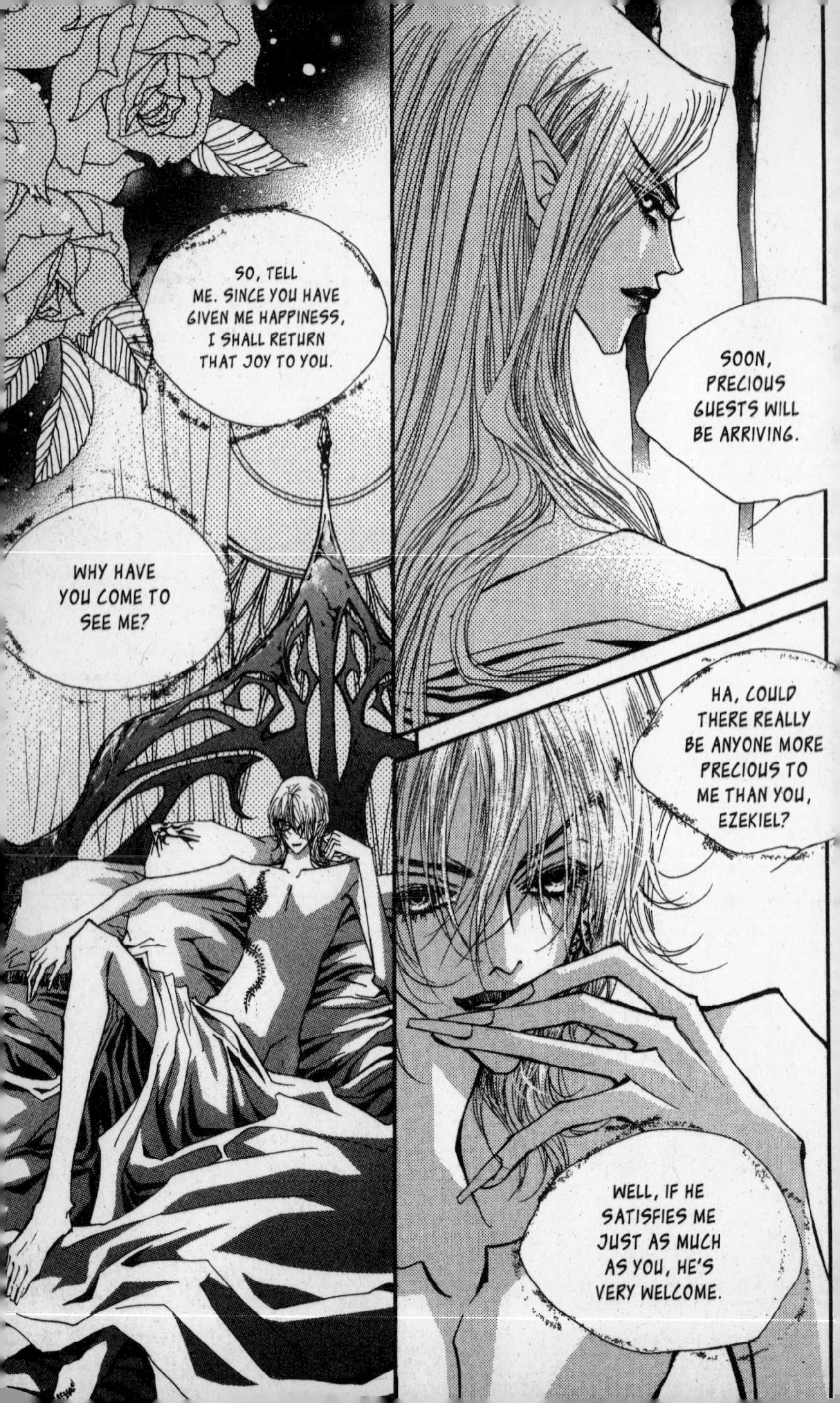
SO, TELL ME. SINCE YOU HAVE GIVEN ME HAPPINESS, I SHALL RETURN THAT JOY TO YOU.
WHY HAVE YOU COME TO SEE ME?
SOON, PRECIOUS GUESTS WILL BE ARRIVING.
HA, COULD THERE REALLY BE ANYONE MORE PRECIOUS TO ME THAN YOU, EZEKIEL?
WELL, IF HE SATISFIES ME JUST AS MUCH AS YOU, HE'S VERY WELCOME.

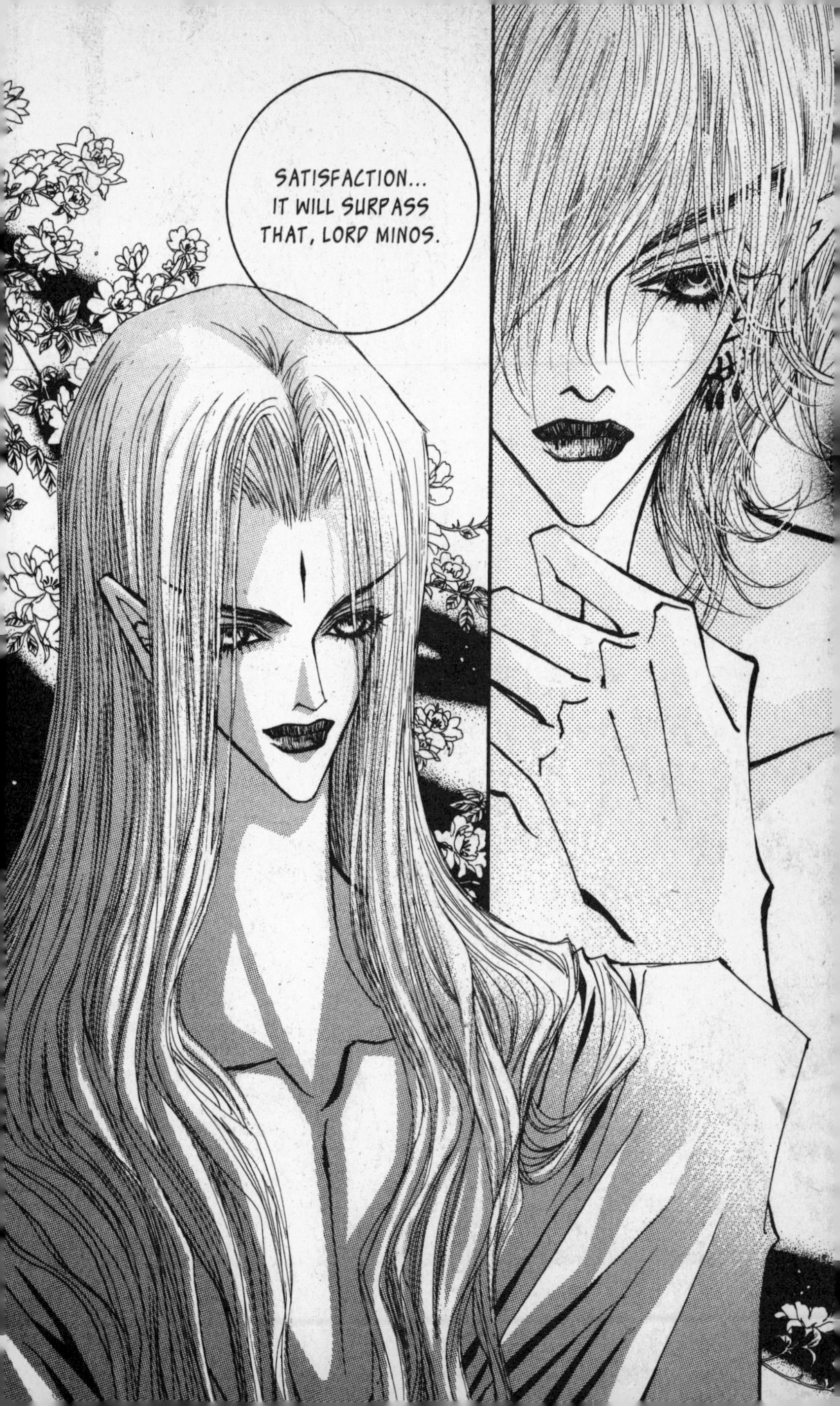
SATISFACTION... IT WILL SURPASS THAT, LORD MINOS.

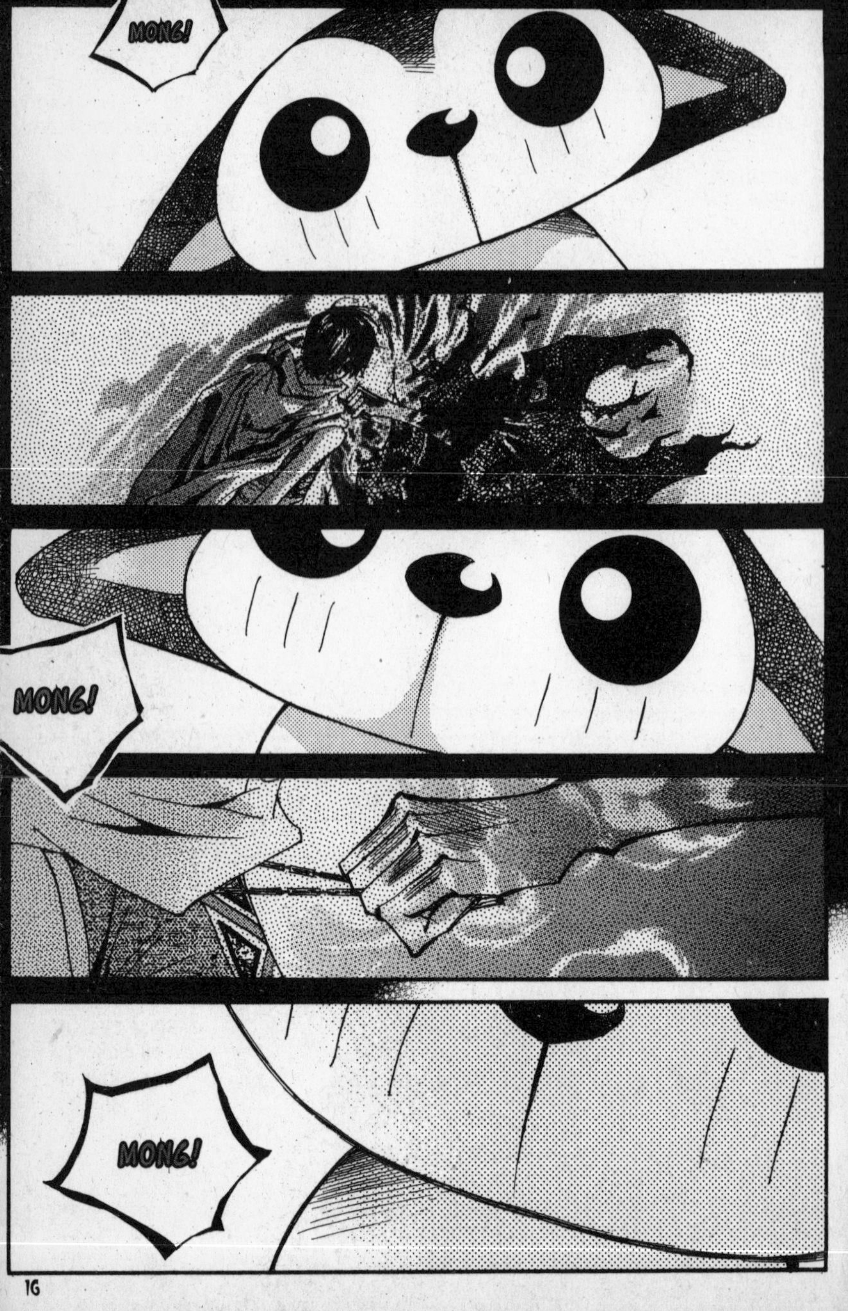
MONG!
MONG!
MONG!

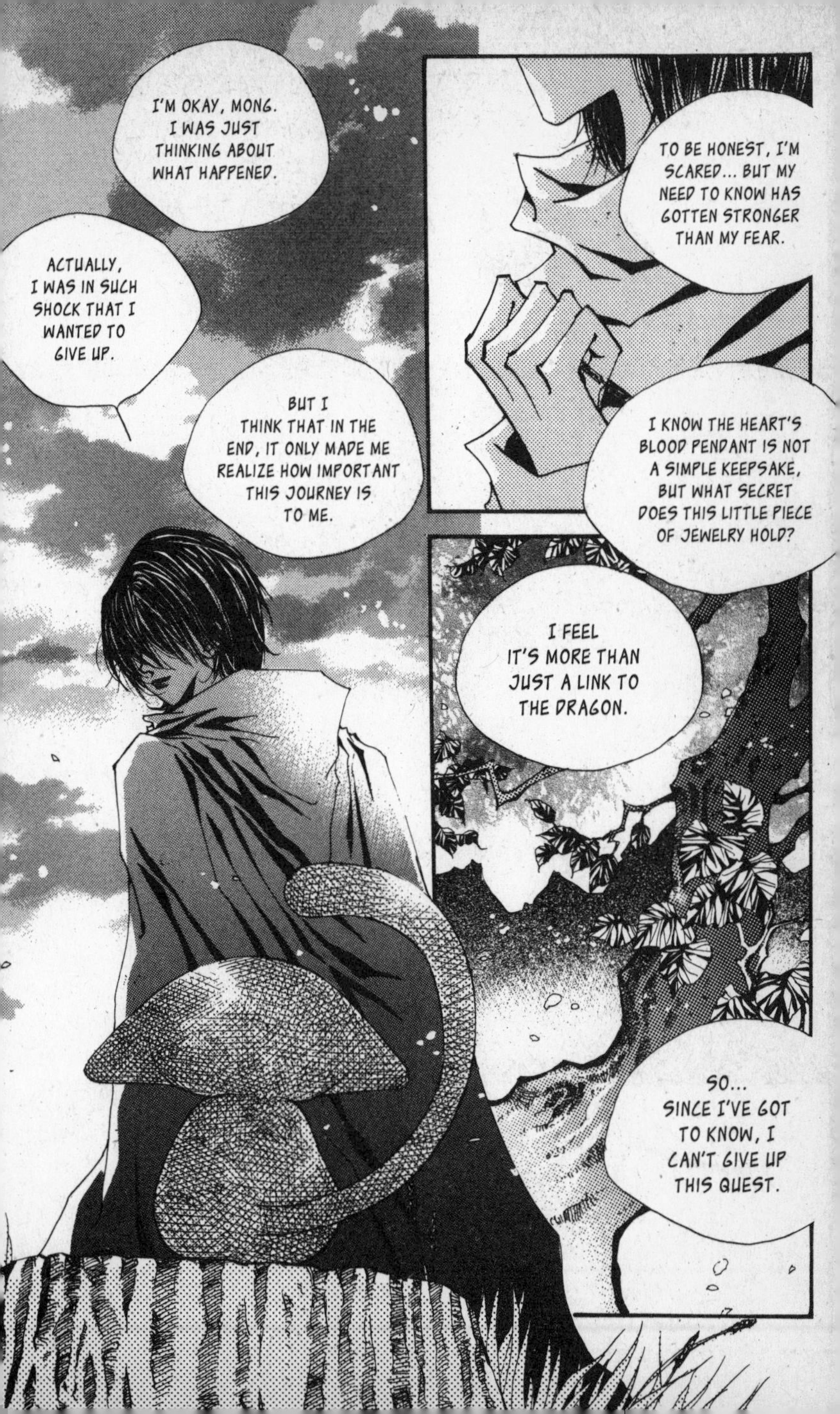
I'M OKAY, MONG. I WAS JUST THINKING ABOUT WHAT HAPPENED.
ACTUALLY, I WAS IN SUCH SHOCK THAT I WANTED TO GIVE UP.
BUT I THINK THAT IN THE END, IT ONLY MADE ME REALIZE HOW IMPORTANT THIS JOURNEY IS TO ME.
TO BE HONEST, I'M SCARED... BUT MY NEED TO KNOW HAS GOTTEN STRONGER THAN MY FEAR.
I KNOW THE HEART'S BLOOD PENDANT IS NOT A SIMPLE KEEPSAKE, BUT WHAT SECRET DOES THIS LITTLE PIECE OF JEWELRY HOLD?
I FEEL IT'S MORE THAN JUST A LINK TO THE DRAGON.
SO... SINCE I'VE GOT TO KNOW, I CAN'T GIVE UP THIS QUEST.

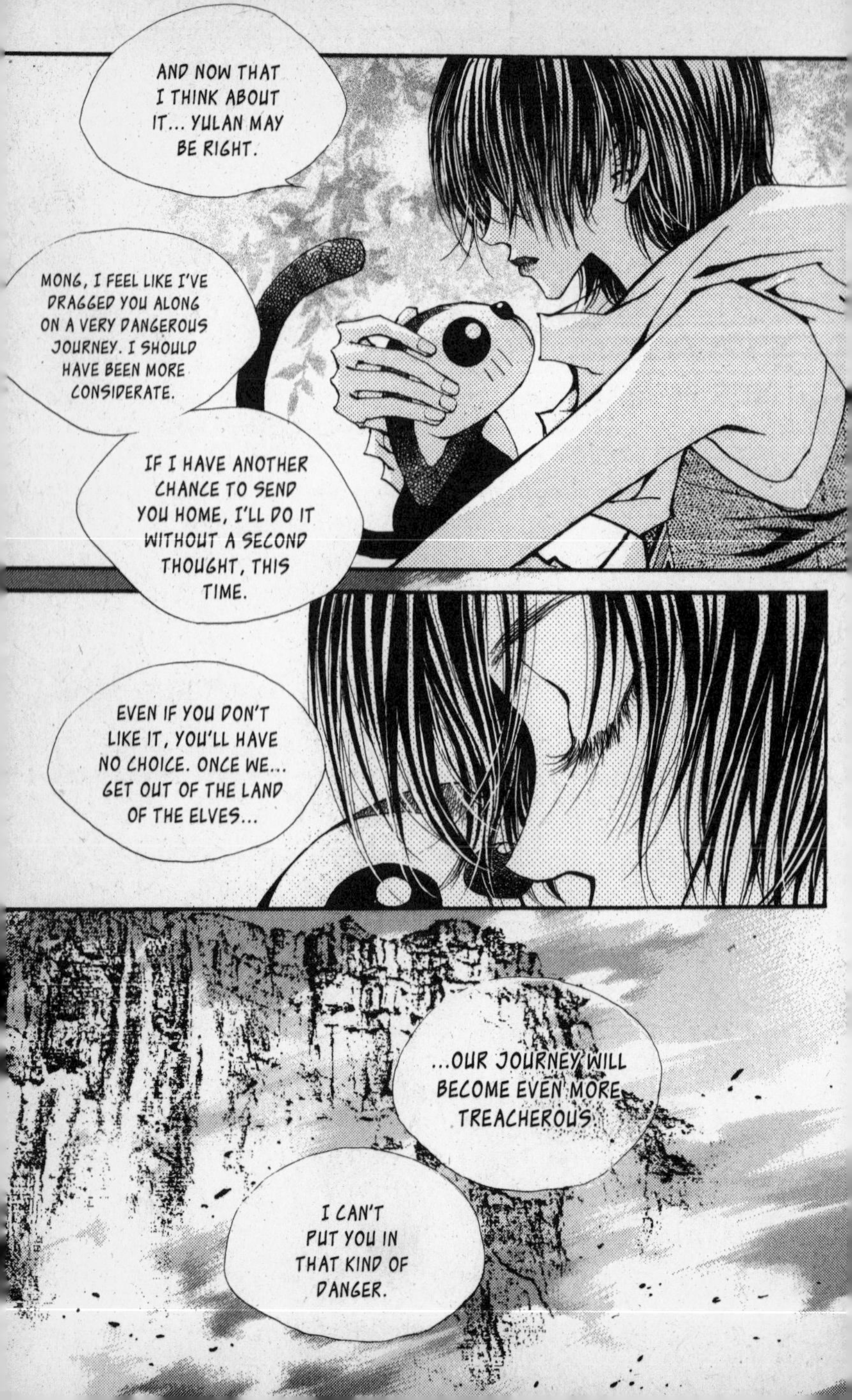
AND NOW THAT I THINK ABOUT IT... YULAN MAY BE RIGHT.
MONG, I FEEL LIKE I'VE DRAGGED YOU ALONG ON A VERY DANGEROUS JOURNEY. I SHOULD HAVE BEEN MORE CONSIDERATE.
IF I HAVE ANOTHER CHANCE TO SEND YOU HOME, I'LL DO IT WITHOUT A SECOND THOUGHT, THIS TIME.
EVEN IF YOU DON'T LIKE IT, YOU'LL HAVE NO CHOICE. ONCE WE... GET OUT OF THE LAND OF THE ELVES...
...OUR JOURNEY WILL BECOME EVEN MORE TREACHEROUS.
I CAN'T PUT YOU IN THAT KIND OF DANGER.

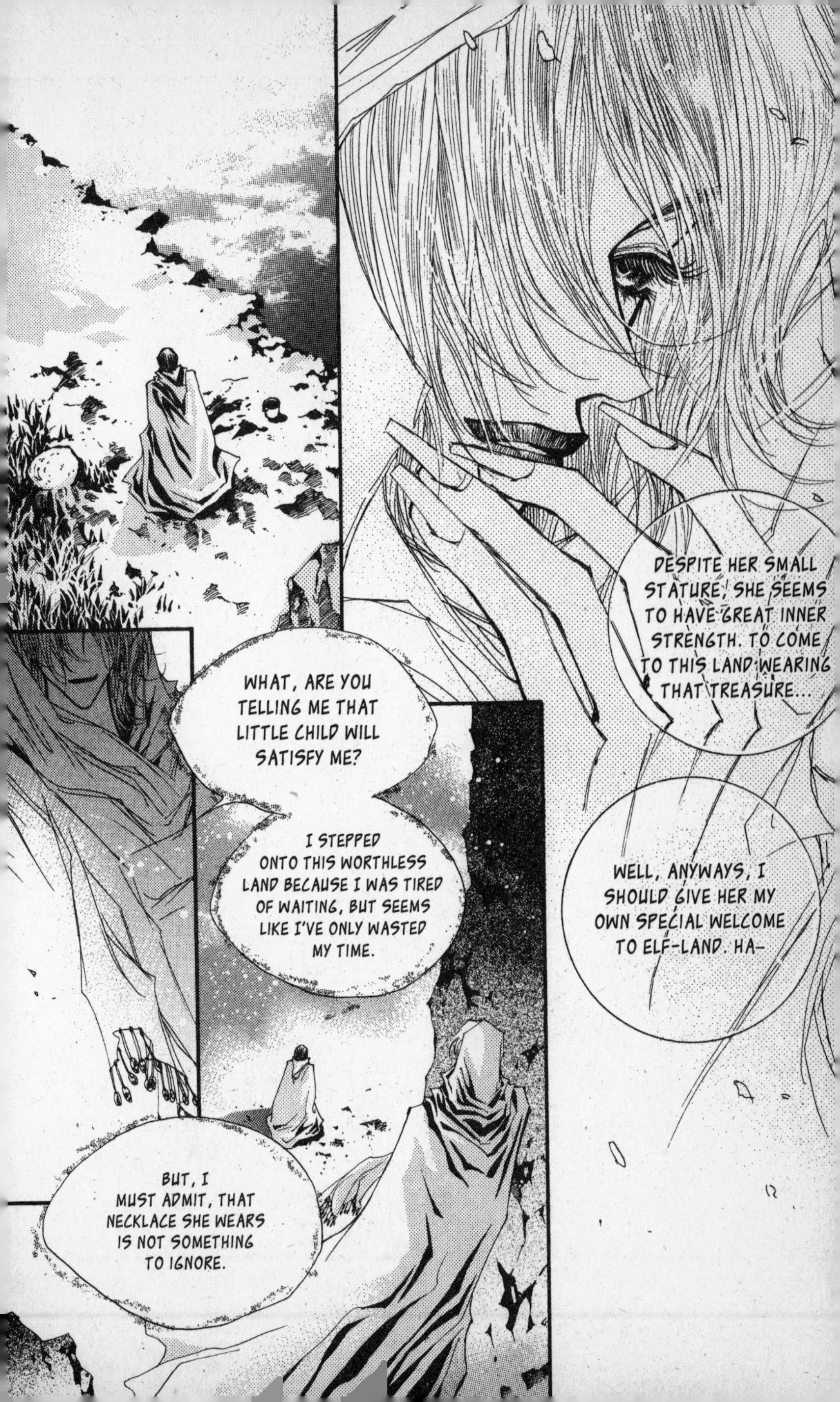
WHAT, ARE YOU TELLING ME THAT LITTLE CHILD WILL SATISFY ME?
I STEPPED ONTO THIS WORTHLESS LAND BECAUSE I WAS TIRED OF WAITING, BUT SEEMS LIKE I'VE ONLY WASTED MY TIME.
BUT, I MUST ADMIT, THAT NECKLACE SHE WEARS IS NOT SOMETHING TO IGNORE.
DESPITE HER SMALL STATURE, SHE SEEMS TO HAVE GREAT INNER STRENGTH. TO COME TO THIS LAND WEARING THAT TREASURE...
WELL, ANYWAYS, I SHOULD GIVE HER MY OWN SPECIAL WELCOME TO ELF-LAND. HA-

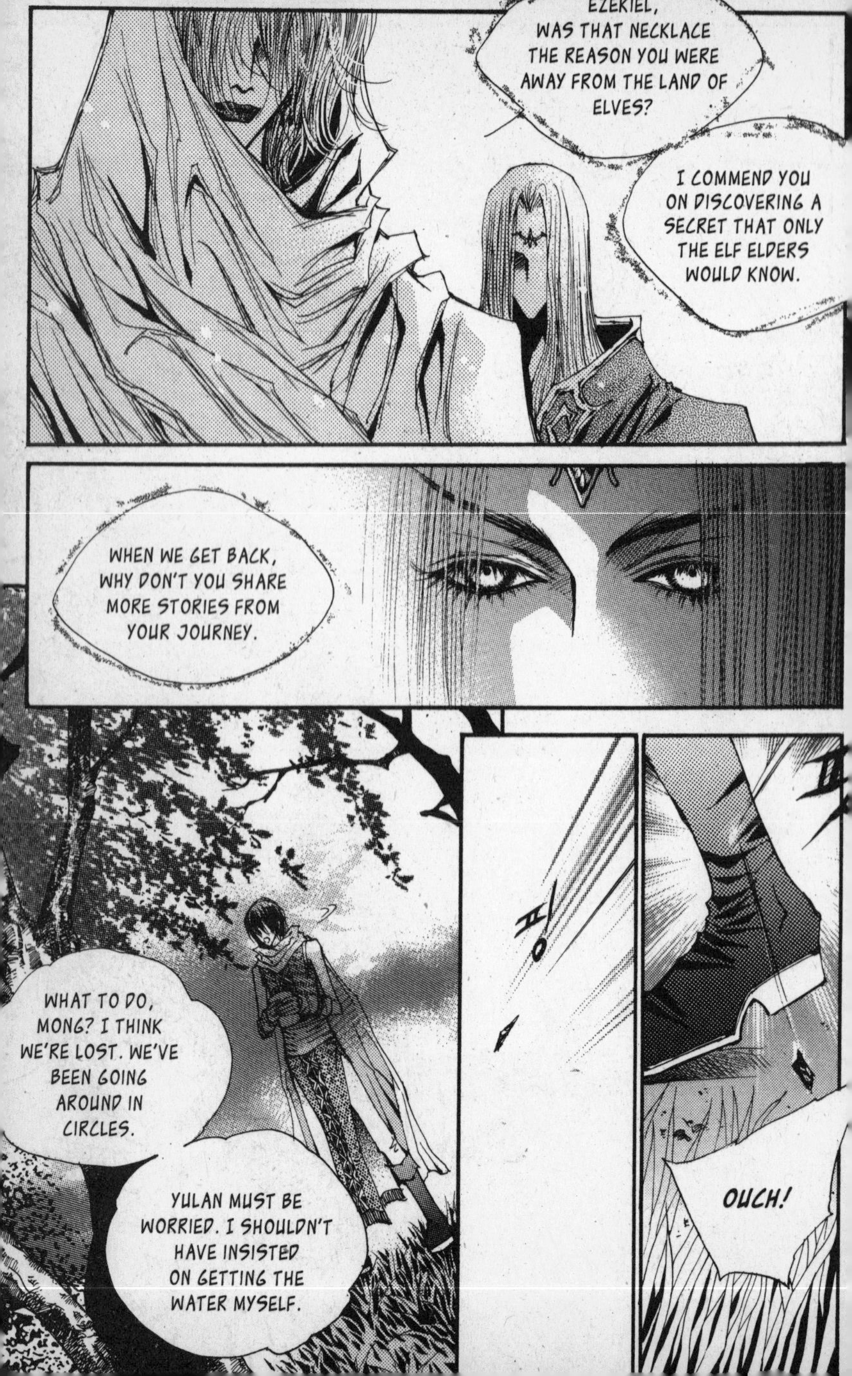
EZEKIEL, WAS THAT NECKLACE THE REASON YOU WERE AWAY FROM THE LAND OF ELVES?
I COMMEND YOU ON DISCOVERING A SECRET THAT ONLY THE ELF ELDERS WOULD KNOW.
WHEN WE GET BACK, WHY DON'T YOU SHARE MORE STORIES FROM YOUR JOURNEY.
WHAT TO DO, MONG? I THINK WE'RE LOST. WE'VE BEEN GOING AROUND IN CIRCLES.
YULAN MUST BE WORRIED. I SHOULDN'T HAVE INSISTED ON GETTING THE WATER MYSELF.
OUCH!

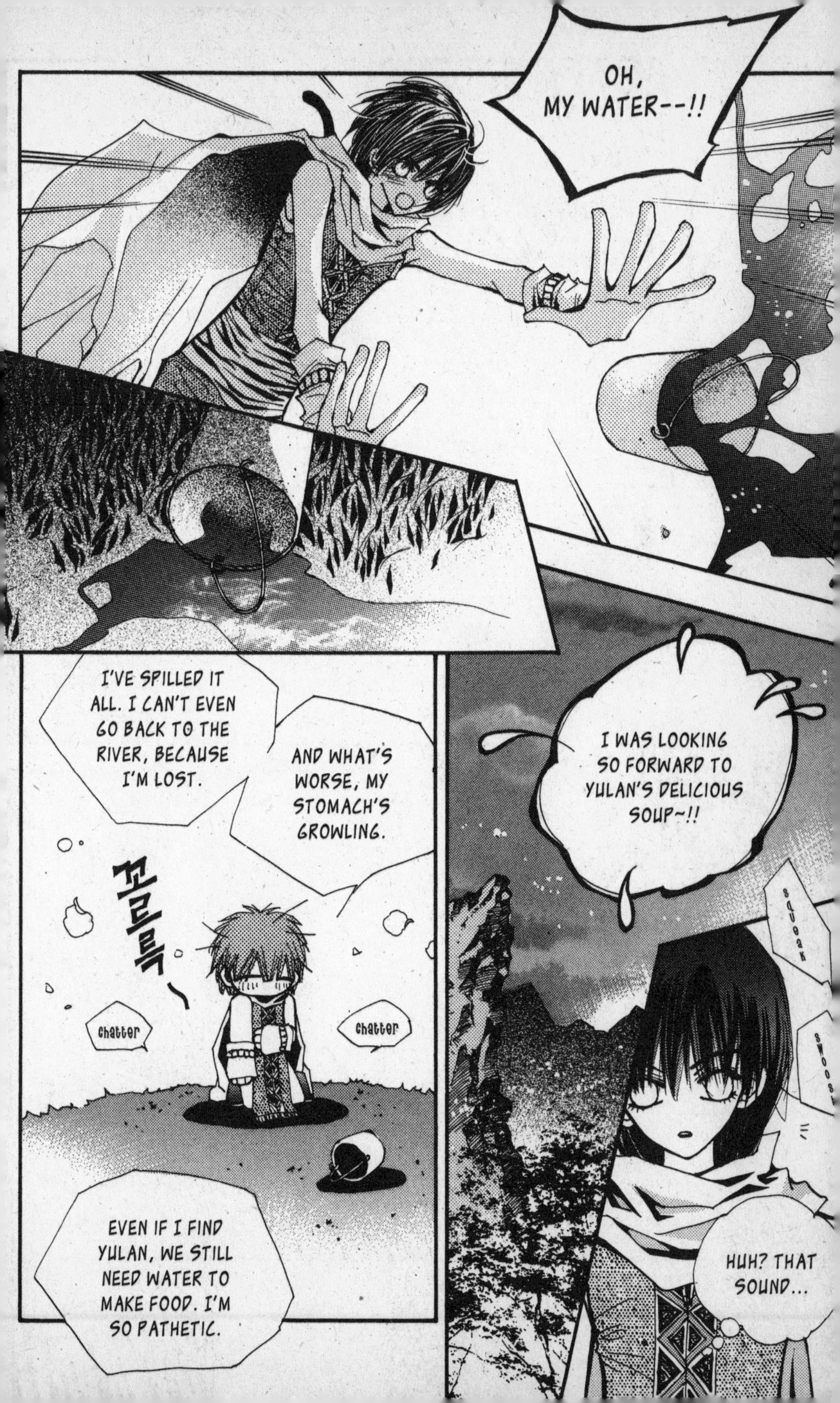
OH, MY WATER--!!
I'VE SPILLED IT ALL. I CAN'T EVEN GO BACK TO THE RIVER, BECAUSE I'M LOST.
AND WHAT'S WORSE, MY STOMACH'S GROWLING.
꼬르륵~
chatter
chatter
EVEN IF I FIND YULAN, WE STILL NEED WATER TO MAKE FOOD. I'M SO PATHETIC.
I WAS LOOKING SO FORWARD TO YULAN'S DELICIOUS SOUP~!!
squeak
HUH? THAT SOUND...

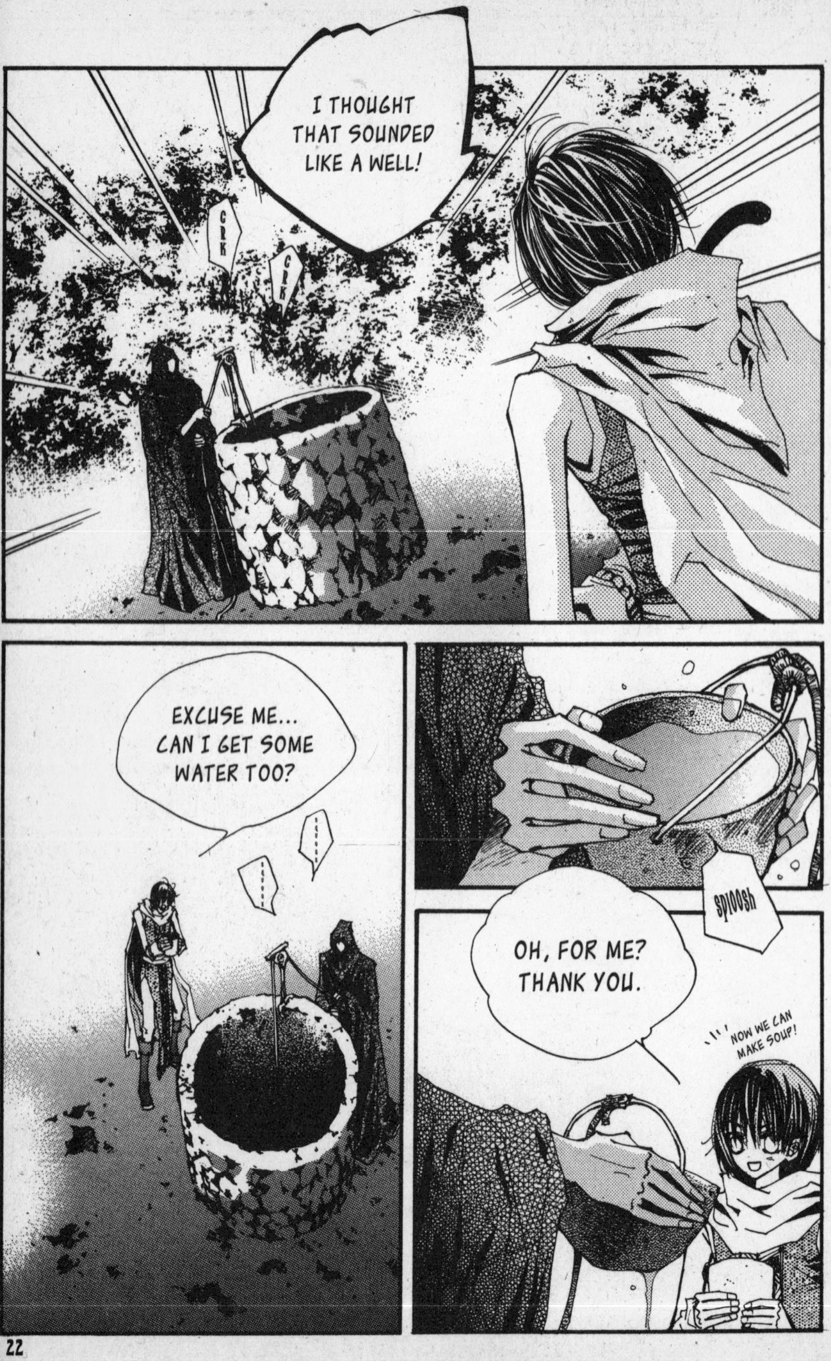
I THOUGHT THAT SOUNDED LIKE A WELL!
CRK
CRK
EXCUSE ME... CAN I GET SOME WATER TOO?
SPLOOSH
OH, FOR ME? THANK YOU.
NOW WE CAN MAKE SOUP!

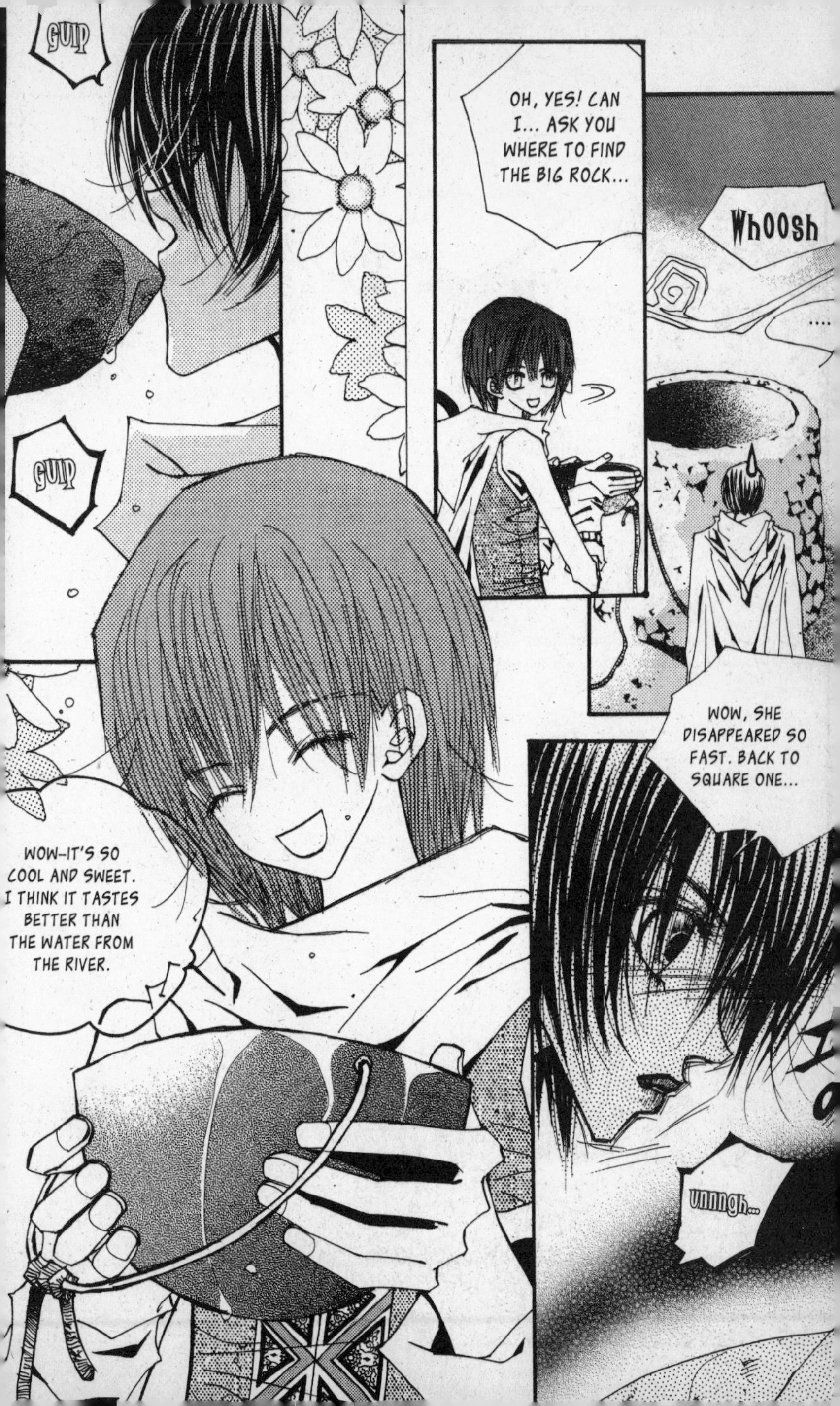
GULP
GULP
OH, YES! CAN I... ASK YOU WHERE TO FIND THE BIG ROCK...
WHOOSH
....
WOW—IT'S SO COOL AND SWEET. I THINK IT TASTES BETTER THAN THE WATER FROM THE RIVER.
WOW, SHE DISAPPEARED SO FAST. BACK TO SQUARE ONE...
UNNNGH...

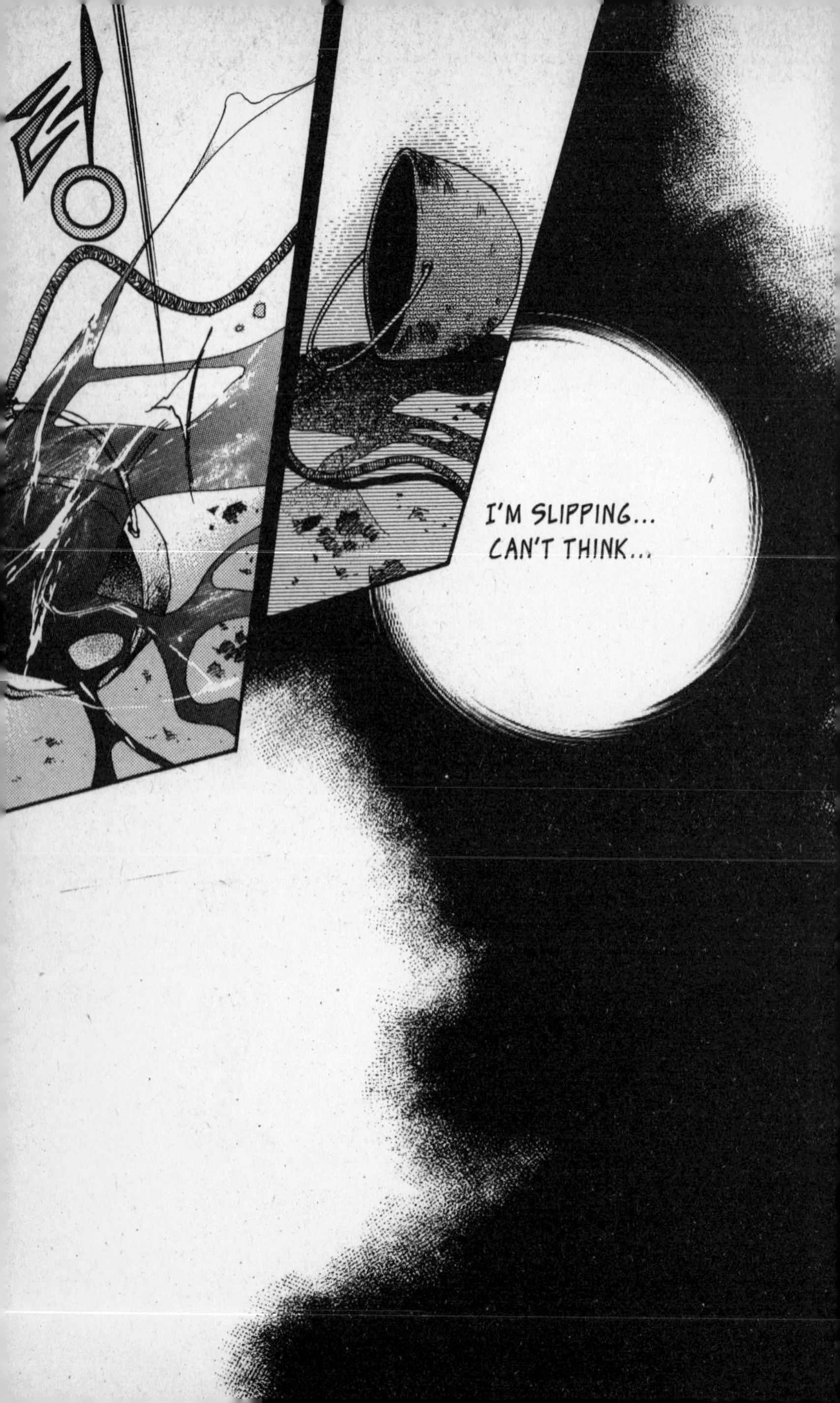
I'M SLIPPING...
CAN'T THINK...

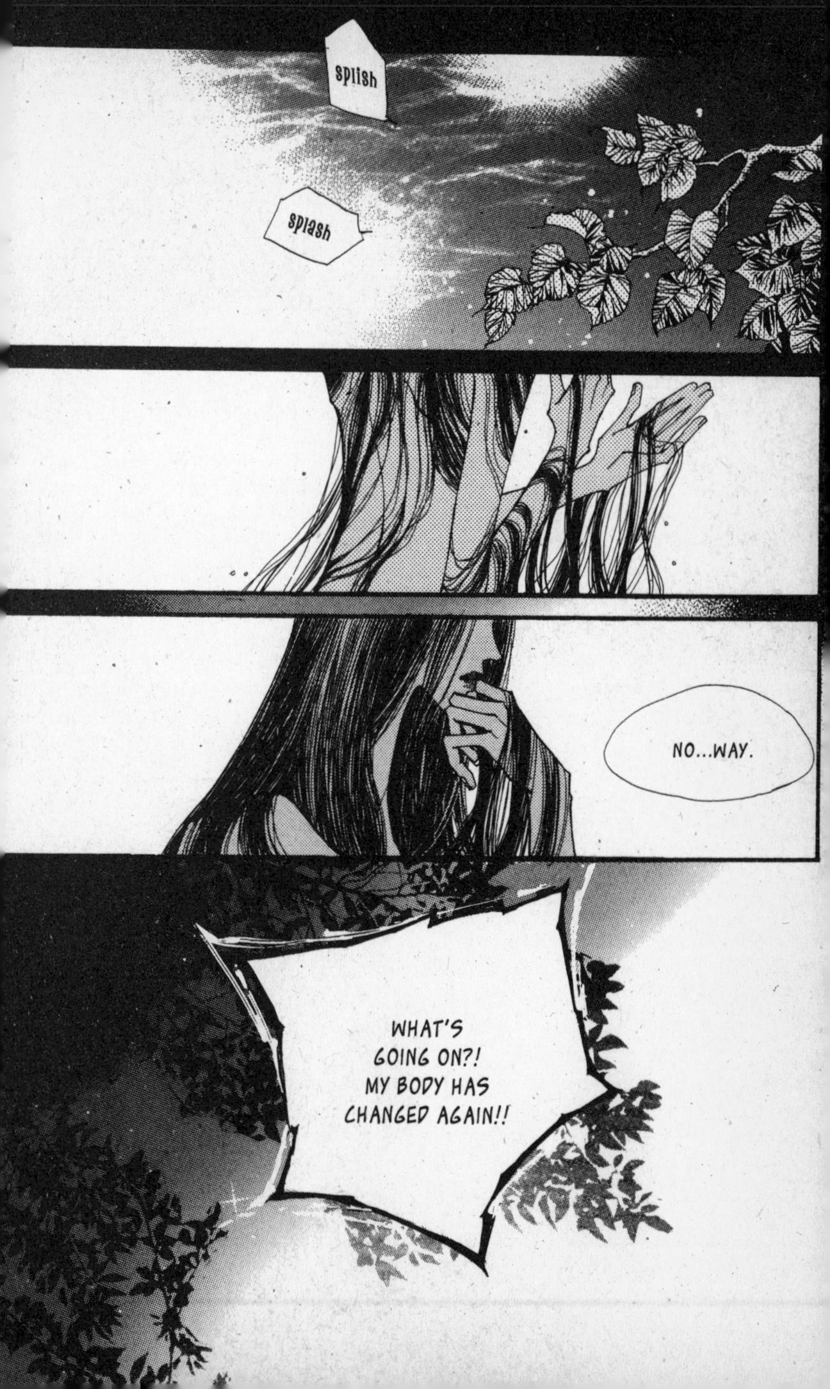
splish
splash
NO...WAY.
WHAT'S GOING ON?! MY BODY HAS CHANGED AGAIN!!

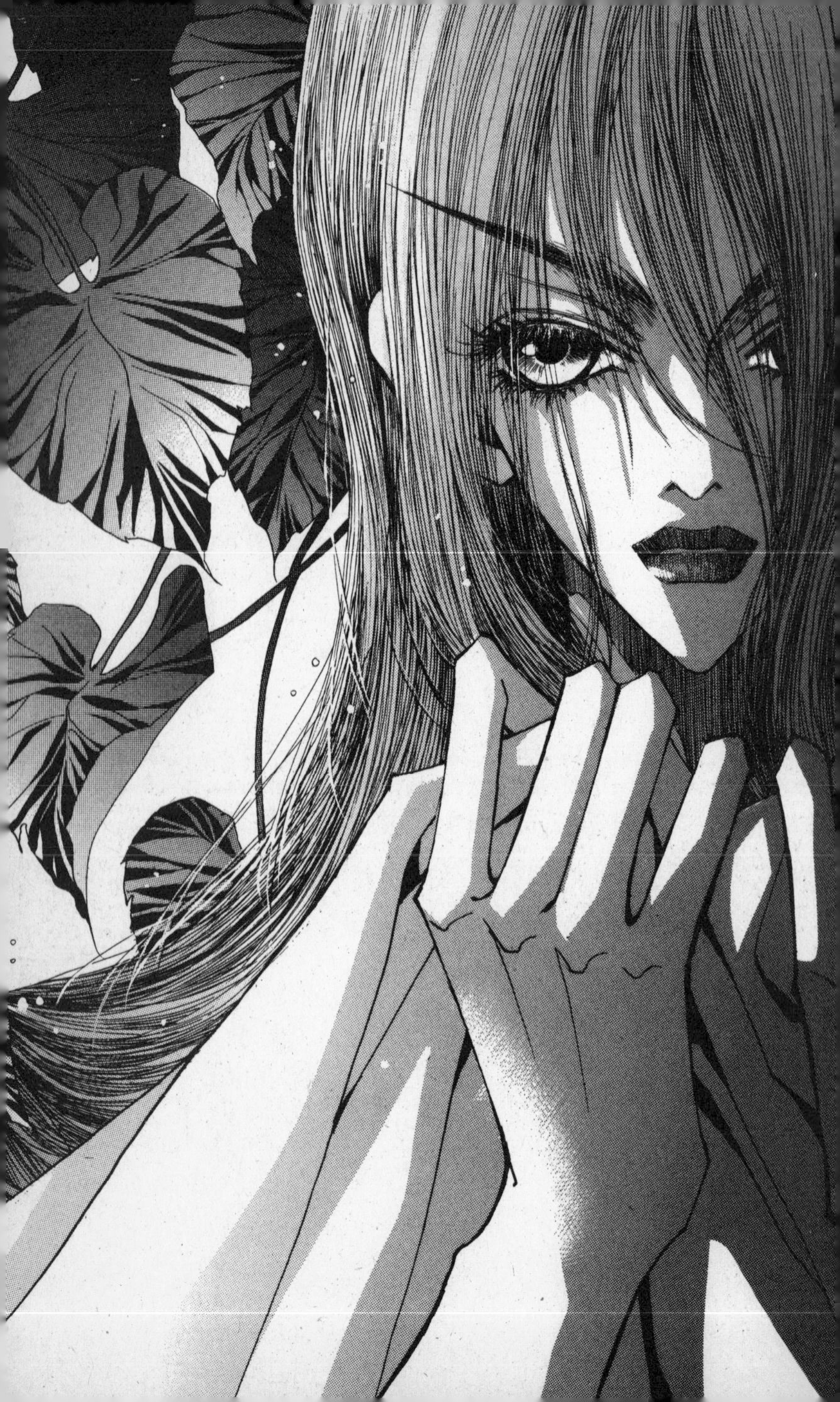

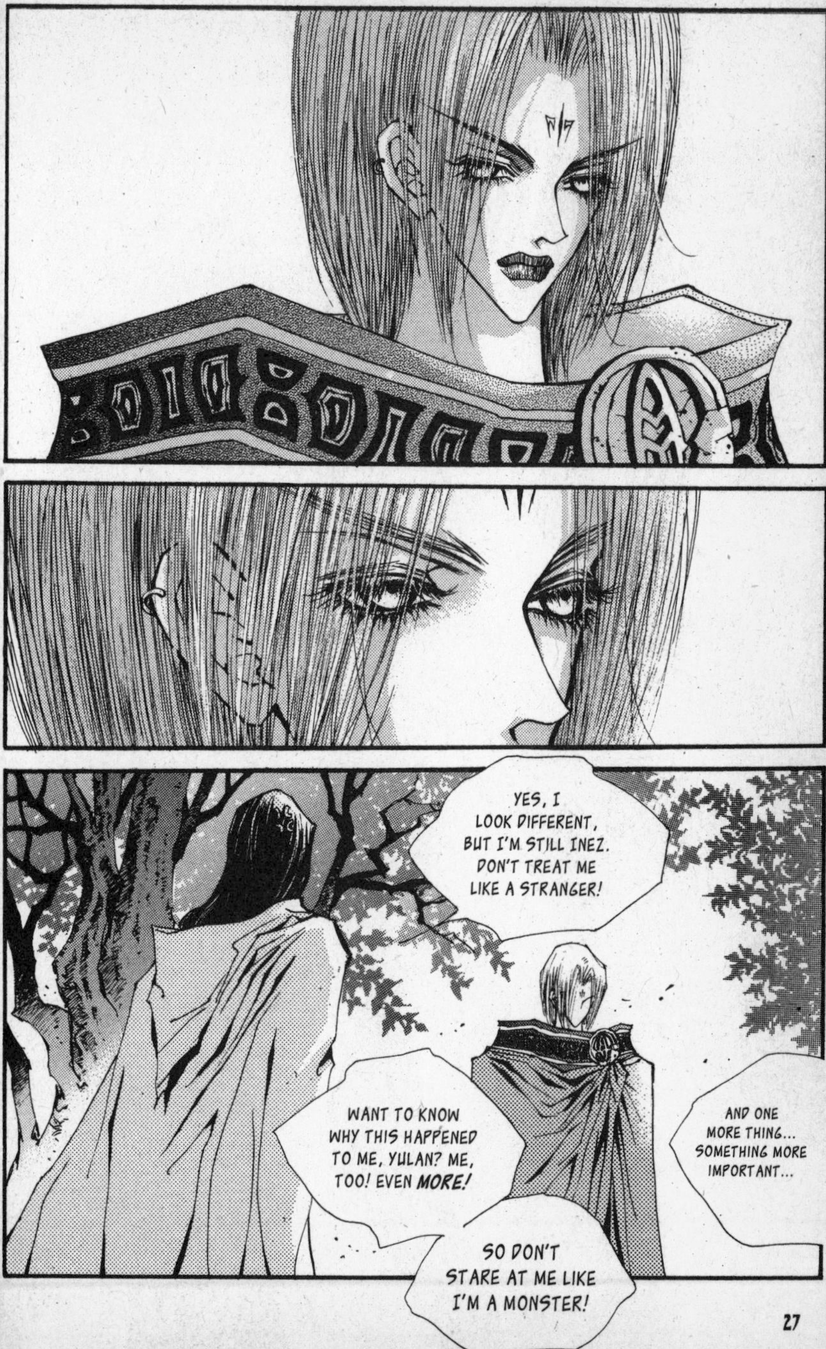
YES, I LOOK DIFFERENT, BUT I'M STILL INEZ. DON'T TREAT ME LIKE A STRANGER!
WANT TO KNOW WHY THIS HAPPENED TO ME, YULAN? ME, TOO! EVEN *MORE!*
SO DON'T STARE AT ME LIKE I'M A MONSTER!
AND ONE MORE THING... SOMETHING MORE IMPORTANT...

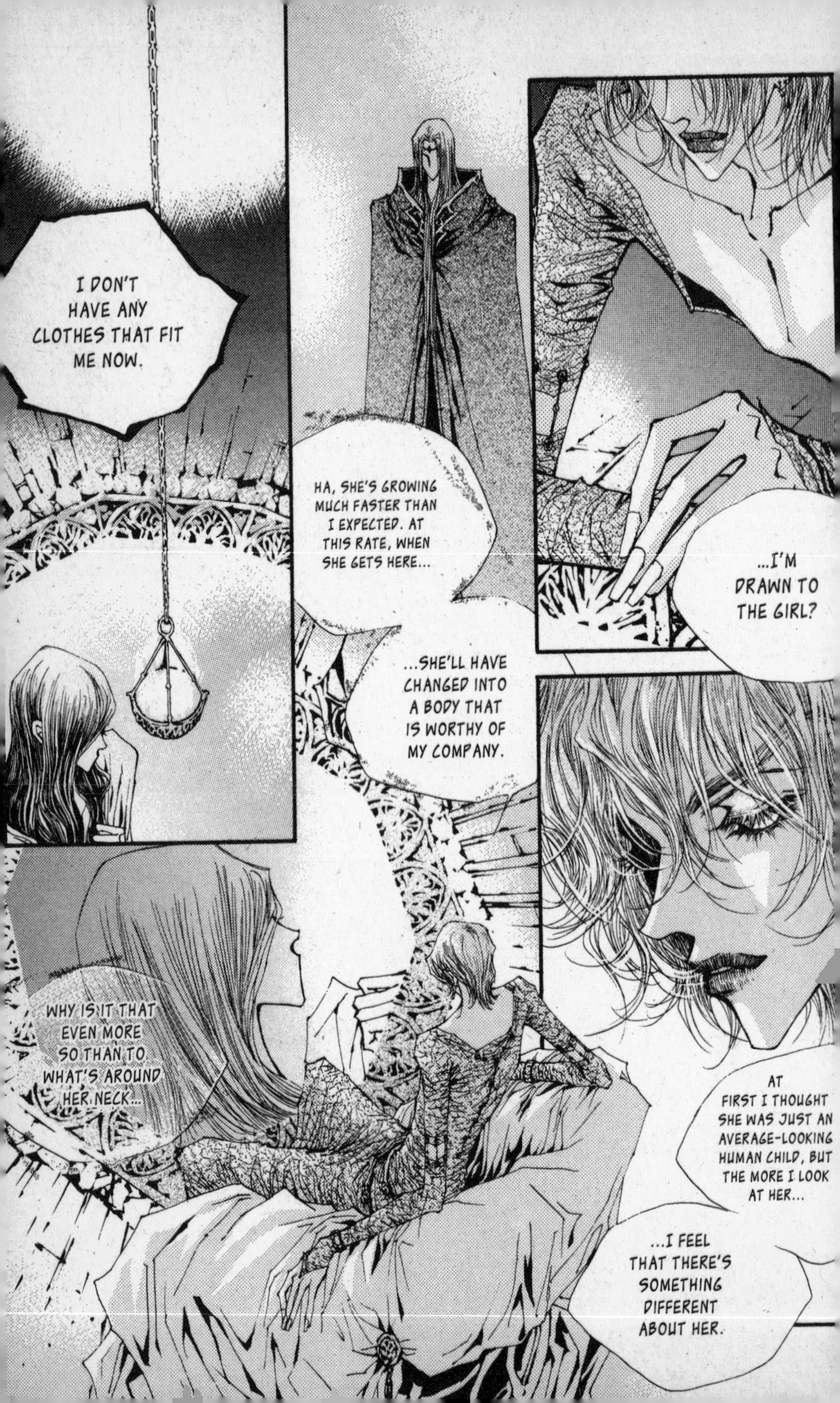

I DON'T HAVE ANY CLOTHES THAT FIT ME NOW.
HA, SHE'S GROWING MUCH FASTER THAN I EXPECTED. AT THIS RATE, WHEN SHE GETS HERE...
...SHE'LL HAVE CHANGED INTO A BODY THAT IS WORTHY OF MY COMPANY.
...I'M DRAWN TO THE GIRL?
WHY IS IT THAT EVEN MORE SO THAN TO WHAT'S AROUND HER NECK...
AT FIRST I THOUGHT SHE WAS JUST AN AVERAGE-LOOKING HUMAN CHILD, BUT THE MORE I LOOK AT HER...
...I FEEL THAT THERE'S SOMETHING DIFFERENT ABOUT HER.

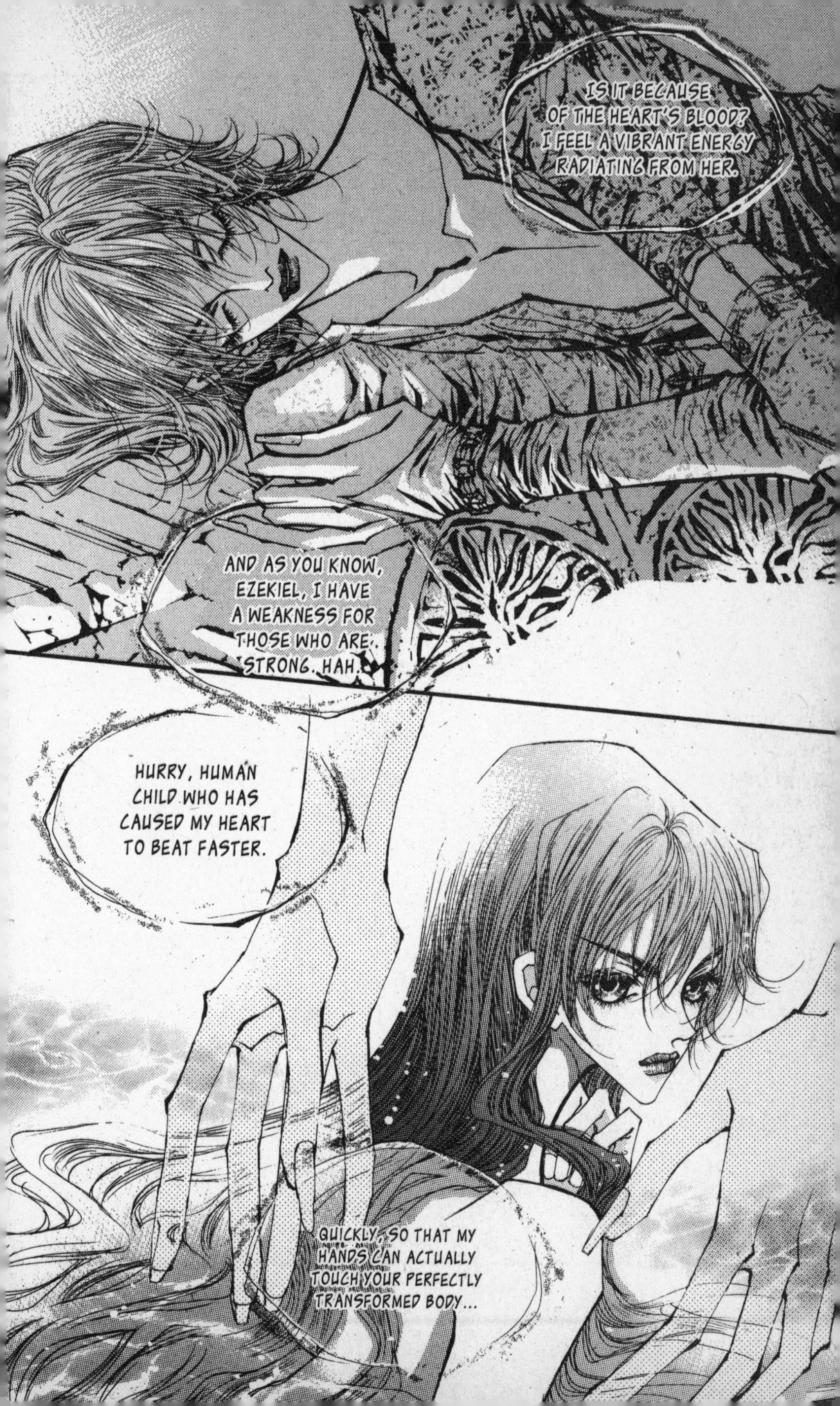
IS IT BECAUSE OF THE HEART'S BLOOD? I FEEL A VIBRANT ENERGY RADIATING FROM HER.
AND AS YOU KNOW, EZEKIEL, I HAVE A WEAKNESS FOR THOSE WHO ARE STRONG. HAH.
HURRY, HUMAN CHILD WHO HAS CAUSED MY HEART TO BEAT FASTER.
QUICKLY, SO THAT MY HANDS CAN ACTUALLY TOUCH YOUR PERFECTLY TRANSFORMED BODY...

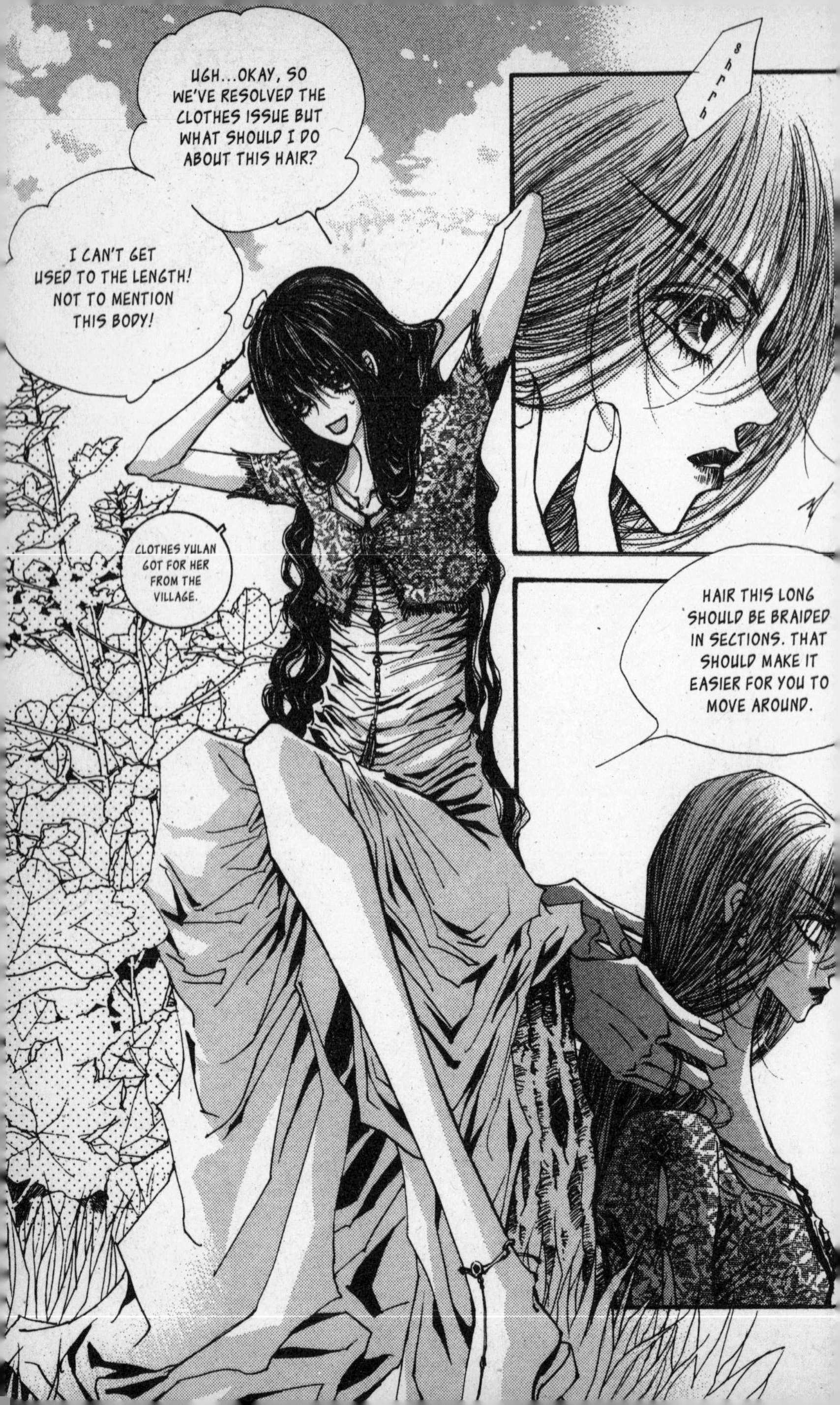

UGH...OKAY, SO WE'VE RESOLVED THE CLOTHES ISSUE BUT WHAT SHOULD I DO ABOUT THIS HAIR?
I CAN'T GET USED TO THE LENGTH! NOT TO MENTION THIS BODY!
CLOTHES YULAN GOT FOR HER FROM THE VILLAGE.
shrrh
HAIR THIS LONG SHOULD BE BRAIDED IN SECTIONS. THAT SHOULD MAKE IT EASIER FOR YOU TO MOVE AROUND.

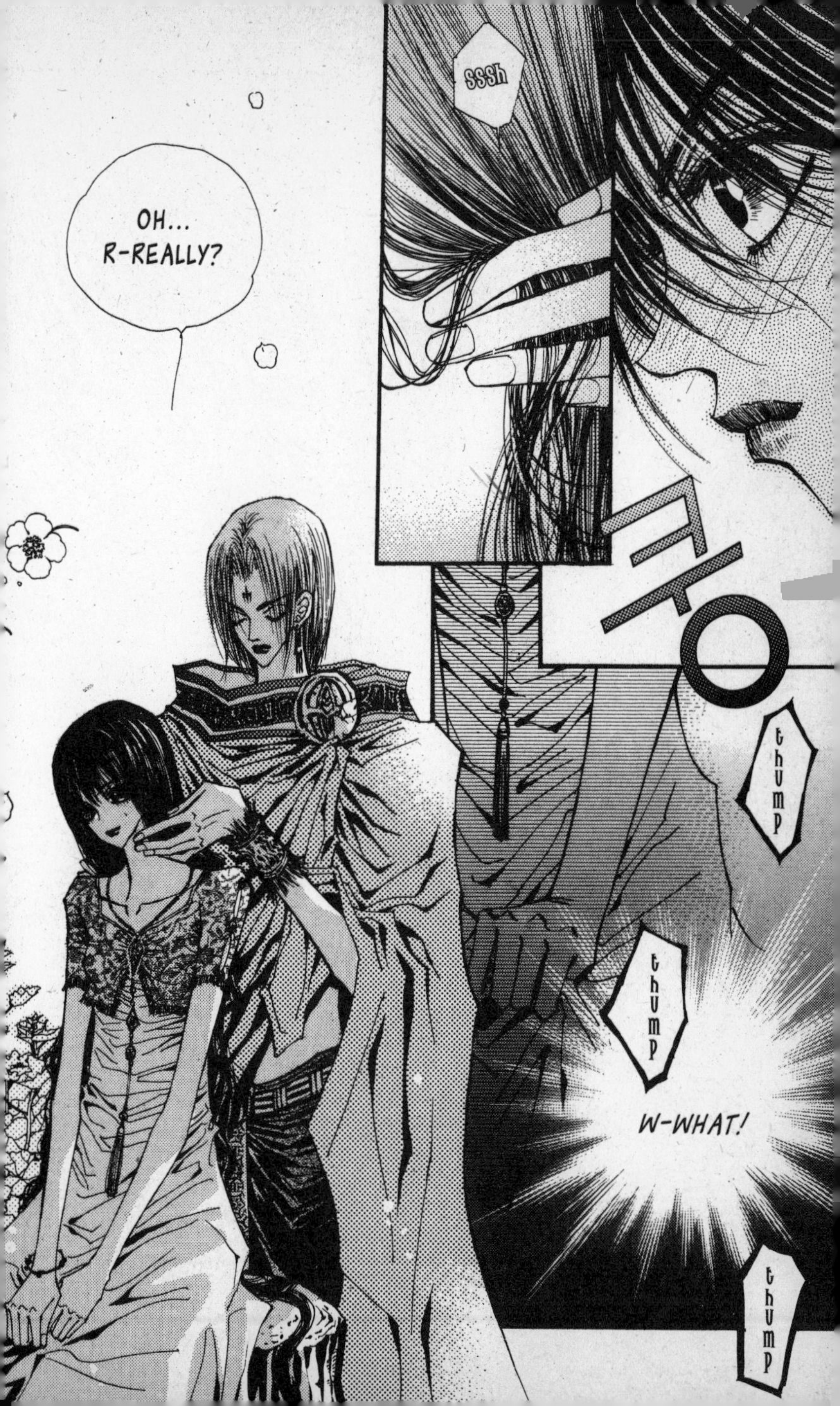
OH... R-REALLY?
SSSh
thump
thump
W-WHAT!
thump

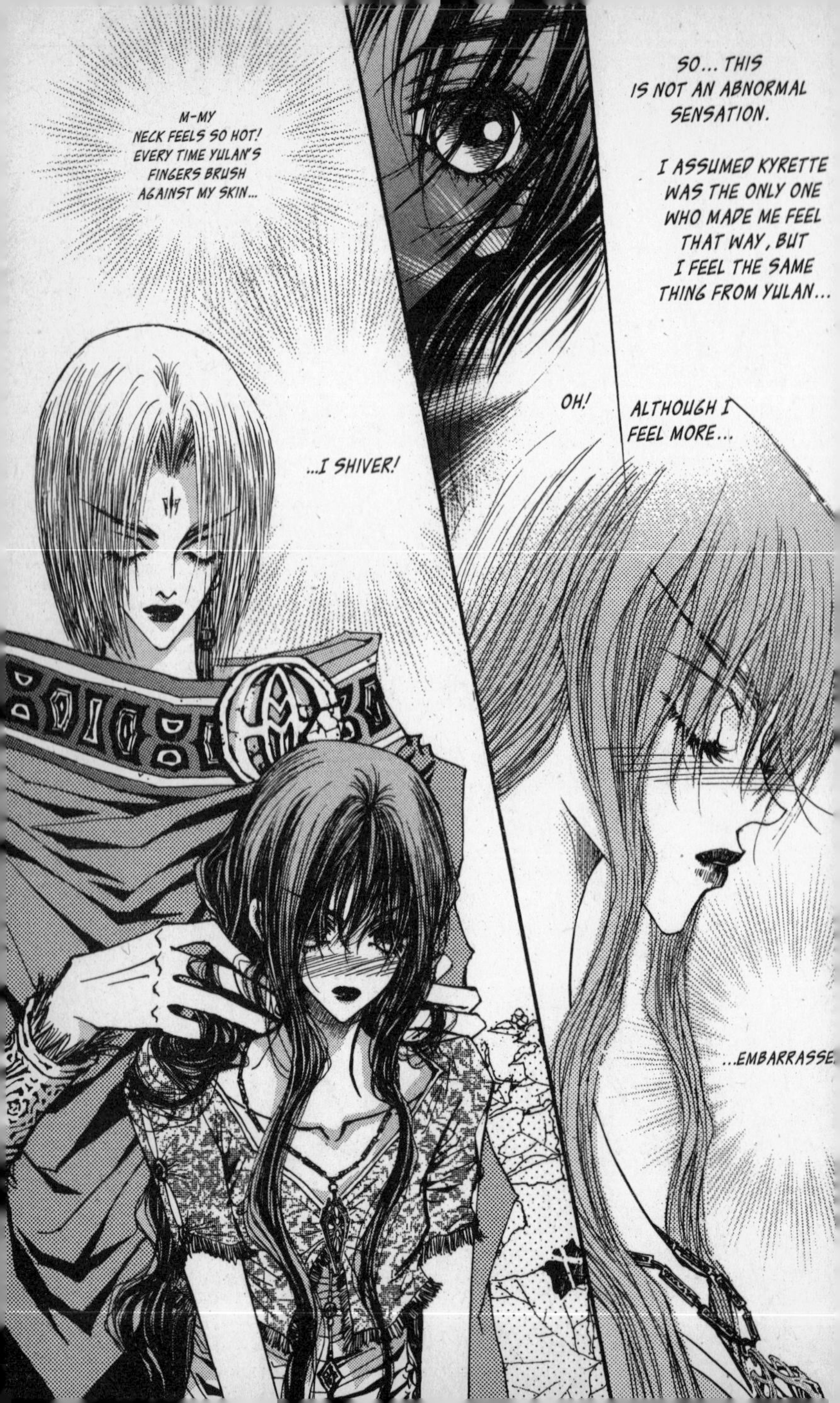
M-MY NECK FEELS SO HOT! EVERY TIME YULAN'S FINGERS BRUSH AGAINST MY SKIN...
...I SHIVER!
SO... THIS IS NOT AN ABNORMAL SENSATION.
I ASSUMED KYRETTE WAS THE ONLY ONE WHO MADE ME FEEL THAT WAY, BUT I FEEL THE SAME THING FROM YULAN...
OH!
ALTHOUGH I FEEL MORE...
...EMBARRASSE

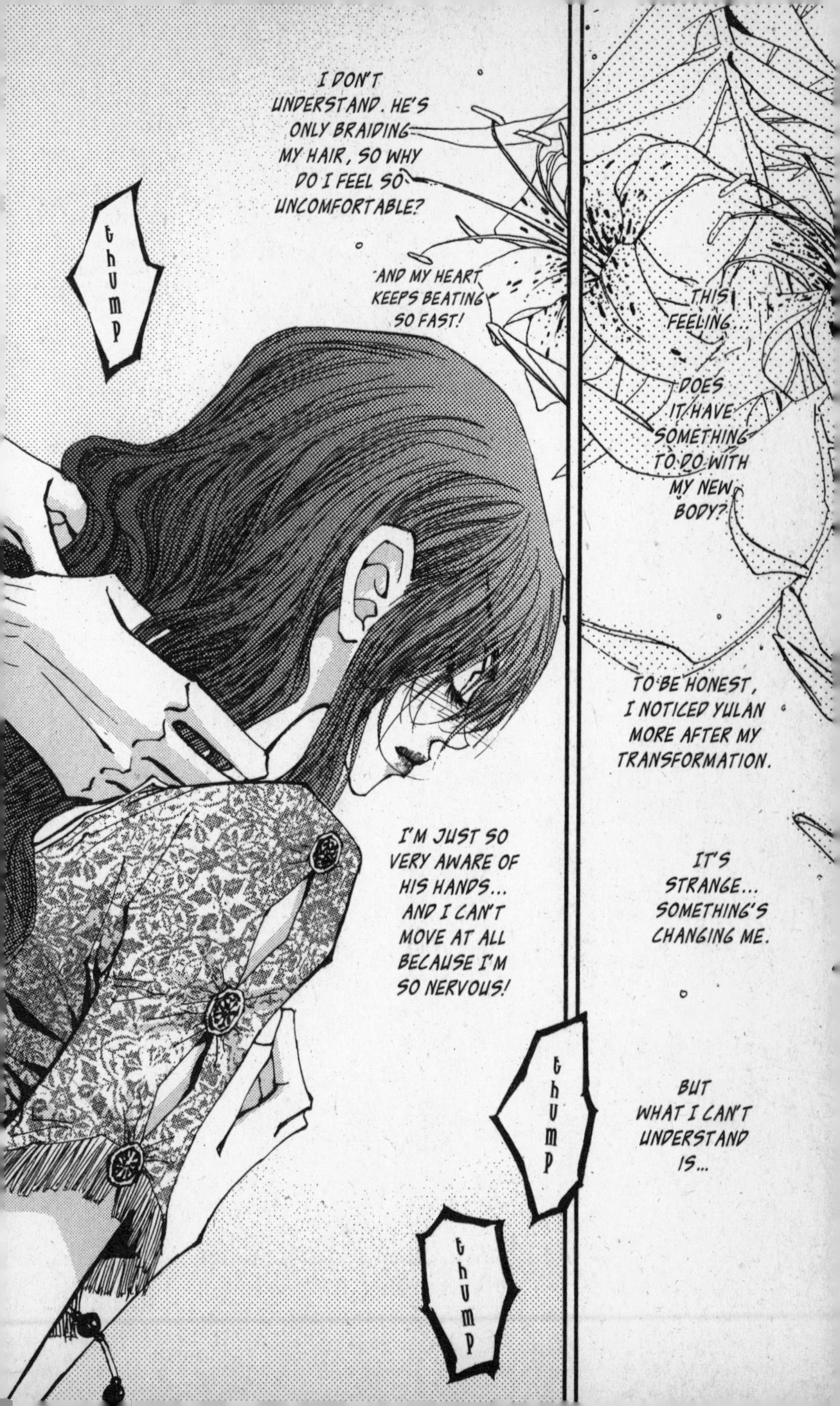
I DON'T UNDERSTAND. HE'S ONLY BRAIDING MY HAIR, SO WHY DO I FEEL SO UNCOMFORTABLE?
THUMP
AND MY HEART KEEPS BEATING SO FAST!
I'M JUST SO VERY AWARE OF HIS HANDS... AND I CAN'T MOVE AT ALL BECAUSE I'M SO NERVOUS!
THUMP
THUMP
THIS FEELING...
DOES IT HAVE SOMETHING TO DO WITH MY NEW BODY?
TO BE HONEST, I NOTICED YULAN MORE AFTER MY TRANSFORMATION.
IT'S STRANGE... SOMETHING'S CHANGING ME.
BUT WHAT I CAN'T UNDERSTAND IS...

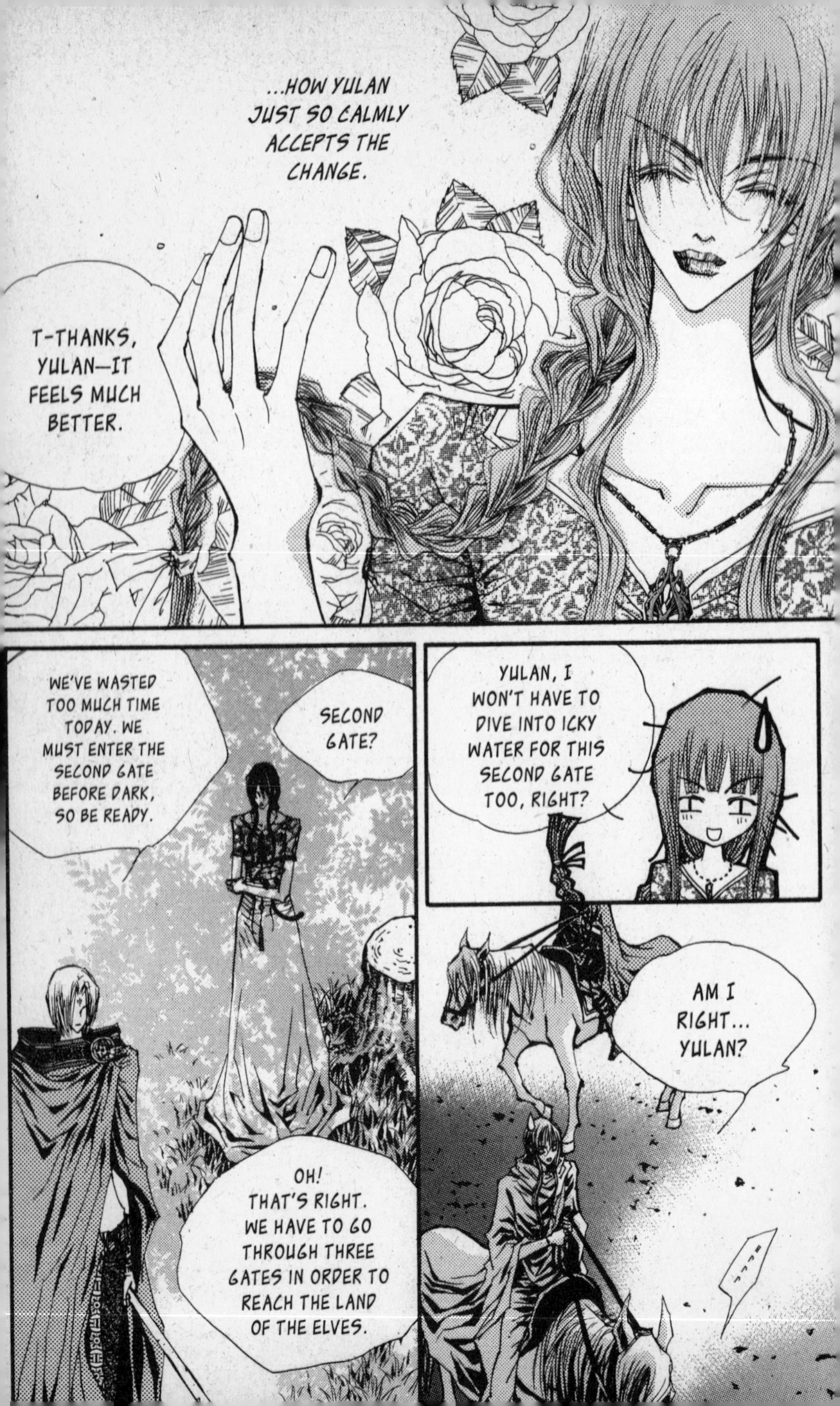
...HOW YULAN JUST SO CALMLY ACCEPTS THE CHANGE.
T-THANKS, YULAN—IT FEELS MUCH BETTER.
WE'VE WASTED TOO MUCH TIME TODAY. WE MUST ENTER THE SECOND GATE BEFORE DARK, SO BE READY.
SECOND GATE?
OH! THAT'S RIGHT. WE HAVE TO GO THROUGH THREE GATES IN ORDER TO REACH THE LAND OF THE ELVES.
YULAN, I WON'T HAVE TO DIVE INTO ICKY WATER FOR THIS SECOND GATE TOO, RIGHT?
AM I RIGHT... YULAN?

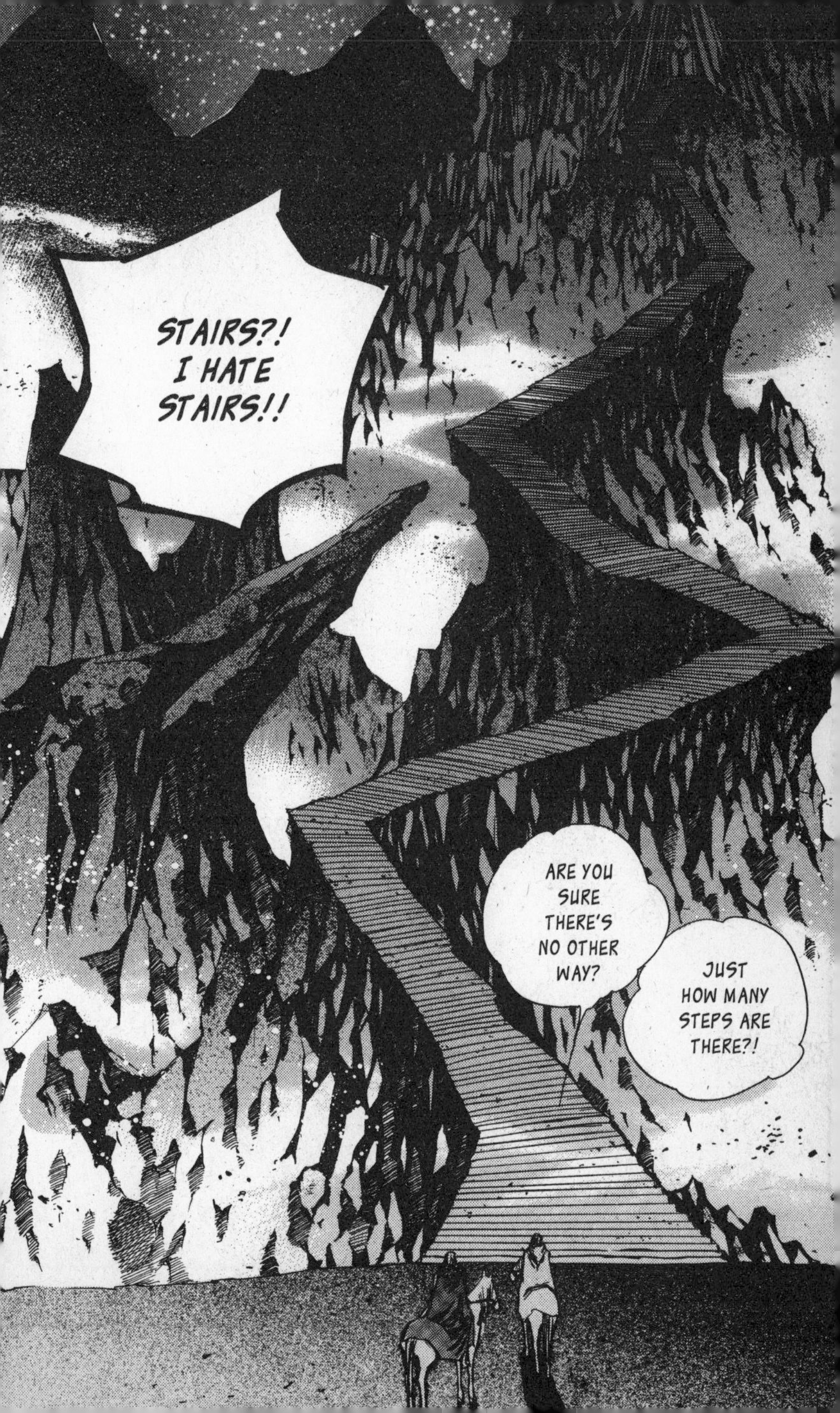
STAIRS?! I HATE STAIRS!!
ARE YOU SURE THERE'S NO OTHER WAY?
JUST HOW MANY STEPS ARE THERE?!

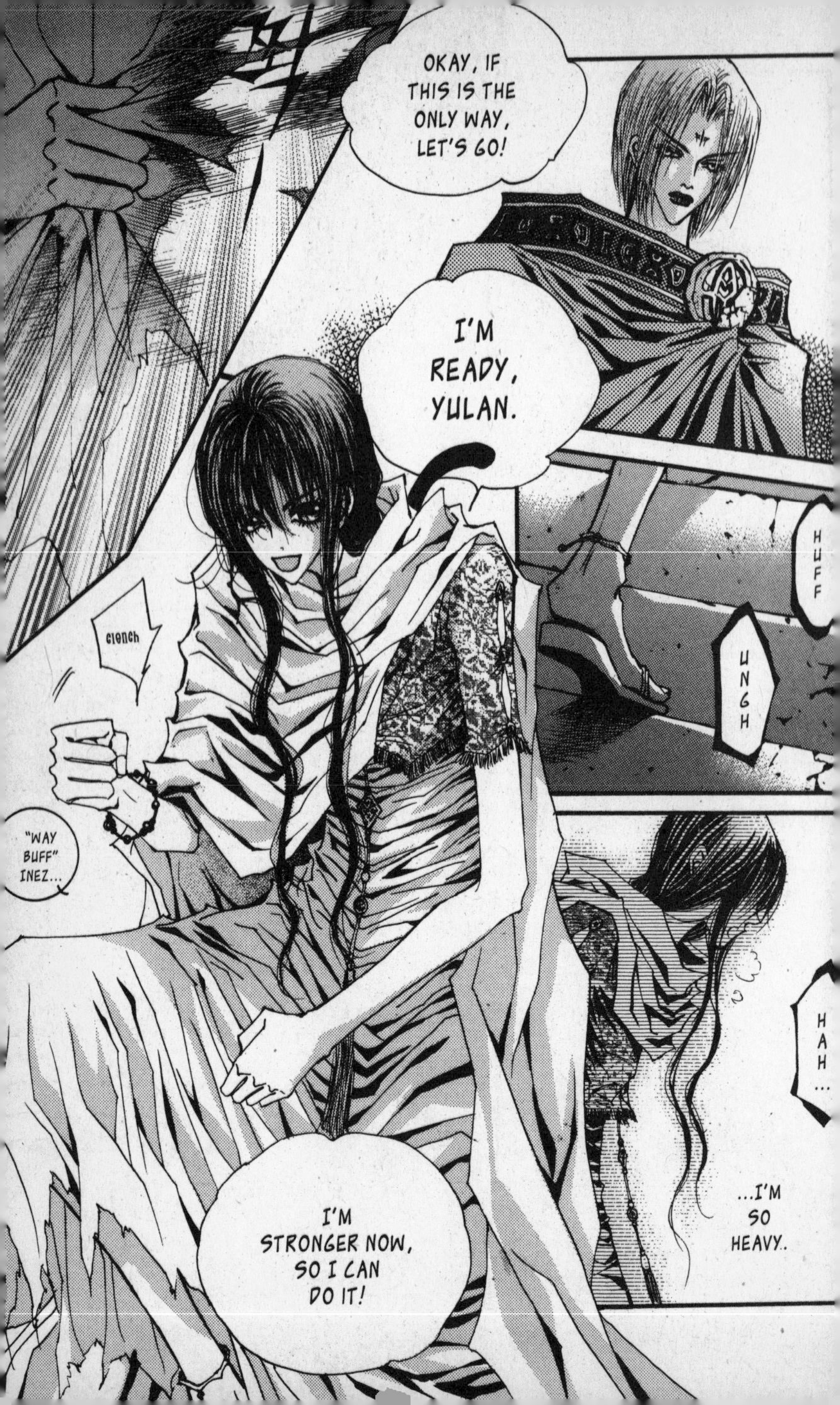
OKAY, IF THIS IS THE ONLY WAY, LET'S GO!
I'M READY, YULAN.
clench
"WAY BUFF" INEZ...
I'M STRONGER NOW, SO I CAN DO IT!
HUFF
UNGH
HAH...
...I'M SO HEAVY.

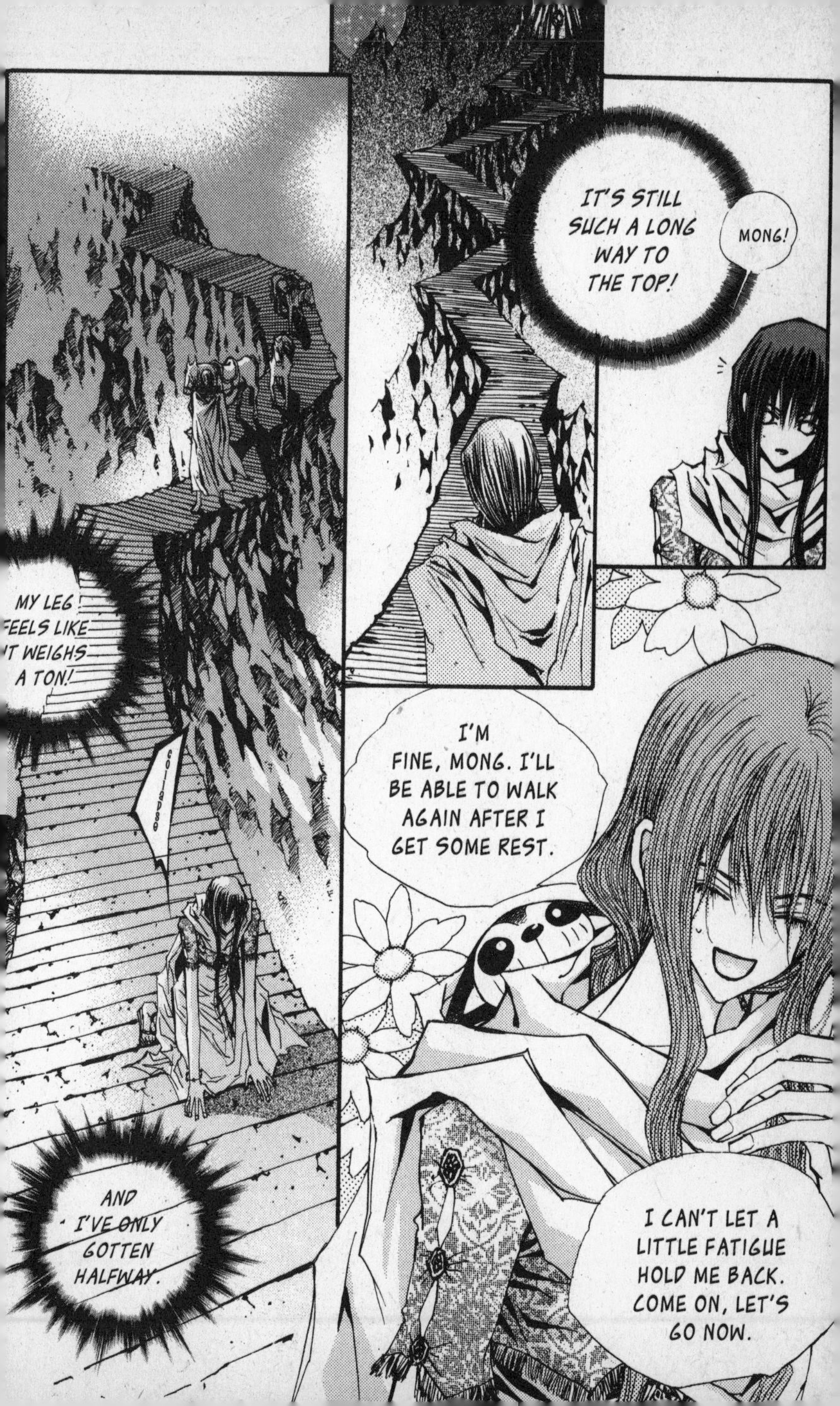
MY LEG FEELS LIKE IT WEIGHS A TON!
COLLAPSE
AND I'VE ONLY GOTTEN HALFWAY.
IT'S STILL SUCH A LONG WAY TO THE TOP!
MONG!
I'M FINE, MONG. I'LL BE ABLE TO WALK AGAIN AFTER I GET SOME REST.
I CAN'T LET A LITTLE FATIGUE HOLD ME BACK. COME ON, LET'S GO NOW.

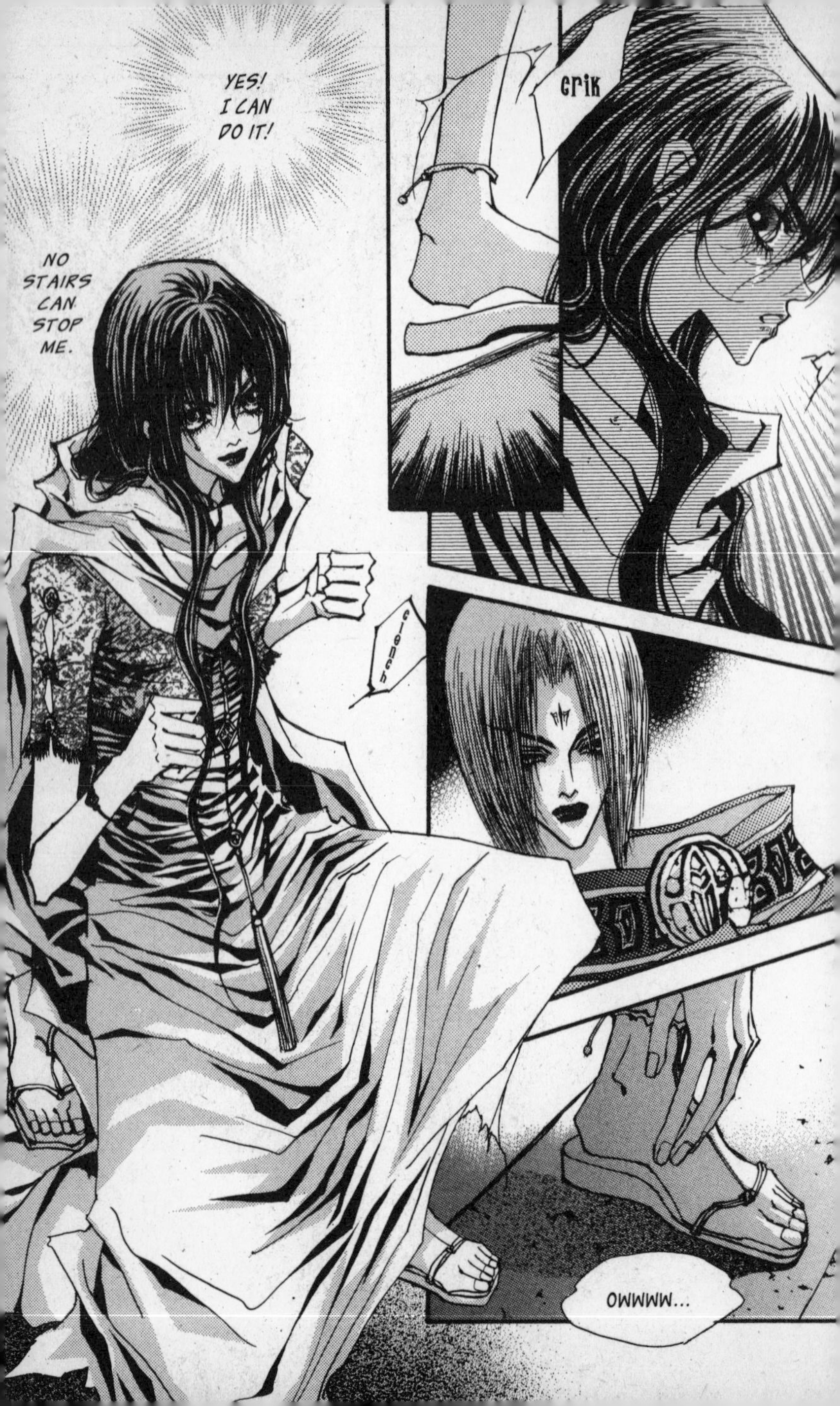
YES! I CAN DO IT!
NO STAIRS CAN STOP ME.
clench
Erik
OWWWW...

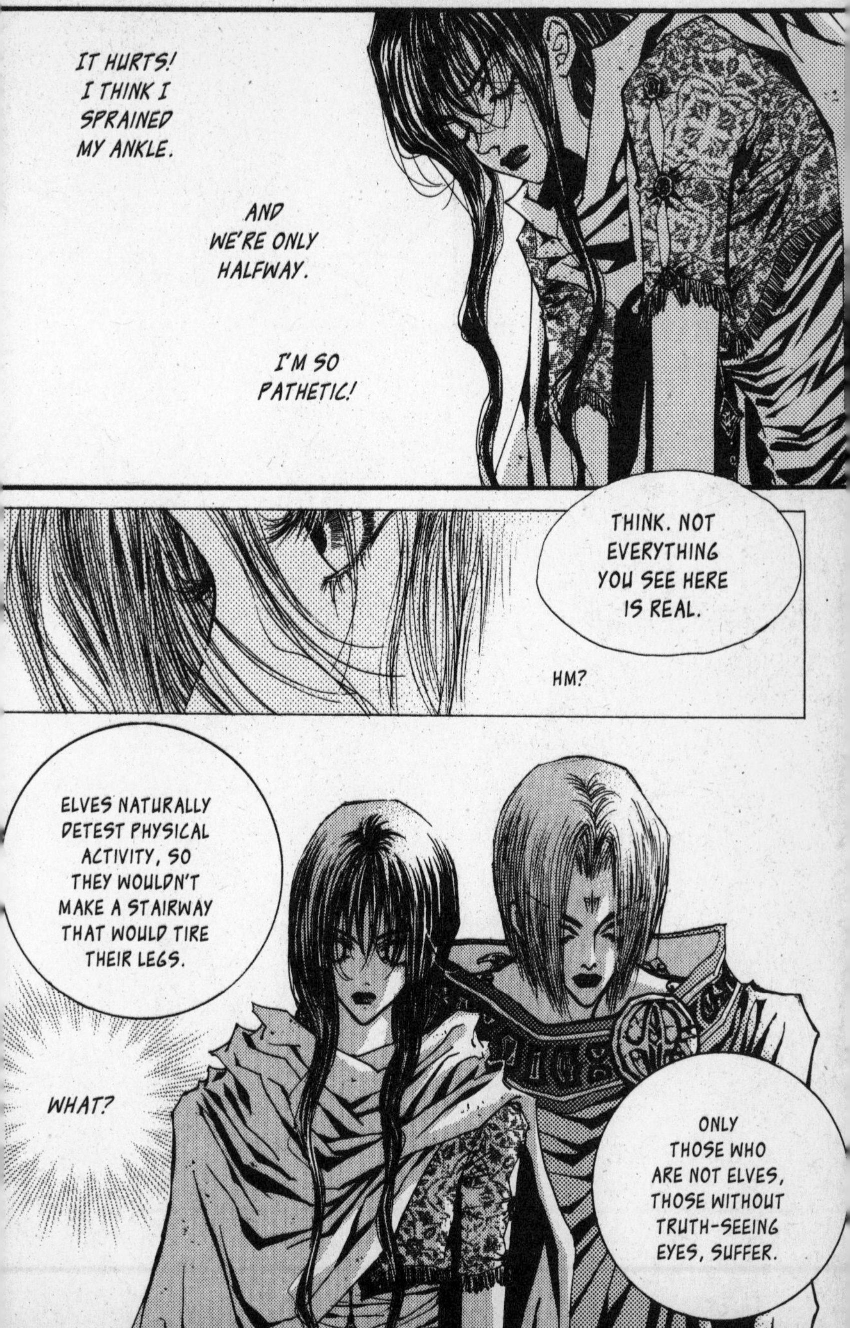
IT HURTS! I THINK I SPRAINED MY ANKLE.
AND WE'RE ONLY HALFWAY.
I'M SO PATHETIC!
THINK. NOT EVERYTHING YOU SEE HERE IS REAL.
HM?
ELVES NATURALLY DETEST PHYSICAL ACTIVITY, SO THEY WOULDN'T MAKE A STAIRWAY THAT WOULD TIRE THEIR LEGS.
WHAT?
ONLY THOSE WHO ARE NOT ELVES, THOSE WITHOUT TRUTH-SEEING EYES, SUFFER.

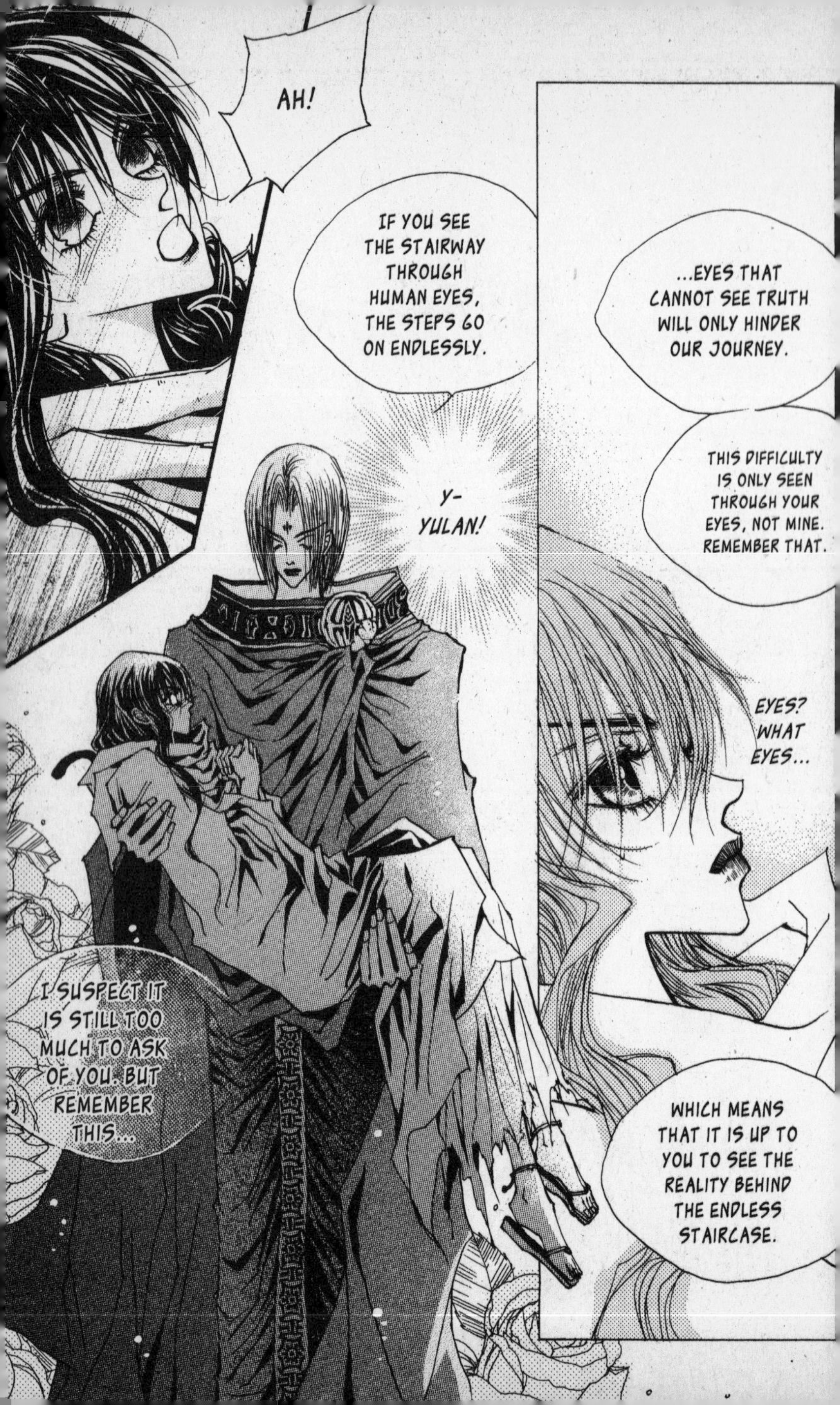

AH!
IF YOU SEE THE STAIRWAY THROUGH HUMAN EYES, THE STEPS GO ON ENDLESSLY.
Y- YULAN!
I SUSPECT IT IS STILL TOO MUCH TO ASK OF YOU. BUT REMEMBER THIS...
...EYES THAT CANNOT SEE TRUTH WILL ONLY HINDER OUR JOURNEY.
THIS DIFFICULTY IS ONLY SEEN THROUGH YOUR EYES, NOT MINE. REMEMBER THAT.
EYES? WHAT EYES...
WHICH MEANS THAT IT IS UP TO YOU TO SEE THE REALITY BEHIND THE ENDLESS STAIRCASE.

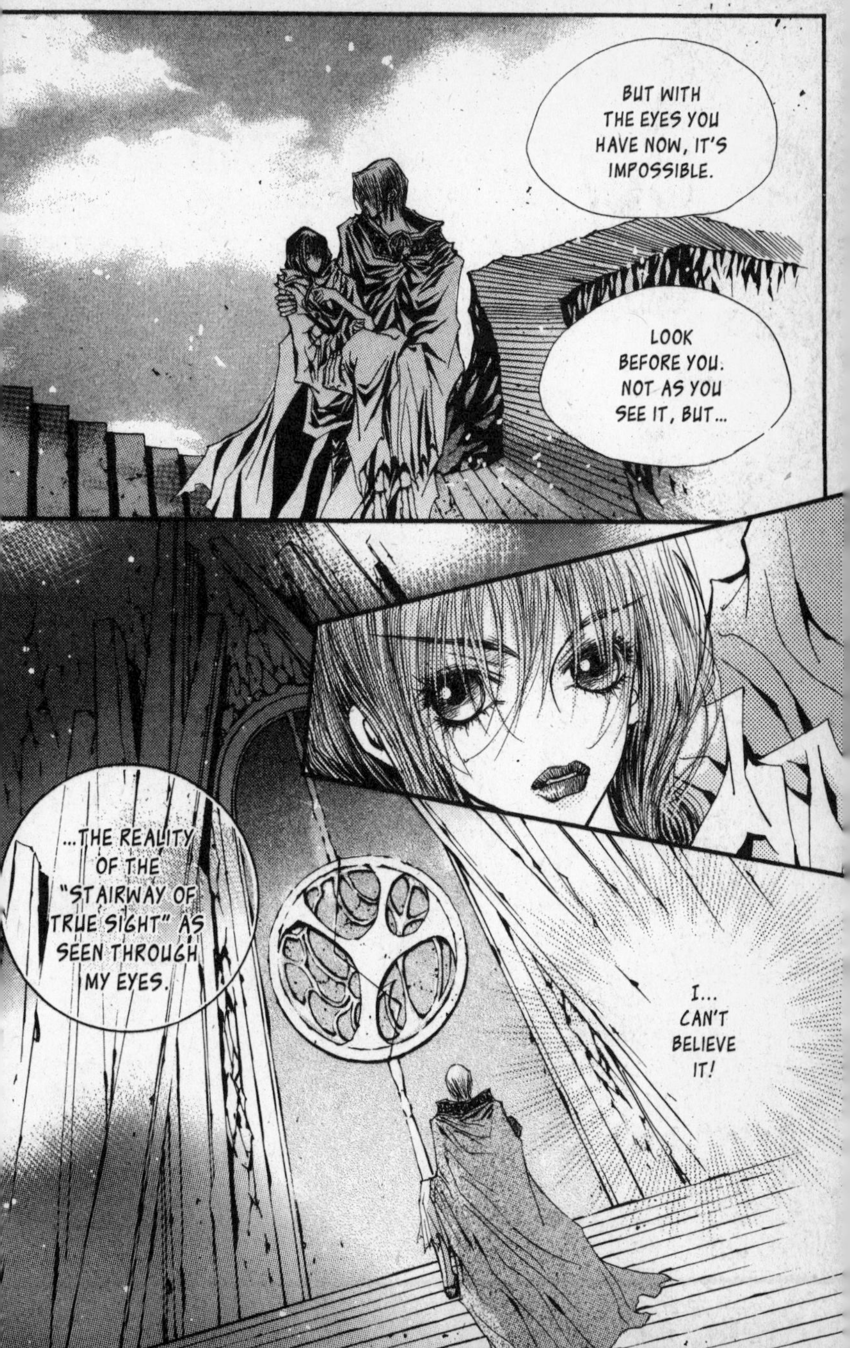
BUT WITH THE EYES YOU HAVE NOW, IT'S IMPOSSIBLE.
LOOK BEFORE YOU. NOT AS YOU SEE IT, BUT...
...THE REALITY OF THE "STAIRWAY OF TRUE SIGHT" AS SEEN THROUGH MY EYES.
I... CAN'T BELIEVE IT!

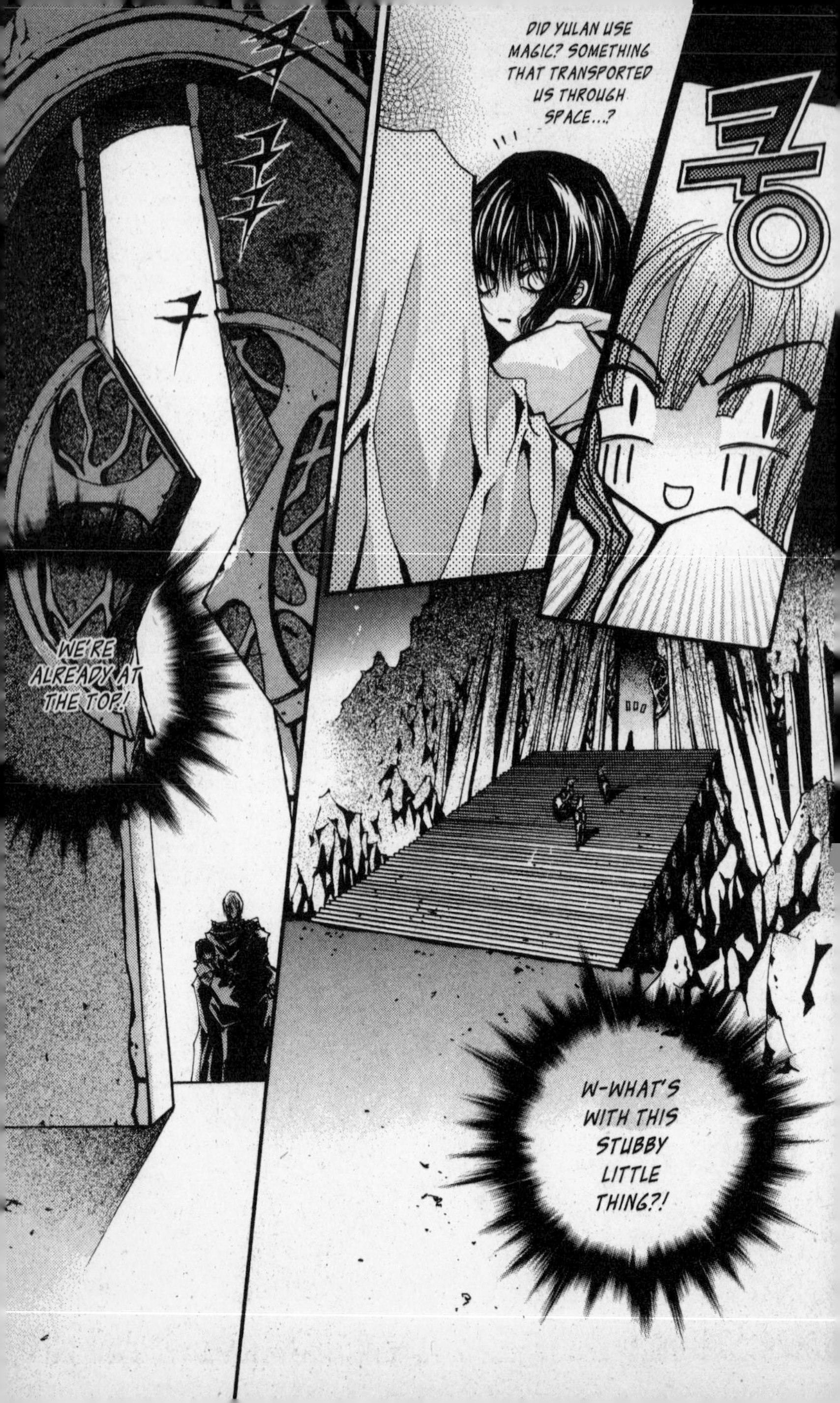
WE'RE ALREADY AT THE TOP!
DID YULAN USE MAGIC? SOMETHING THAT TRANSPORTED US THROUGH SPACE...?
W-WHAT'S WITH THIS STUBBY LITTLE THING?!

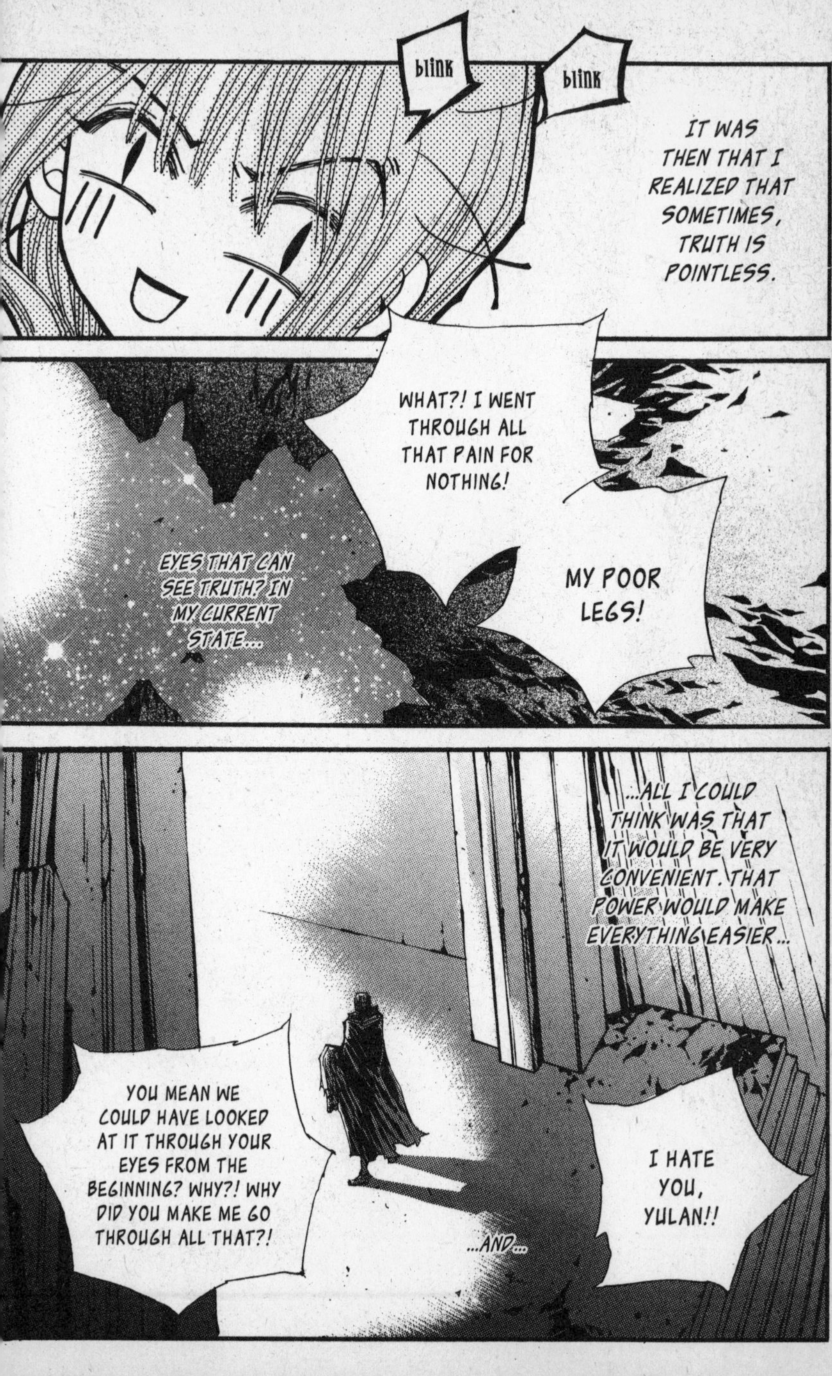
blink
blink
IT WAS THEN THAT I REALIZED THAT SOMETIMES, TRUTH IS POINTLESS.
EYES THAT CAN SEE TRUTH? IN MY CURRENT STATE...
WHAT?! I WENT THROUGH ALL THAT PAIN FOR NOTHING!
MY POOR LEGS!
...ALL I COULD THINK WAS THAT IT WOULD BE VERY CONVENIENT. THAT POWER WOULD MAKE EVERYTHING EASIER...
YOU MEAN WE COULD HAVE LOOKED AT IT THROUGH YOUR EYES FROM THE BEGINNING? WHY?! WHY DID YOU MAKE ME GO THROUGH ALL THAT?!
...AND...
I HATE YOU, YULAN!!

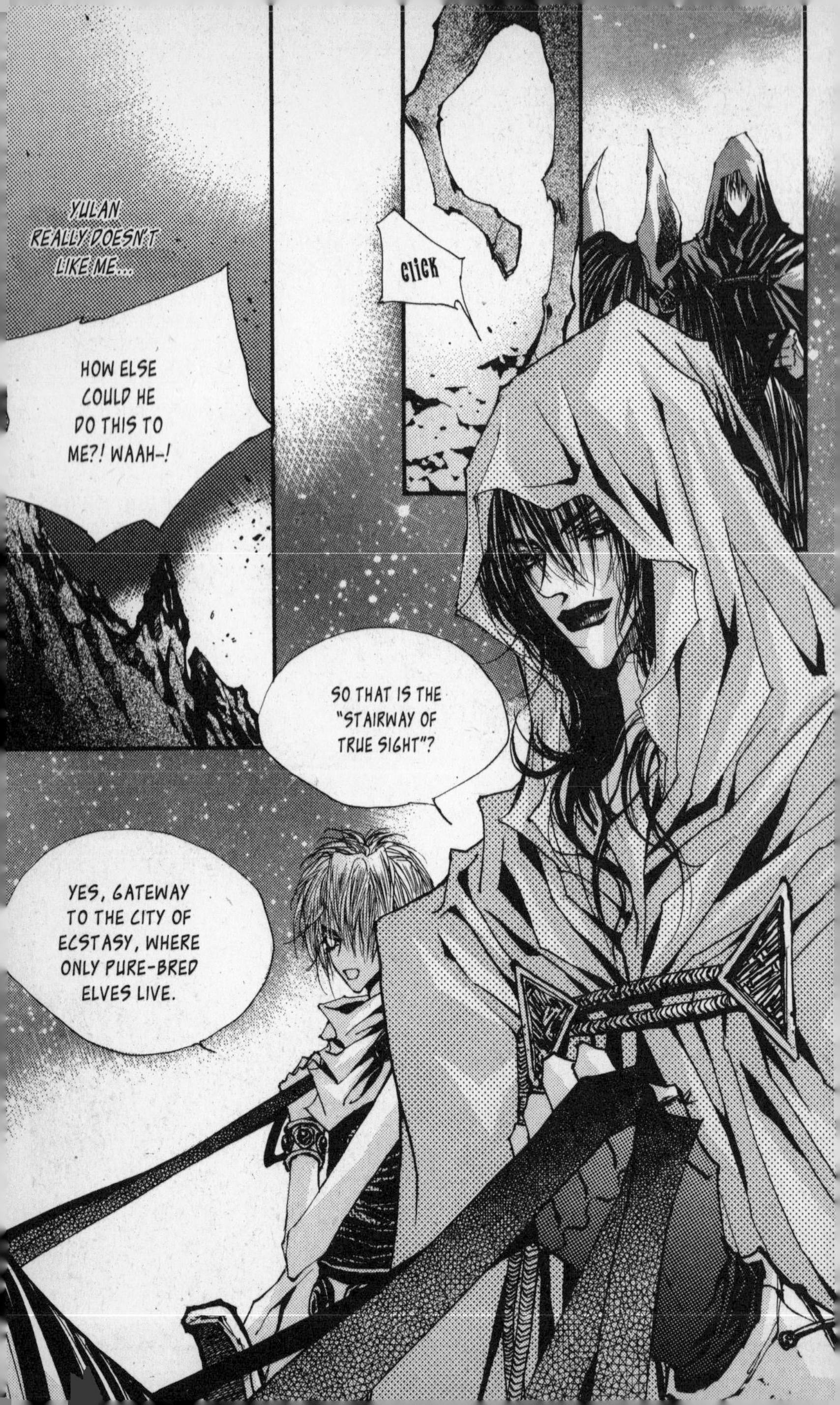
YULAN REALLY DOESN'T LIKE ME...
HOW ELSE COULD HE DO THIS TO ME?! WAAH-!
CLICK
SO THAT IS THE "STAIRWAY OF TRUE SIGHT"?
YES, GATEWAY TO THE CITY OF ECSTASY, WHERE ONLY PURE-BRED ELVES LIVE.

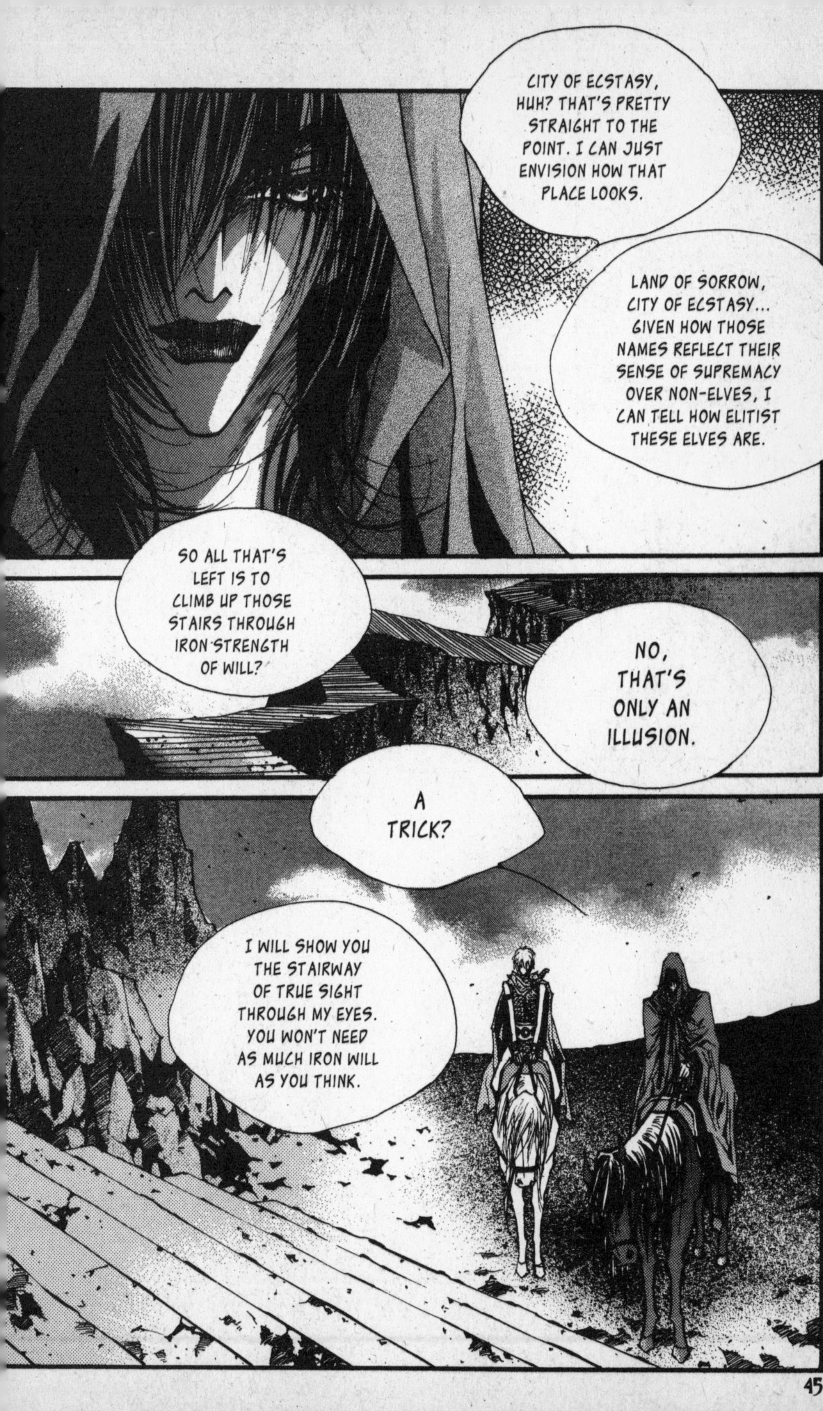
CITY OF ECSTASY, HUH? THAT'S PRETTY STRAIGHT TO THE POINT. I CAN JUST ENVISION HOW THAT PLACE LOOKS.
LAND OF SORROW, CITY OF ECSTASY... GIVEN HOW THOSE NAMES REFLECT THEIR SENSE OF SUPREMACY OVER NON-ELVES, I CAN TELL HOW ELITIST THESE ELVES ARE.
SO ALL THAT'S LEFT IS TO CLIMB UP THOSE STAIRS THROUGH IRON STRENGTH OF WILL?
NO, THAT'S ONLY AN ILLUSION.
A TRICK?
I WILL SHOW YOU THE STAIRWAY OF TRUE SIGHT THROUGH MY EYES. YOU WON'T NEED AS MUCH IRON WILL AS YOU THINK.

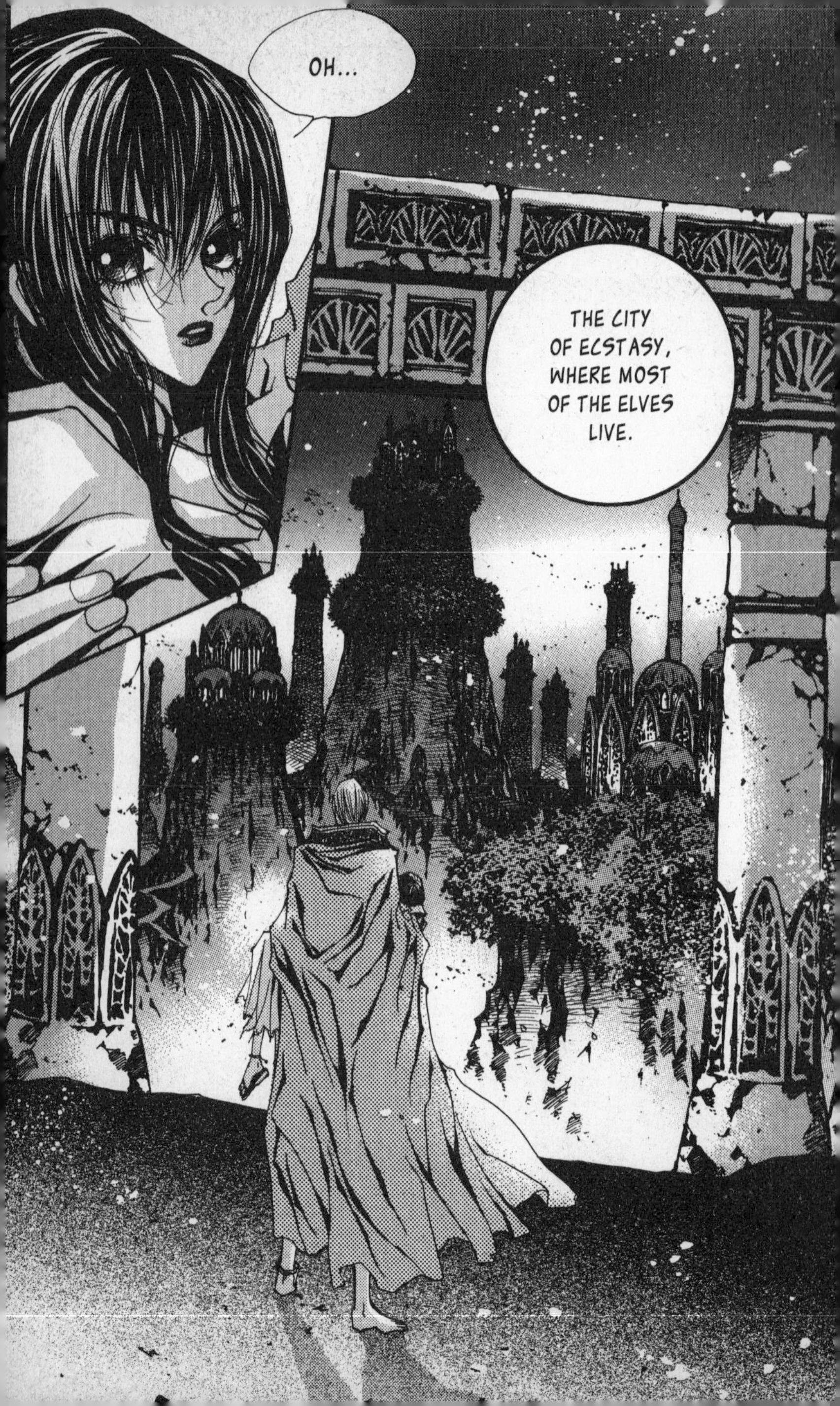
OH...
THE CITY OF ECSTASY, WHERE MOST OF THE ELVES LIVE.

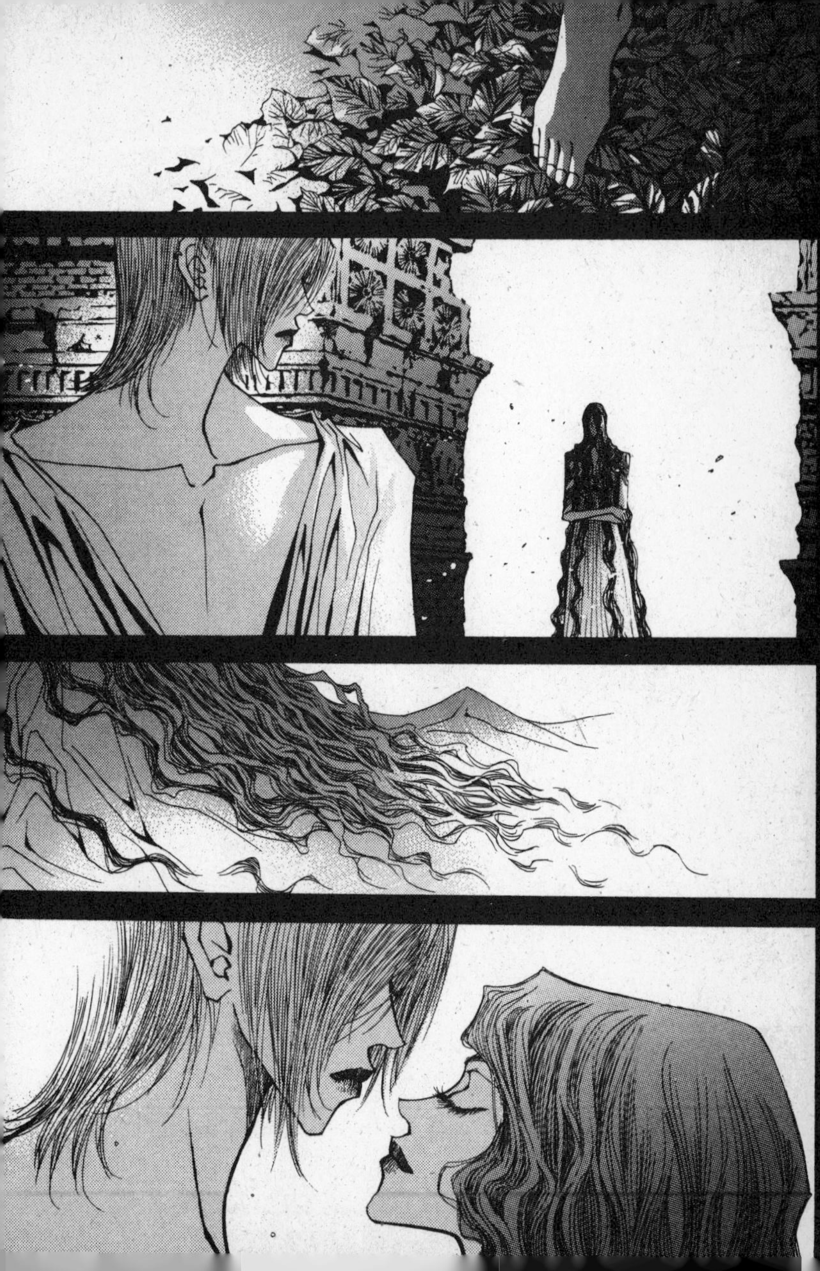

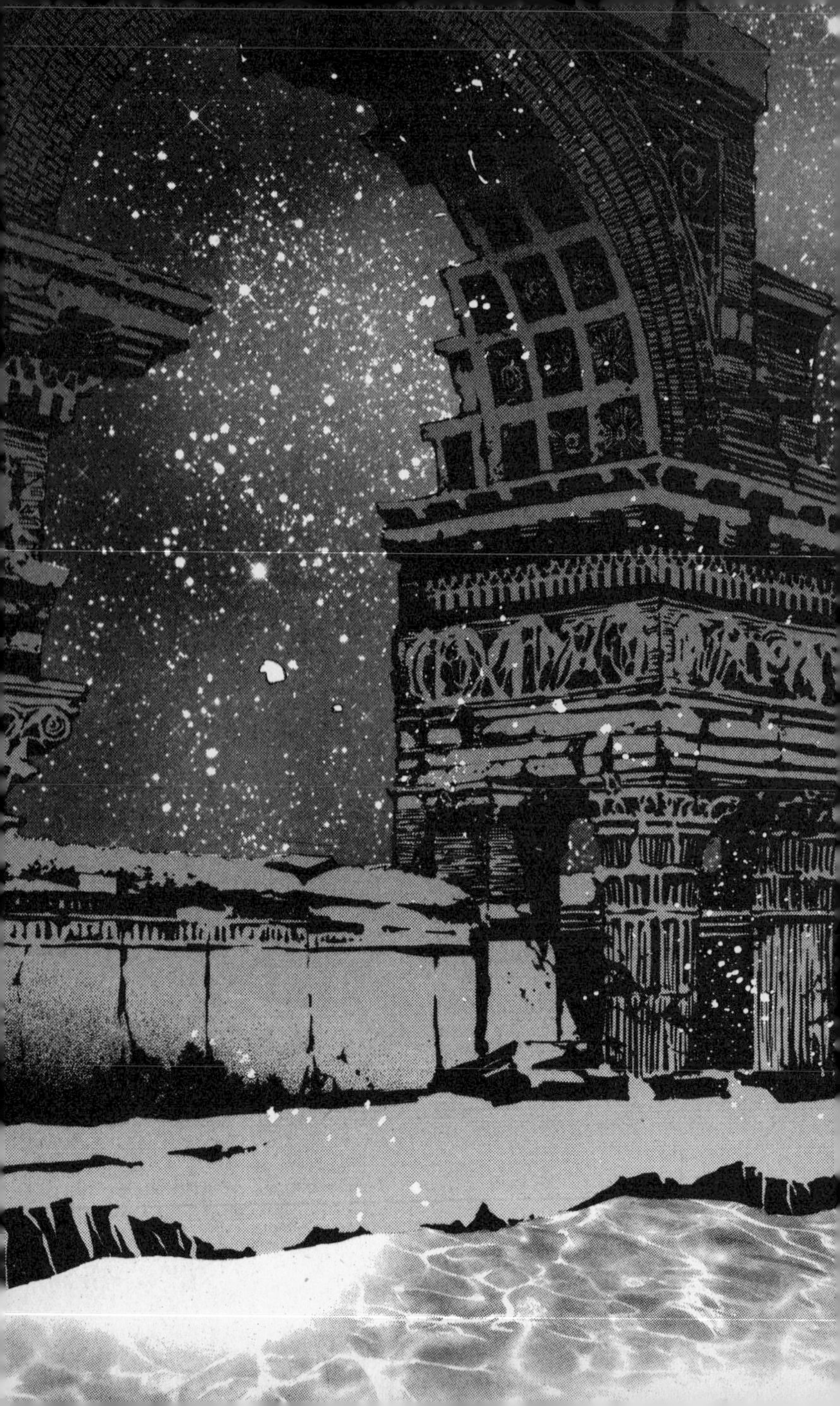

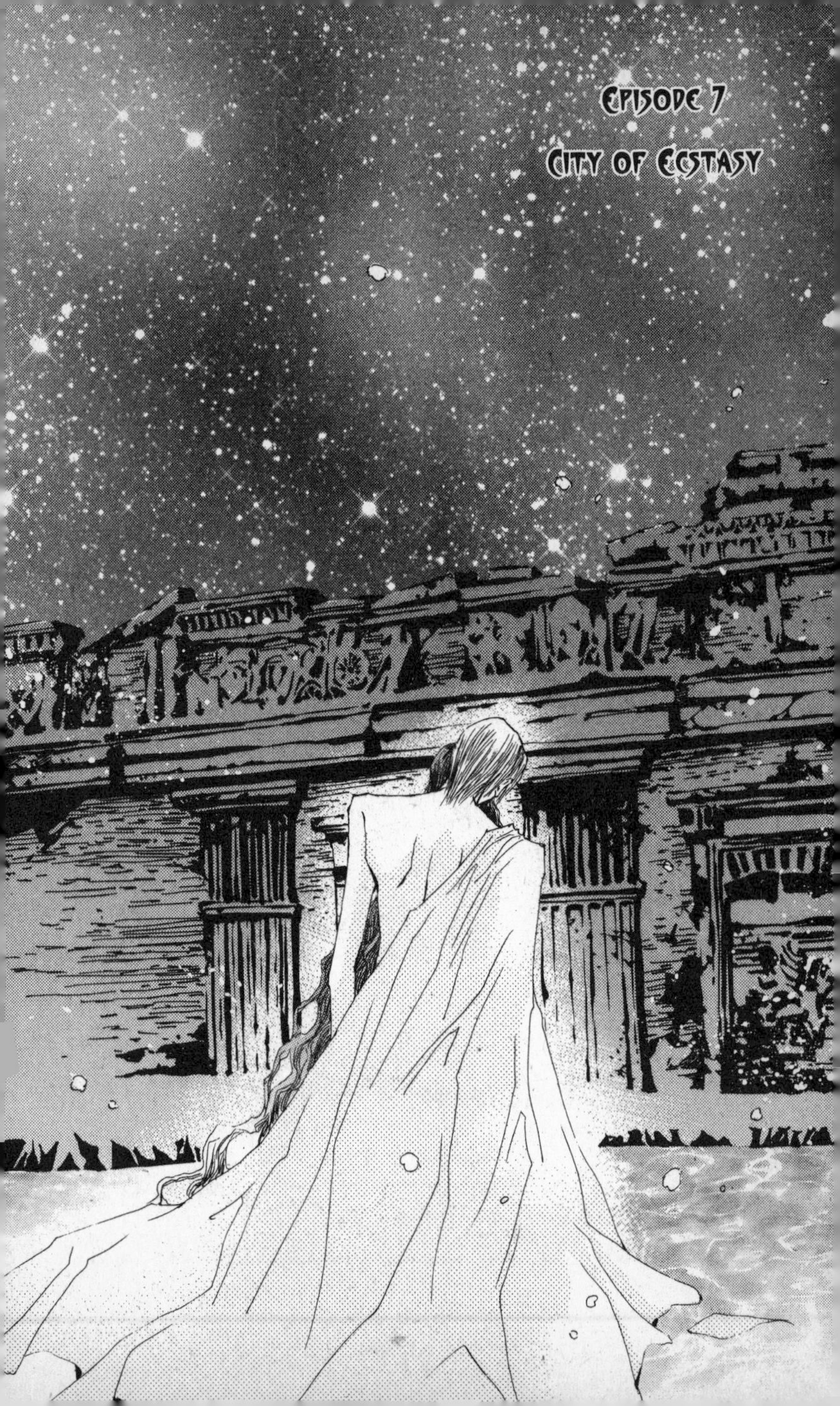
Episode 7
City of Ecstasy

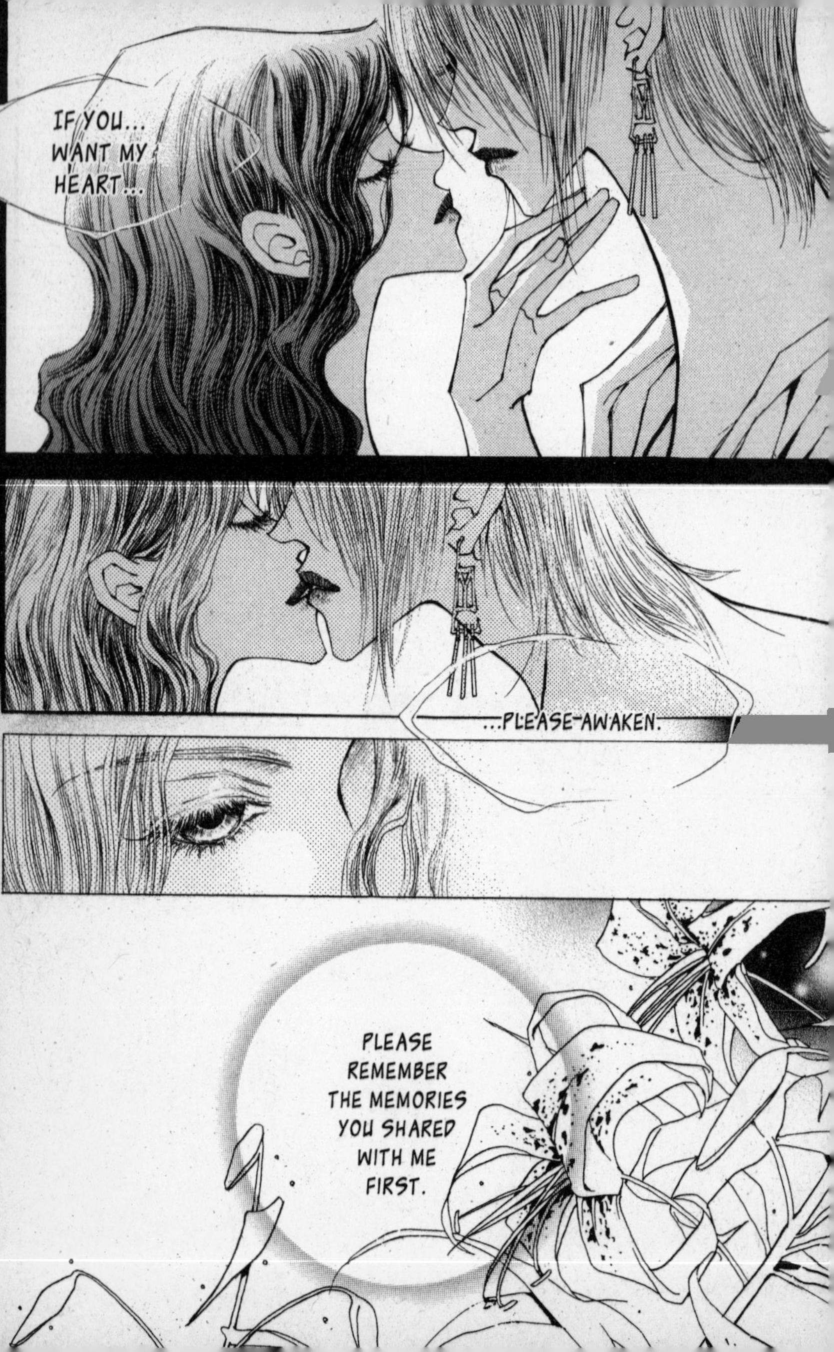
IF YOU... WANT MY HEART...
...PLEASE AWAKEN.
PLEASE REMEMBER THE MEMORIES YOU SHARED WITH ME FIRST.

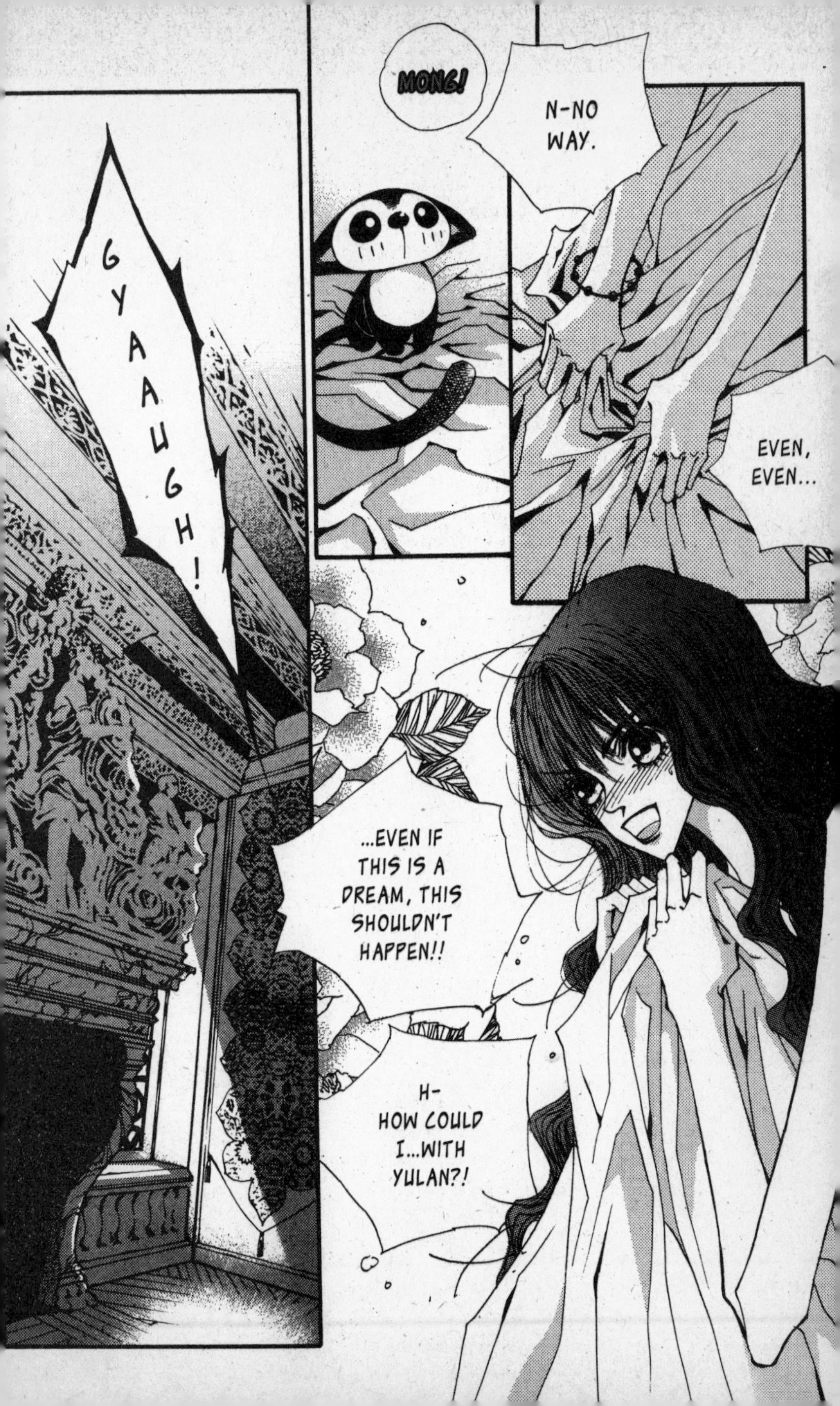
GYAAUGH!
MONG!
N-NO WAY.
EVEN, EVEN...
...EVEN IF THIS IS A DREAM, THIS SHOULDN'T HAPPEN!!
H- HOW COULD I...WITH YULAN?!

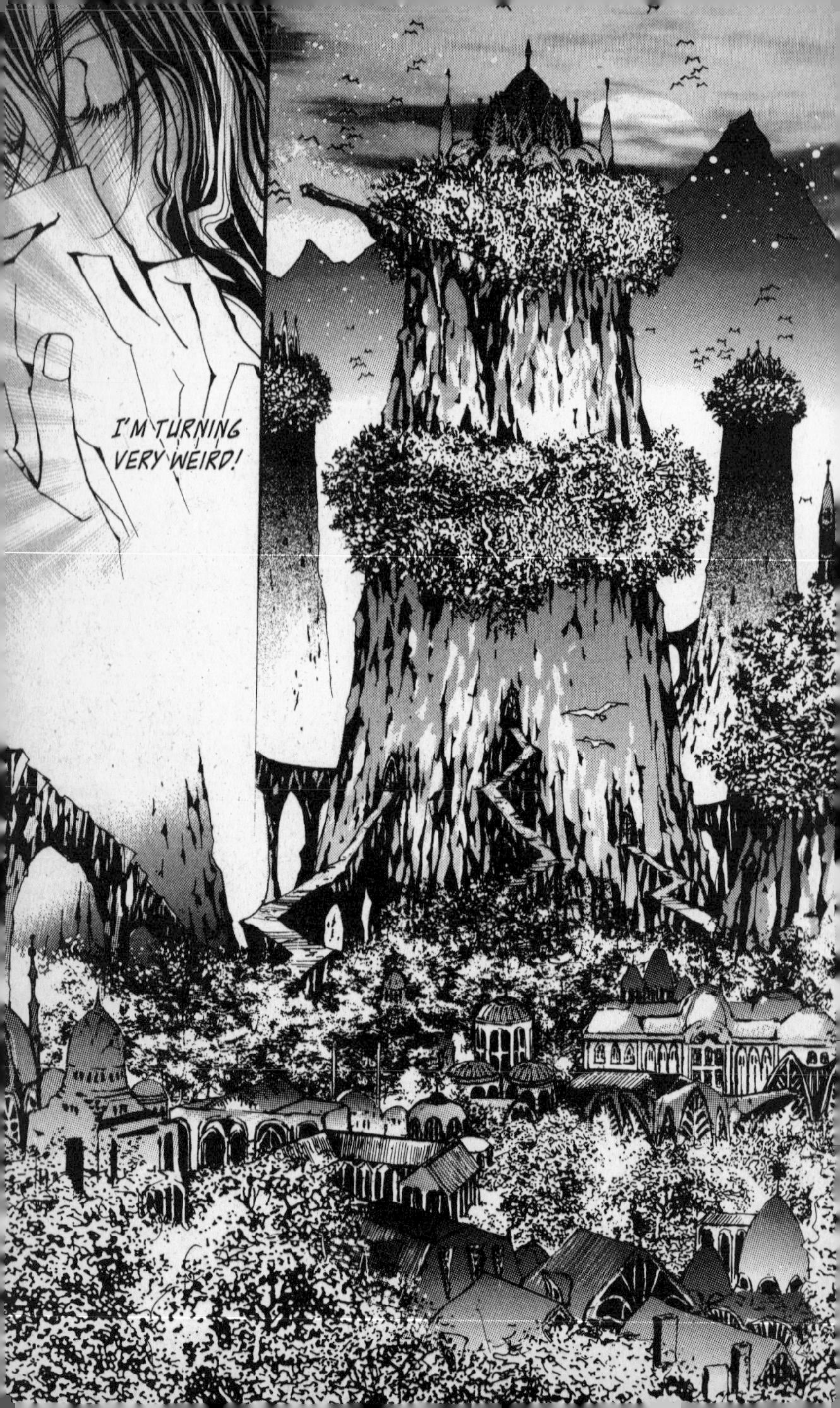
I'M TURNING VERY WEIRD!

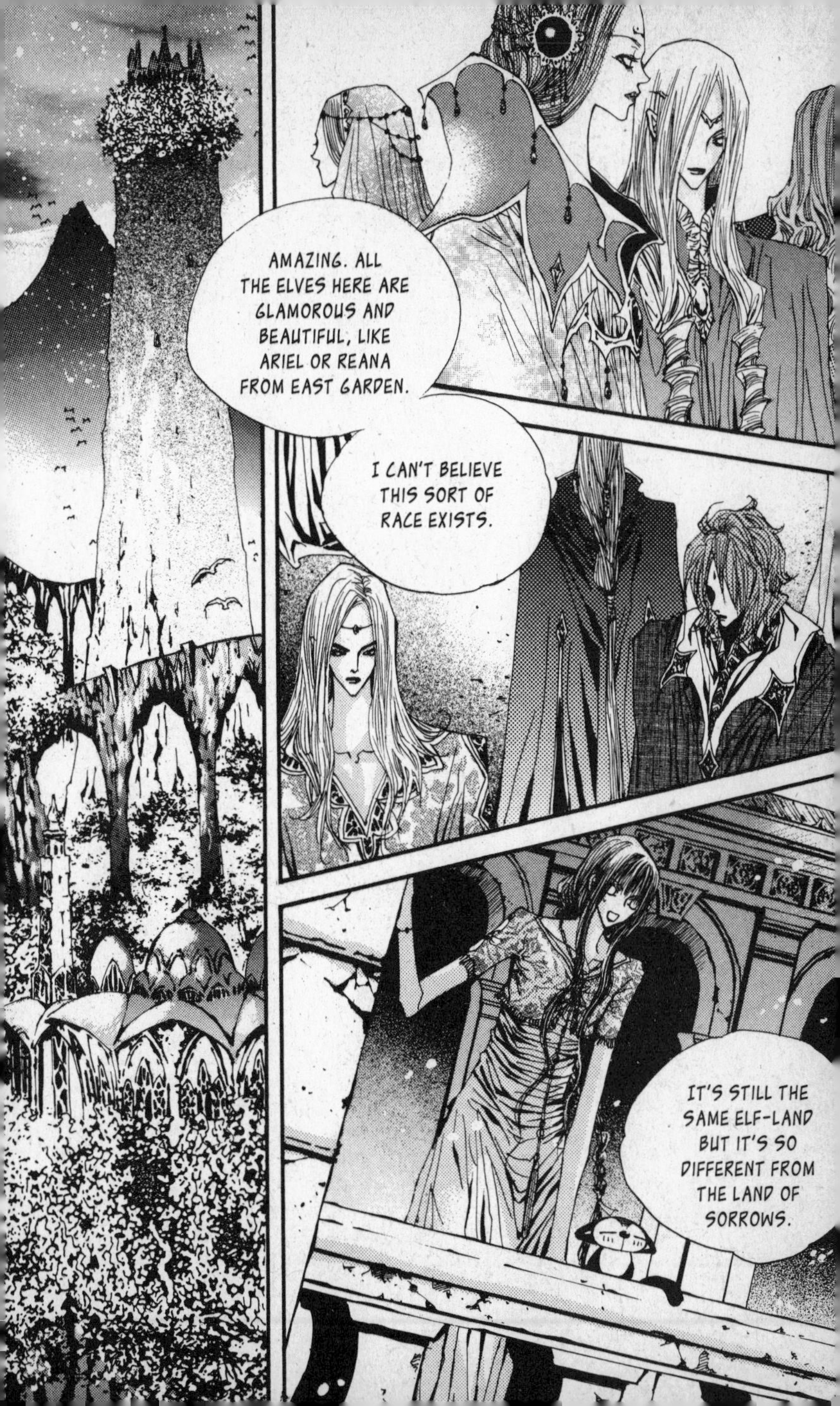
AMAZING. ALL THE ELVES HERE ARE GLAMOROUS AND BEAUTIFUL, LIKE ARIEL OR REANA FROM EAST GARDEN.
I CAN'T BELIEVE THIS SORT OF RACE EXISTS.
IT'S STILL THE SAME ELF-LAND BUT IT'S SO DIFFERENT FROM THE LAND OF SORROWS.

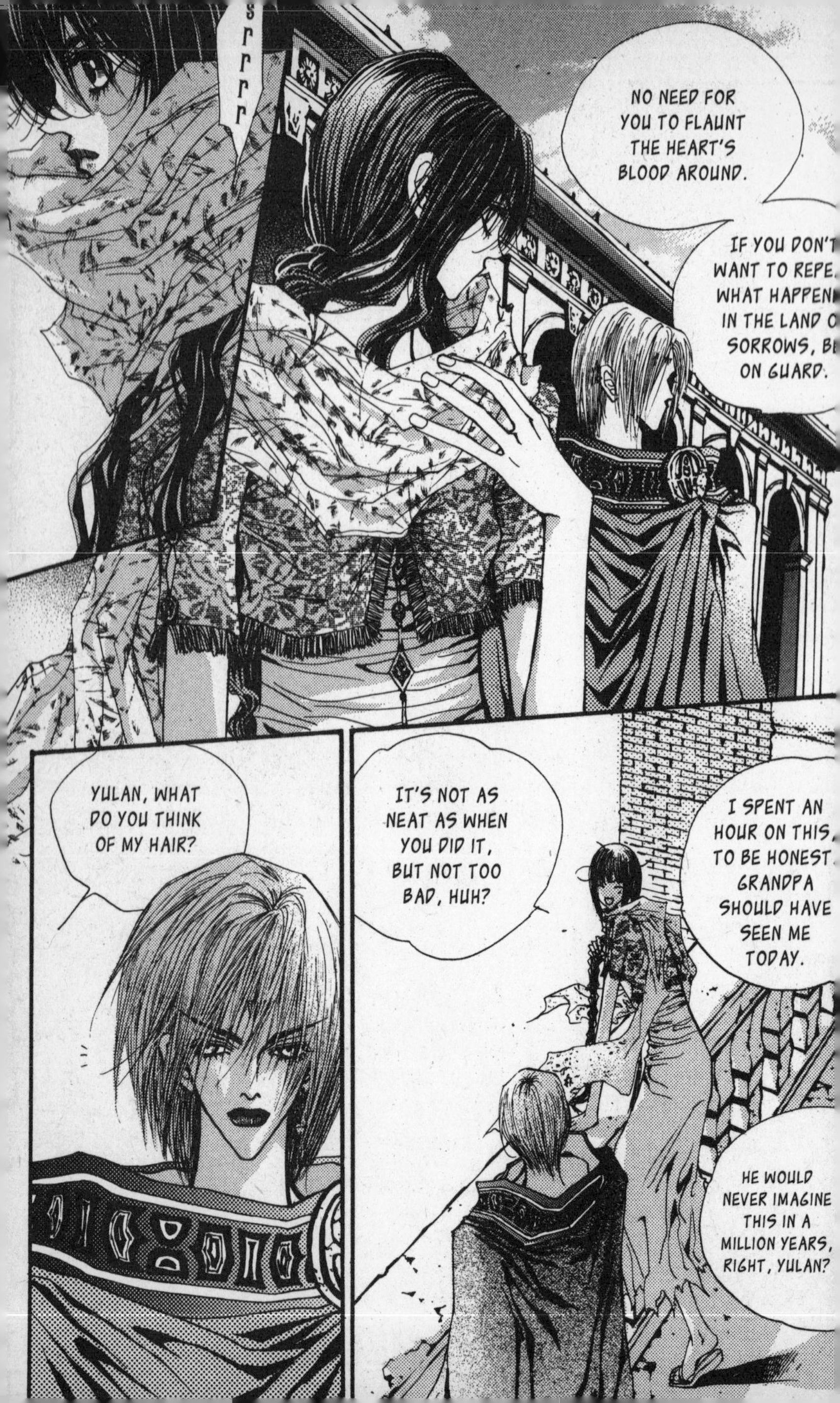
SRRRR
NO NEED FOR YOU TO FLAUNT THE HEART'S BLOOD AROUND.
IF YOU DON'T WANT TO REPE WHAT HAPPEN IN THE LAND O SORROWS, B ON GUARD.
YULAN, WHAT DO YOU THINK OF MY HAIR?
IT'S NOT AS NEAT AS WHEN YOU DID IT, BUT NOT TOO BAD, HUH?
I SPENT AN HOUR ON THIS, TO BE HONEST. GRANDPA SHOULD HAVE SEEN ME TODAY.
HE WOULD NEVER IMAGINE THIS IN A MILLION YEARS, RIGHT, YULAN?

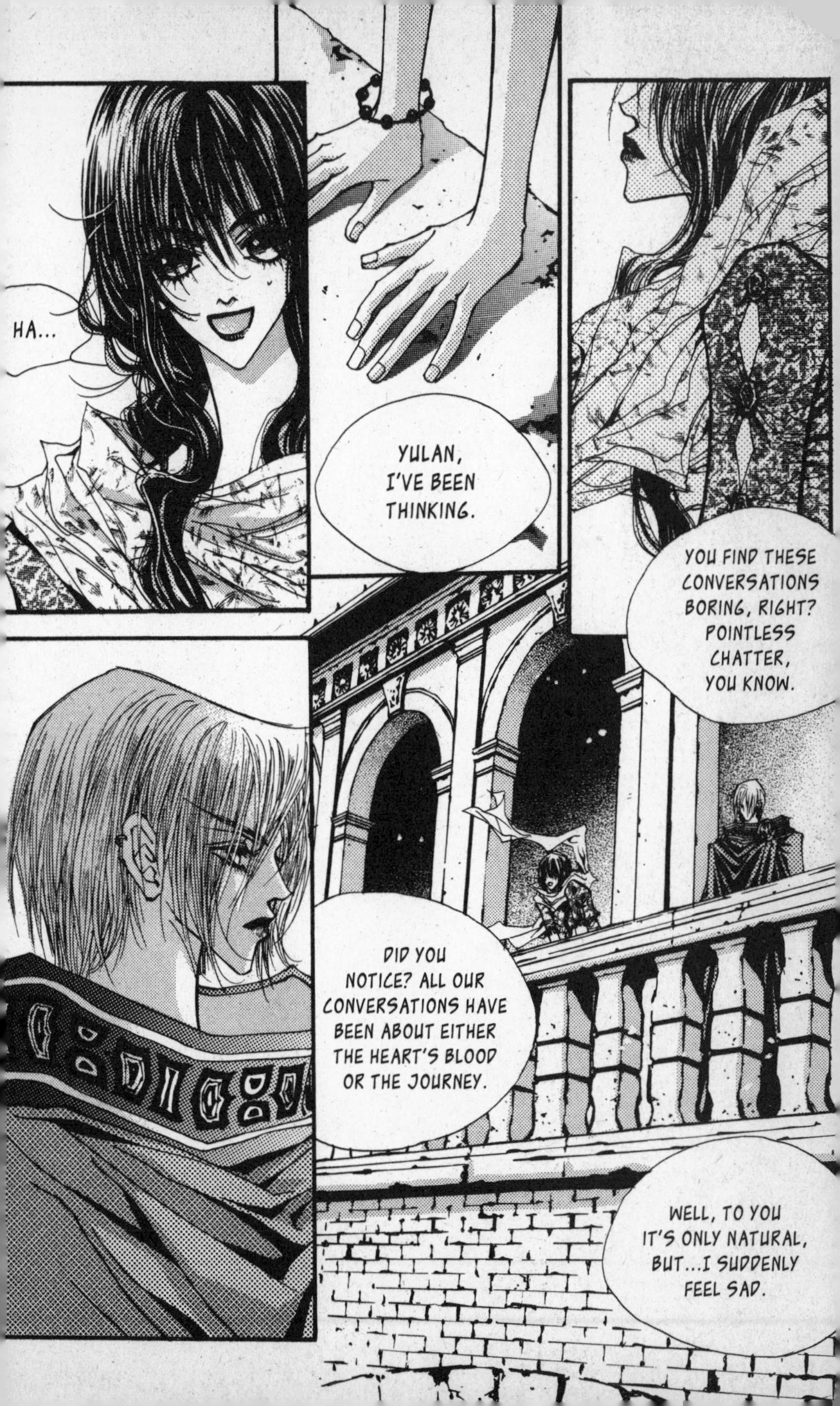
HA...
YULAN, I'VE BEEN THINKING.
YOU FIND THESE CONVERSATIONS BORING, RIGHT? POINTLESS CHATTER, YOU KNOW.
DID YOU NOTICE? ALL OUR CONVERSATIONS HAVE BEEN ABOUT EITHER THE HEART'S BLOOD OR THE JOURNEY.
WELL, TO YOU IT'S ONLY NATURAL, BUT...I SUDDENLY FEEL SAD.

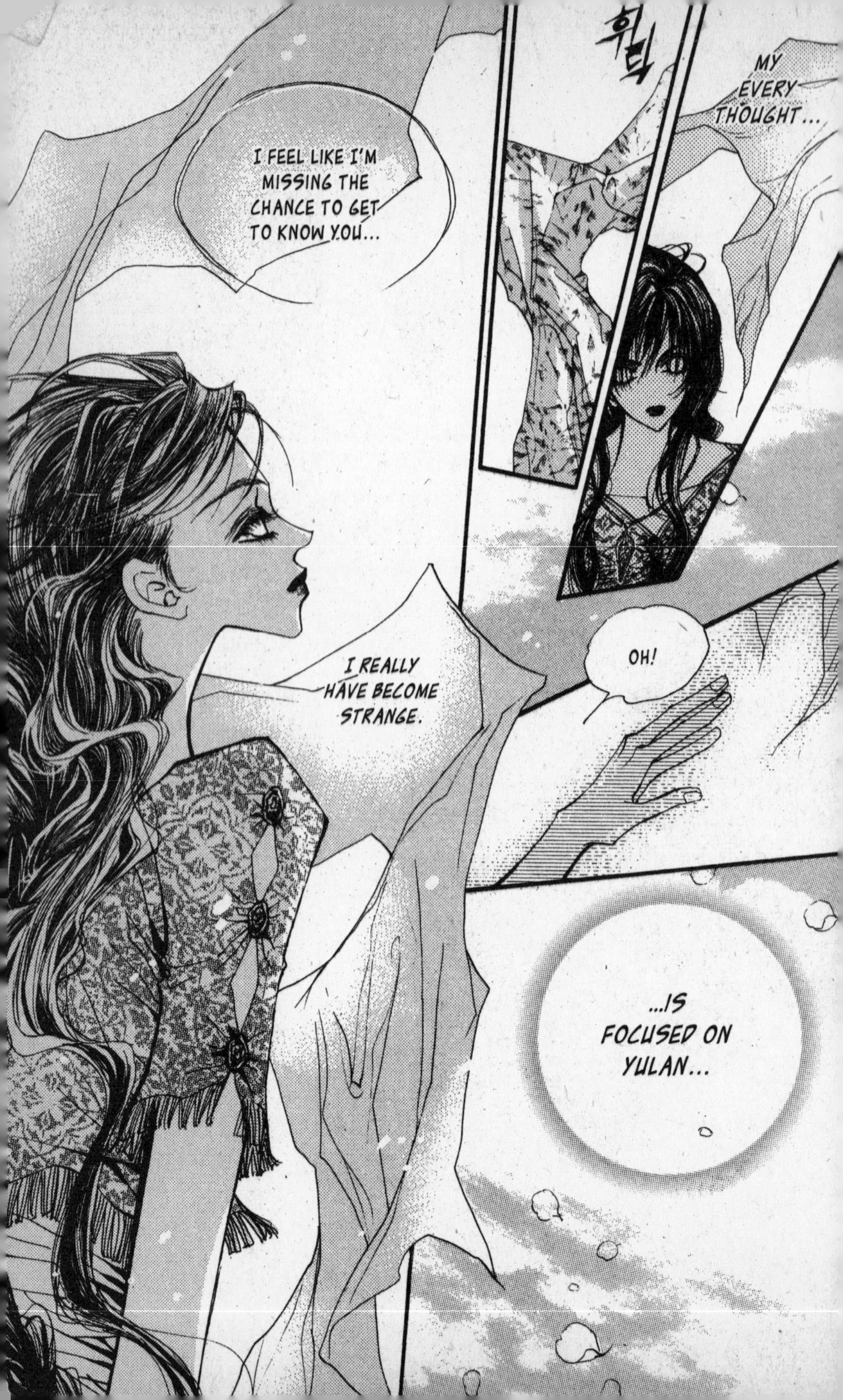
I FEEL LIKE I'M MISSING THE CHANCE TO GET TO KNOW YOU...
I REALLY HAVE BECOME STRANGE.
휘릭
MY EVERY THOUGHT...
OH!
...IS FOCUSED ON YULAN...

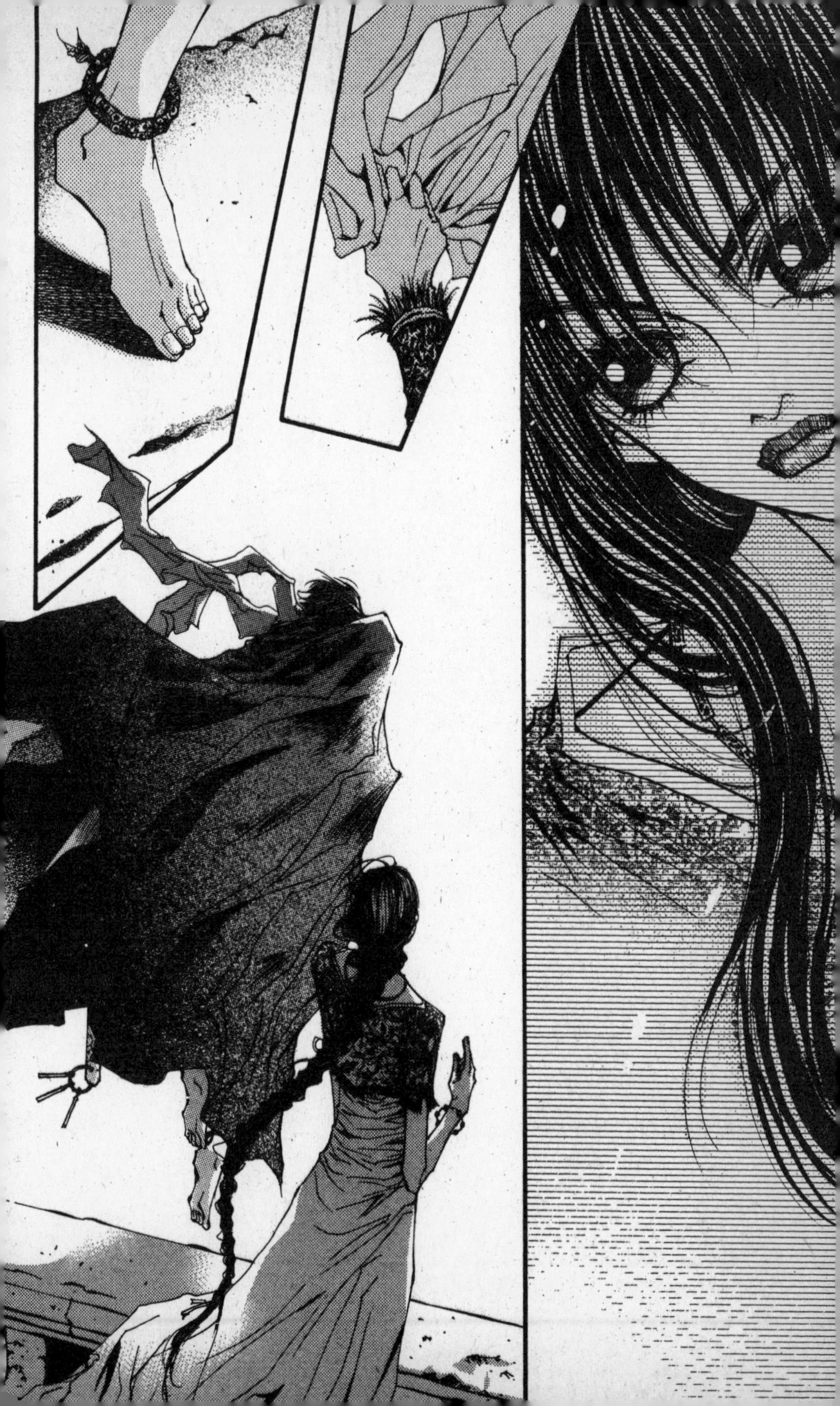

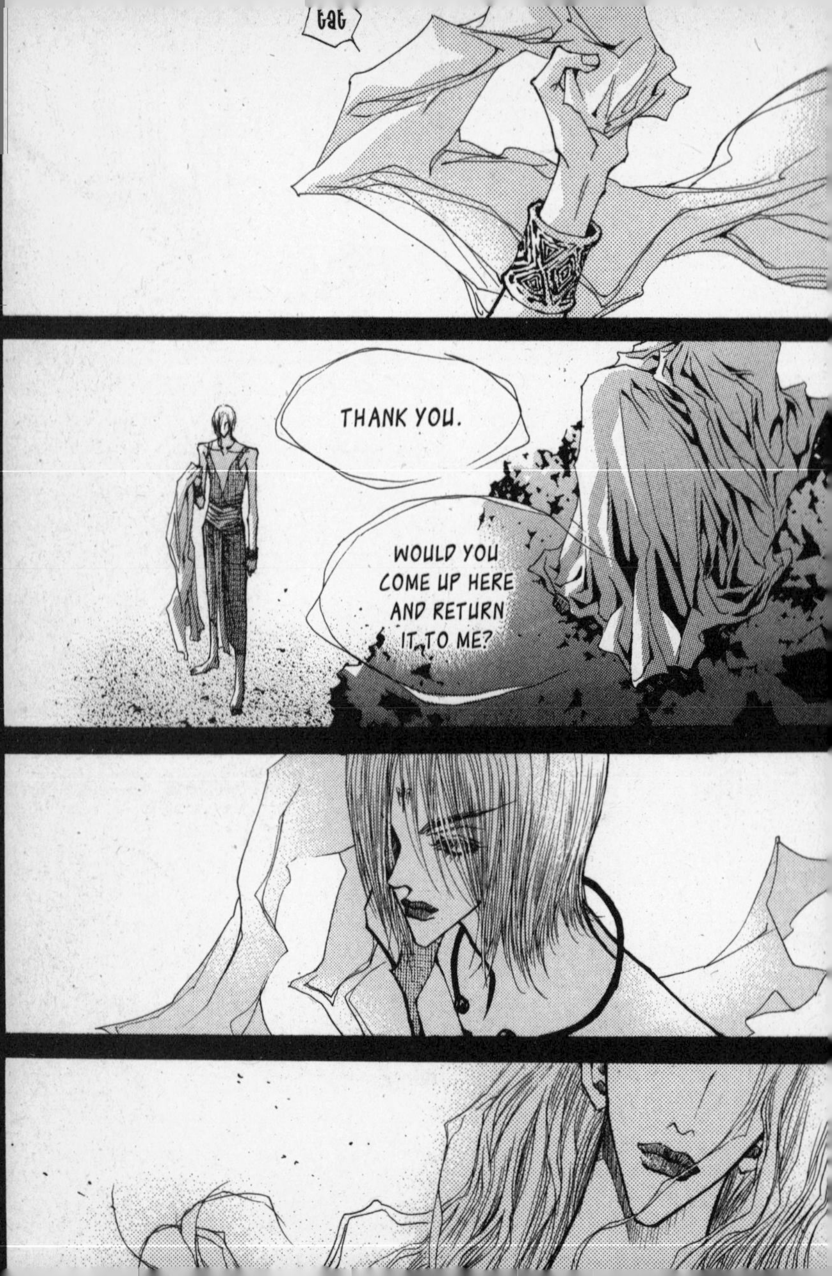
tat
THANK YOU.
WOULD YOU COME UP HERE AND RETURN IT TO ME?

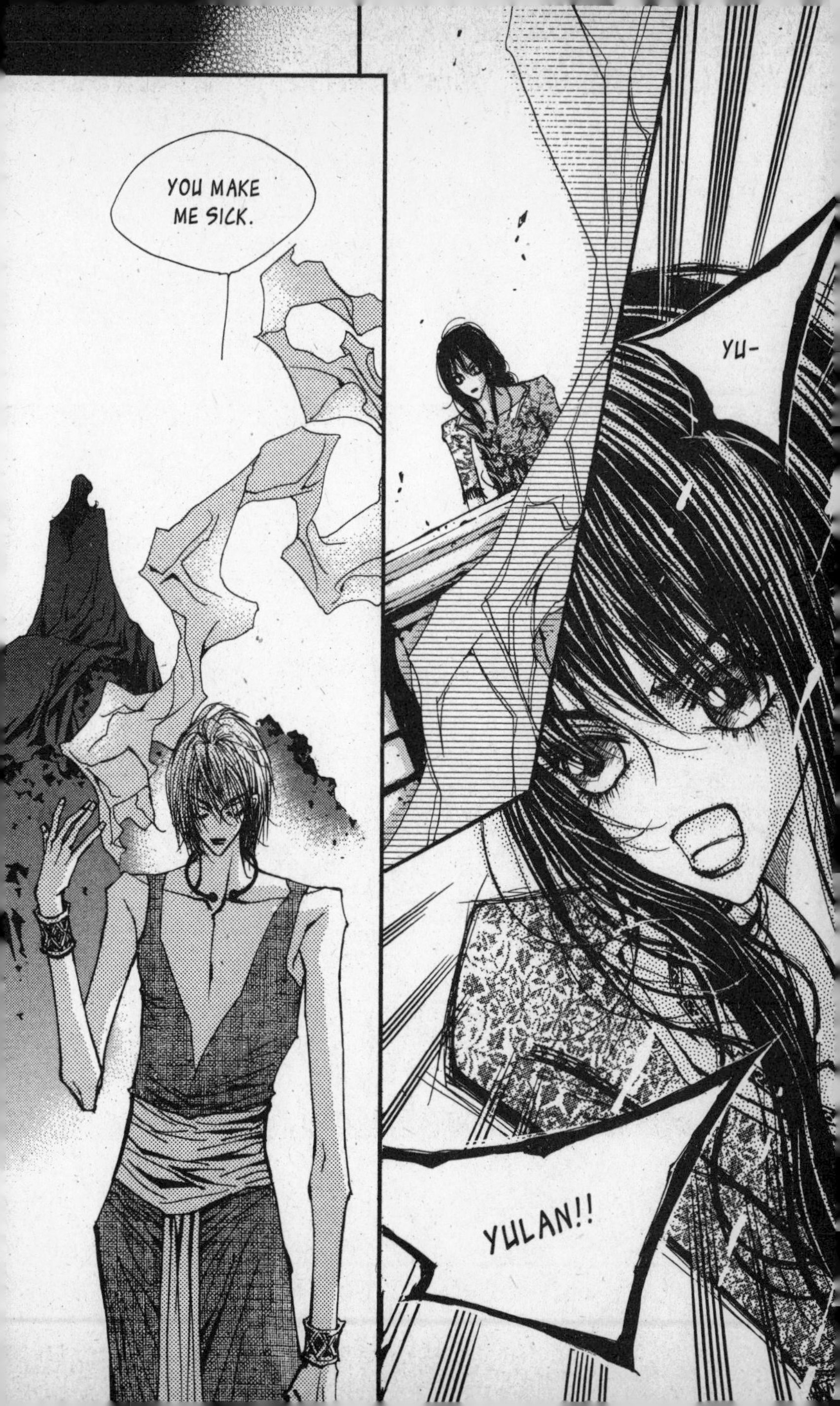
YOU MAKE ME SICK.
YU-
YULAN!!

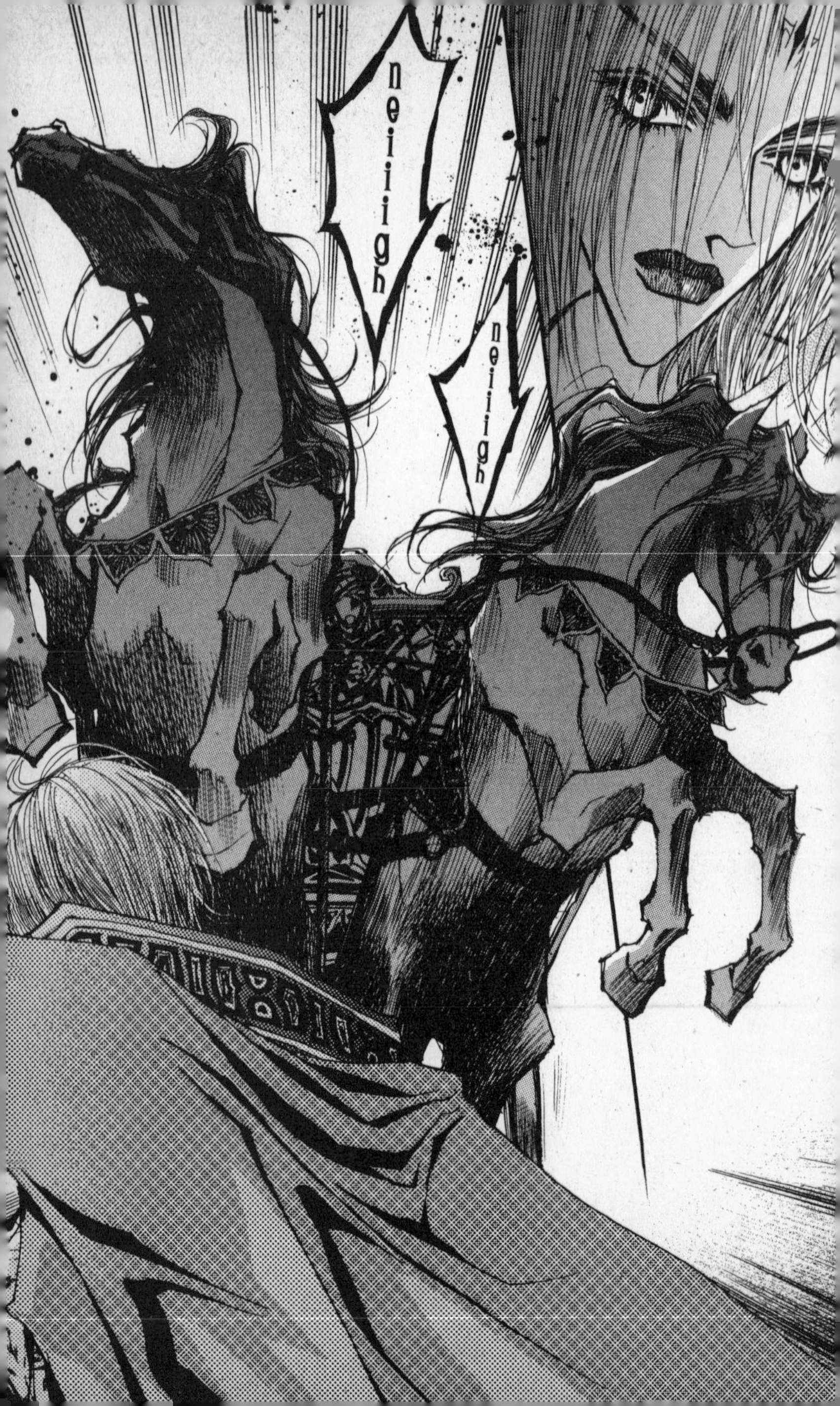
neiiigh
neiiigh

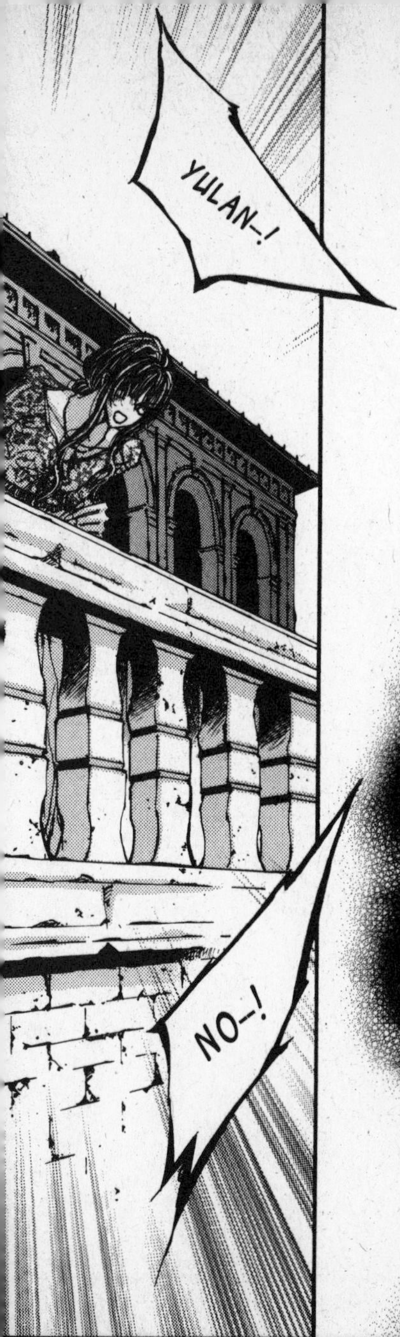
YULAN-!
NO-!
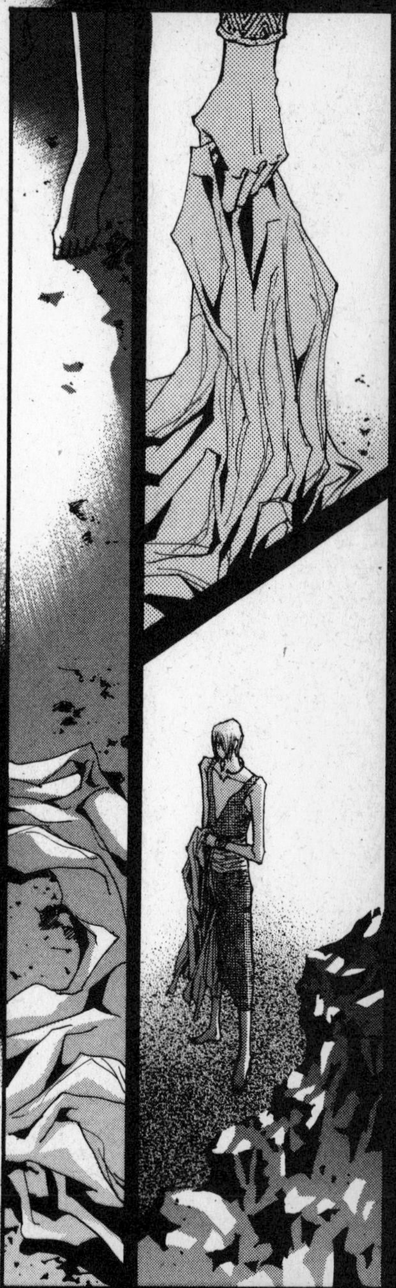

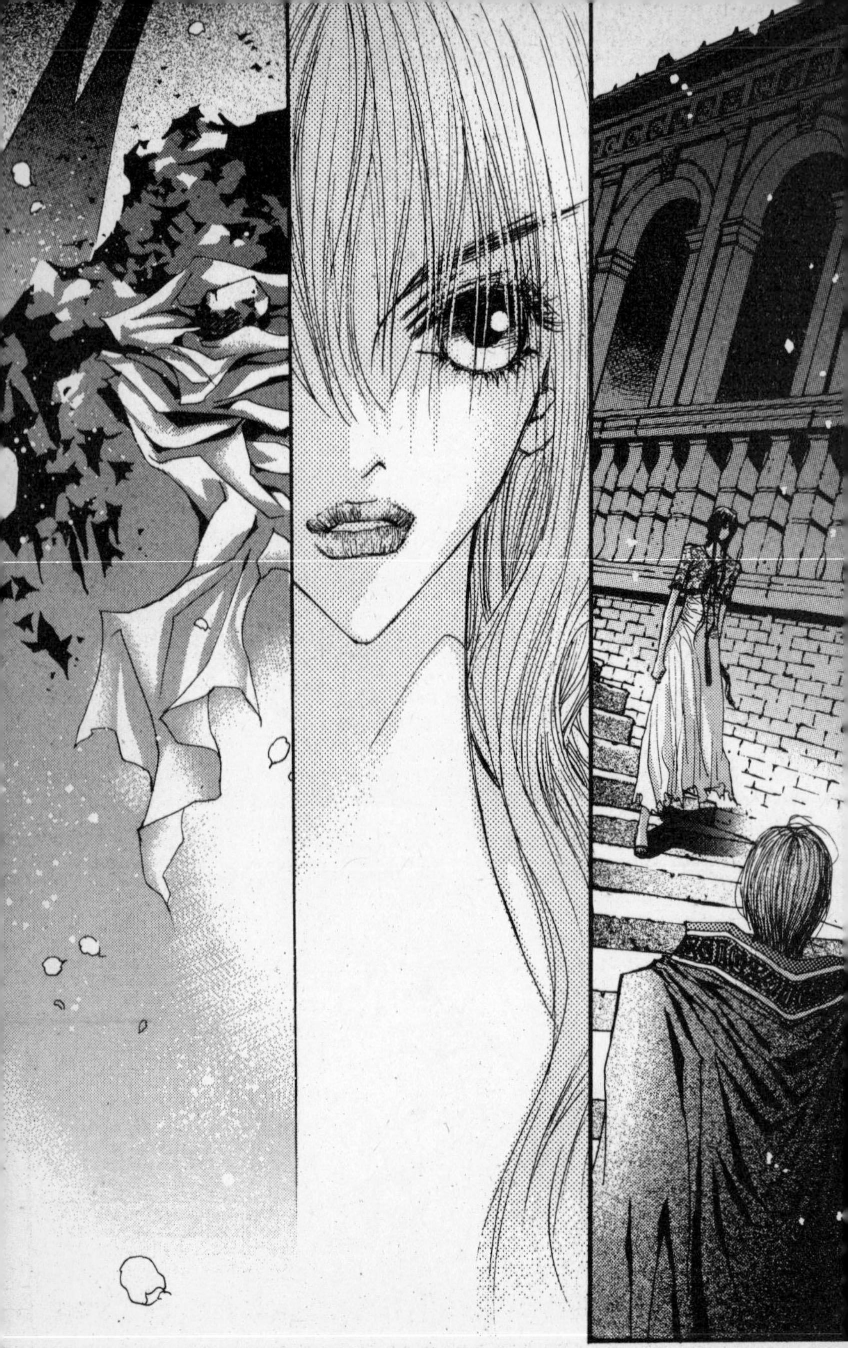

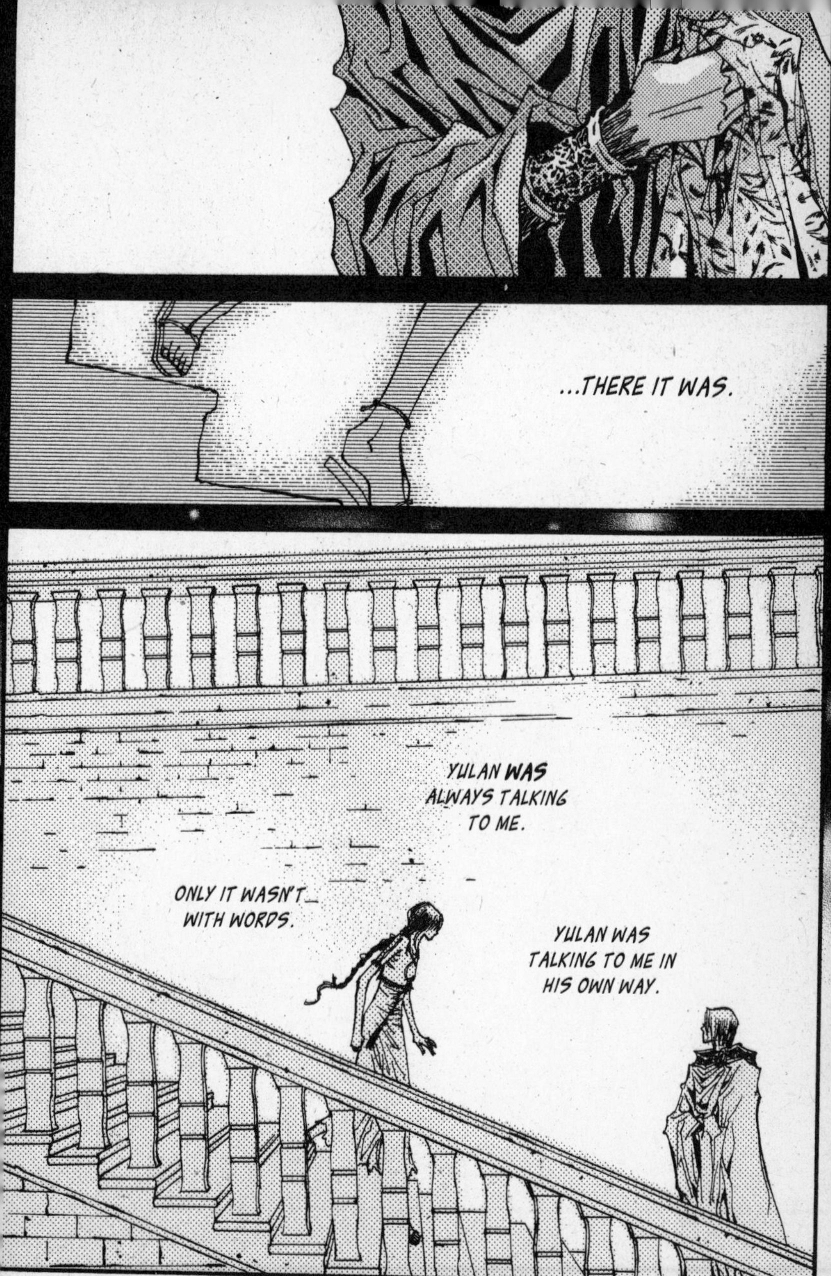
...THERE IT WAS.
YULAN WAS ALWAYS TALKING TO ME.
ONLY IT WASN'T WITH WORDS.
YULAN WAS TALKING TO ME IN HIS OWN WAY.

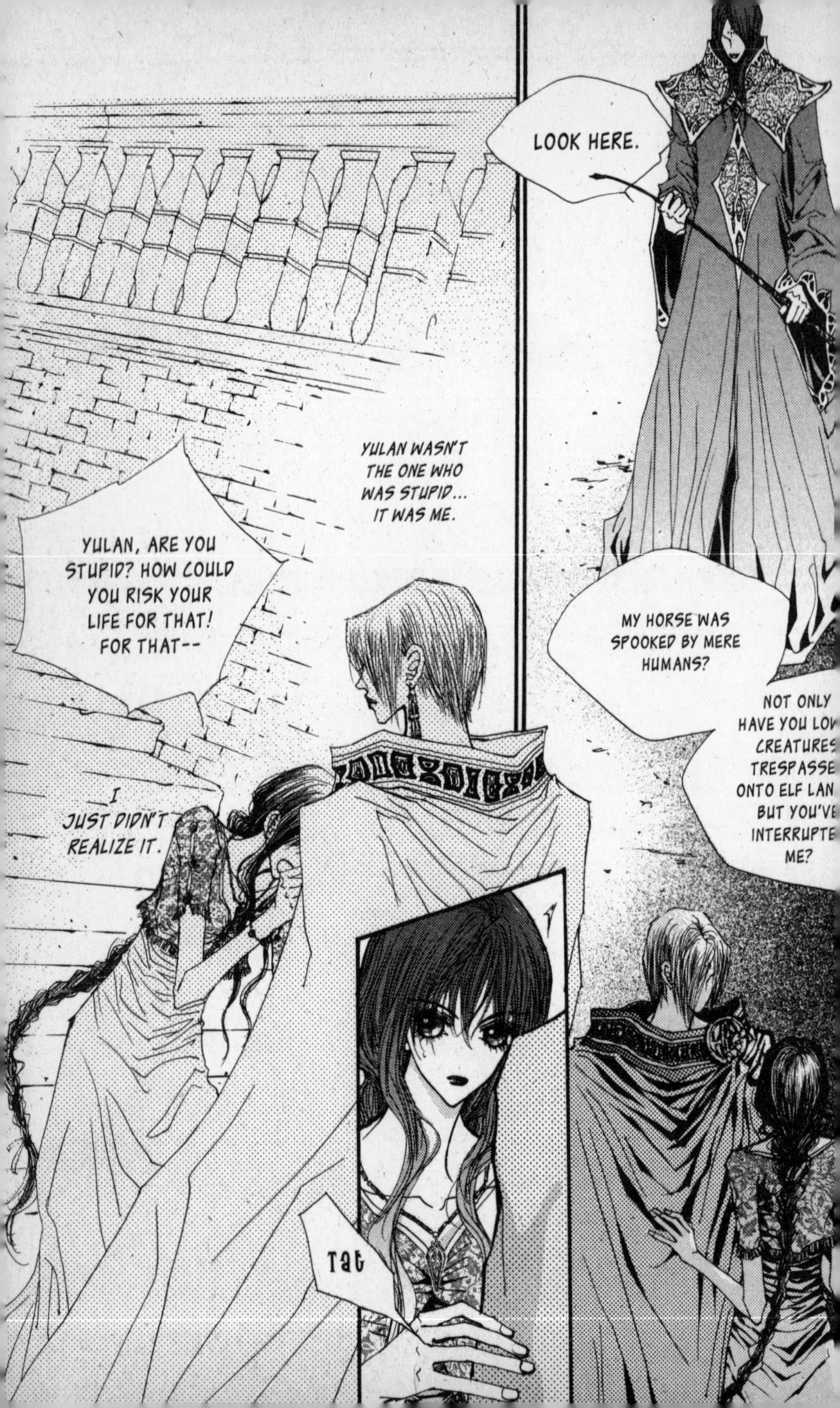
YULAN, ARE YOU STUPID? HOW COULD YOU RISK YOUR LIFE FOR THAT! FOR THAT--
YULAN WASN'T THE ONE WHO WAS STUPID... IT WAS ME.
I JUST DIDN'T REALIZE IT.
Tat
LOOK HERE.
MY HORSE WAS SPOOKED BY MERE HUMANS?
NOT ONLY HAVE YOU LOW CREATURES TRESPASSE ONTO ELF LAN BUT YOU'VE INTERRUPTE ME?

OH...WHAT'S THIS? NOW THAT I LOOK, I SEE YOU'RE NOT A HUMAN...

...BUT A HALF-ELF

EEDA: A SHAWL

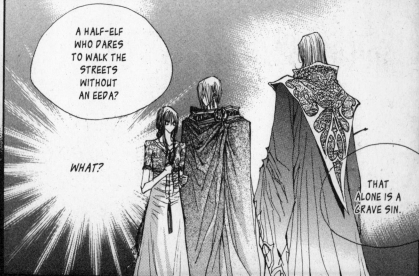

A HALF-ELF WHO DARES TO WALK THE STREETS WITHOUT AN EEDA?

WHAT?

THAT ALONE IS A GRAVE SIN.

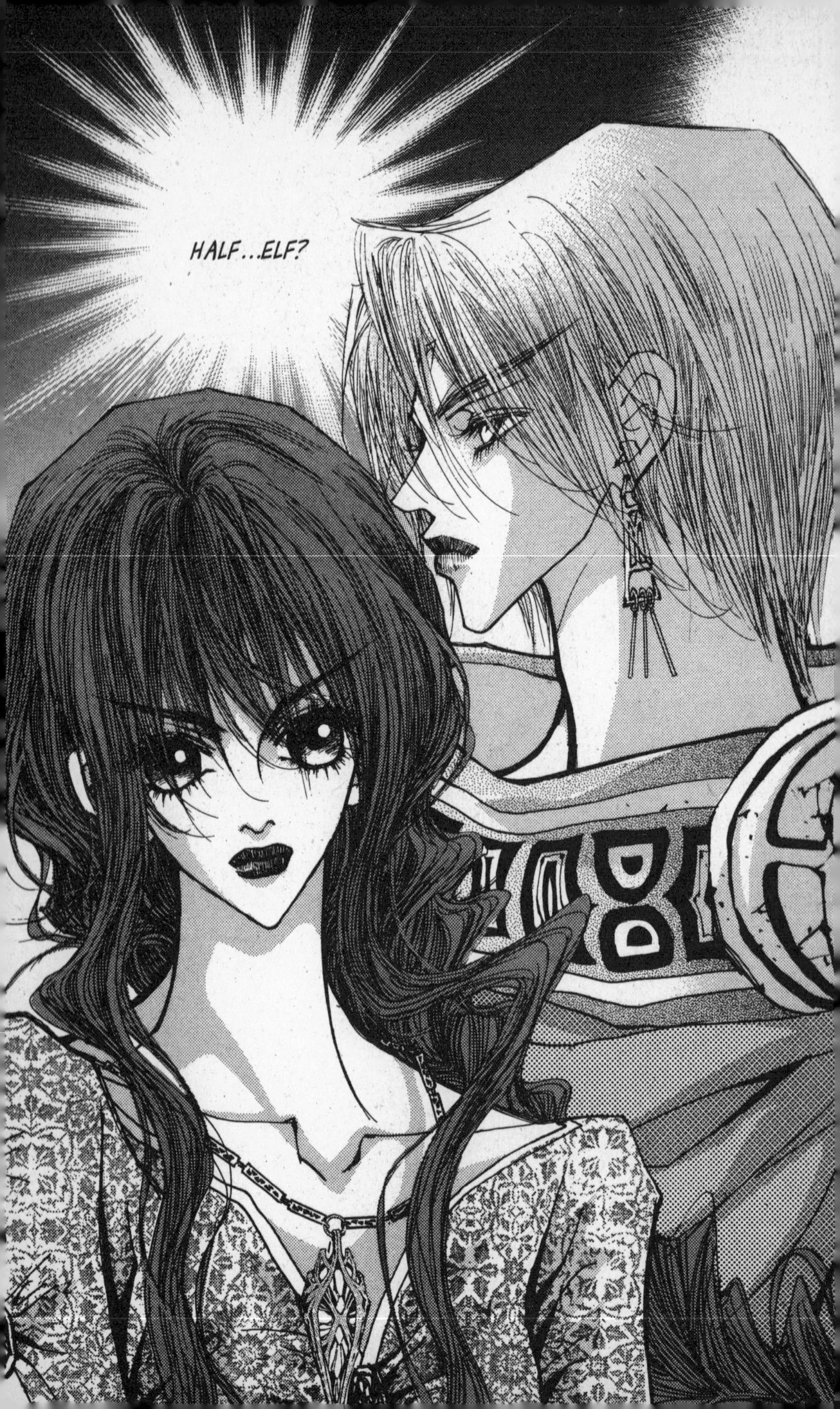
HALF...ELF?

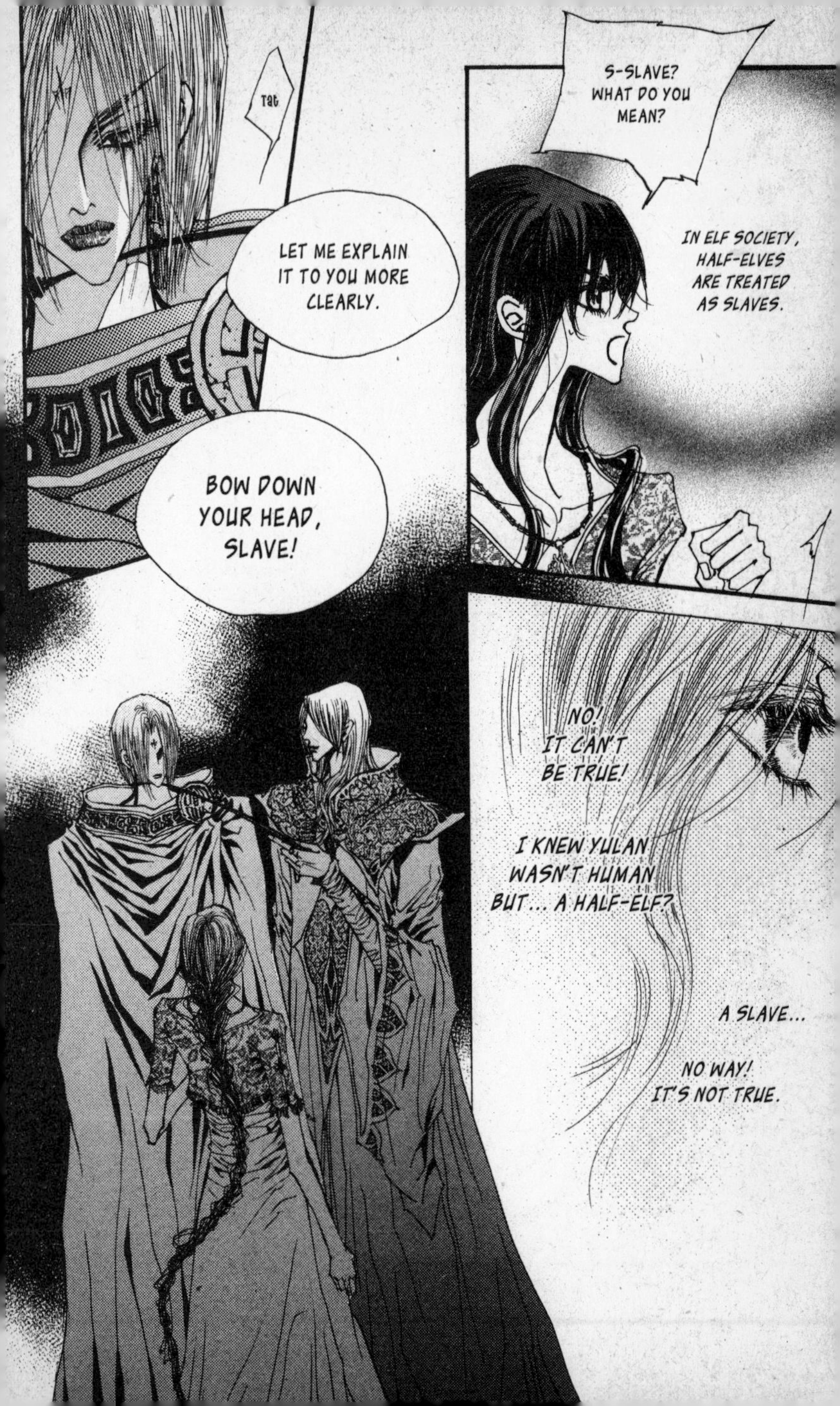
Tat
LET ME EXPLAIN IT TO YOU MORE CLEARLY.
BOW DOWN YOUR HEAD, SLAVE!
S-SLAVE? WHAT DO YOU MEAN?
IN ELF SOCIETY, HALF-ELVES ARE TREATED AS SLAVES.
NO! IT CAN'T BE TRUE!
I KNEW YULAN WASN'T HUMAN BUT ... A HALF-ELF?
A SLAVE...
NO WAY! IT'S NOT TRUE.

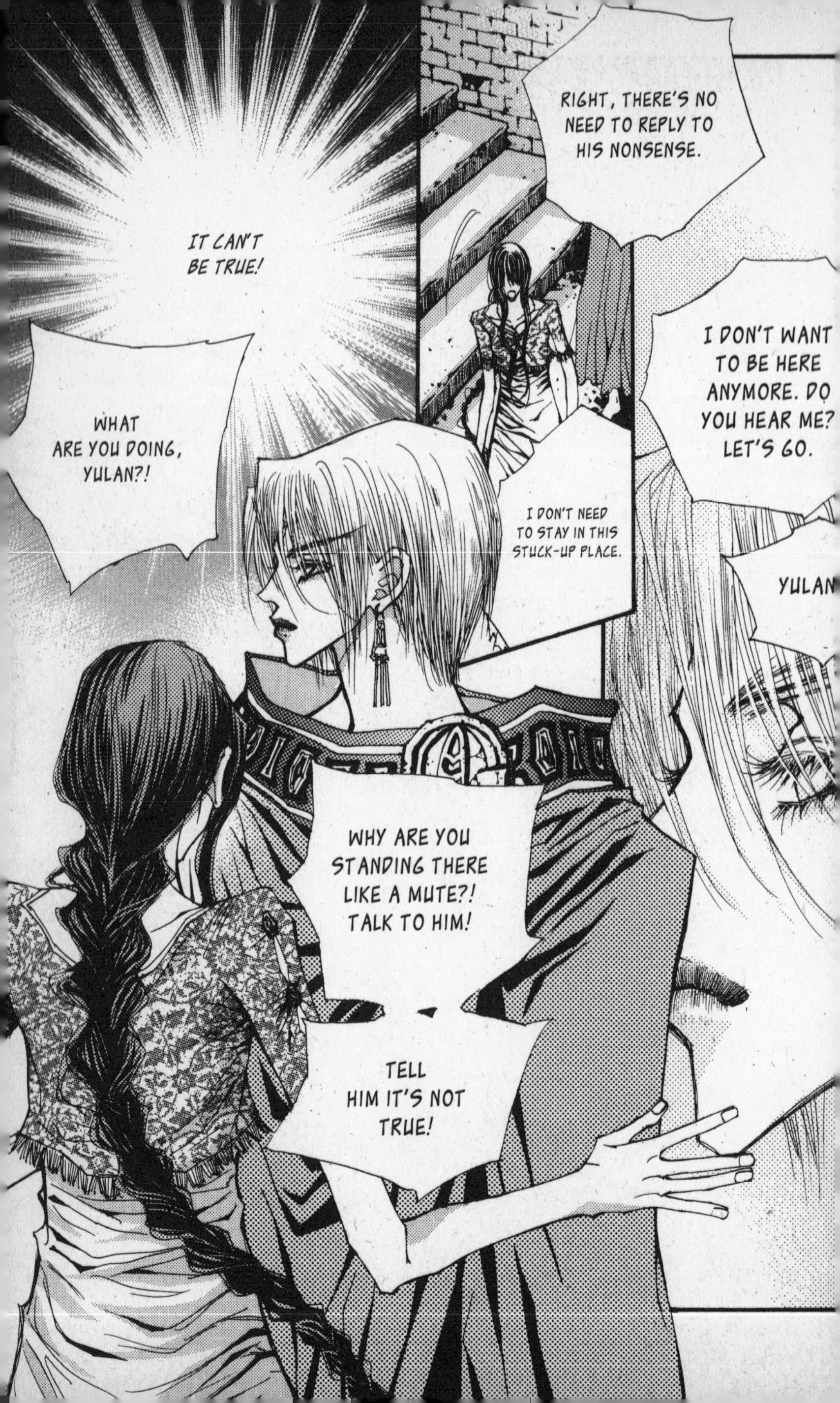
IT CAN'T BE TRUE!
WHAT ARE YOU DOING, YULAN?!
RIGHT, THERE'S NO NEED TO REPLY TO HIS NONSENSE.
I DON'T WANT TO BE HERE ANYMORE. DO YOU HEAR ME? LET'S GO.
I DON'T NEED TO STAY IN THIS STUCK-UP PLACE.
YULAN
WHY ARE YOU STANDING THERE LIKE A MUTE?! TALK TO HIM!
TELL HIM IT'S NOT TRUE!

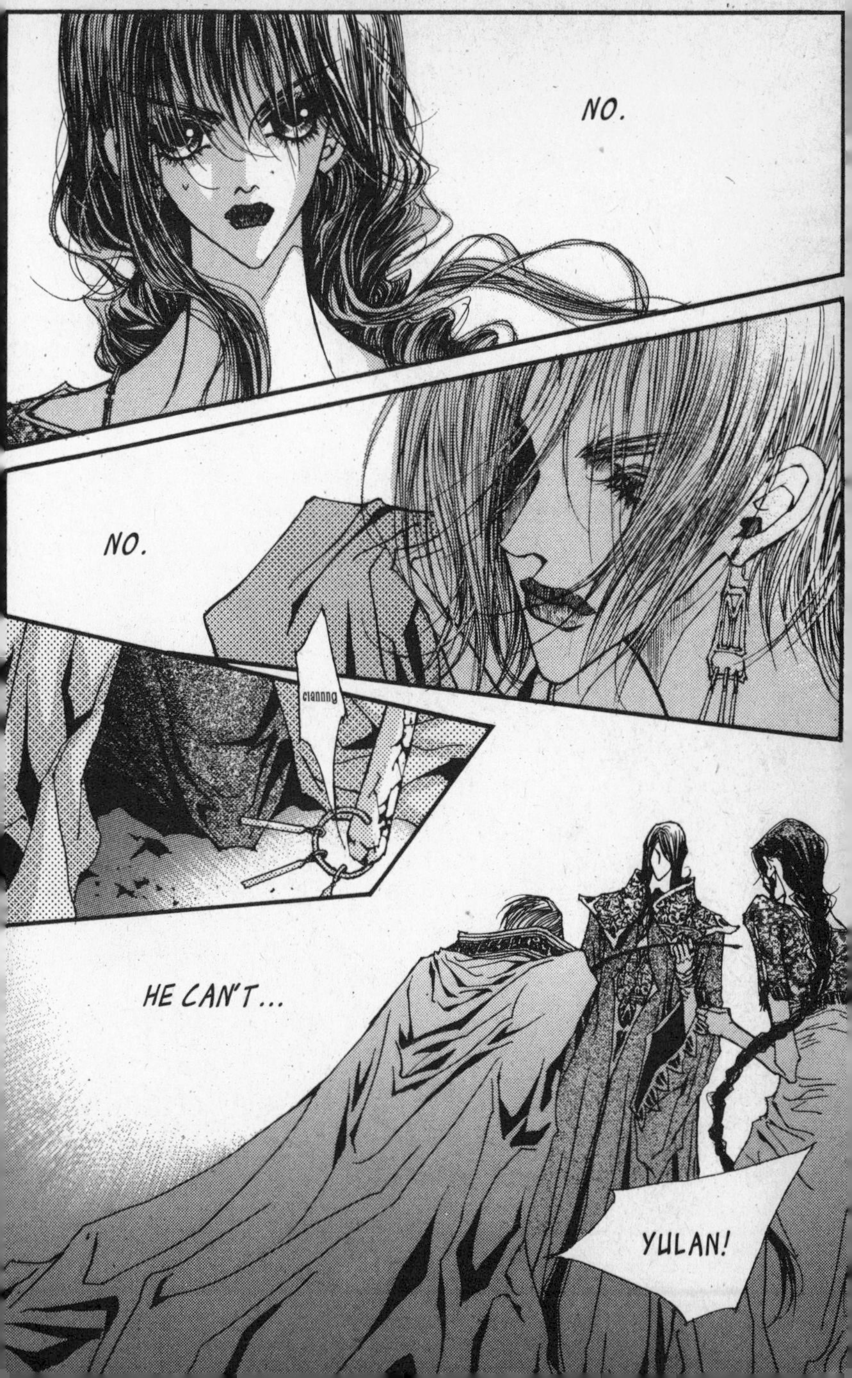
NO.
NO.
clannng
HE CAN'T...
YULAN!

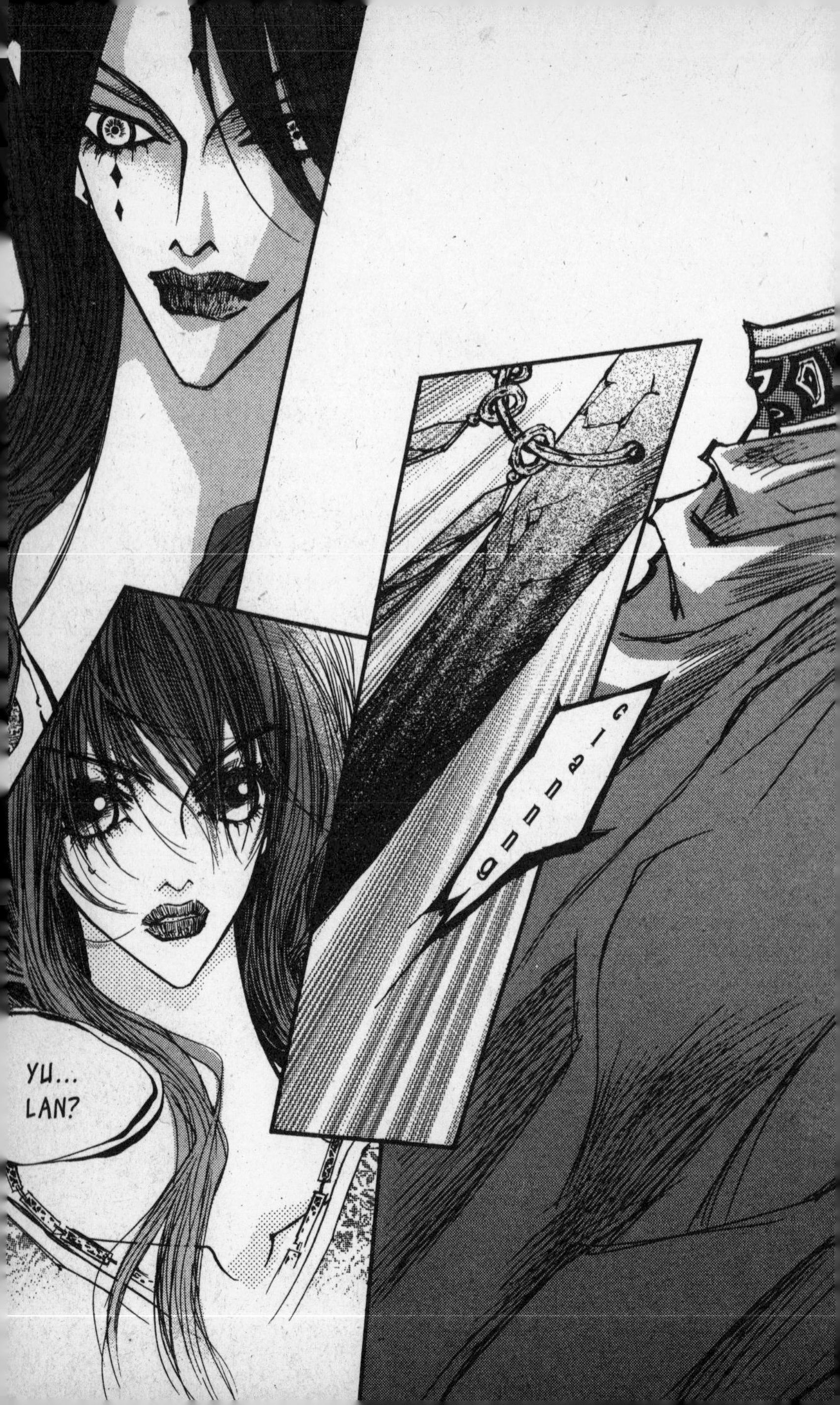
Clannng
YU... LAN?

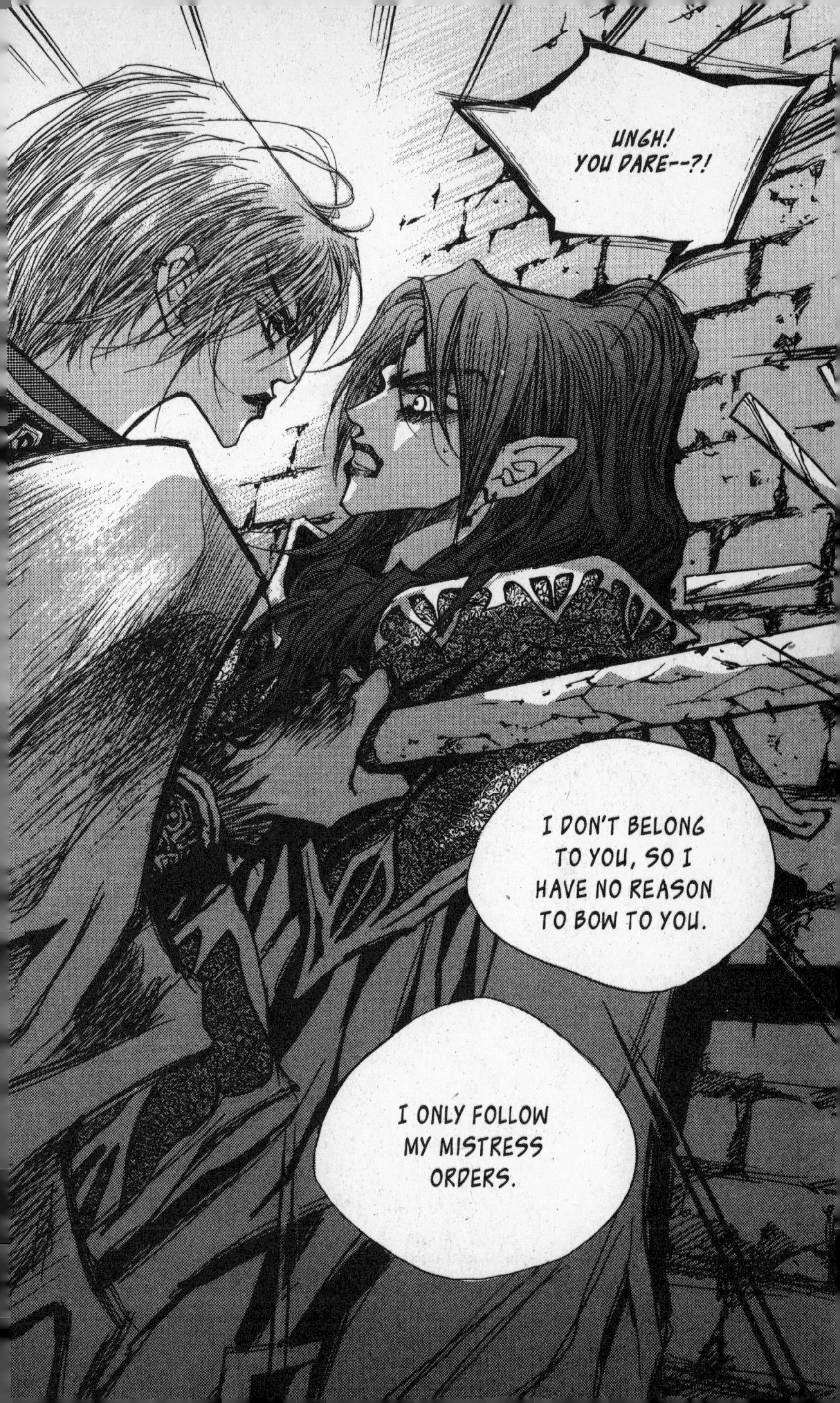
UNGH! YOU DARE--?!
I DON'T BELONG TO YOU, SO I HAVE NO REASON TO BOW TO YOU.
I ONLY FOLLOW MY MISTRESS ORDERS.

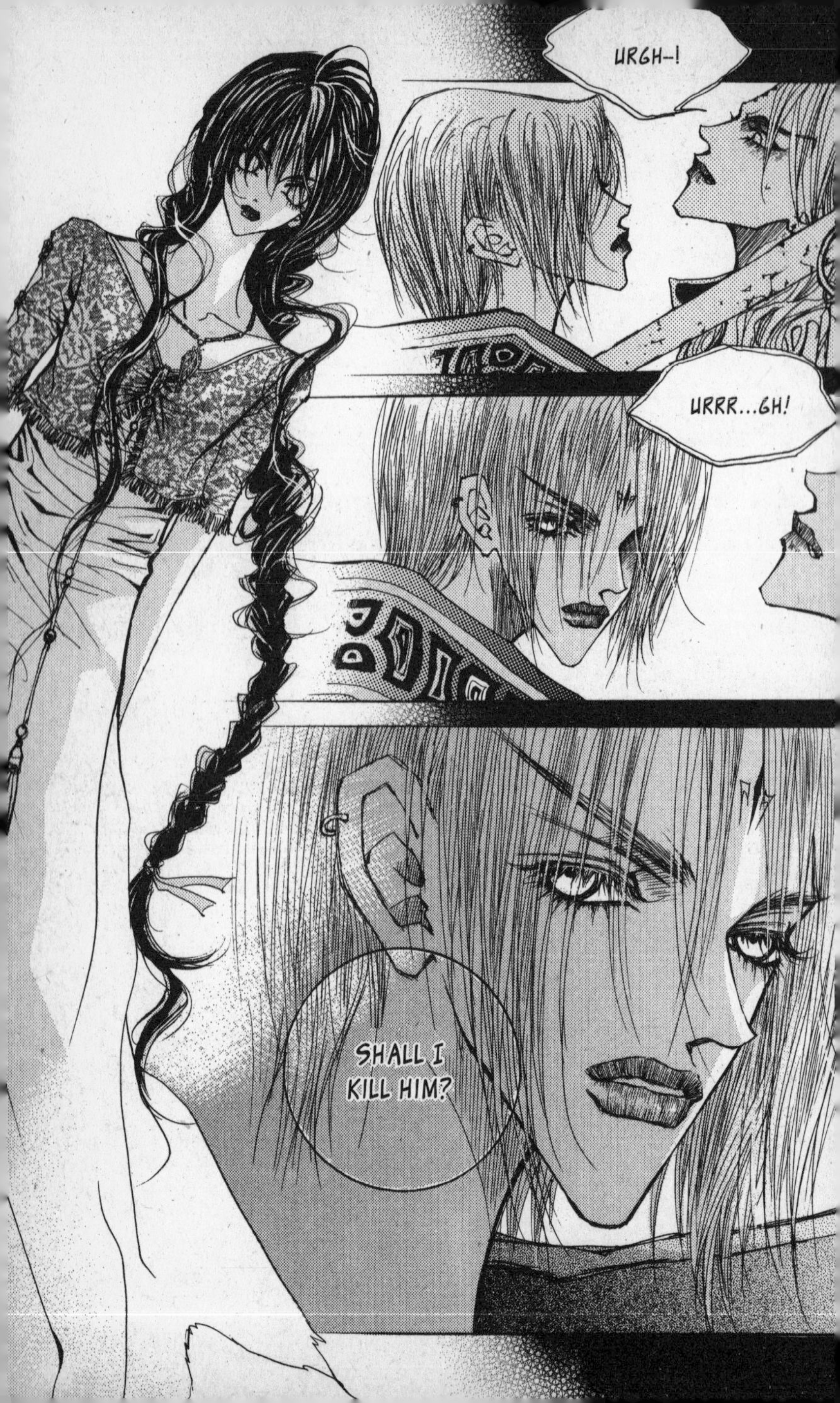
URGH-!
URRR...GH!
SHALL I KILL HIM?

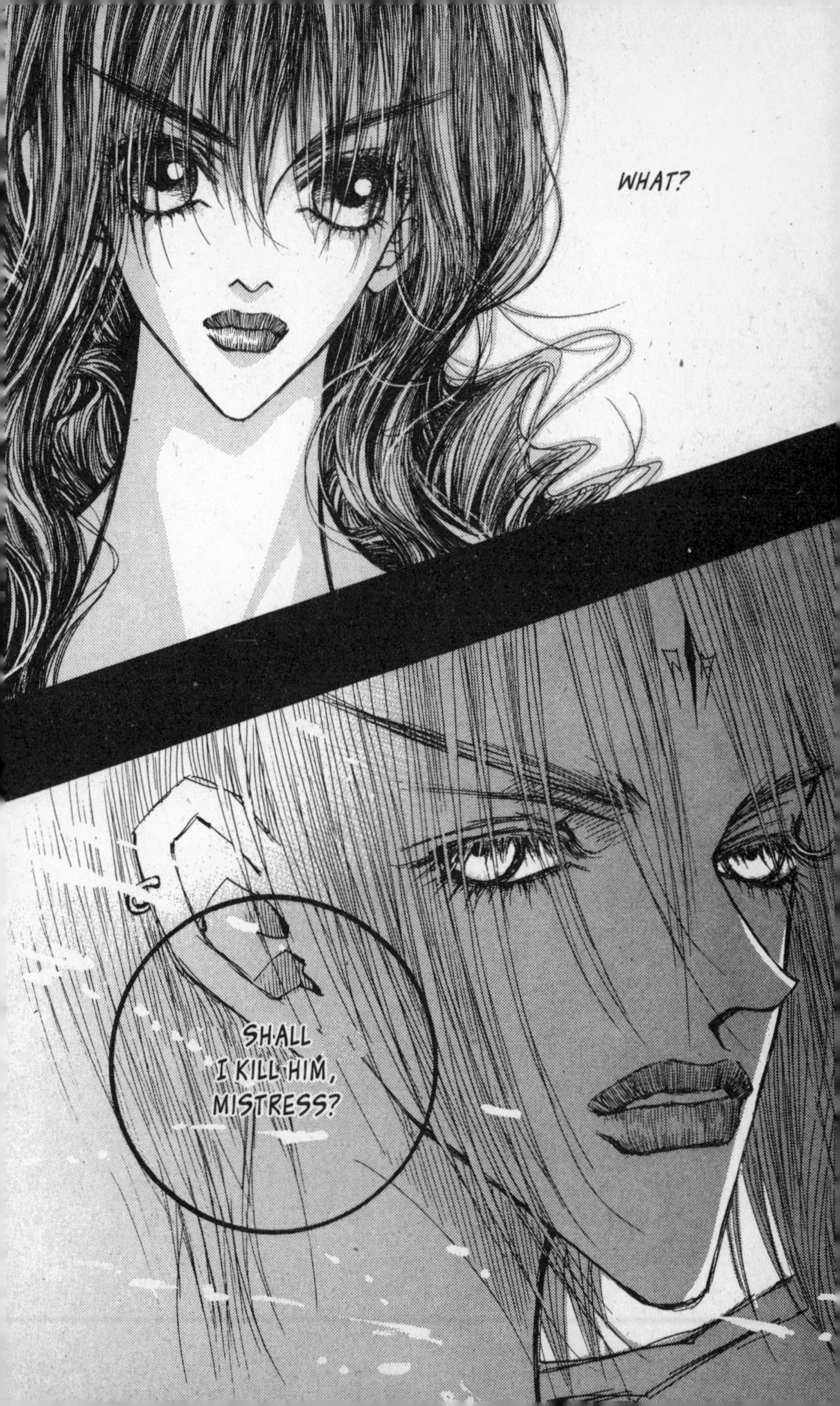
WHAT?
SHALL I KILL HIM, MISTRESS?

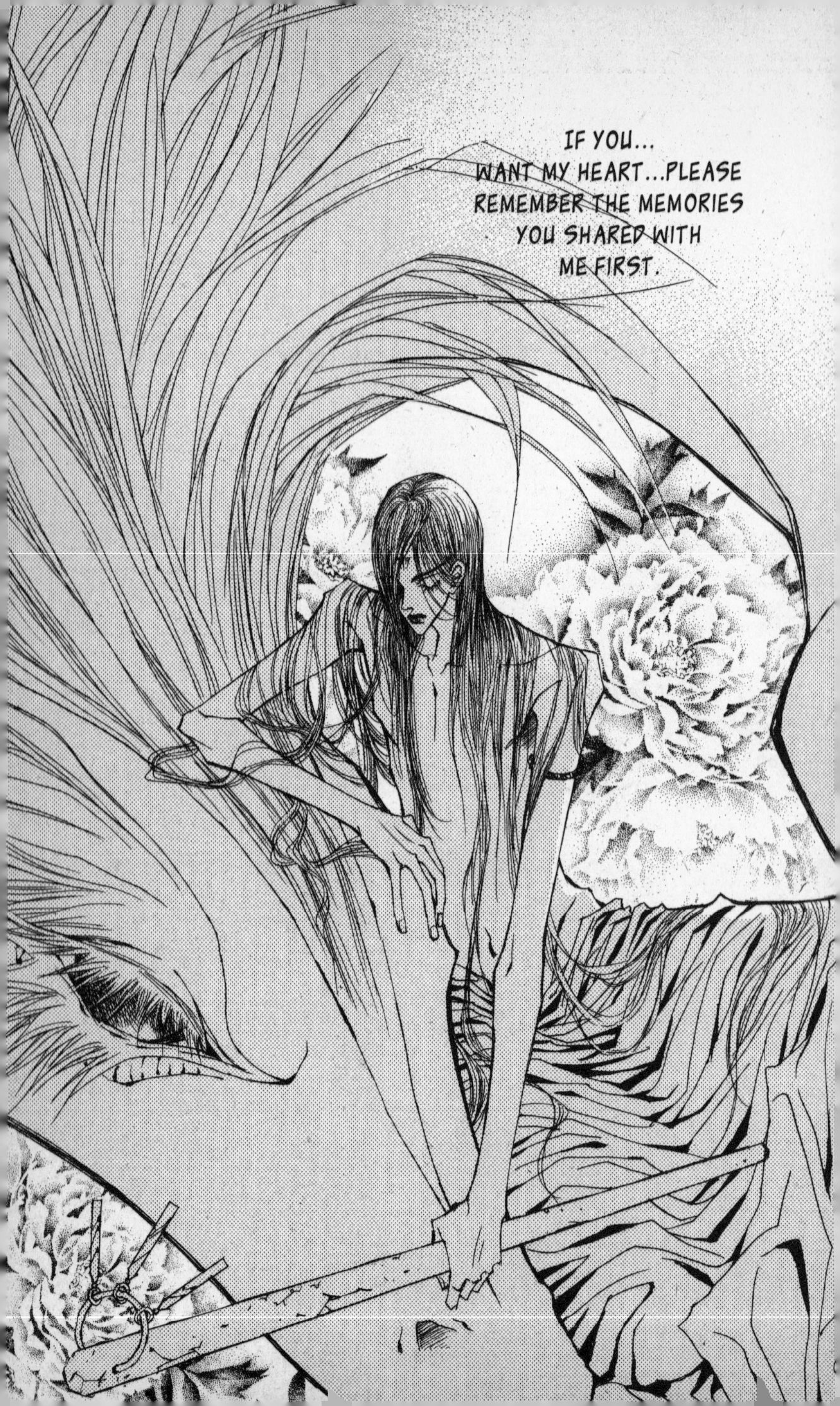
IF YOU... WANT MY HEART...PLEASE REMEMBER THE MEMORIES YOU SHARED WITH ME FIRST.

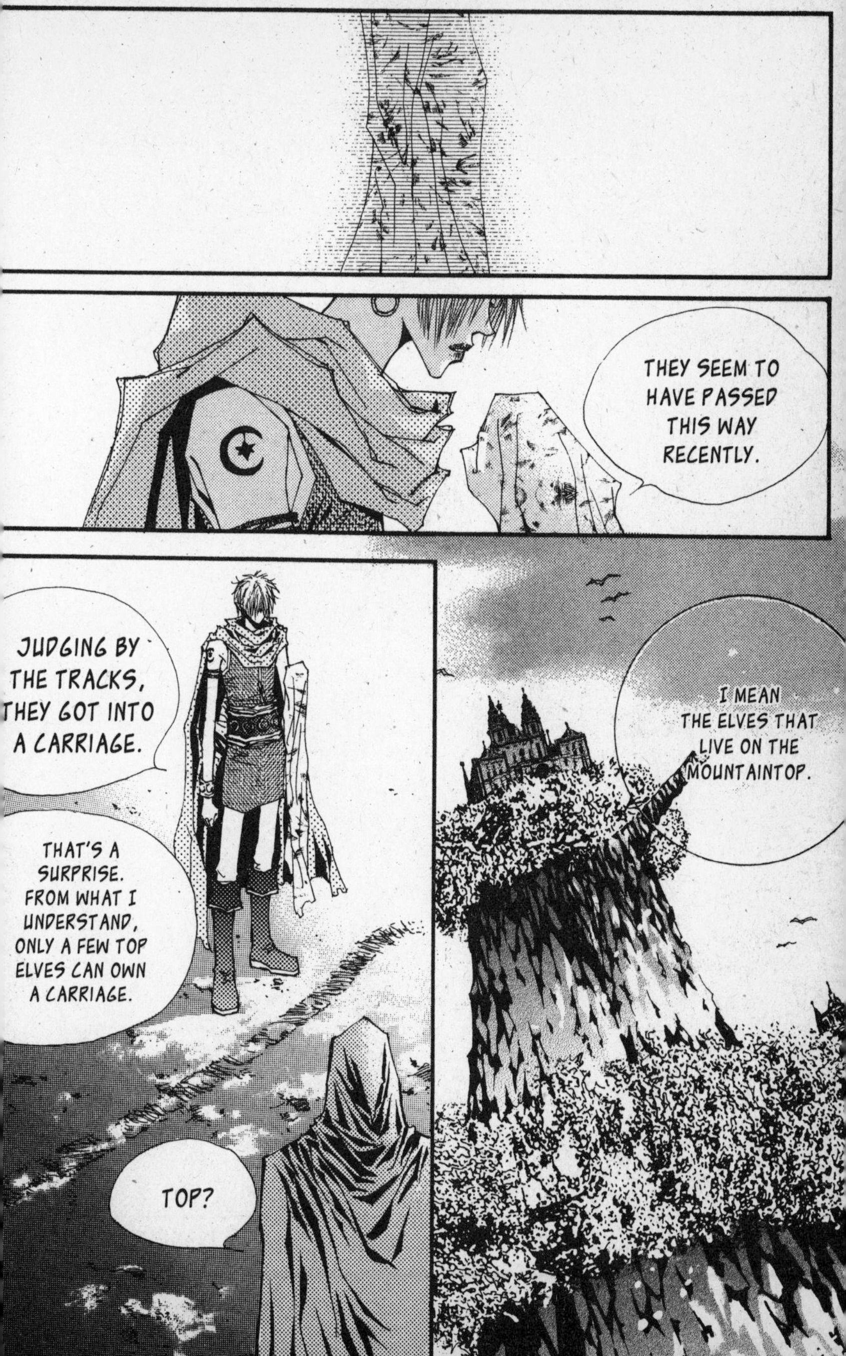
THEY SEEM TO HAVE PASSED THIS WAY RECENTLY.
JUDGING BY THE TRACKS, THEY GOT INTO A CARRIAGE.
THAT'S A SURPRISE. FROM WHAT I UNDERSTAND, ONLY A FEW TOP ELVES CAN OWN A CARRIAGE.
TOP?
I MEAN THE ELVES THAT LIVE ON THE MOUNTAINTOP.

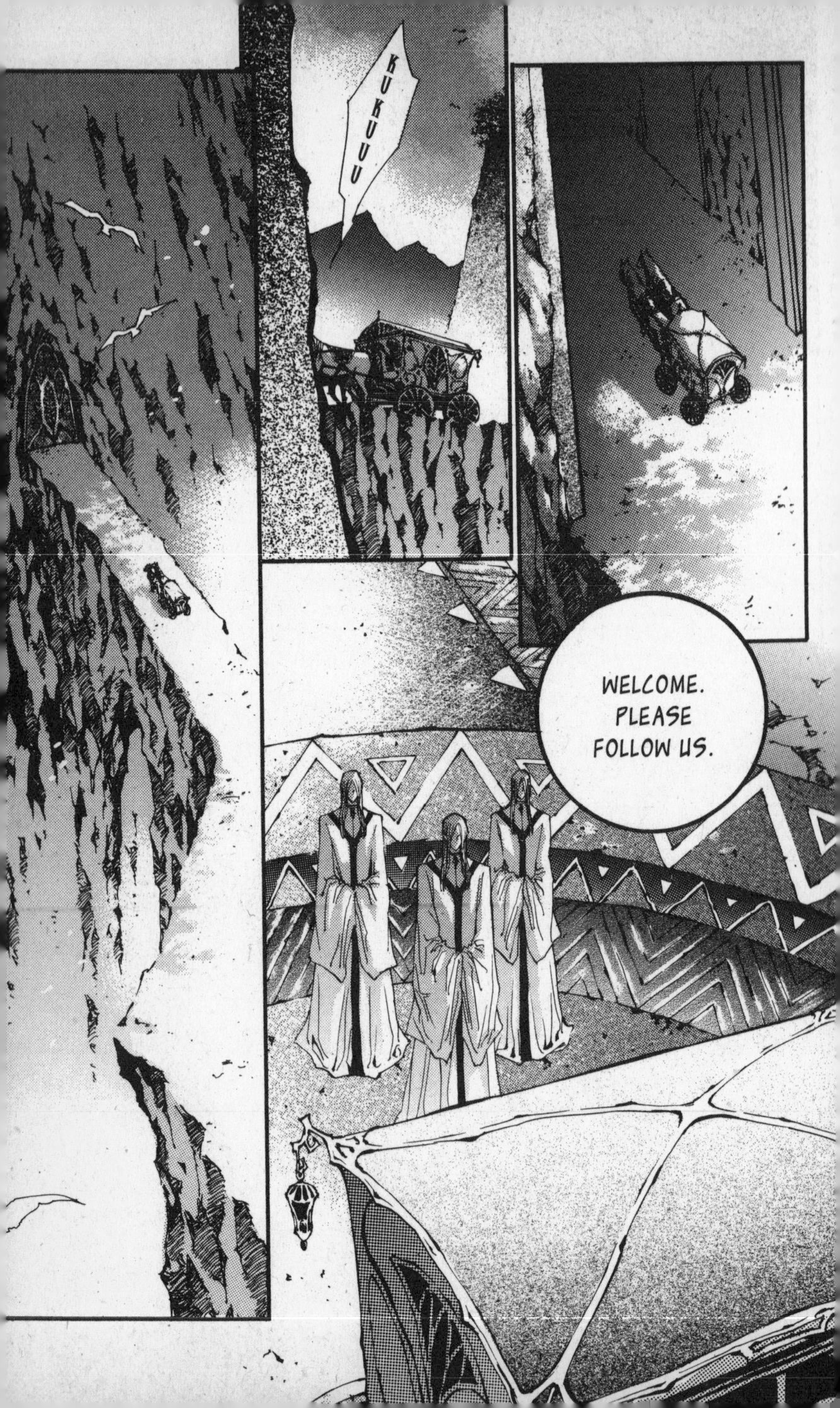
KUKUUUU
WELCOME. PLEASE FOLLOW US.

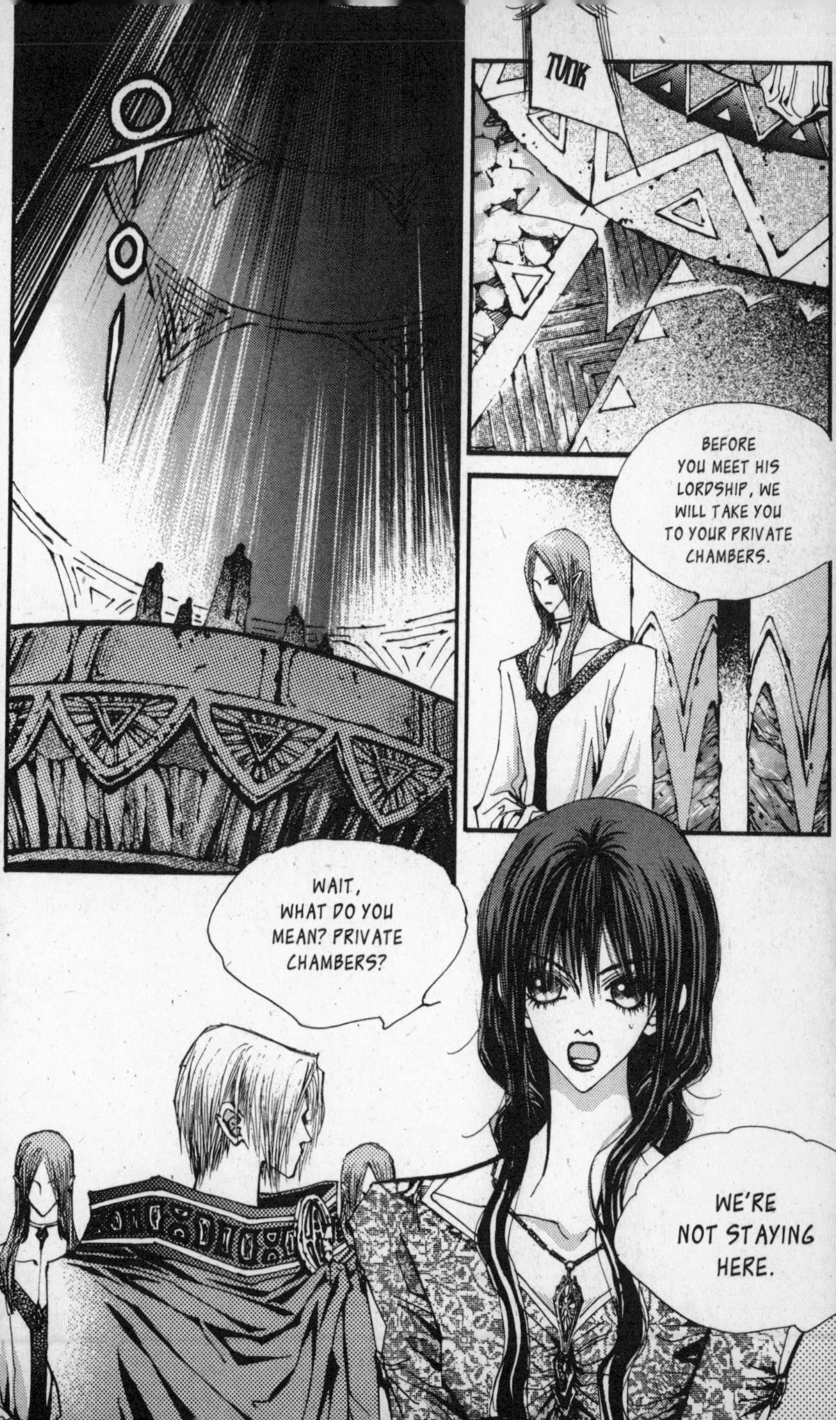
TUNK
BEFORE YOU MEET HIS LORDSHIP, WE WILL TAKE YOU TO YOUR PRIVATE CHAMBERS.
WAIT, WHAT DO YOU MEAN? PRIVATE CHAMBERS?
WE'RE NOT STAYING HERE.

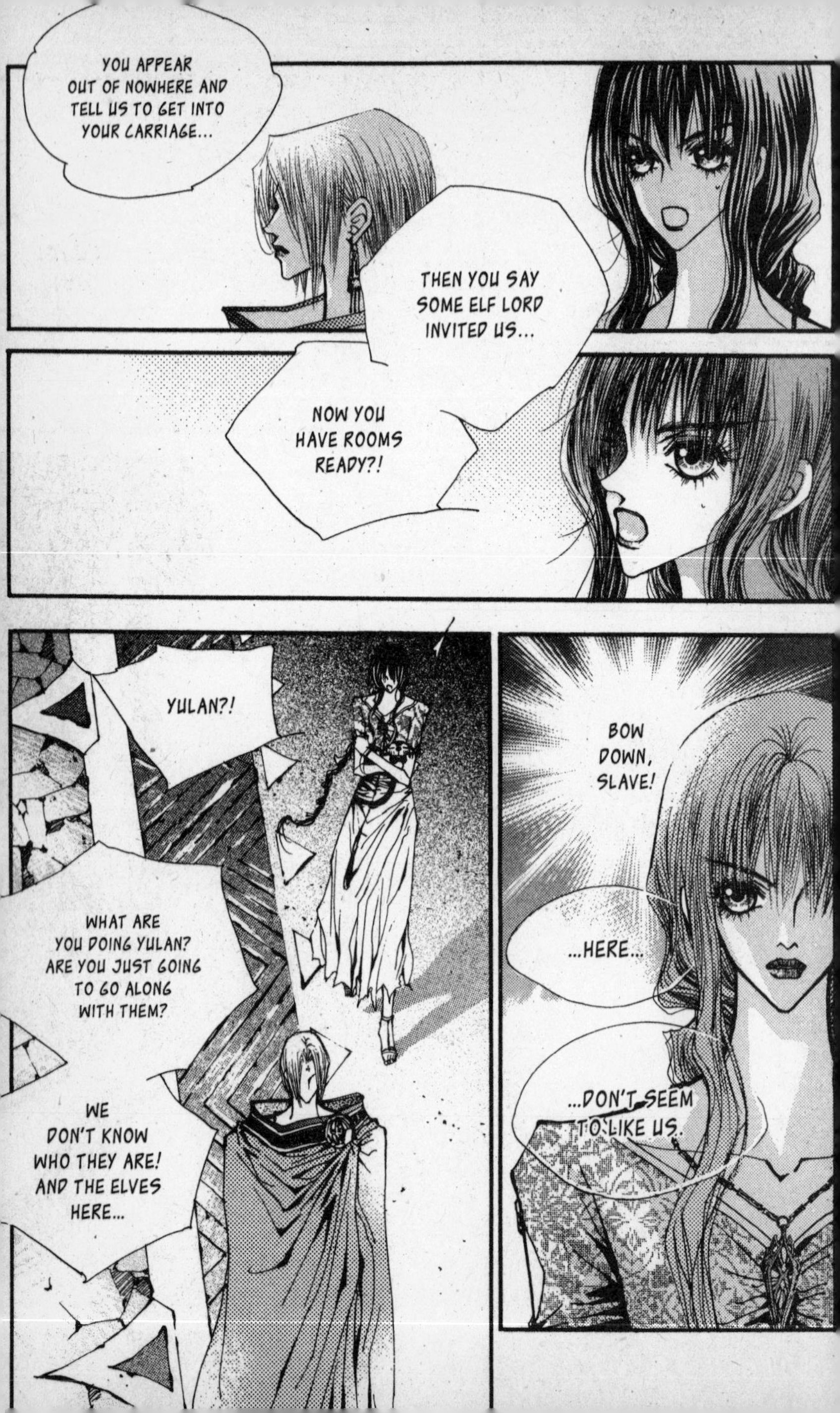
YOU APPEAR OUT OF NOWHERE AND TELL US TO GET INTO YOUR CARRIAGE...
THEN YOU SAY SOME ELF LORD INVITED US...
NOW YOU HAVE ROOMS READY?!
YULAN?!
WHAT ARE YOU DOING YULAN? ARE YOU JUST GOING TO GO ALONG WITH THEM?
WE DON'T KNOW WHO THEY ARE! AND THE ELVES HERE...
BOW DOWN, SLAVE!
...HERE...
...DON'T SEEM TO LIKE US.

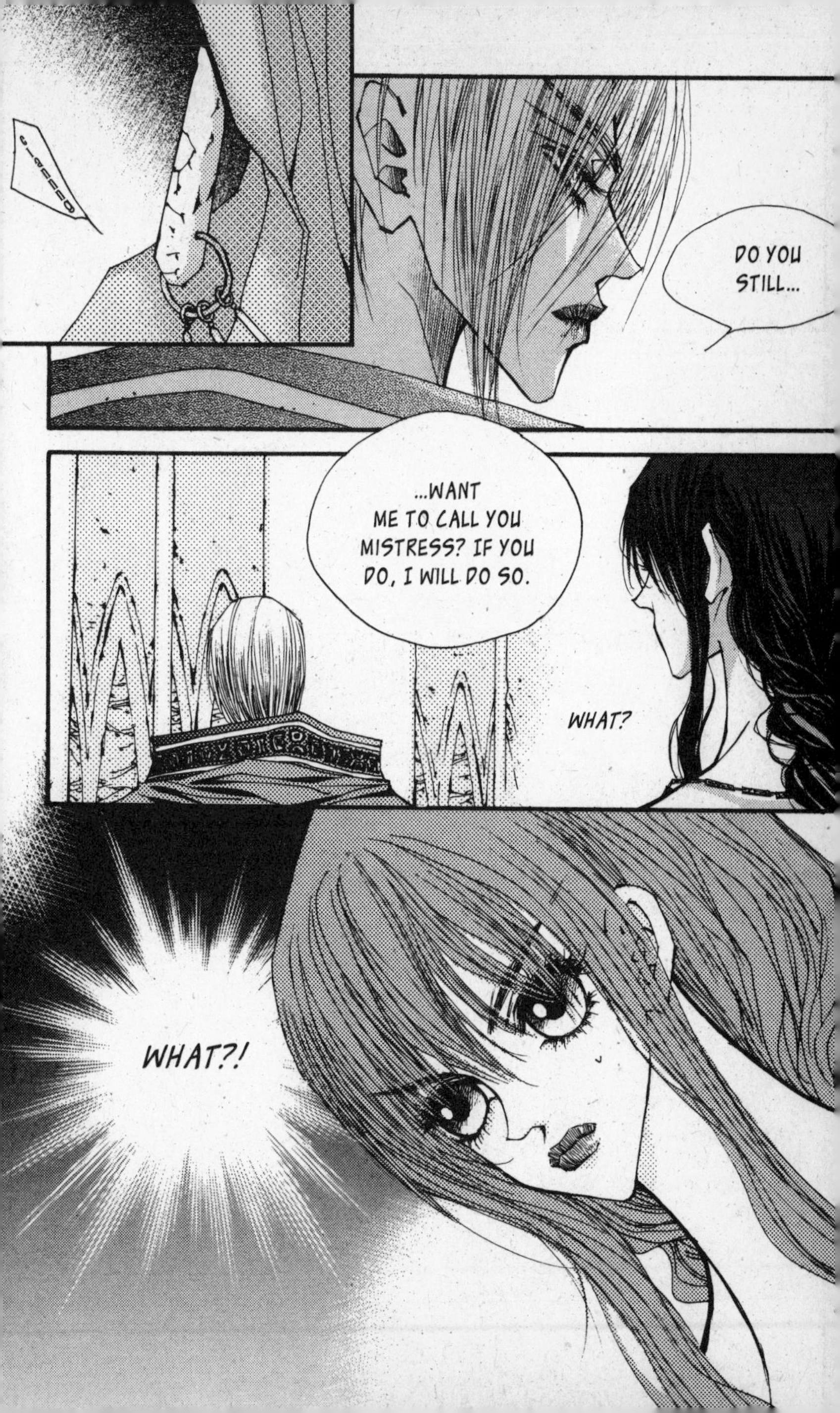
DO YOU STILL...
...WANT ME TO CALL YOU MISTRESS? IF YOU DO, I WILL DO SO.
WHAT?
WHAT?!

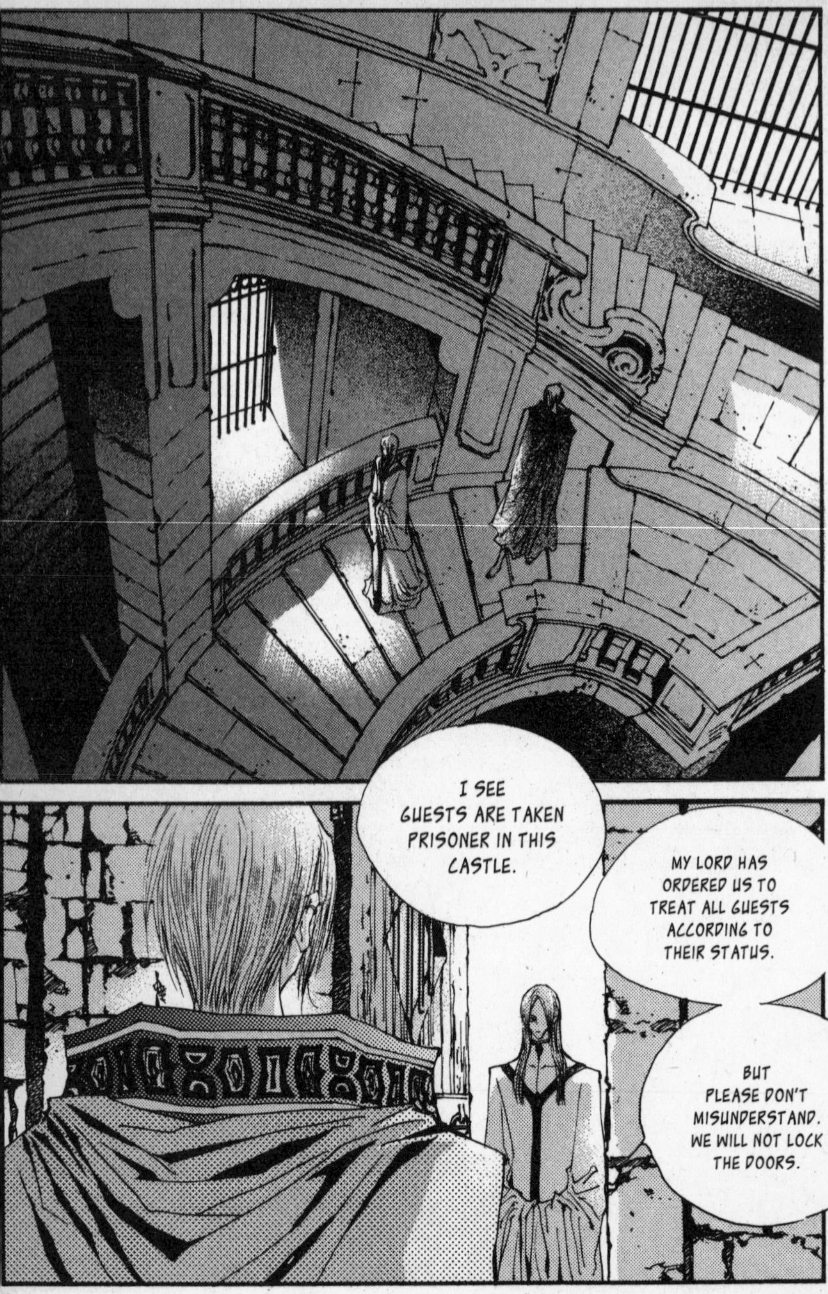
I SEE GUESTS ARE TAKEN PRISONER IN THIS CASTLE.
MY LORD HAS ORDERED US TO TREAT ALL GUESTS ACCORDING TO THEIR STATUS.
BUT PLEASE DON'T MISUNDERSTAND. WE WILL NOT LOCK THE DOORS.

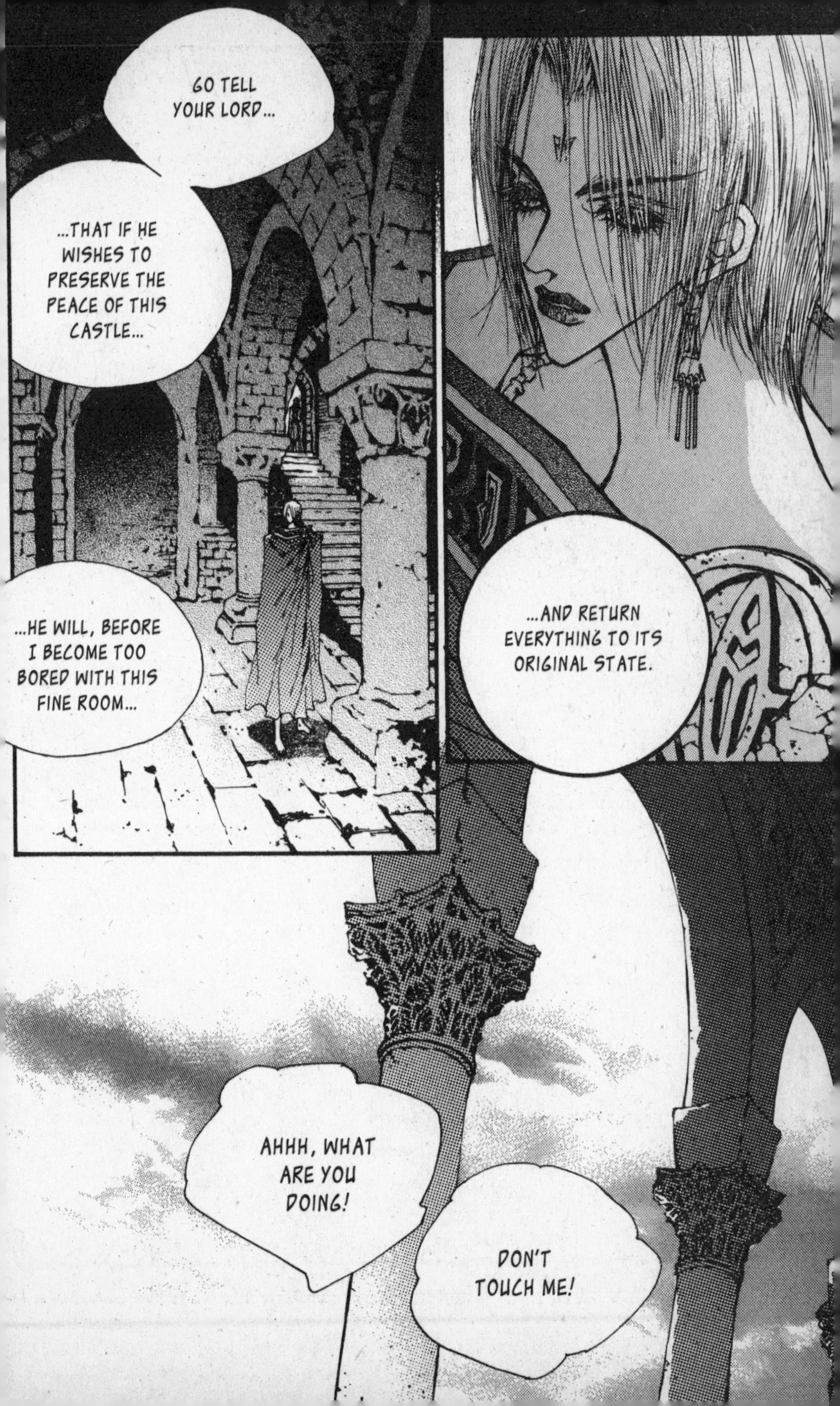
GO TELL YOUR LORD...
...THAT IF HE WISHES TO PRESERVE THE PEACE OF THIS CASTLE...
...HE WILL, BEFORE I BECOME TOO BORED WITH THIS FINE ROOM...
...AND RETURN EVERYTHING TO ITS ORIGINAL STATE.
AHHH, WHAT ARE YOU DOING!
DON'T TOUCH ME!

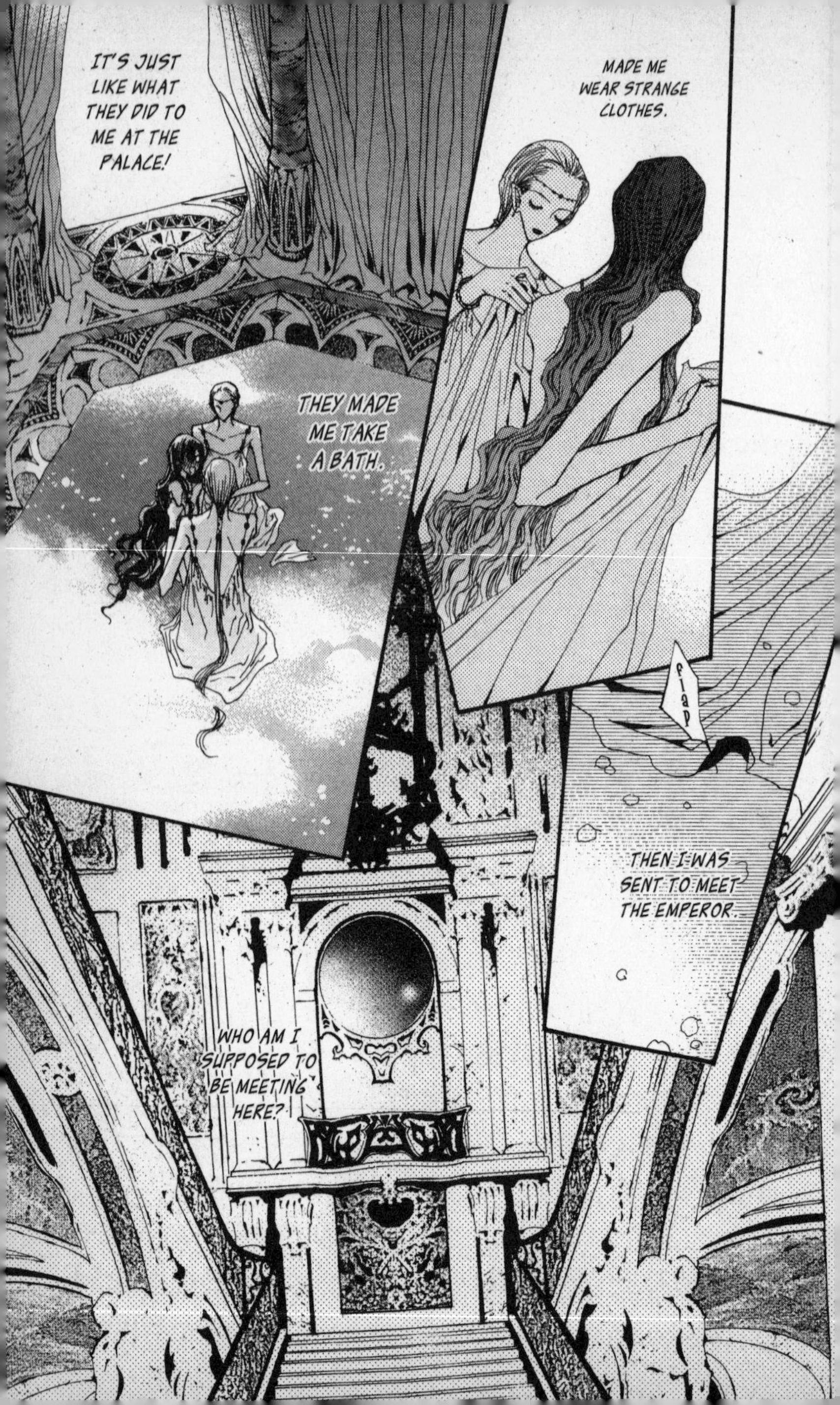
IT'S JUST LIKE WHAT THEY DID TO ME AT THE PALACE!
THEY MADE ME TAKE A BATH.
MADE ME WEAR STRANGE CLOTHES.
flap
THEN I WAS SENT TO MEET THE EMPEROR.
WHO AM I SUPPOSED TO BE MEETING HERE?

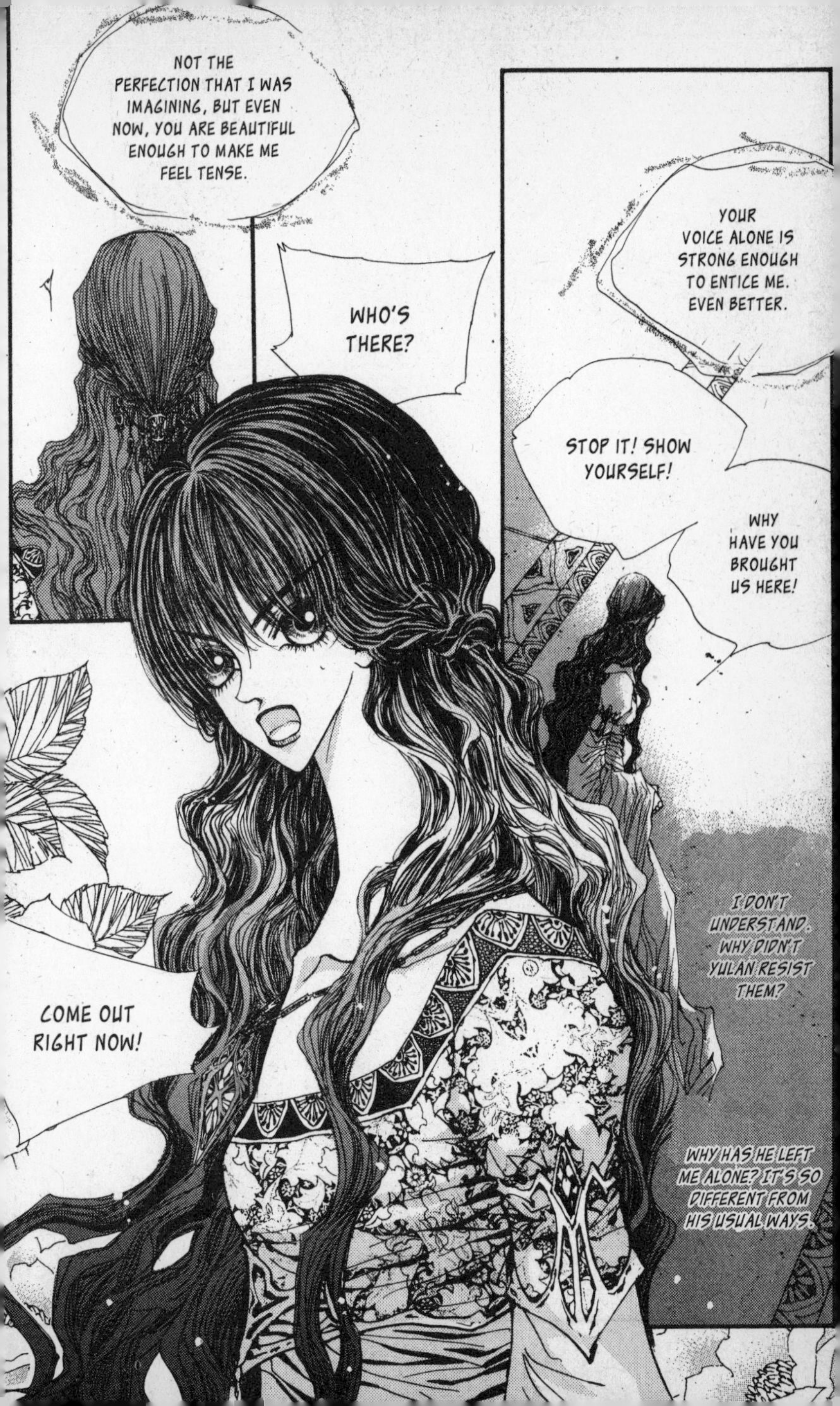
NOT THE PERFECTION THAT I WAS IMAGINING, BUT EVEN NOW, YOU ARE BEAUTIFUL ENOUGH TO MAKE ME FEEL TENSE.
WHO'S THERE?
YOUR VOICE ALONE IS STRONG ENOUGH TO ENTICE ME. EVEN BETTER.
STOP IT! SHOW YOURSELF!
WHY HAVE YOU BROUGHT US HERE!
COME OUT RIGHT NOW!
I DON'T UNDERSTAND. WHY DIDN'T YULAN RESIST THEM?
WHY HAS HE LEFT ME ALONE? IT'S SO DIFFERENT FROM HIS USUAL WAYS.

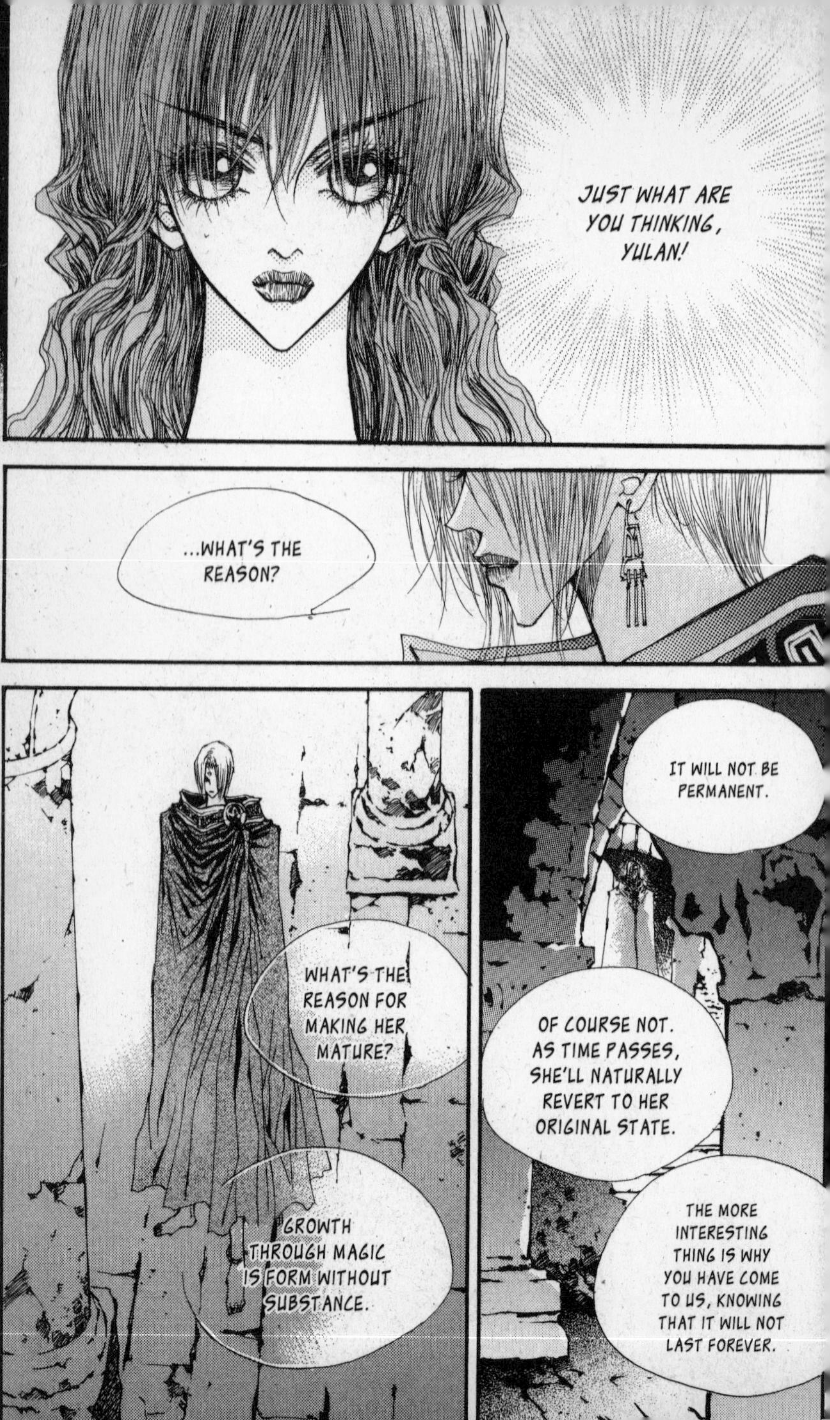
JUST WHAT ARE YOU THINKING, YULAN!
...WHAT'S THE REASON?
WHAT'S THE REASON FOR MAKING HER MATURE?
GROWTH THROUGH MAGIC IS FORM WITHOUT SUBSTANCE.
IT WILL NOT BE PERMANENT.
OF COURSE NOT. AS TIME PASSES, SHE'LL NATURALLY REVERT TO HER ORIGINAL STATE.
THE MORE INTERESTING THING IS WHY YOU HAVE COME TO US, KNOWING THAT IT WILL NOT LAST FOREVER.

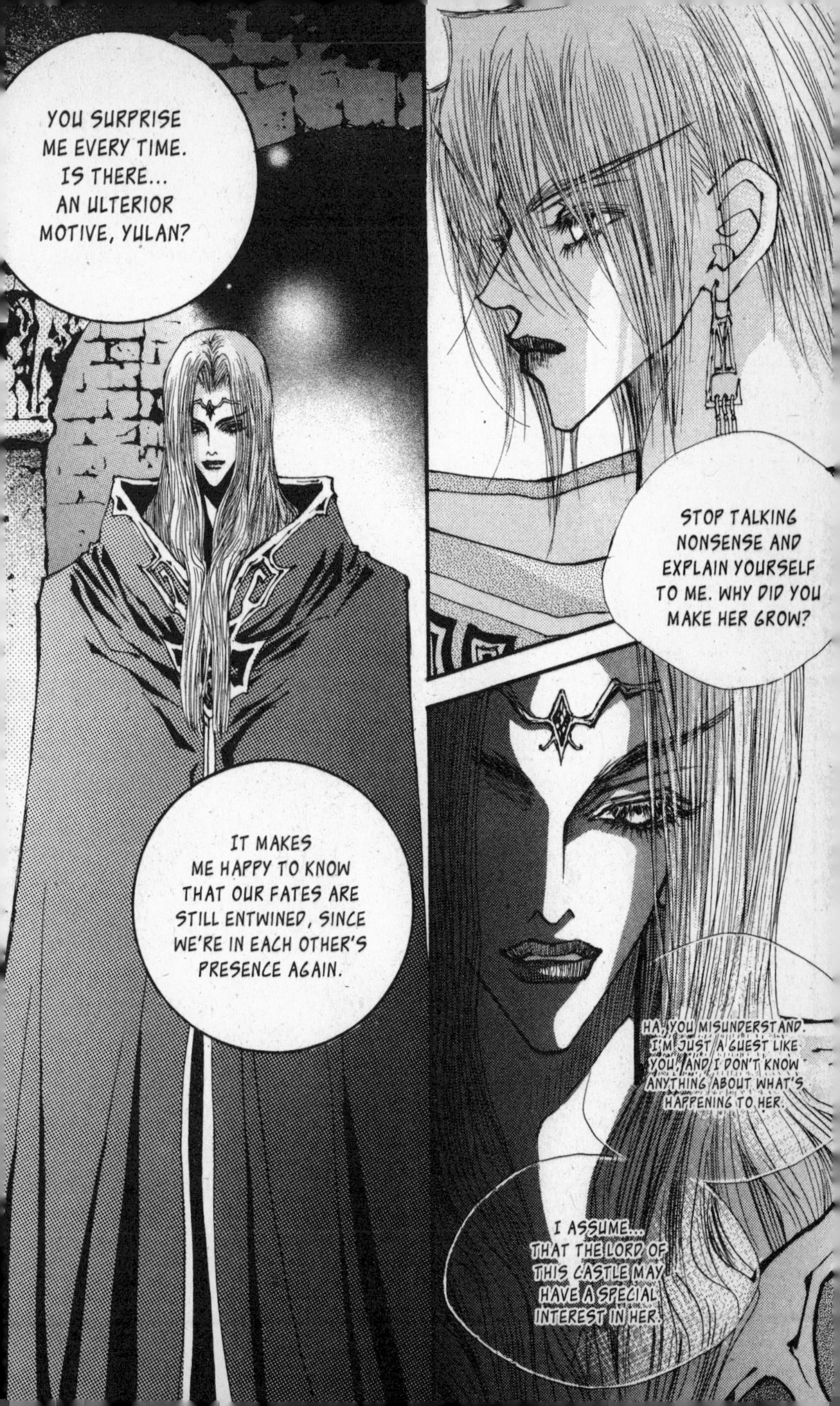
YOU SURPRISE ME EVERY TIME. IS THERE... AN ULTERIOR MOTIVE, YULAN?
IT MAKES ME HAPPY TO KNOW THAT OUR FATES ARE STILL ENTWINED, SINCE WE'RE IN EACH OTHER'S PRESENCE AGAIN.
STOP TALKING NONSENSE AND EXPLAIN YOURSELF TO ME. WHY DID YOU MAKE HER GROW?
HA, YOU MISUNDERSTAND. I'M JUST A GUEST LIKE YOU, AND I DON'T KNOW ANYTHING ABOUT WHAT'S HAPPENING TO HER.
I ASSUME... THAT THE LORD OF THIS CASTLE MAY HAVE A SPECIAL INTEREST IN HER.

THE LORD OF THIS CASTLE IS ONLY INTERESTED IN FUN, PLEASURE, AND EVERLASTING YOUTH.

SO WHY DO YOU THINK HE WOULD MADE A GIRL GROW INTO A WOMAN?

I'M SURE YOU'RE NOT LEAVING HER UNGUARDED WITHOUT ANY SUSPICIONS OF YOUR OWN...

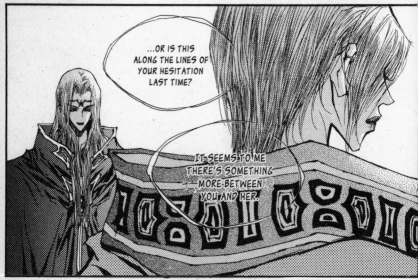

...OR IS THIS ALONG THE LINES OF YOUR HESITATION LAST TIME?

IT SEEMS TO ME THERE'S SOMETHING MORE BETWEEN YOU AND HER.

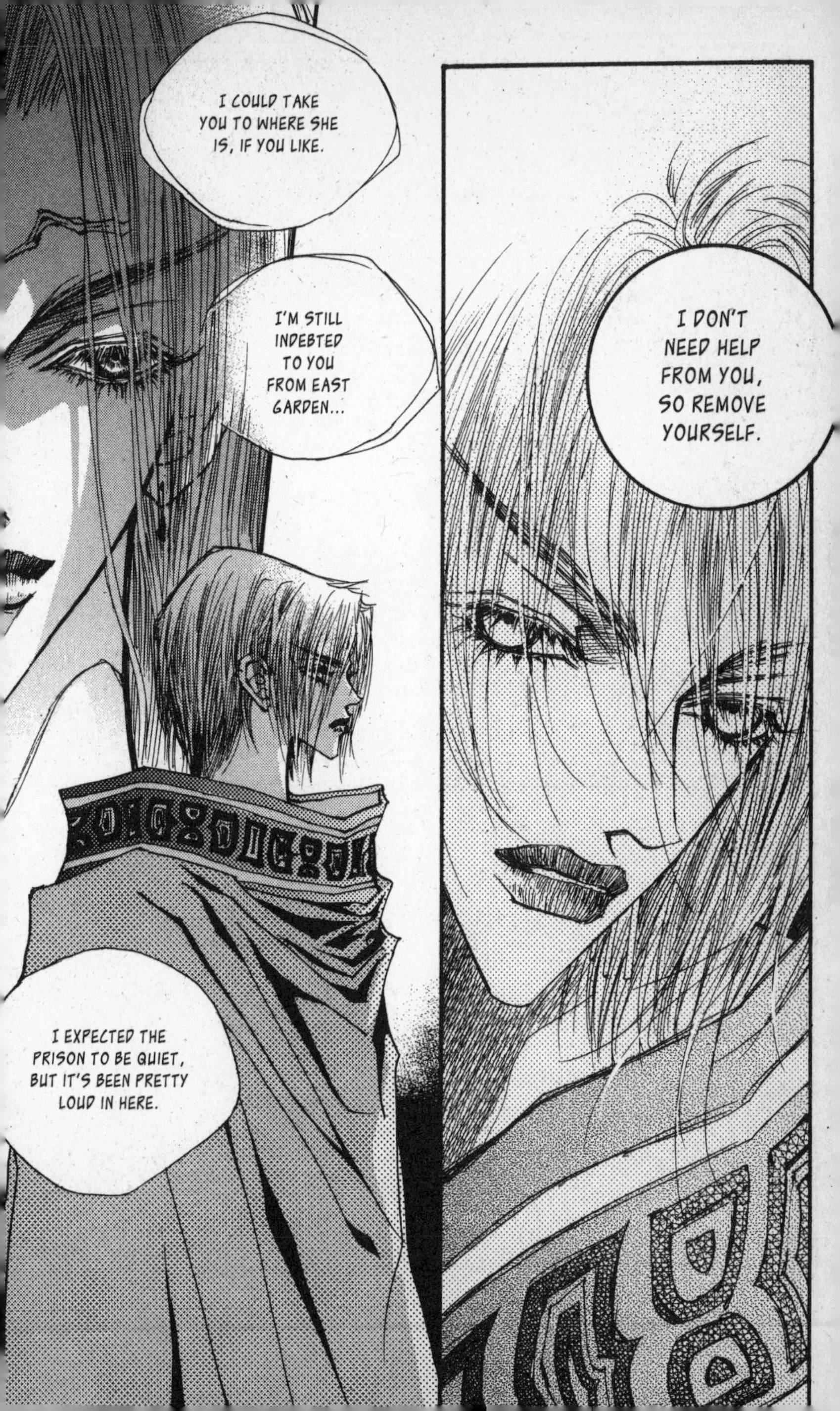
I COULD TAKE YOU TO WHERE SHE IS, IF YOU LIKE.
I'M STILL INDEBTED TO YOU FROM EAST GARDEN...
I EXPECTED THE PRISON TO BE QUIET, BUT IT'S BEEN PRETTY LOUD IN HERE.
I DON'T NEED HELP FROM YOU, SO REMOVE YOURSELF.

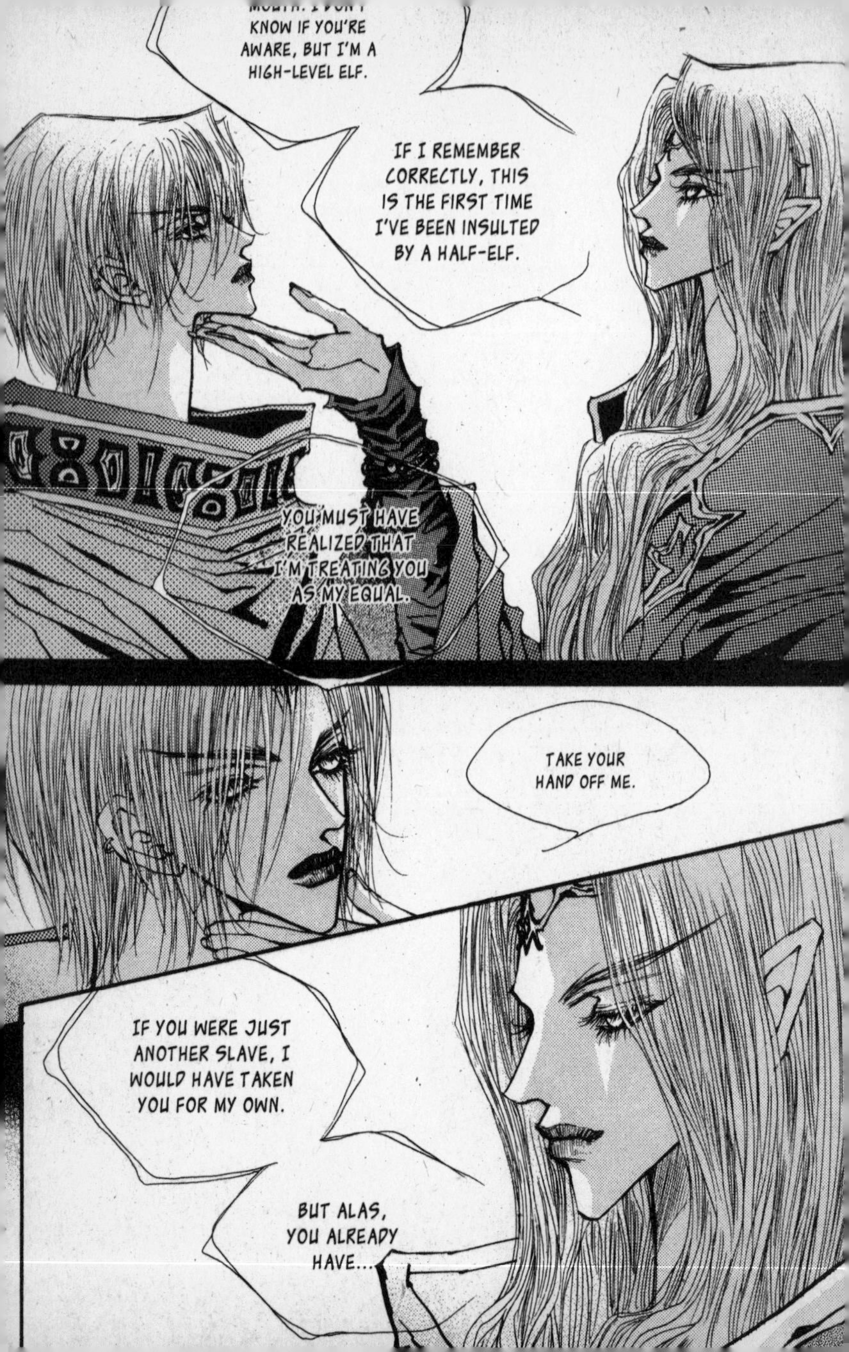
KNOW IF YOU'RE AWARE, BUT I'M A HIGH-LEVEL ELF.
IF I REMEMBER CORRECTLY, THIS IS THE FIRST TIME I'VE BEEN INSULTED BY A HALF-ELF.
YOU MUST HAVE REALIZED THAT I'M TREATING YOU AS MY EQUAL.
TAKE YOUR HAND OFF ME.
IF YOU WERE JUST ANOTHER SLAVE, I WOULD HAVE TAKEN YOU FOR MY OWN.
BUT ALAS, YOU ALREADY HAVE...

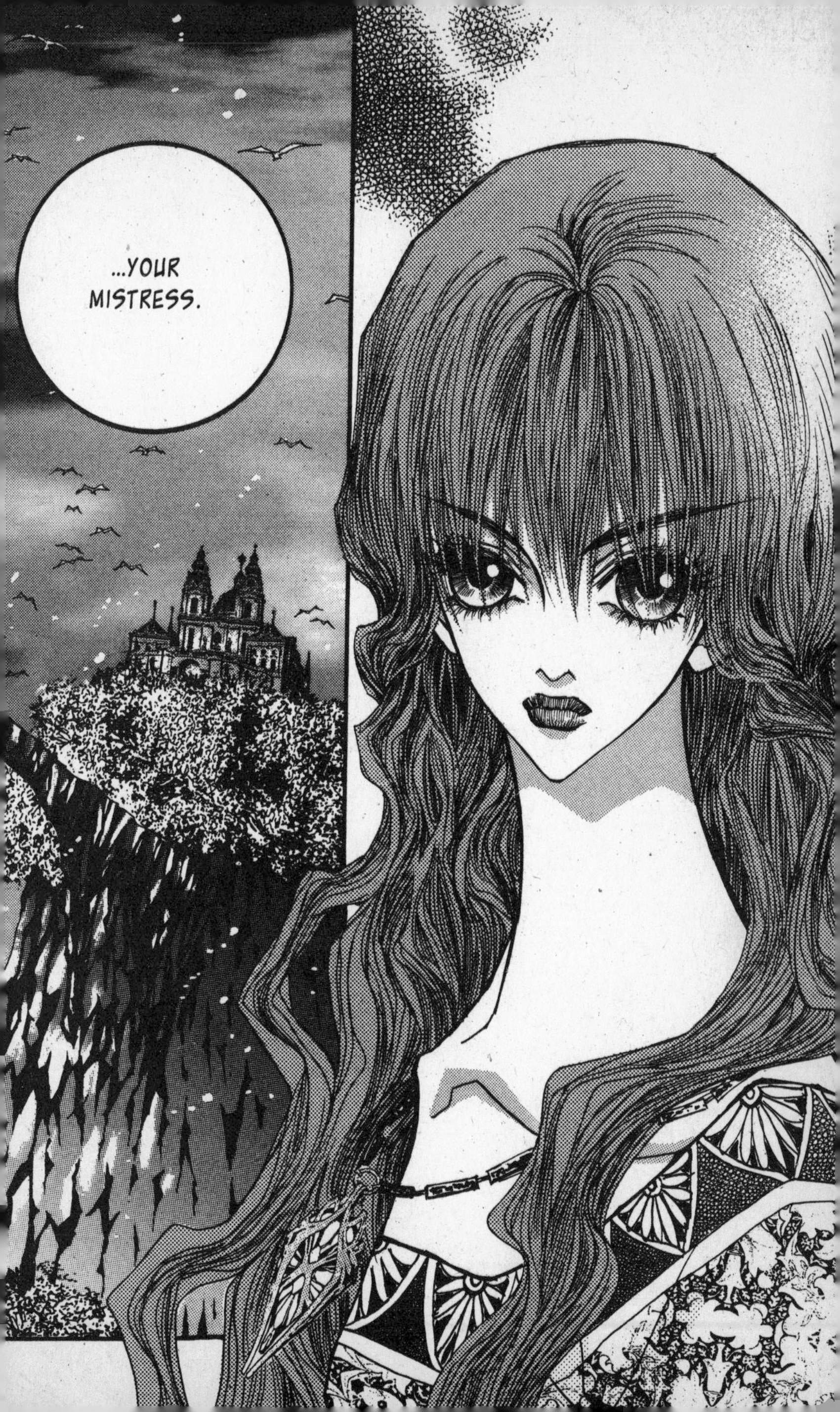
...YOUR MISTRESS.

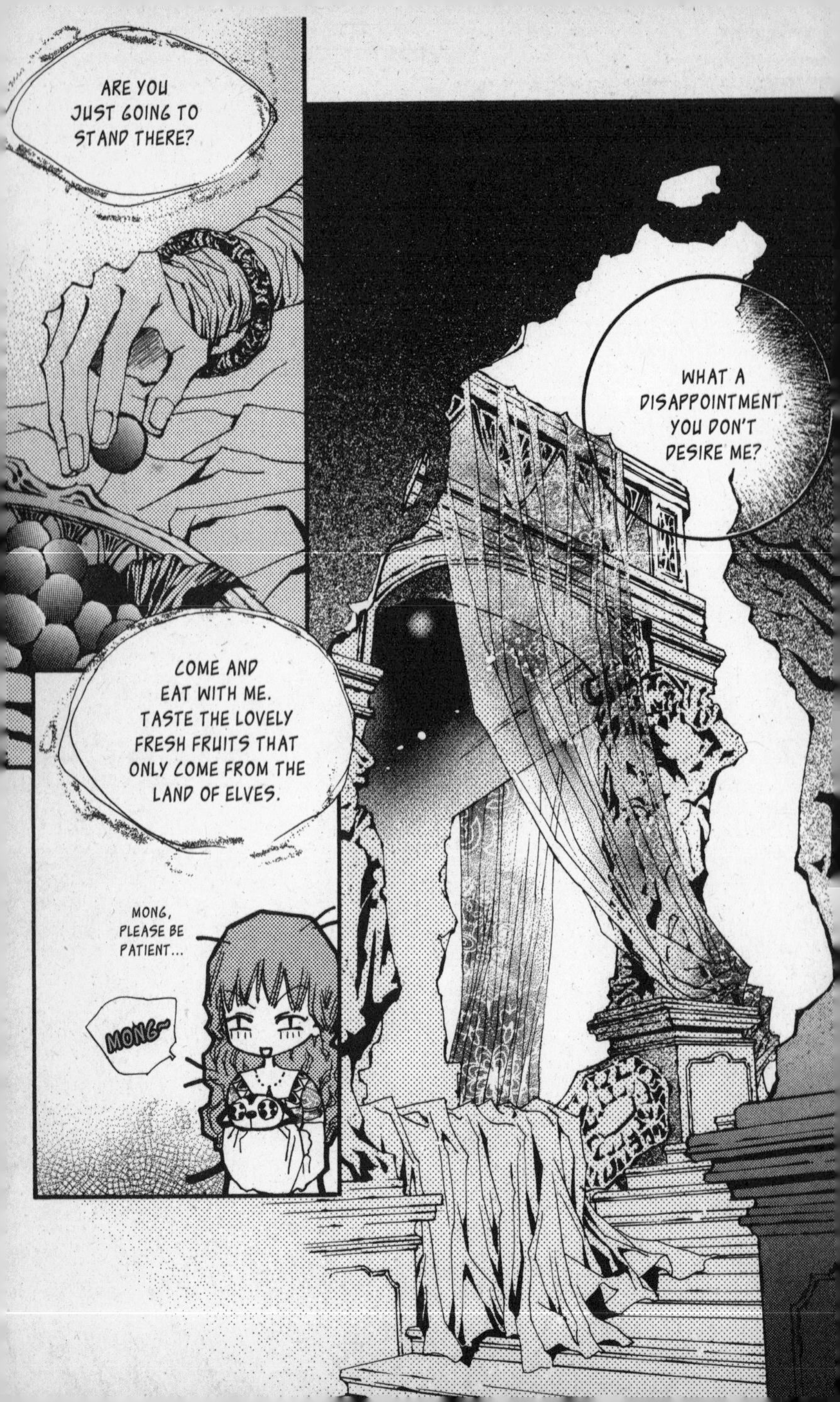
ARE YOU JUST GOING TO STAND THERE?
WHAT A DISAPPOINTMENT. YOU DON'T DESIRE ME?
COME AND EAT WITH ME. TASTE THE LOVELY FRESH FRUITS THAT ONLY COME FROM THE LAND OF ELVES.
MONG, PLEASE BE PATIENT...
MONG~

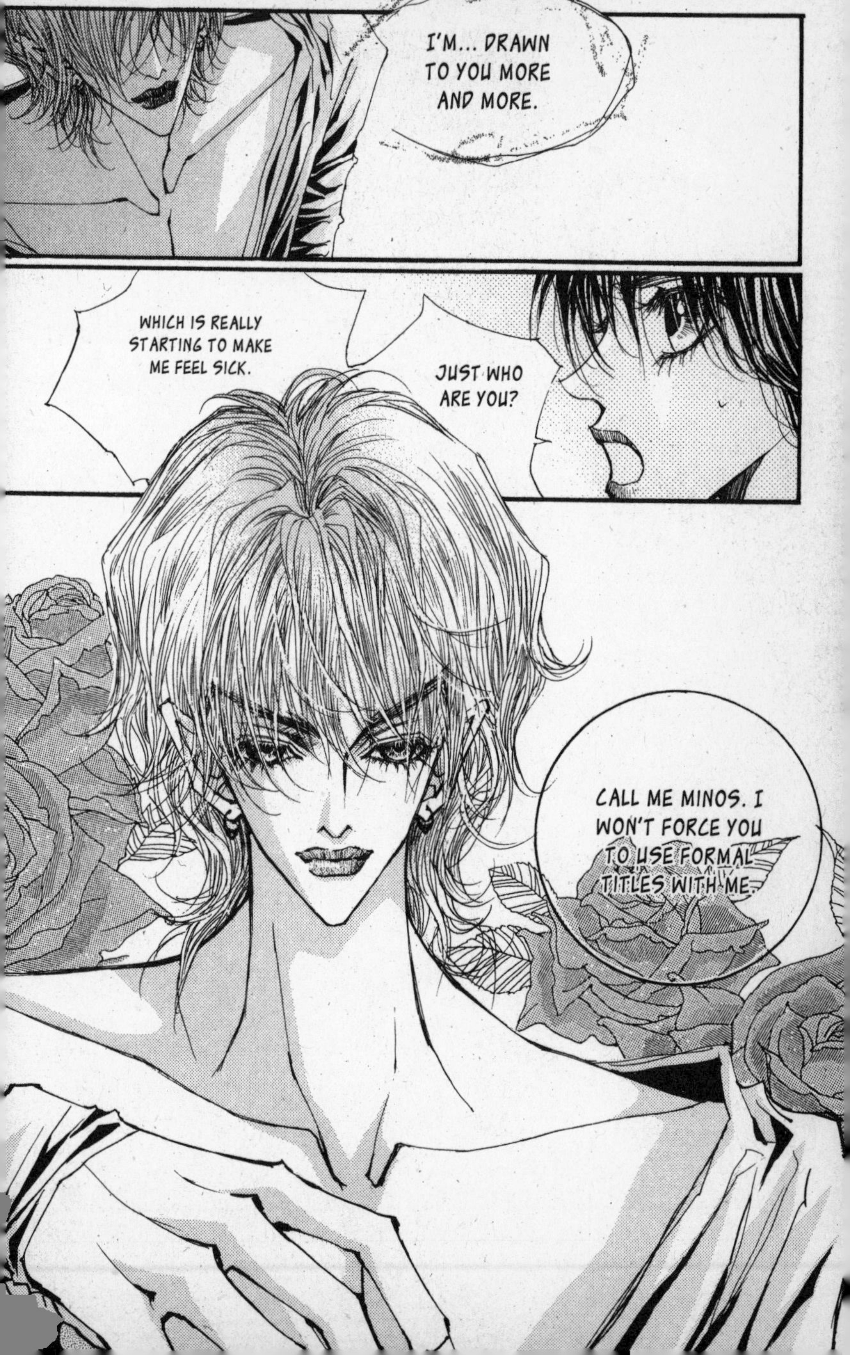
I'M... DRAWN TO YOU MORE AND MORE.
WHICH IS REALLY STARTING TO MAKE ME FEEL SICK.
JUST WHO ARE YOU?
CALL ME MINOS. I WON'T FORCE YOU TO USE FORMAL TITLES WITH ME.

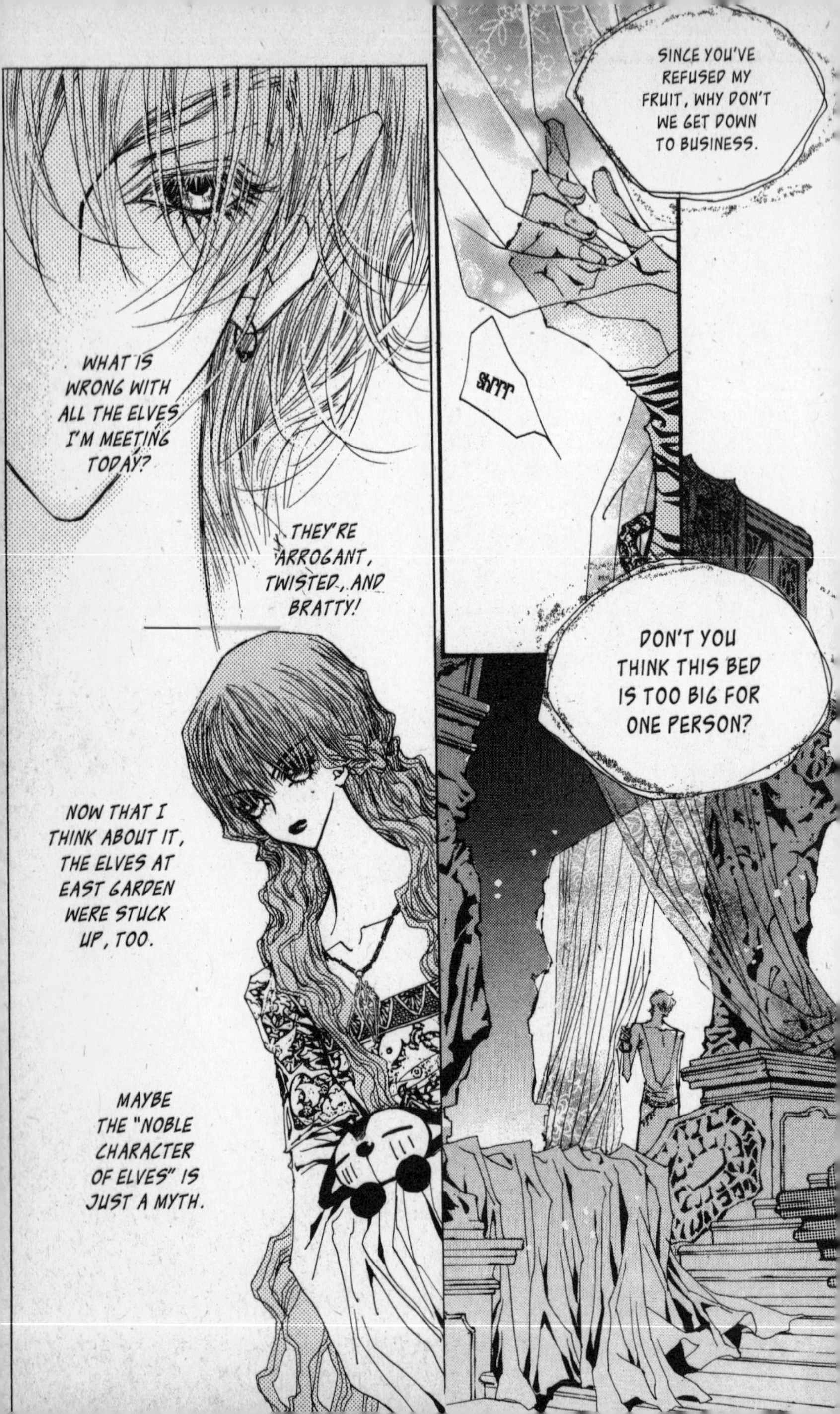
WHAT IS WRONG WITH ALL THE ELVES I'M MEETING TODAY?
THEY'RE ARROGANT, TWISTED, AND BRATTY!
NOW THAT I THINK ABOUT IT, THE ELVES AT EAST GARDEN WERE STUCK UP, TOO.
MAYBE THE "NOBLE CHARACTER OF ELVES" IS JUST A MYTH.
SINCE YOU'VE REFUSED MY FRUIT, WHY DON'T WE GET DOWN TO BUSINESS.
Shrrr
DON'T YOU THINK THIS BED IS TOO BIG FOR ONE PERSON?

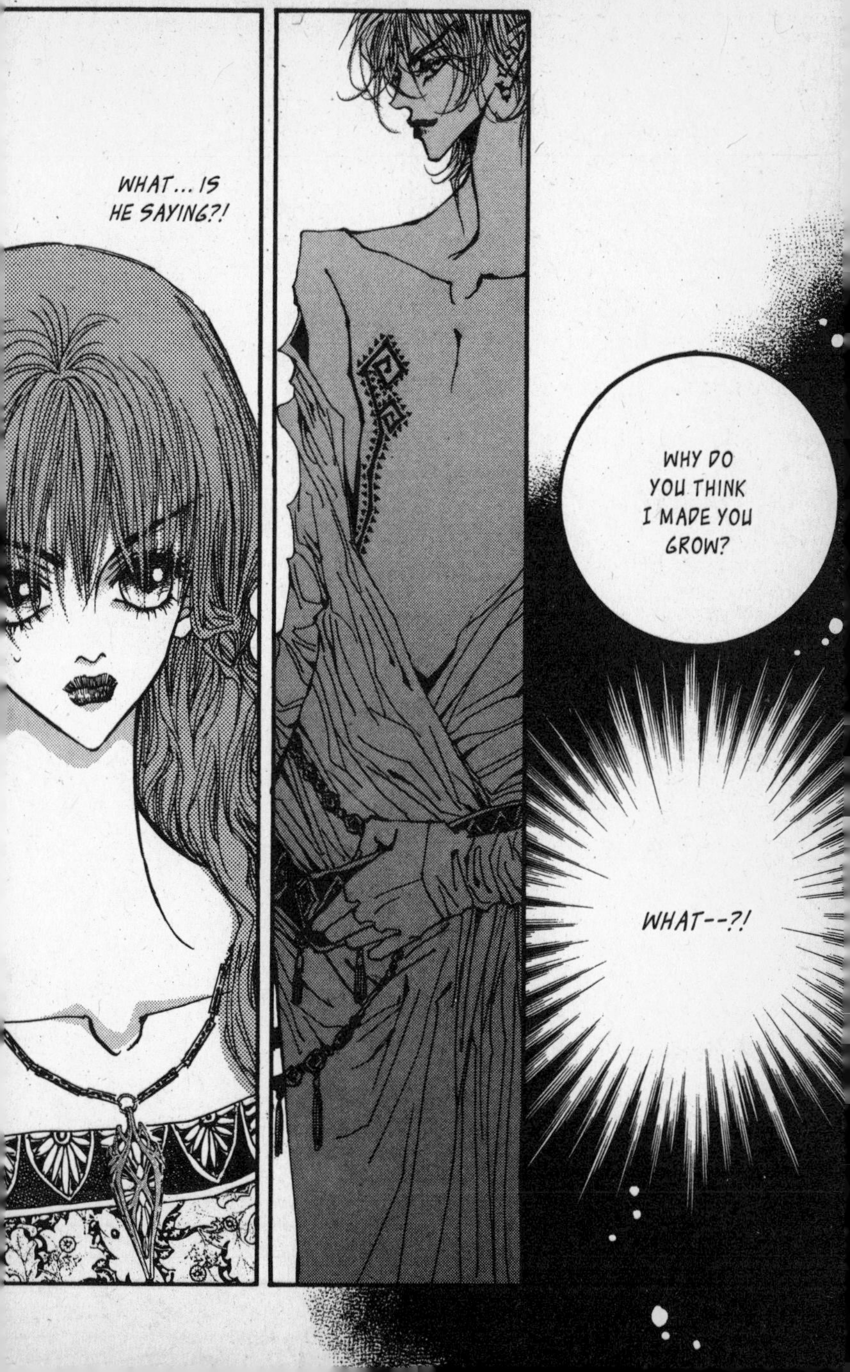
WHAT... IS HE SAYING?!
WHY DO YOU THINK I MADE YOU GROW?
WHAT--?!

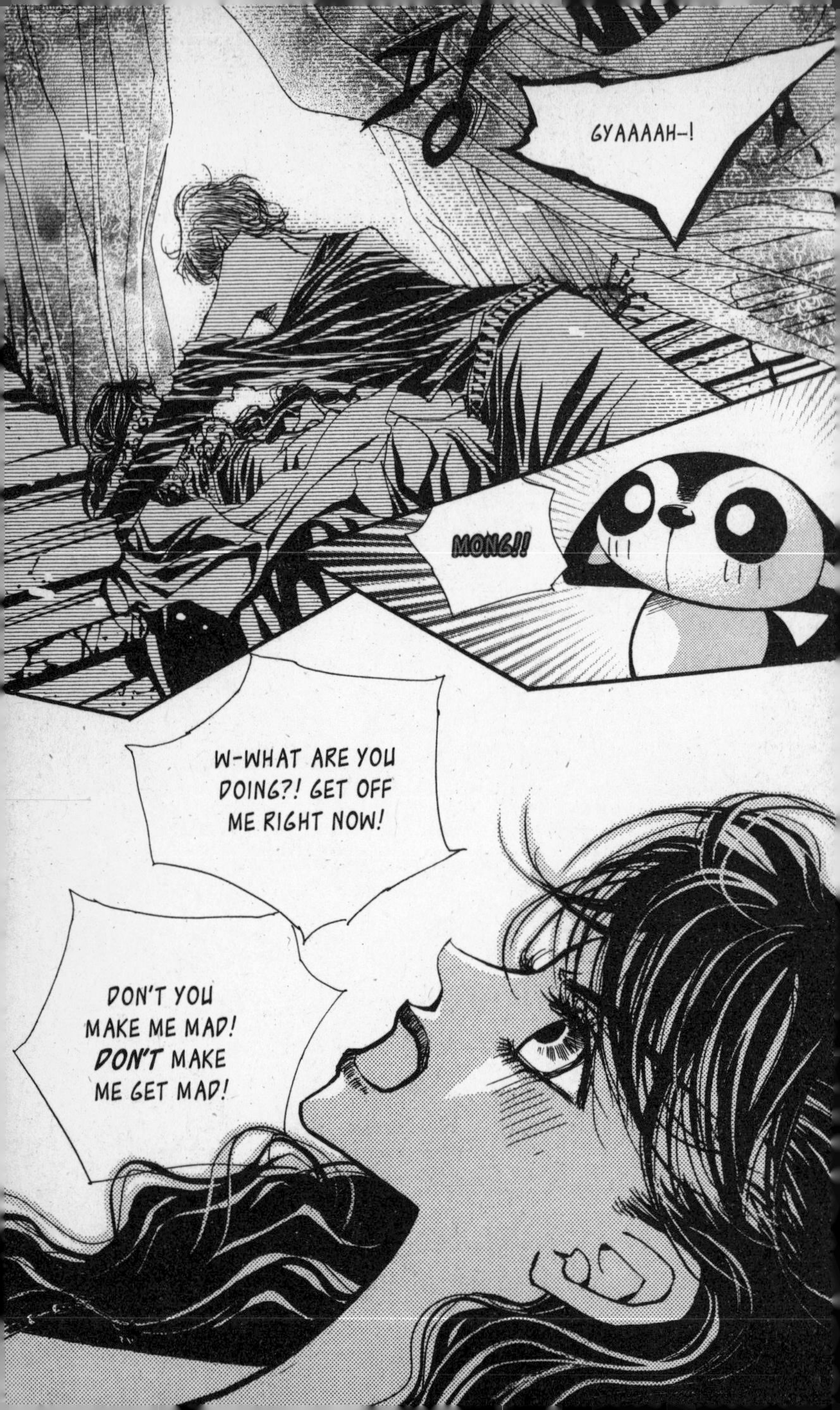
GYAAAAH-!
MONG!!
W-WHAT ARE YOU DOING?! GET OFF ME RIGHT NOW!
DON'T YOU MAKE ME MAD! **DON'T** MAKE ME GET MAD!

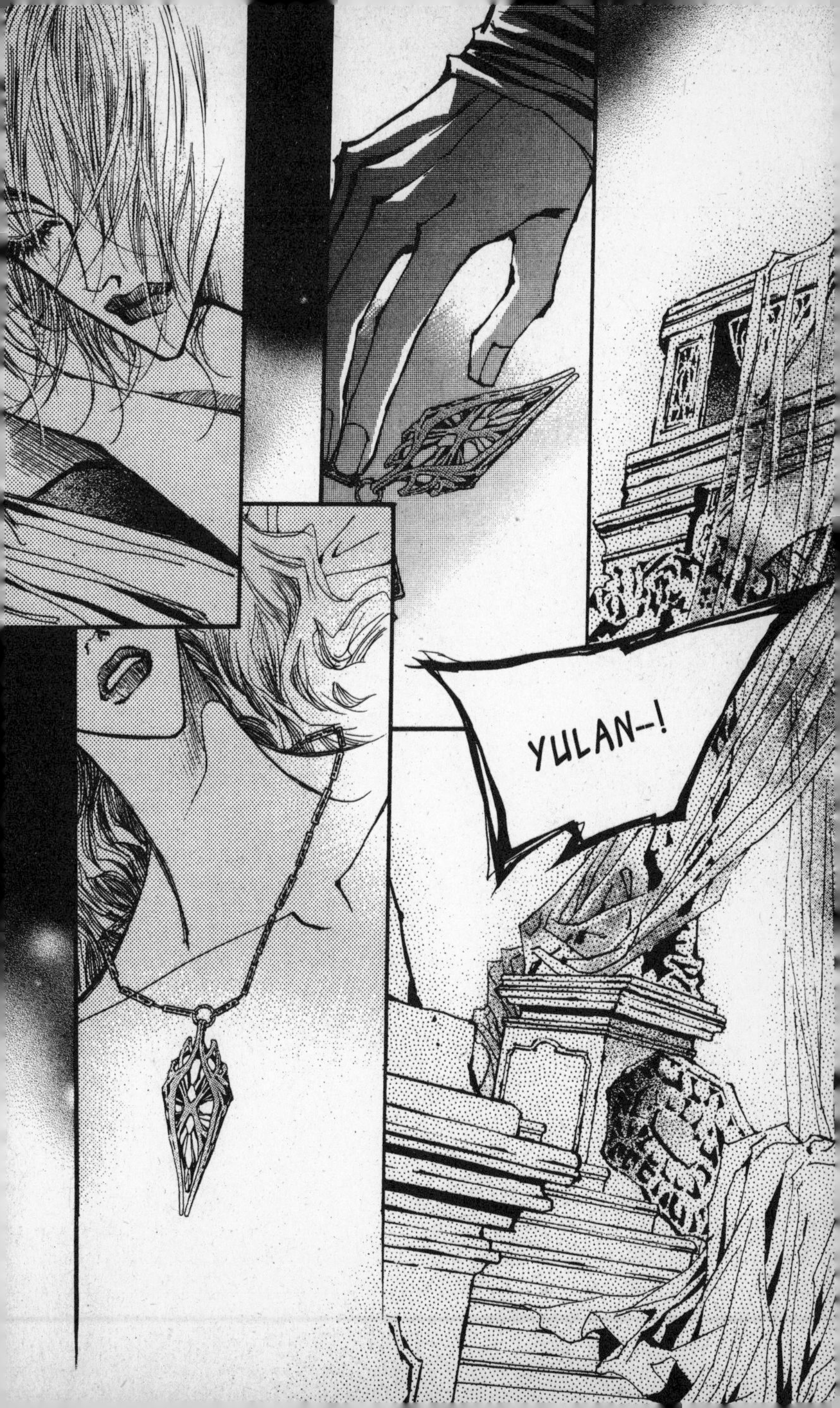
YULAN--!

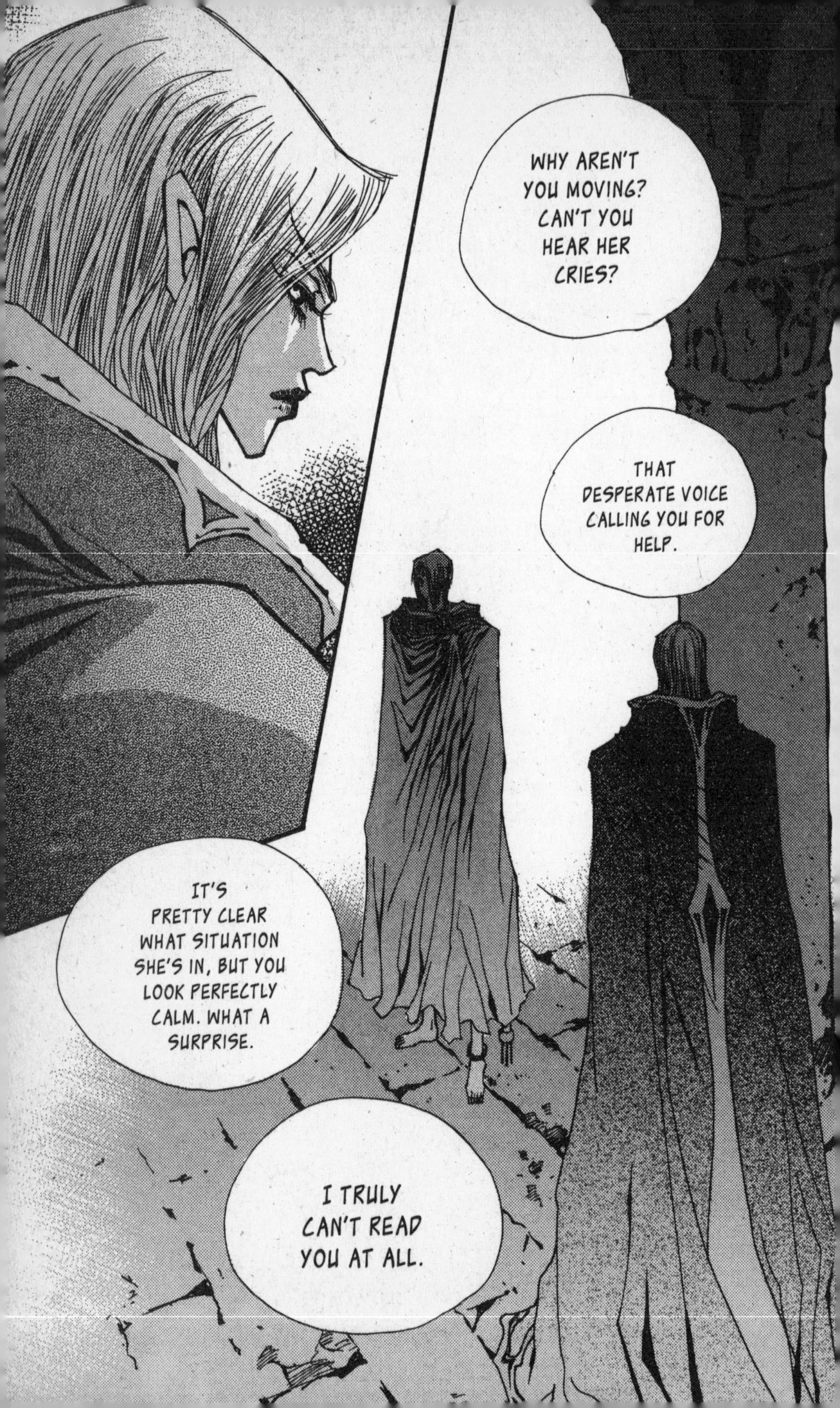
WHY AREN'T YOU MOVING? CAN'T YOU HEAR HER CRIES?
THAT DESPERATE VOICE CALLING YOU FOR HELP.
IT'S PRETTY CLEAR WHAT SITUATION SHE'S IN, BUT YOU LOOK PERFECTLY CALM. WHAT A SURPRISE.
I TRULY CAN'T READ YOU AT ALL.

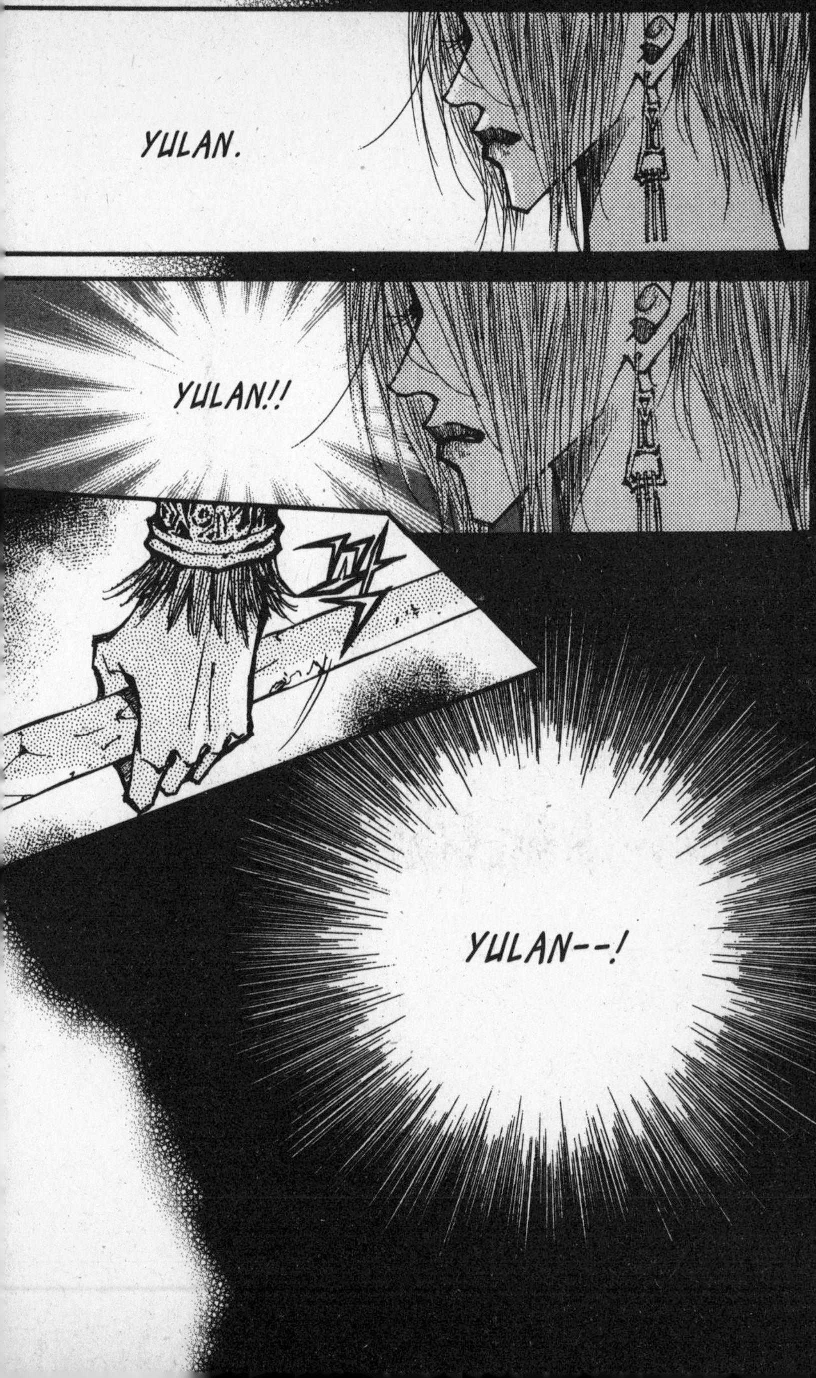
YULAN.
YULAN!!
YULAN--!

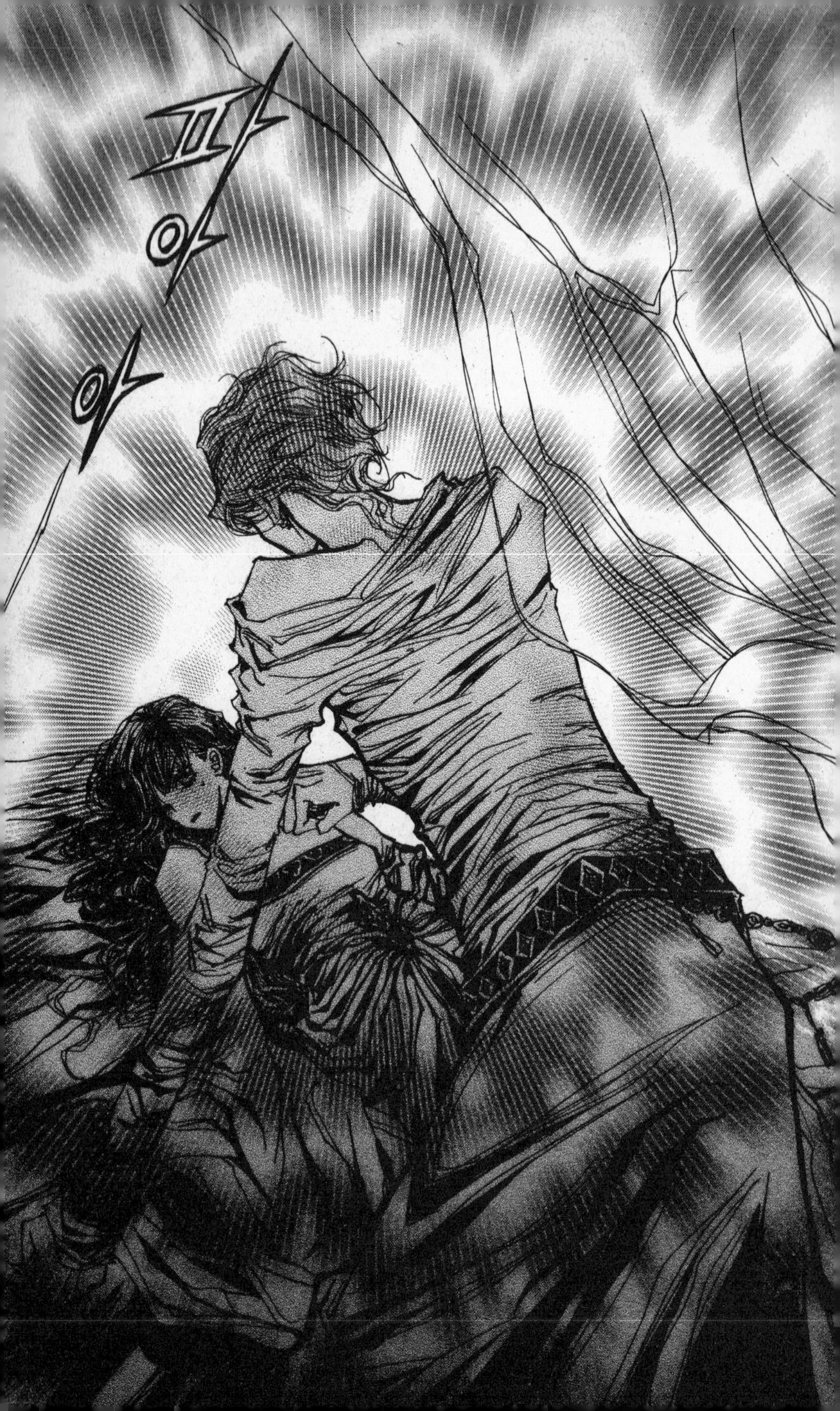
파아아

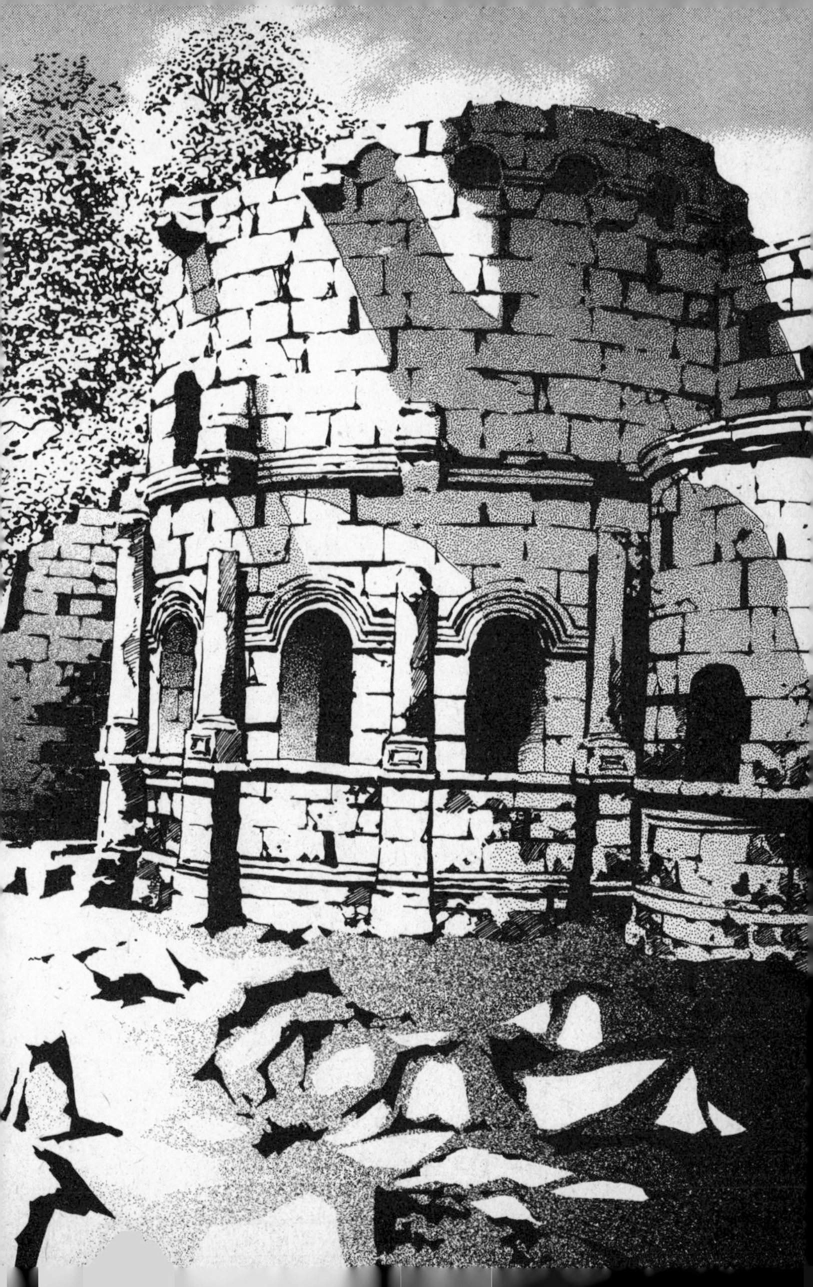

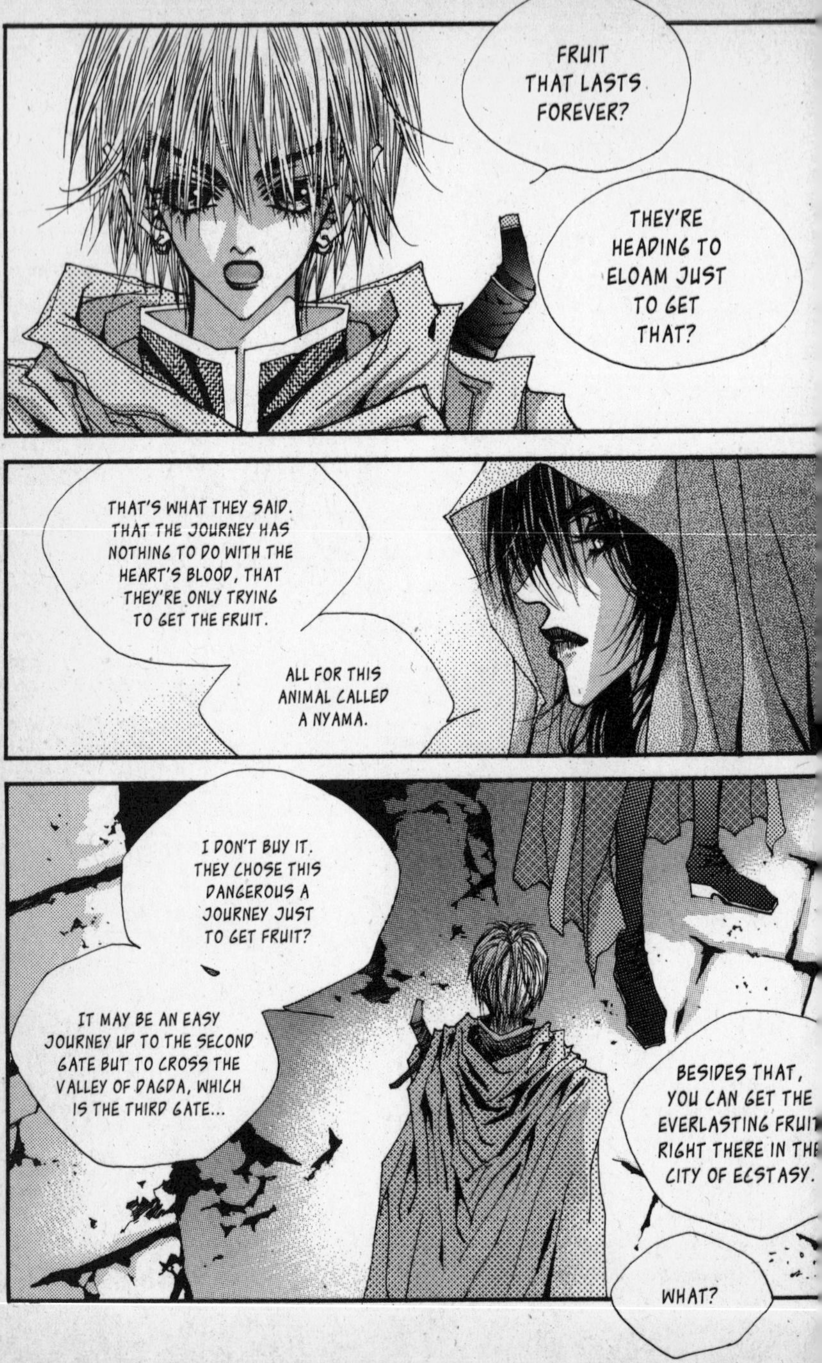
FRUIT THAT LASTS FOREVER?
THEY'RE HEADING TO ELOAM JUST TO GET THAT?
THAT'S WHAT THEY SAID. THAT THE JOURNEY HAS NOTHING TO DO WITH THE HEART'S BLOOD, THAT THEY'RE ONLY TRYING TO GET THE FRUIT.
ALL FOR THIS ANIMAL CALLED A NYAMA.
I DON'T BUY IT. THEY CHOSE THIS DANGEROUS A JOURNEY JUST TO GET FRUIT?
IT MAY BE AN EASY JOURNEY UP TO THE SECOND GATE BUT TO CROSS THE VALLEY OF DAGDA, WHICH IS THE THIRD GATE...
BESIDES THAT, YOU CAN GET THE EVERLASTING FRUIT RIGHT THERE IN THE CITY OF ECSTASY.
WHAT?

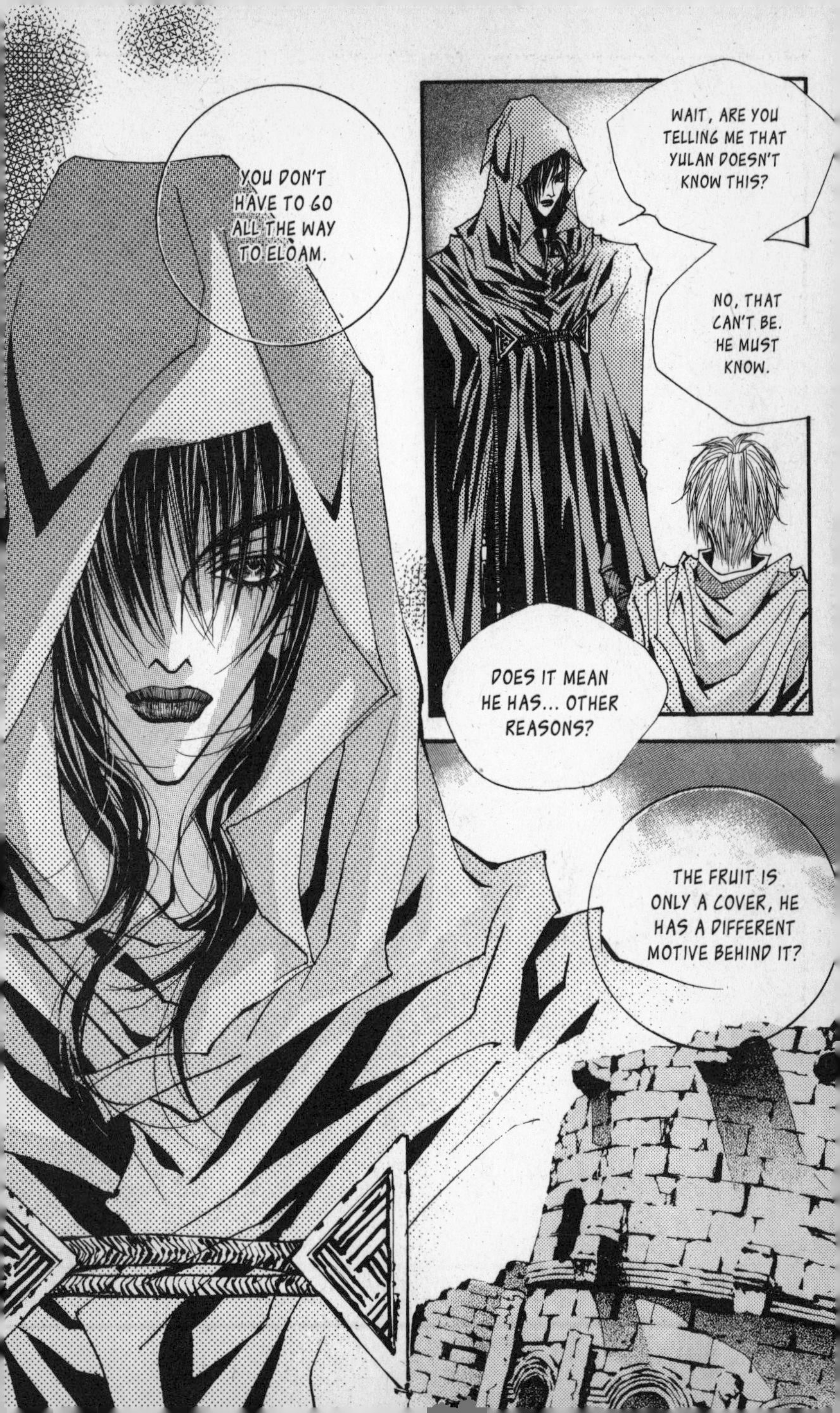
YOU DON'T HAVE TO GO ALL THE WAY TO ELOAM.
WAIT, ARE YOU TELLING ME THAT YULAN DOESN'T KNOW THIS?
NO, THAT CAN'T BE. HE MUST KNOW.
DOES IT MEAN HE HAS... OTHER REASONS?
THE FRUIT IS ONLY A COVER, HE HAS A DIFFERENT MOTIVE BEHIND IT?

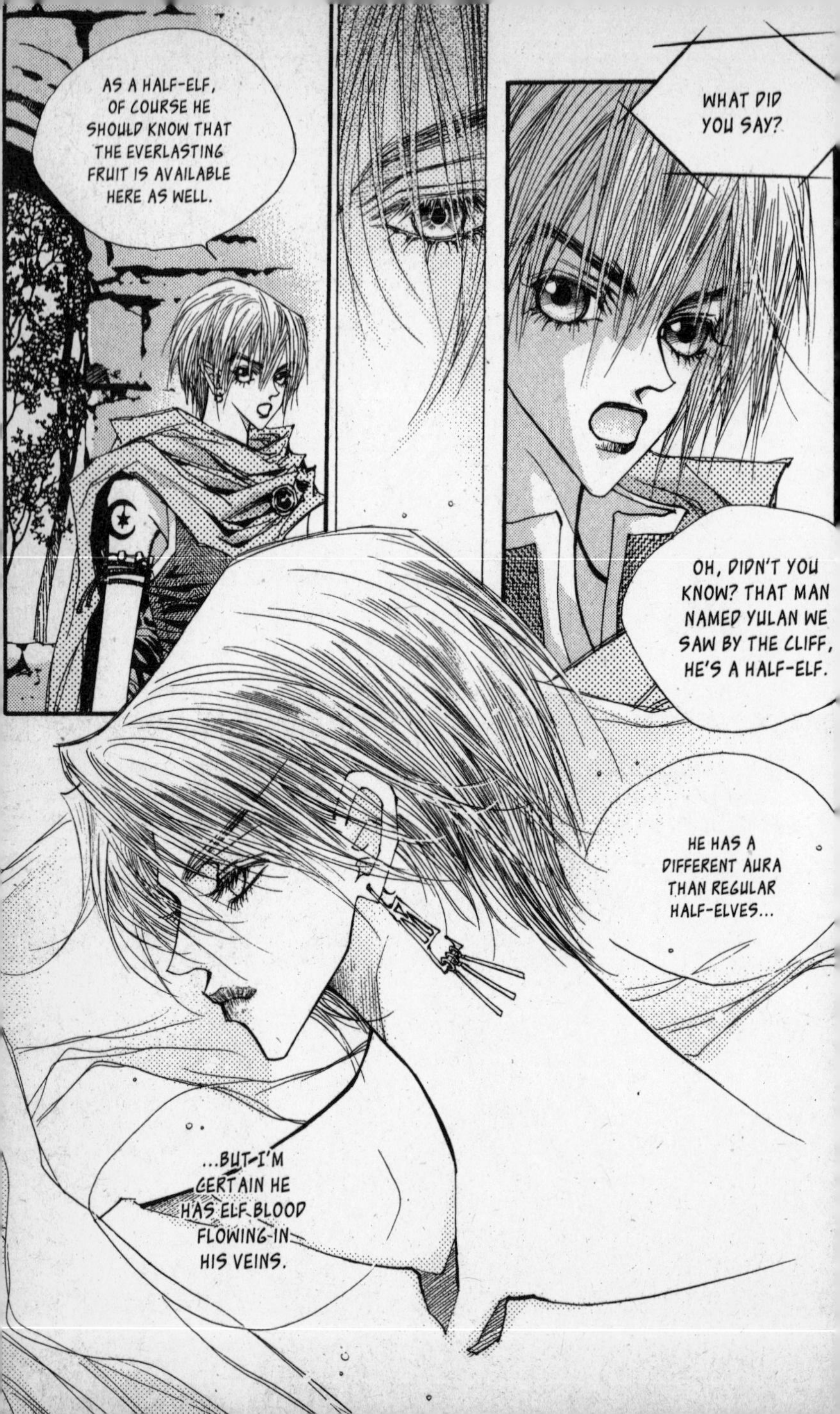
AS A HALF-ELF, OF COURSE HE SHOULD KNOW THAT THE EVERLASTING FRUIT IS AVAILABLE HERE AS WELL.
WHAT DID YOU SAY?
OH, DIDN'T YOU KNOW? THAT MAN NAMED YULAN WE SAW BY THE CLIFF, HE'S A HALF-ELF.
HE HAS A DIFFERENT AURA THAN REGULAR HALF-ELVES...
...BUT I'M CERTAIN HE HAS ELF BLOOD FLOWING IN HIS VEINS.

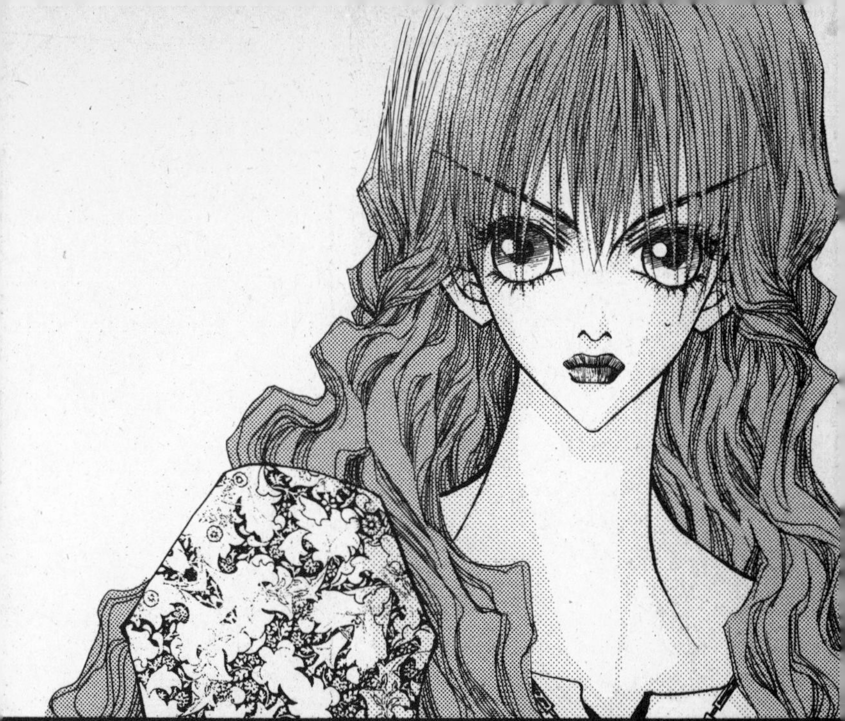
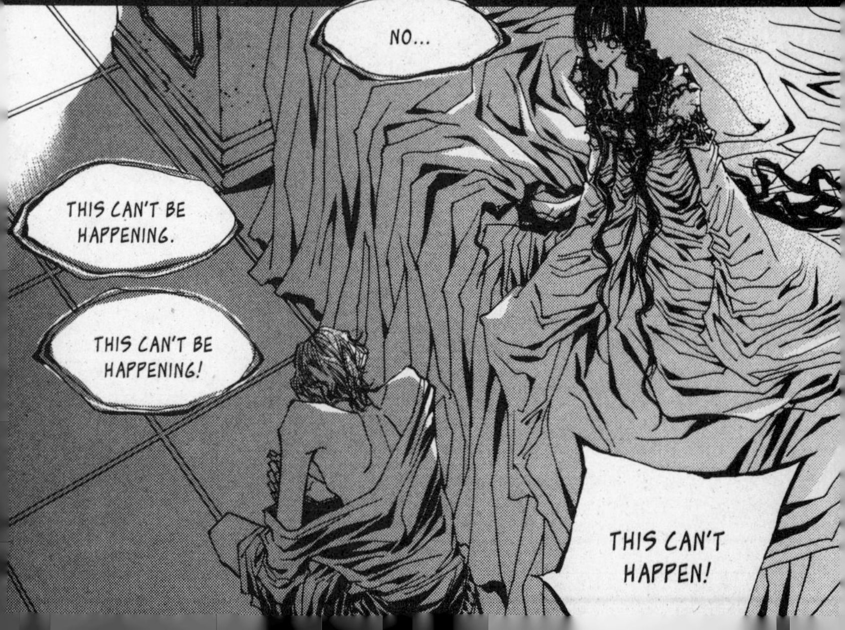
NO...
THIS CAN'T BE HAPPENING.
THIS CAN'T BE HAPPENING!
THIS CAN'T HAPPEN!

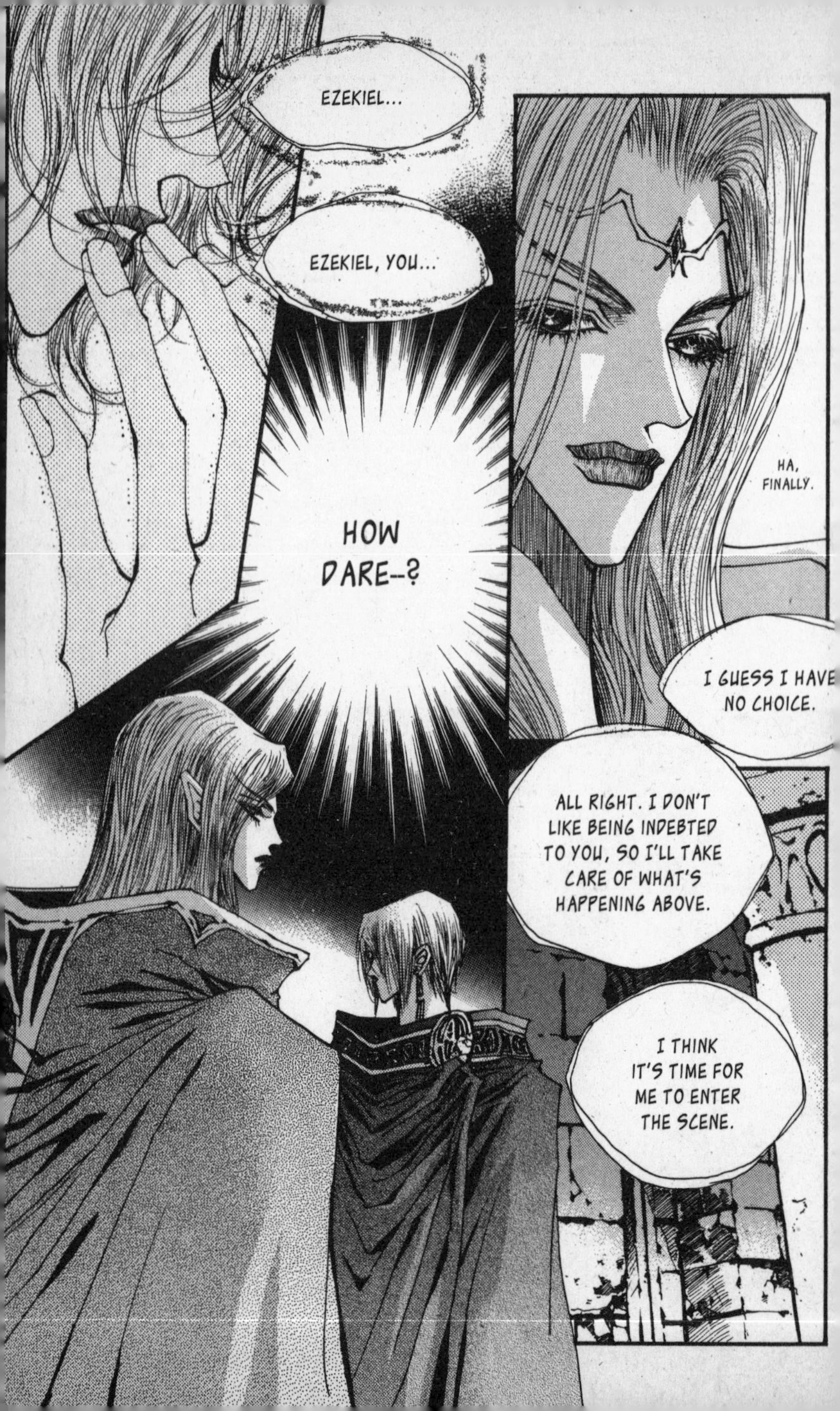
EZEKIEL...
EZEKIEL, YOU...
HOW DARE--?
HA, FINALLY.
I GUESS I HAVE NO CHOICE.
ALL RIGHT. I DON'T LIKE BEING INDEBTED TO YOU, SO I'LL TAKE CARE OF WHAT'S HAPPENING ABOVE.
I THINK IT'S TIME FOR ME TO ENTER THE SCENE.

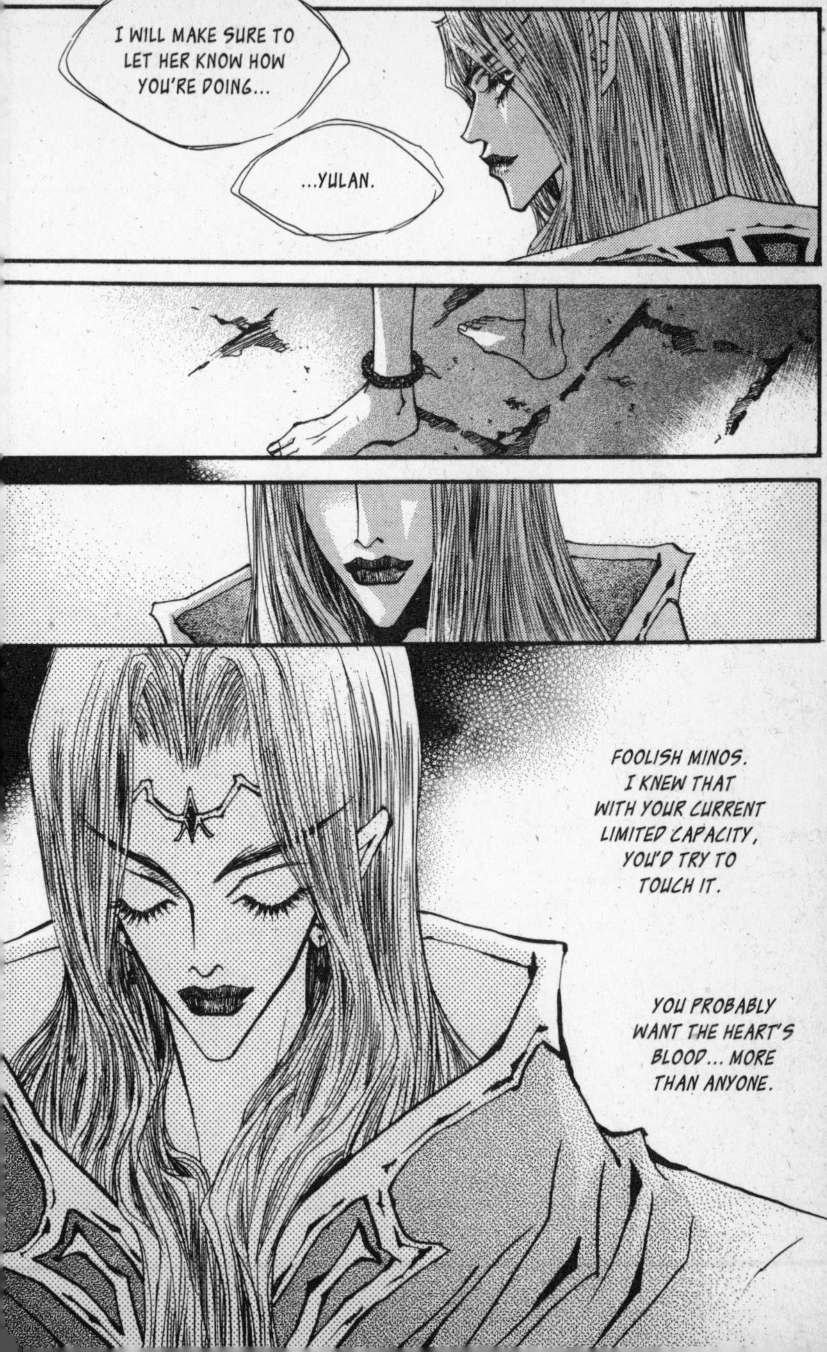
I WILL MAKE SURE TO LET HER KNOW HOW YOU'RE DOING...
...YULAN.
FOOLISH MINOS. I KNEW THAT WITH YOUR CURRENT LIMITED CAPACITY, YOU'D TRY TO TOUCH IT.
YOU PROBABLY WANT THE HEART'S BLOOD... MORE THAN ANYONE.

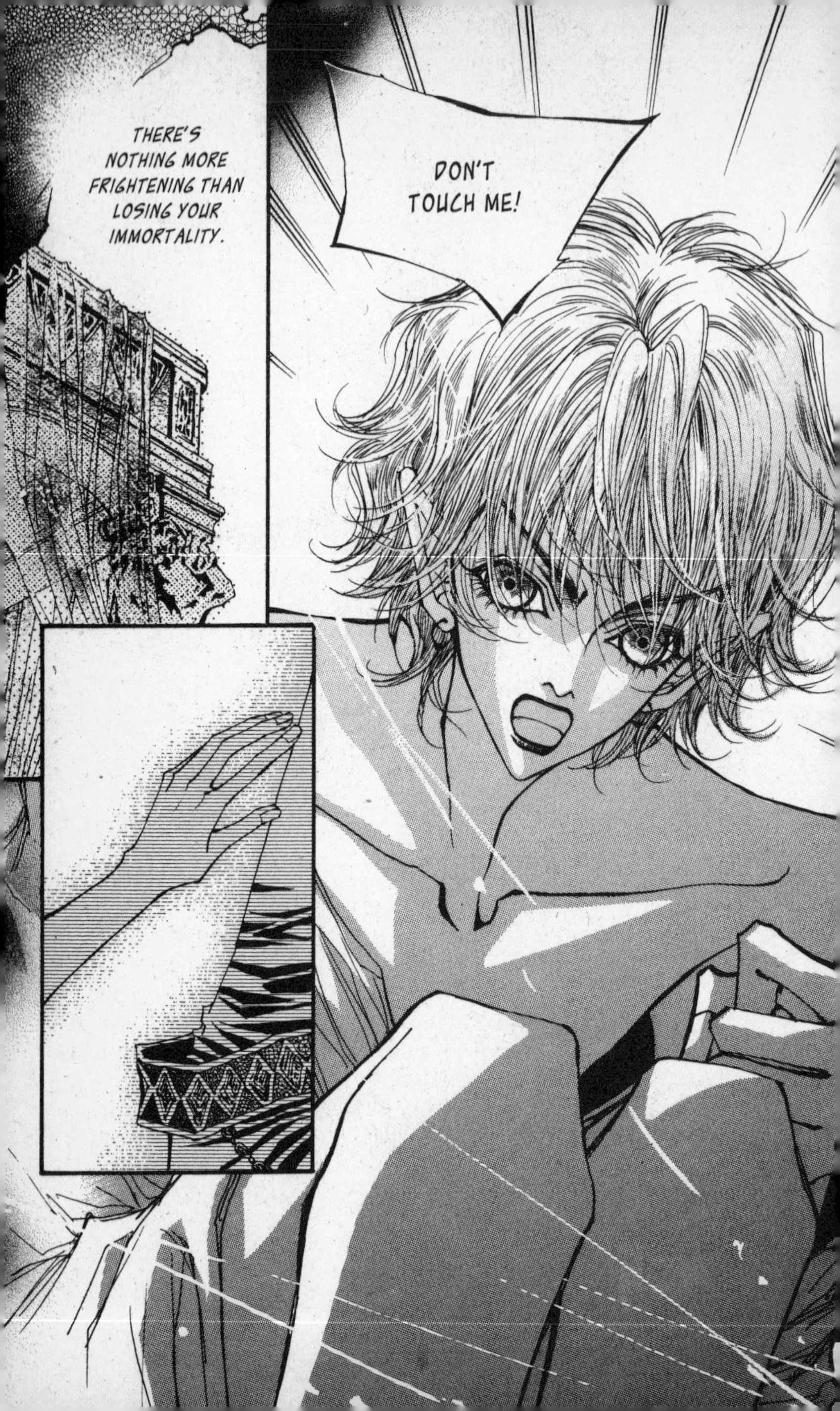
THERE'S NOTHING MORE FRIGHTENING THAN LOSING YOUR IMMORTALITY.
DON'T TOUCH ME!

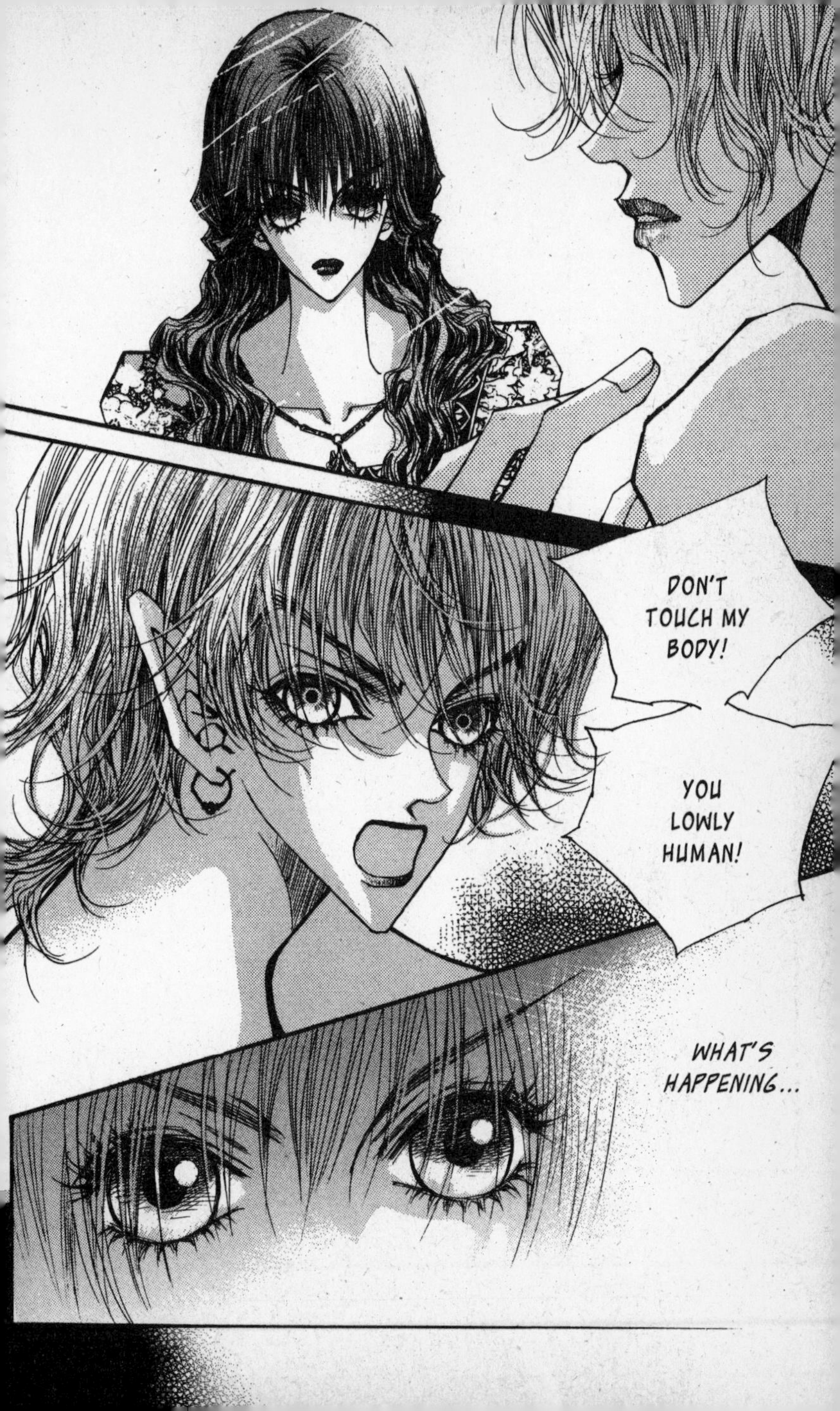
DON'T TOUCH MY BODY!
YOU LOWLY HUMAN!
WHAT'S HAPPENING...

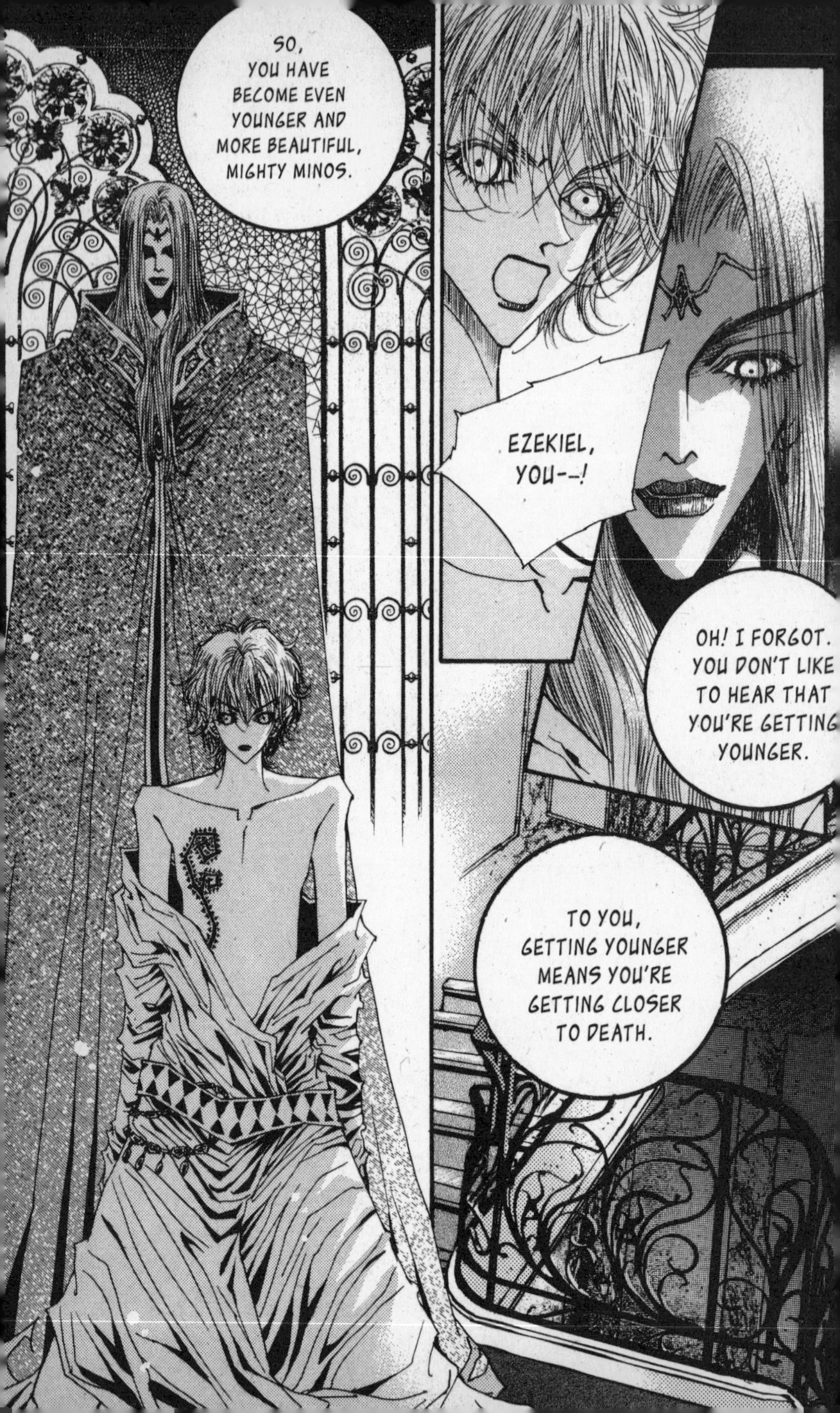
SO, YOU HAVE BECOME EVEN YOUNGER AND MORE BEAUTIFUL, MIGHTY MINOS.
EZEKIEL, YOU--!
OH! I FORGOT. YOU DON'T LIKE TO HEAR THAT YOU'RE GETTING YOUNGER.
TO YOU, GETTING YOUNGER MEANS YOU'RE GETTING CLOSER TO DEATH.

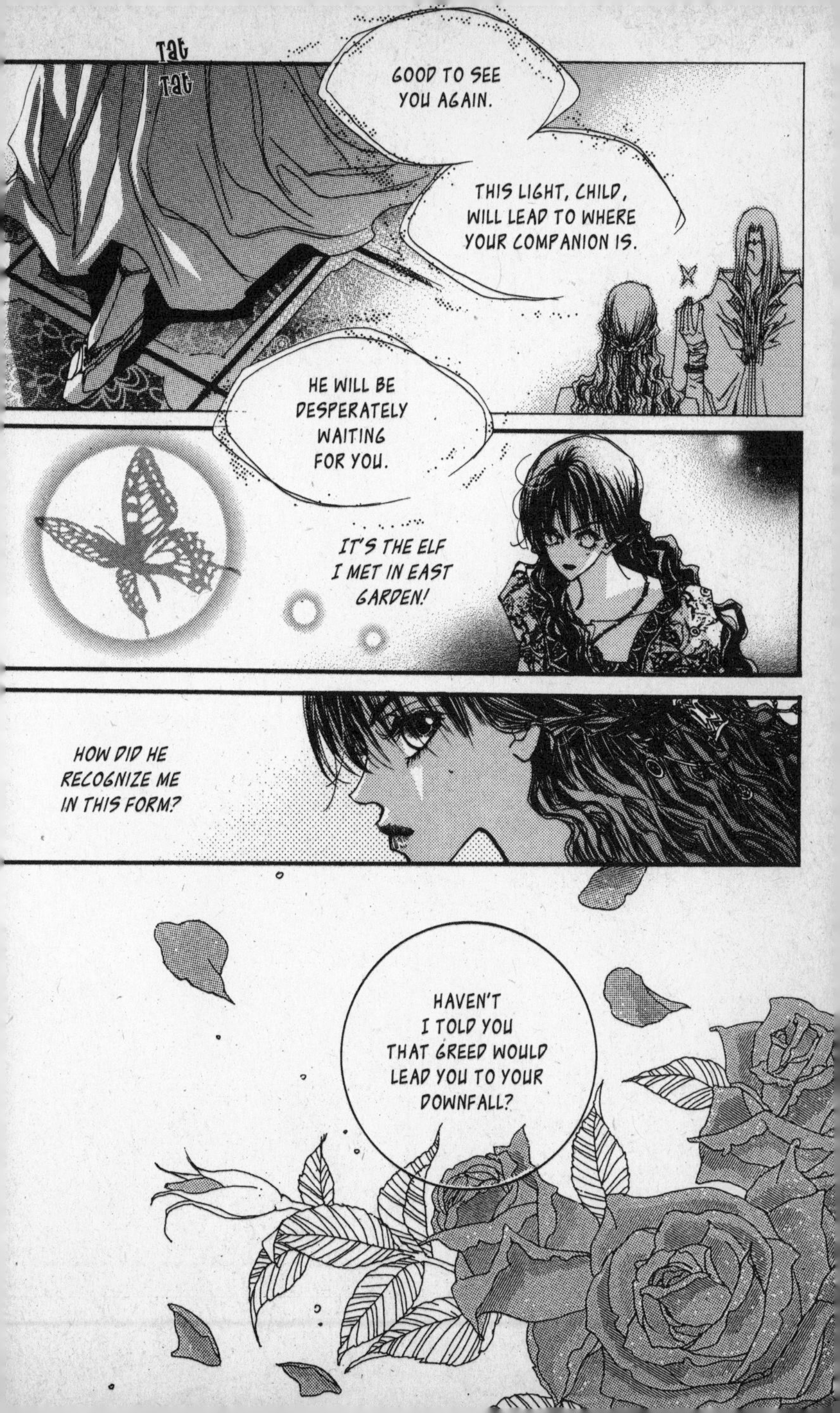
TAT TAT
GOOD TO SEE YOU AGAIN.
THIS LIGHT, CHILD, WILL LEAD TO WHERE YOUR COMPANION IS.
HE WILL BE DESPERATELY WAITING FOR YOU.
IT'S THE ELF I MET IN EAST GARDEN!
HOW DID HE RECOGNIZE ME IN THIS FORM?
HAVEN'T I TOLD YOU THAT GREED WOULD LEAD YOU TO YOUR DOWNFALL?

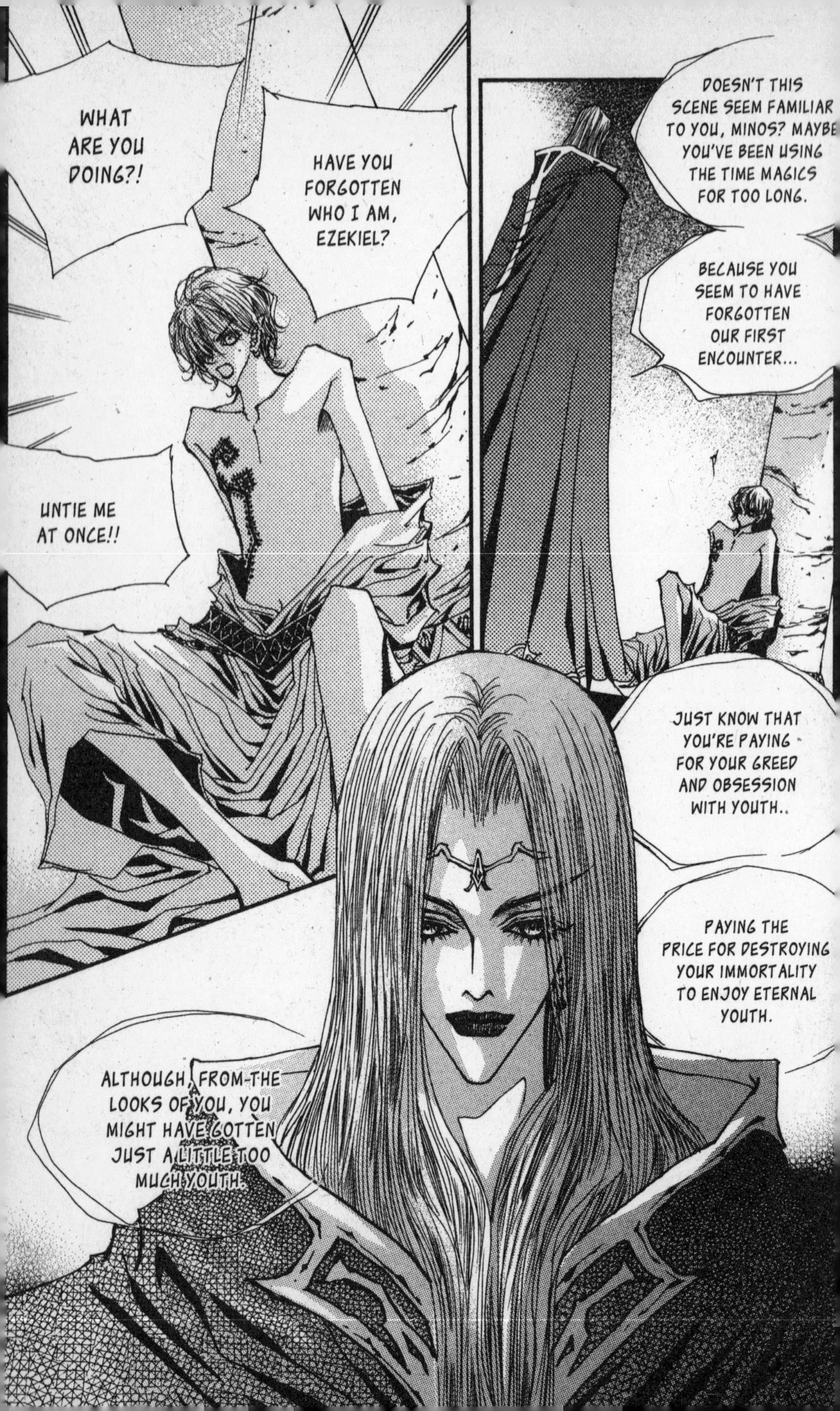
WHAT ARE YOU DOING?!
HAVE YOU FORGOTTEN WHO I AM, EZEKIEL?
UNTIE ME AT ONCE!!
DOESN'T THIS SCENE SEEM FAMILIAR TO YOU, MINOS? MAYBE YOU'VE BEEN USING THE TIME MAGICS FOR TOO LONG.
BECAUSE YOU SEEM TO HAVE FORGOTTEN OUR FIRST ENCOUNTER...
JUST KNOW THAT YOU'RE PAYING FOR YOUR GREED AND OBSESSION WITH YOUTH..
PAYING THE PRICE FOR DESTROYING YOUR IMMORTALITY TO ENJOY ETERNAL YOUTH.
ALTHOUGH, FROM THE LOOKS OF YOU, YOU MIGHT HAVE GOTTEN JUST A LITTLE TOO MUCH YOUTH.

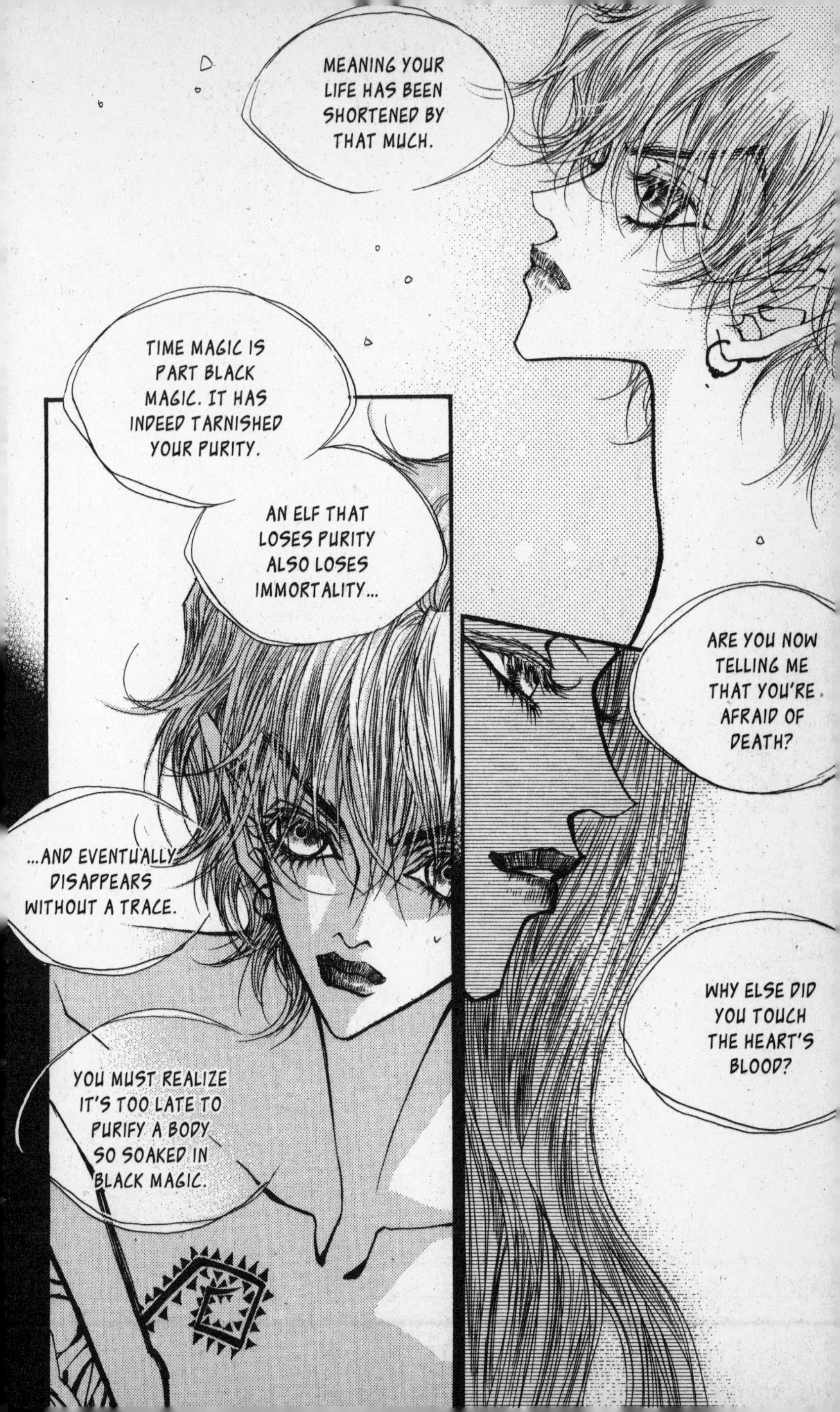
MEANING YOUR LIFE HAS BEEN SHORTENED BY THAT MUCH.
TIME MAGIC IS PART BLACK MAGIC. IT HAS INDEED TARNISHED YOUR PURITY.
AN ELF THAT LOSES PURITY ALSO LOSES IMMORTALITY...
...AND EVENTUALLY DISAPPEARS WITHOUT A TRACE.
YOU MUST REALIZE IT'S TOO LATE TO PURIFY A BODY SO SOAKED IN BLACK MAGIC.
ARE YOU NOW TELLING ME THAT YOU'RE AFRAID OF DEATH?
WHY ELSE DID YOU TOUCH THE HEART'S BLOOD?

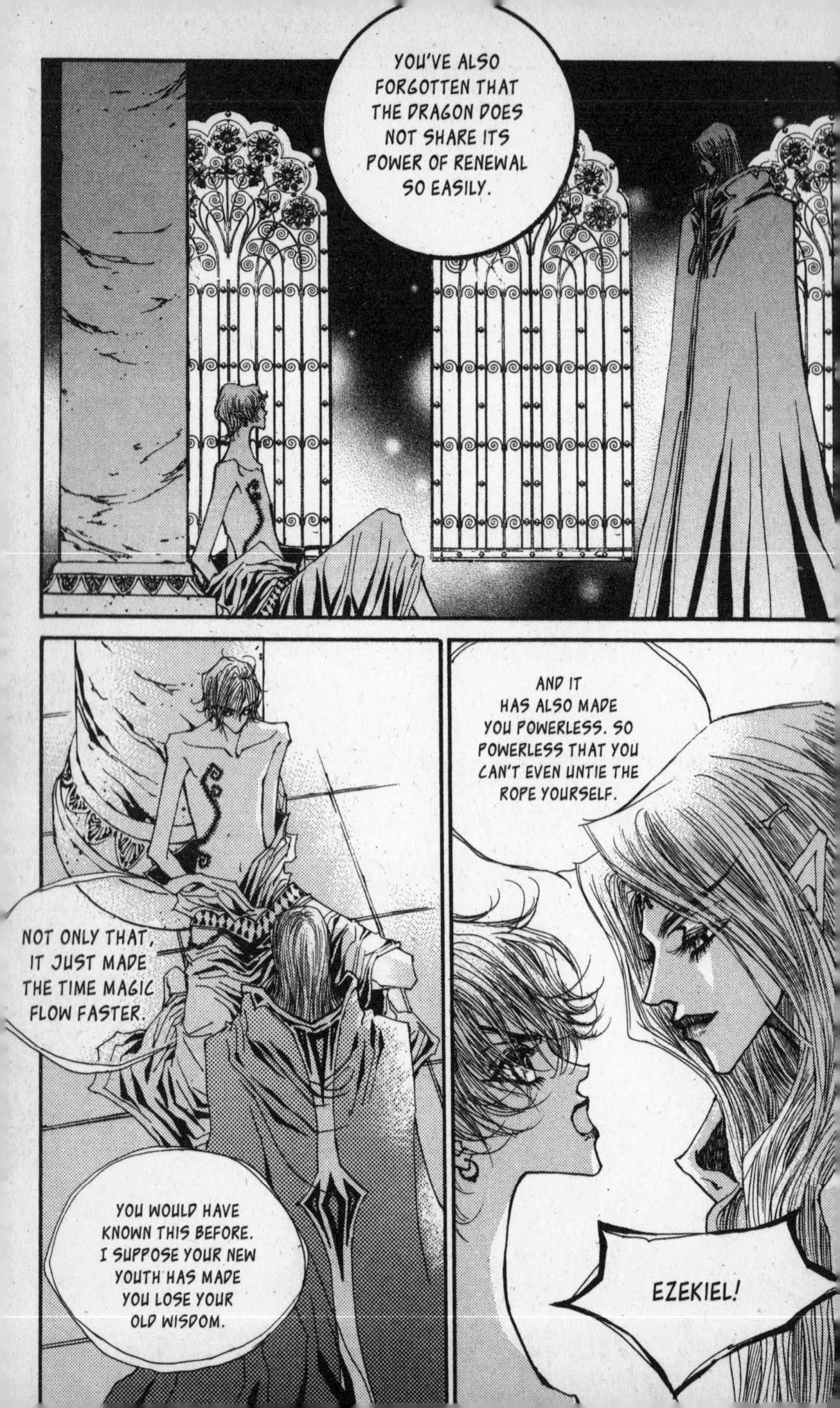
YOU'VE ALSO FORGOTTEN THAT THE DRAGON DOES NOT SHARE ITS POWER OF RENEWAL SO EASILY.
NOT ONLY THAT, IT JUST MADE THE TIME MAGIC FLOW FASTER.
YOU WOULD HAVE KNOWN THIS BEFORE. I SUPPOSE YOUR NEW YOUTH HAS MADE YOU LOSE YOUR OLD WISDOM.
AND IT HAS ALSO MADE YOU POWERLESS. SO POWERLESS THAT YOU CAN'T EVEN UNTIE THE ROPE YOURSELF.
EZEKIEL!

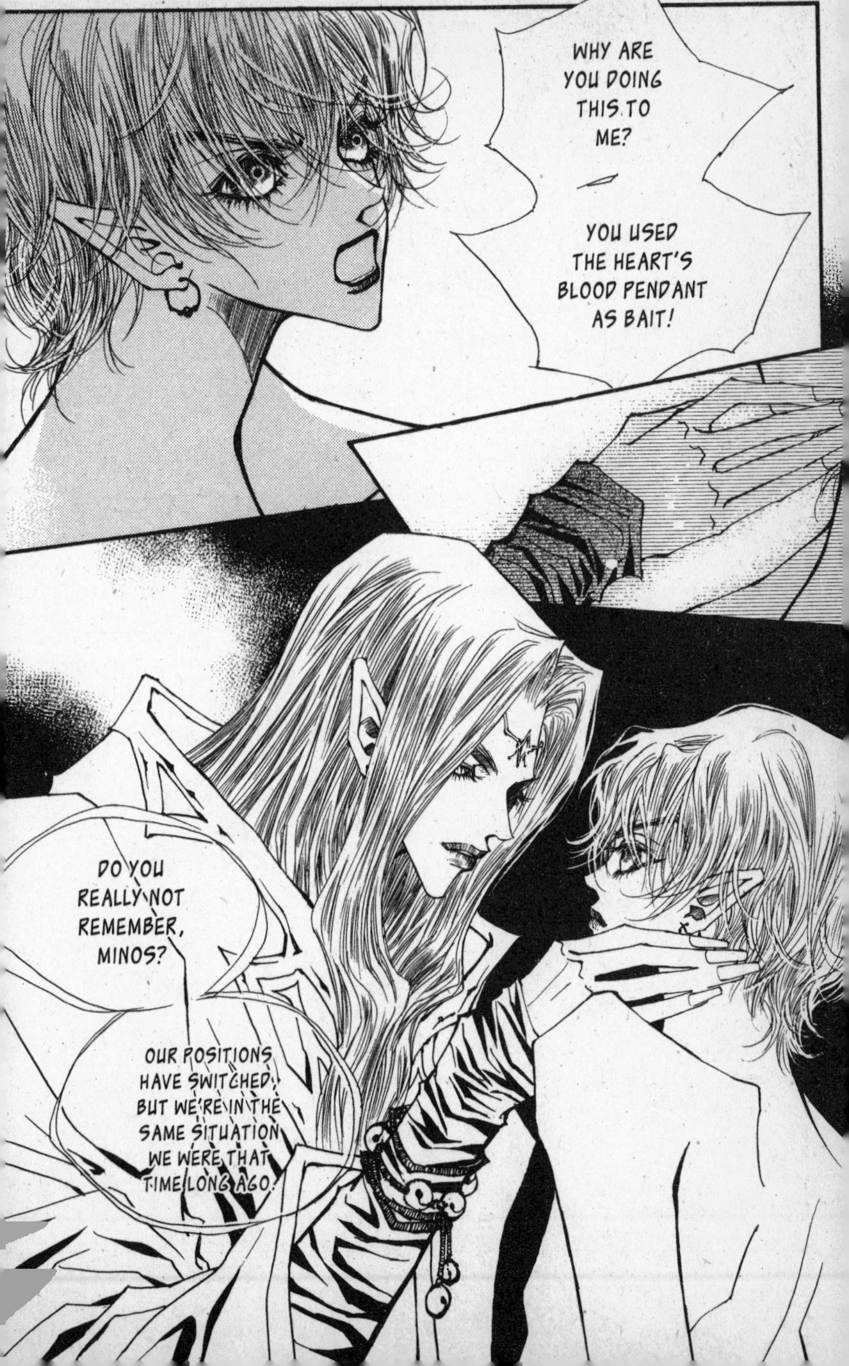
WHY ARE YOU DOING THIS TO ME?
YOU USED THE HEART'S BLOOD PENDANT AS BAIT!
DO YOU REALLY NOT REMEMBER, MINOS?
OUR POSITIONS HAVE SWITCHED, BUT WE'RE IN THE SAME SITUATION WE WERE THAT TIME LONG AGO.

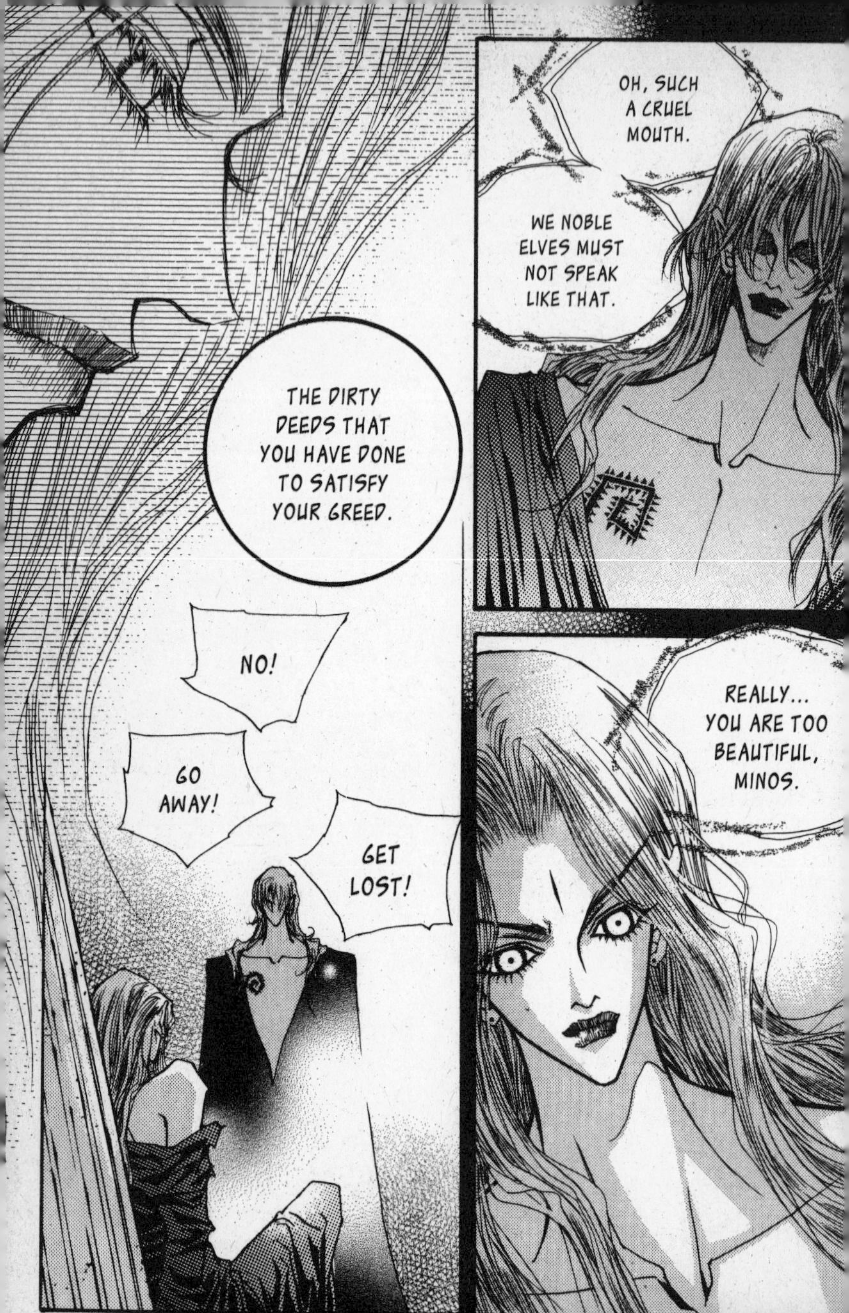
THE DIRTY DEEDS THAT YOU HAVE DONE TO SATISFY YOUR GREED.
NO!
GO AWAY!
GET LOST!
OH, SUCH A CRUEL MOUTH.
WE NOBLE ELVES MUST NOT SPEAK LIKE THAT.
REALLY... YOU ARE TOO BEAUTIFUL, MINOS.

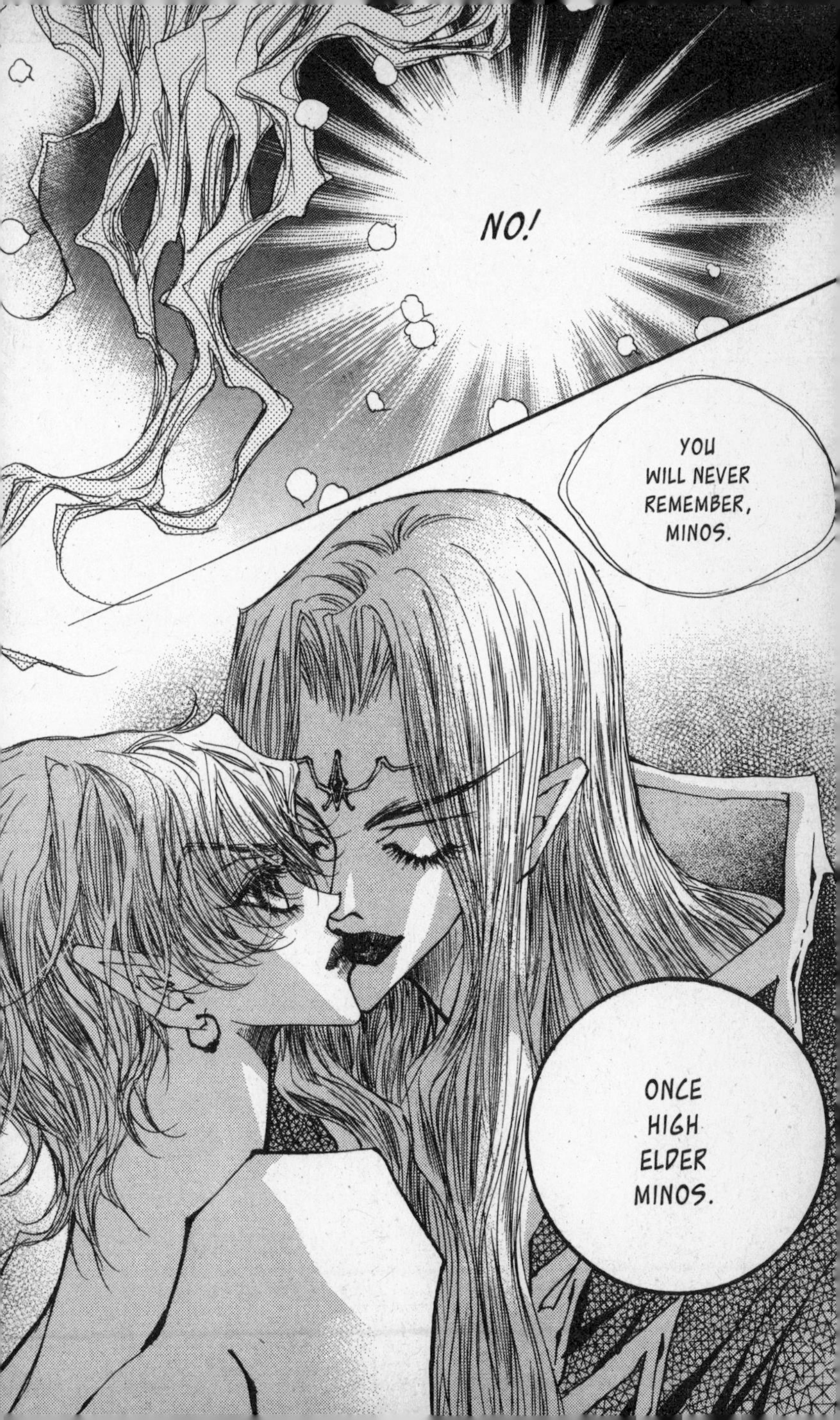
NO!
YOU WILL NEVER REMEMBER, MINOS.
ONCE HIGH ELDER MINOS.

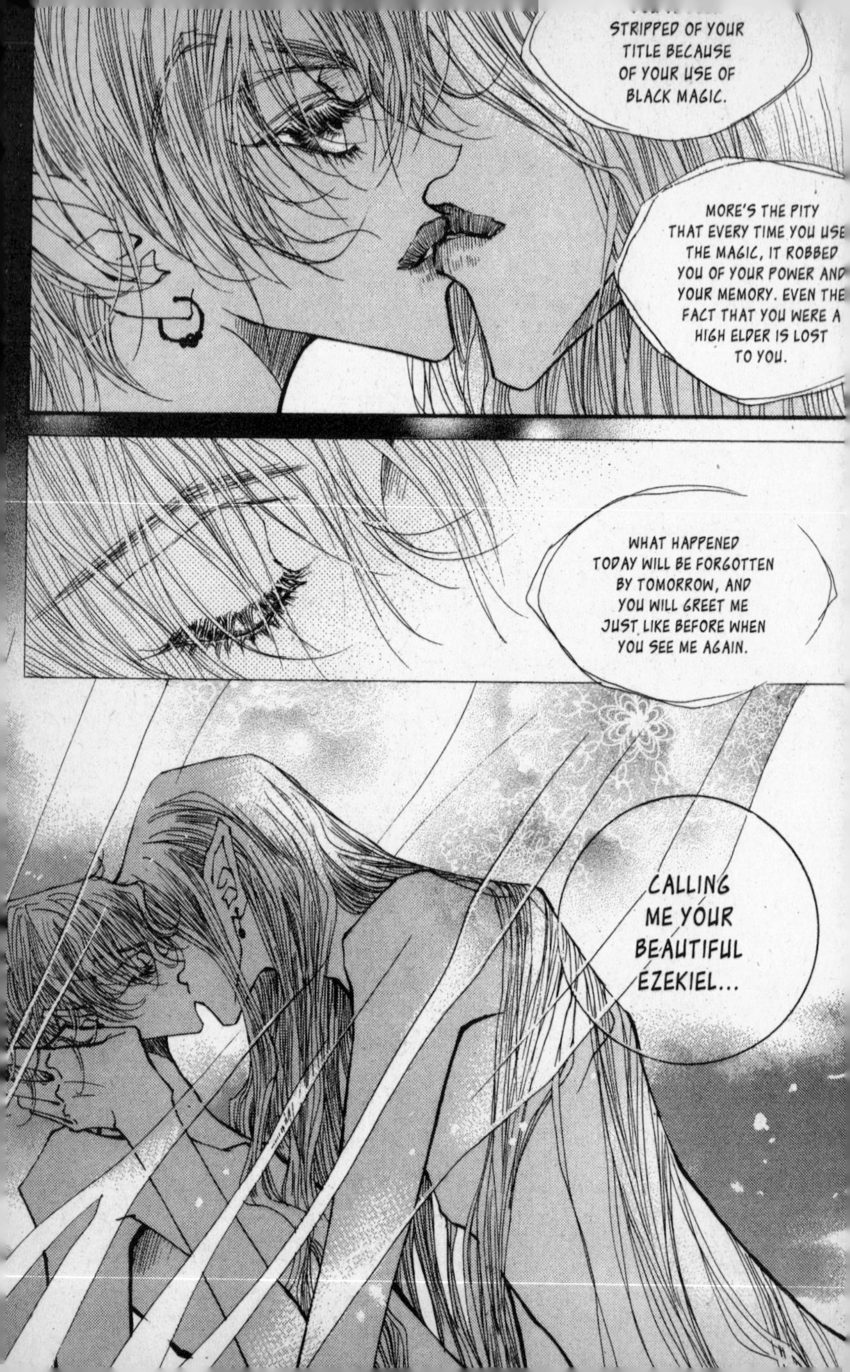
STRIPPED OF YOUR TITLE BECAUSE OF YOUR USE OF BLACK MAGIC.
MORE'S THE PITY THAT EVERY TIME YOU USE THE MAGIC, IT ROBBED YOU OF YOUR POWER AND YOUR MEMORY. EVEN THE FACT THAT YOU WERE A HIGH ELDER IS LOST TO YOU.
WHAT HAPPENED TODAY WILL BE FORGOTTEN BY TOMORROW, AND YOU WILL GREET ME JUST LIKE BEFORE WHEN YOU SEE ME AGAIN.
CALLING ME YOUR BEAUTIFUL EZEKIEL...

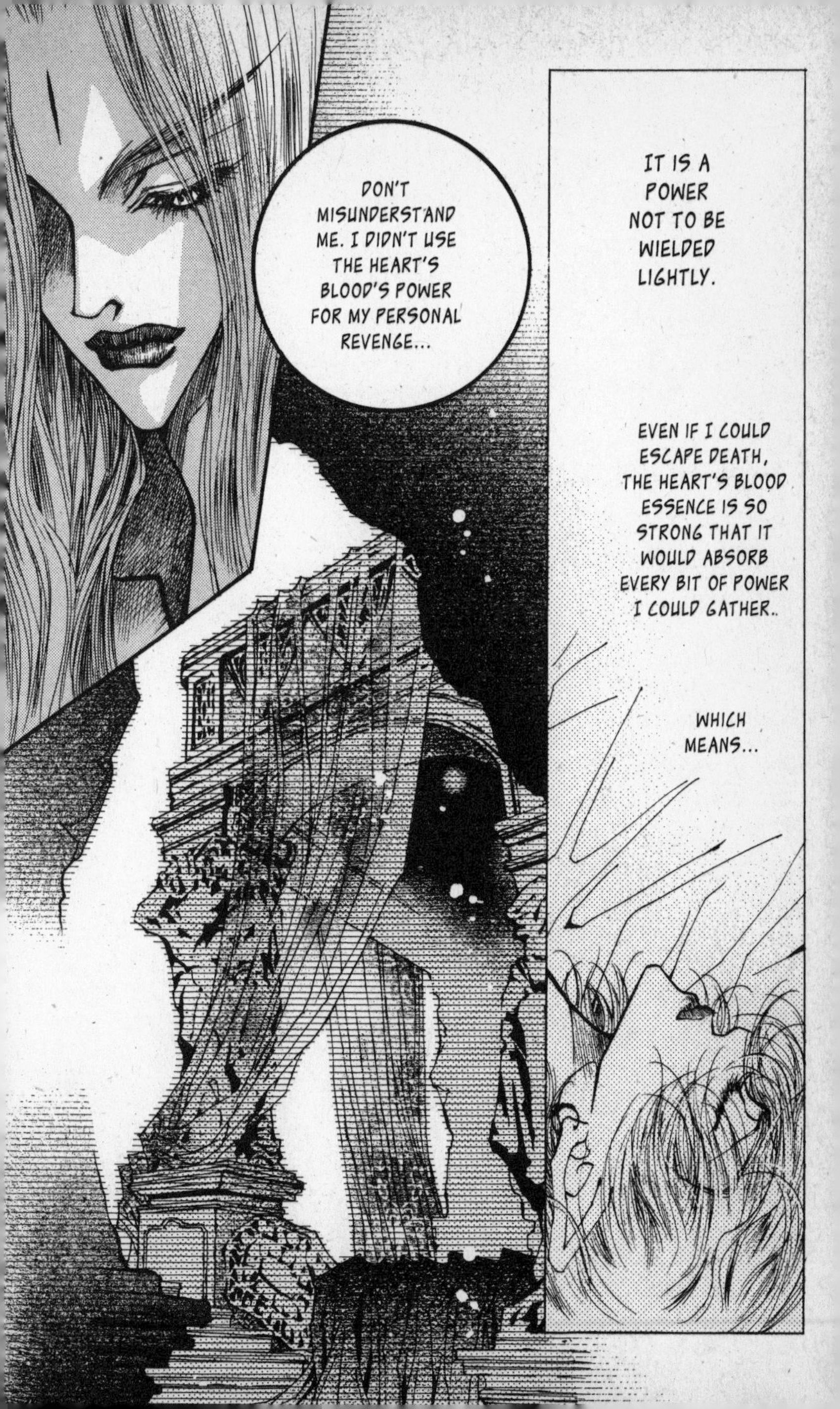
DON'T MISUNDERSTAND ME. I DIDN'T USE THE HEART'S BLOOD'S POWER FOR MY PERSONAL REVENGE...
IT IS A POWER NOT TO BE WIELDED LIGHTLY.
EVEN IF I COULD ESCAPE DEATH, THE HEART'S BLOOD ESSENCE IS SO STRONG THAT IT WOULD ABSORB EVERY BIT OF POWER I COULD GATHER..
WHICH MEANS...

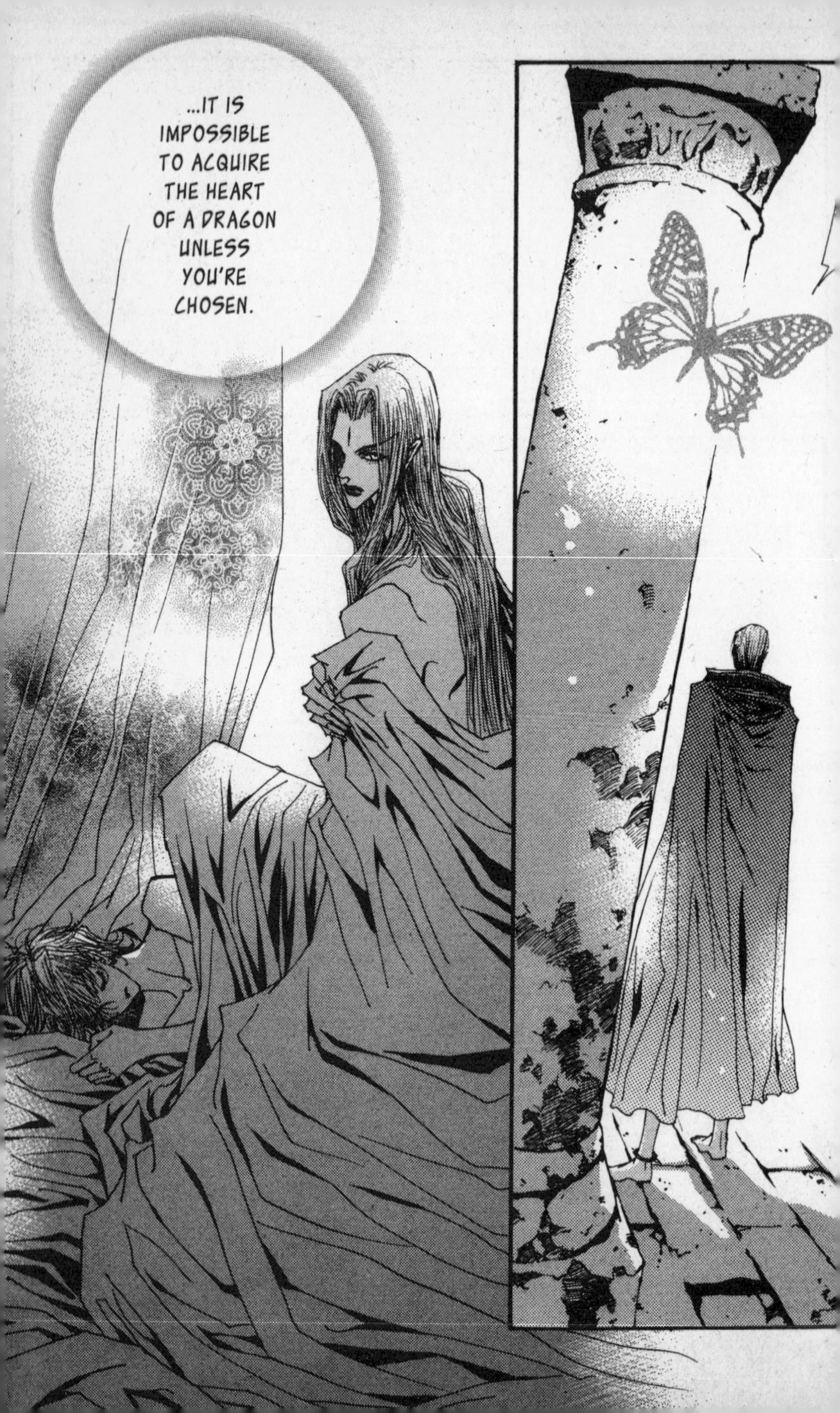
...IT IS IMPOSSIBLE TO ACQUIRE THE HEART OF A DRAGON UNLESS YOU'RE CHOSEN.

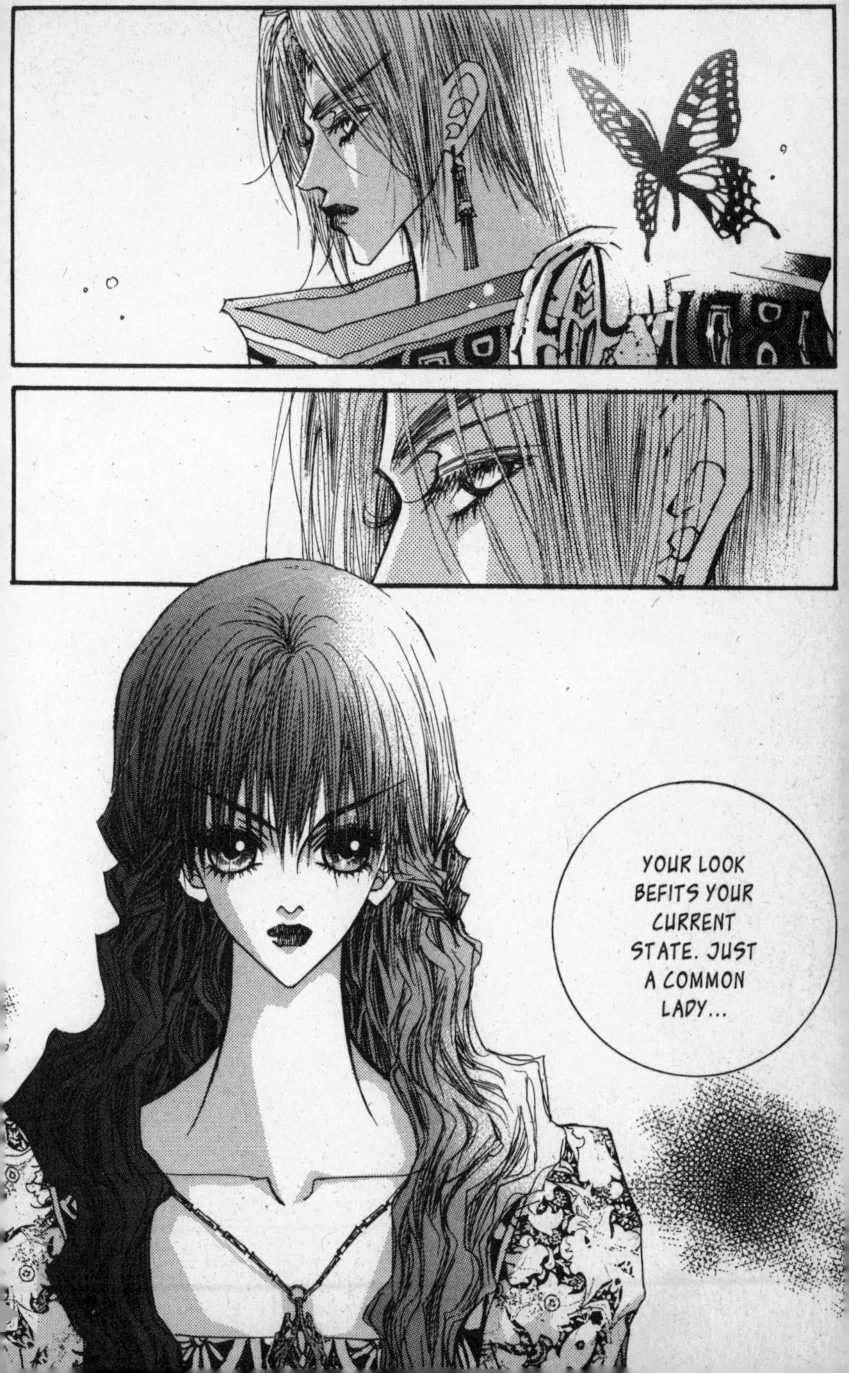
YOUR LOOK BEFITS YOUR CURRENT STATE. JUST A COMMON LADY...

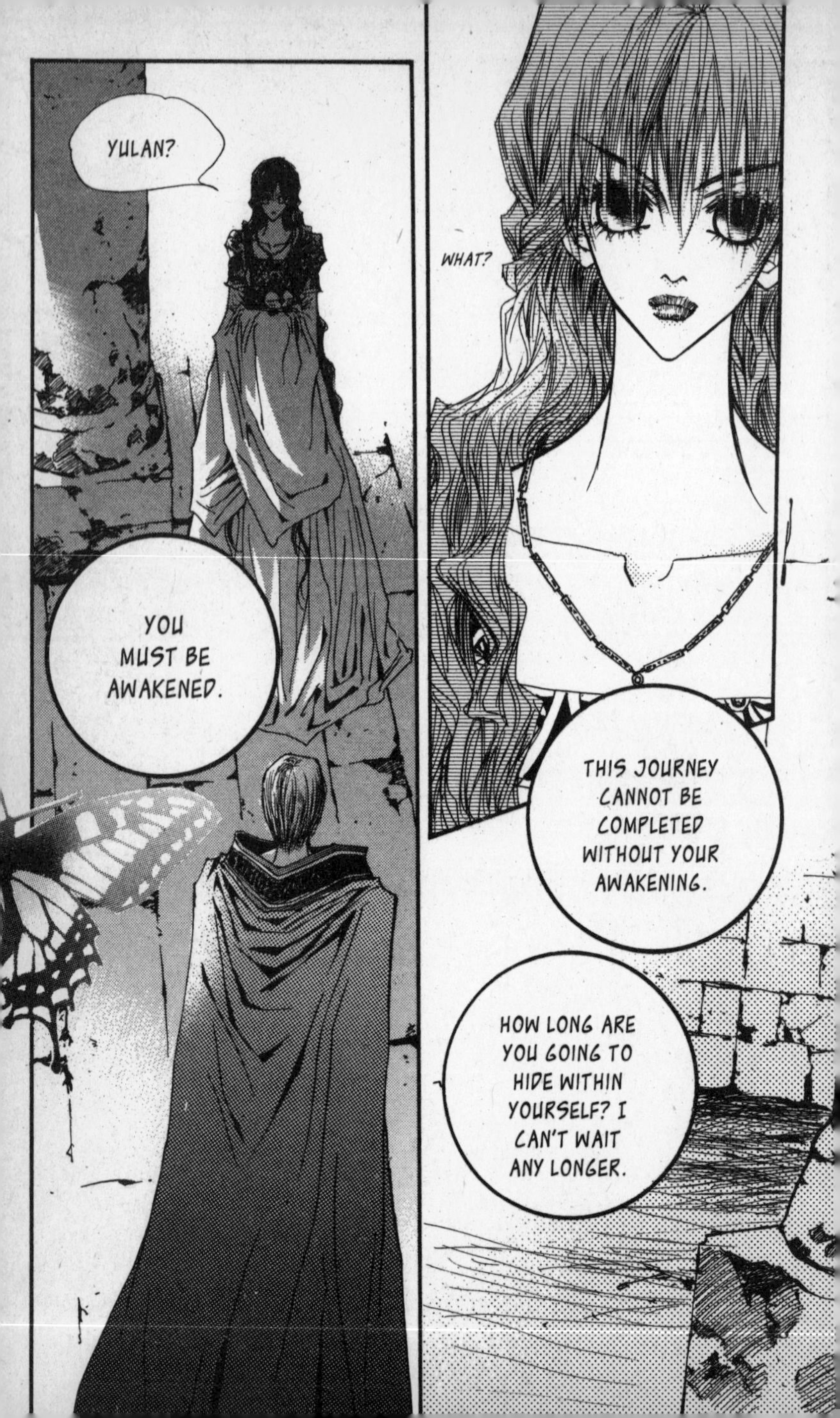
YULAN?
YOU MUST BE AWAKENED.
WHAT?
THIS JOURNEY CANNOT BE COMPLETED WITHOUT YOUR AWAKENING.
HOW LONG ARE YOU GOING TO HIDE WITHIN YOURSELF? I CAN'T WAIT ANY LONGER.

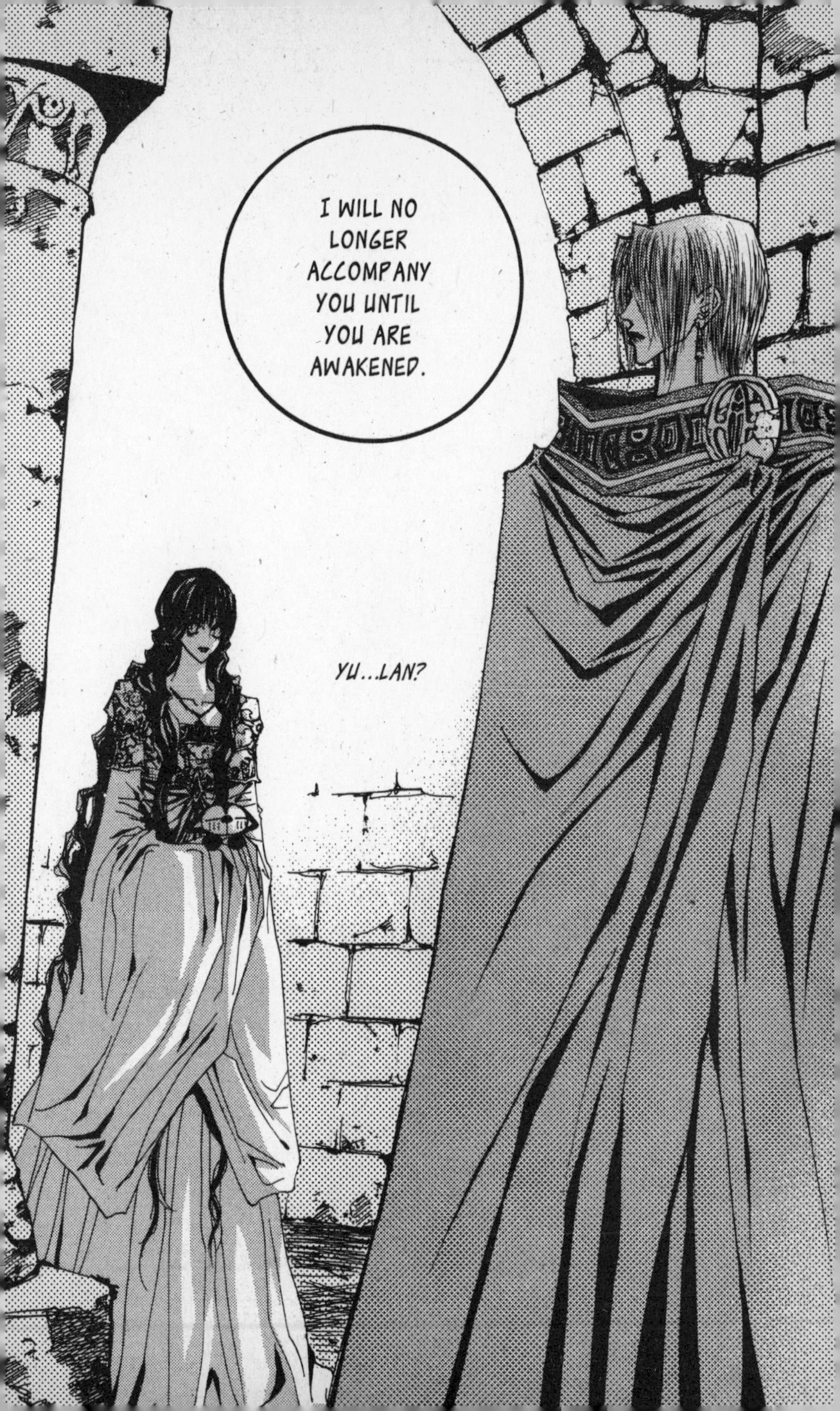
I WILL NO LONGER ACCOMPANY YOU UNTIL YOU ARE AWAKENED.
YU...LAN?

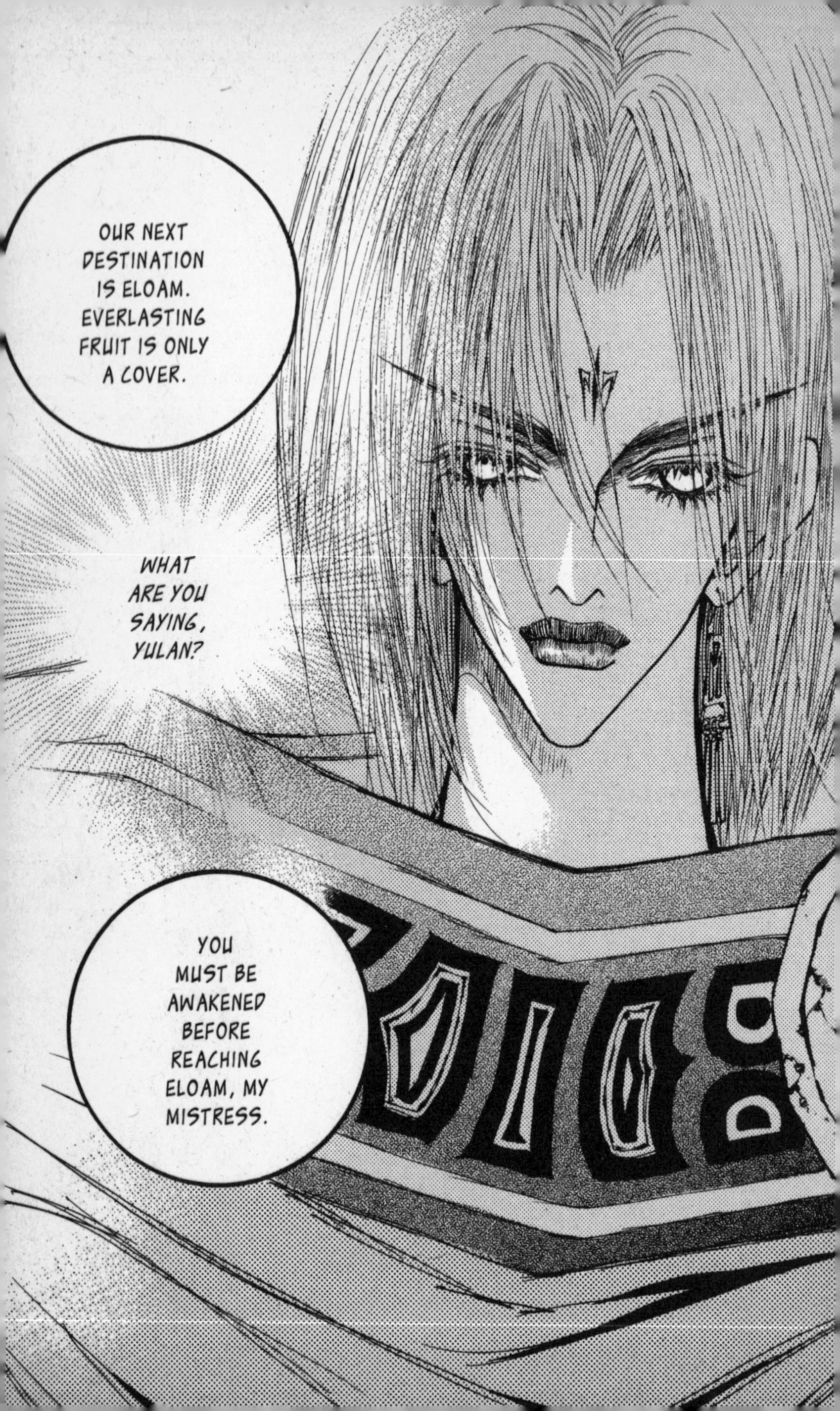
OUR NEXT DESTINATION IS ELOAM. EVERLASTING FRUIT IS ONLY A COVER.
WHAT ARE YOU SAYING, YULAN?
YOU MUST BE AWAKENED BEFORE REACHING ELOAM, MY MISTRESS.

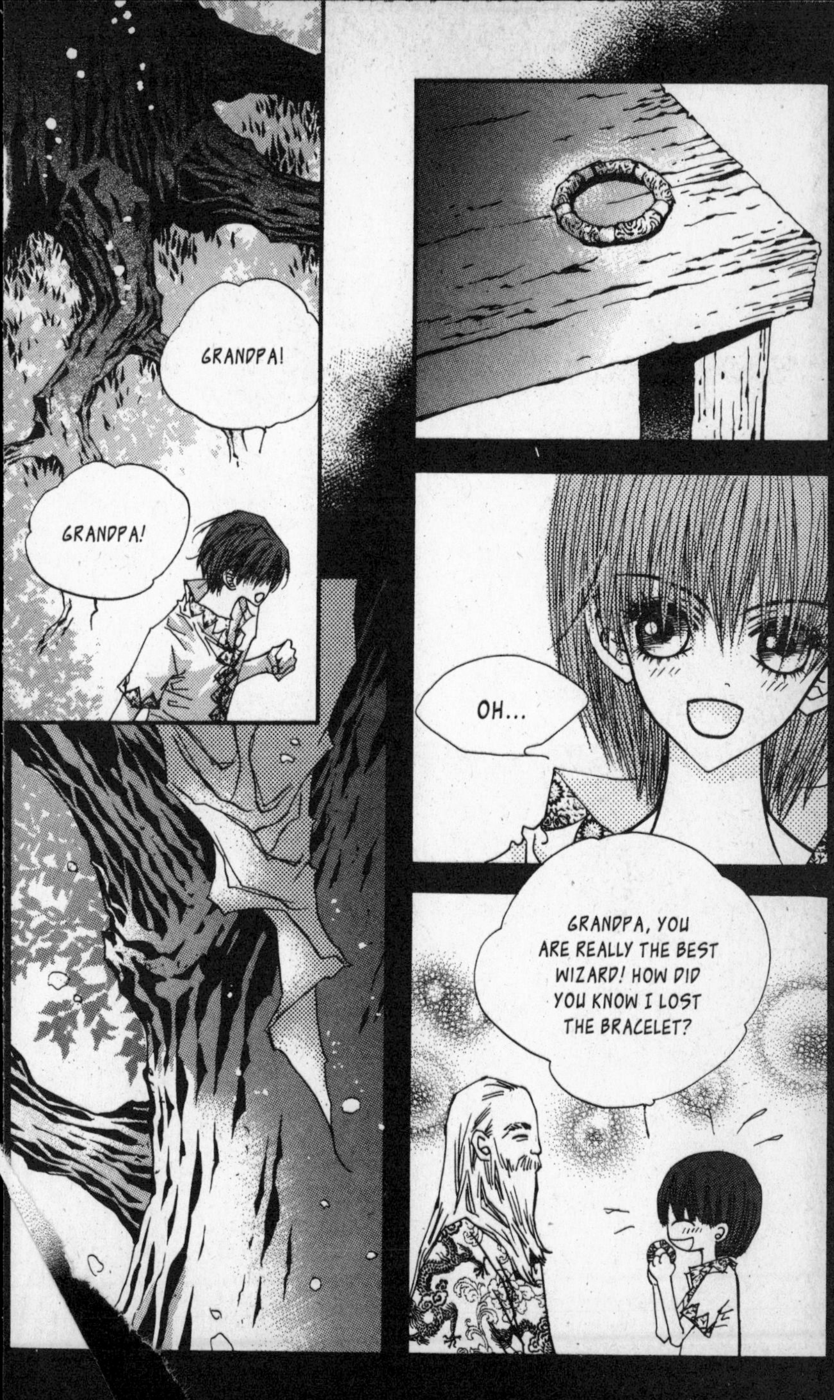
GRANDPA!
GRANDPA!
OH...
GRANDPA, YOU ARE REALLY THE BEST WIZARD! HOW DID YOU KNOW I LOST THE BRACELET?

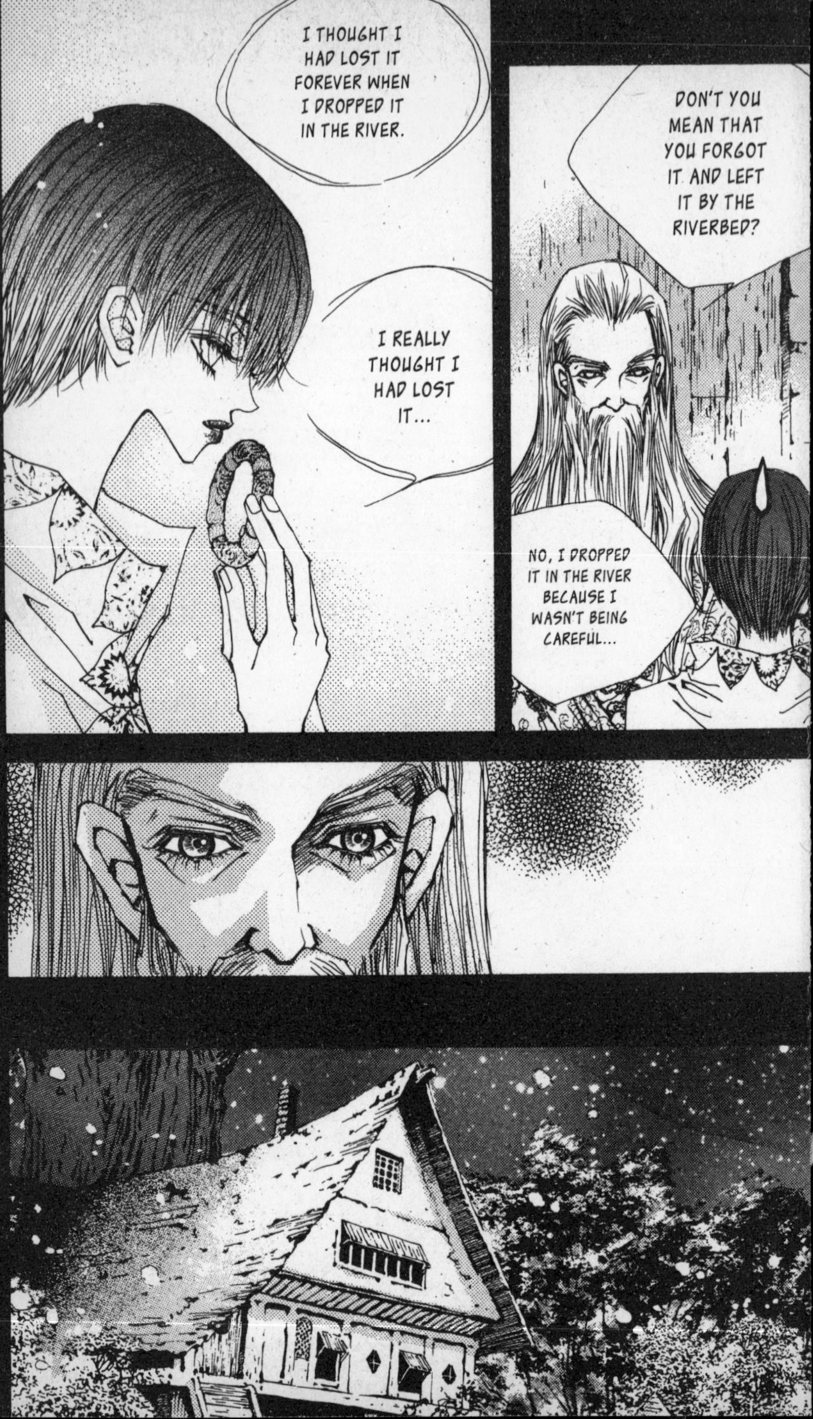
I THOUGHT I HAD LOST IT FOREVER WHEN I DROPPED IT IN THE RIVER.
I REALLY THOUGHT I HAD LOST IT...
DON'T YOU MEAN THAT YOU FORGOT IT AND LEFT IT BY THE RIVERBED?
NO, I DROPPED IT IN THE RIVER BECAUSE I WASN'T BEING CAREFUL...

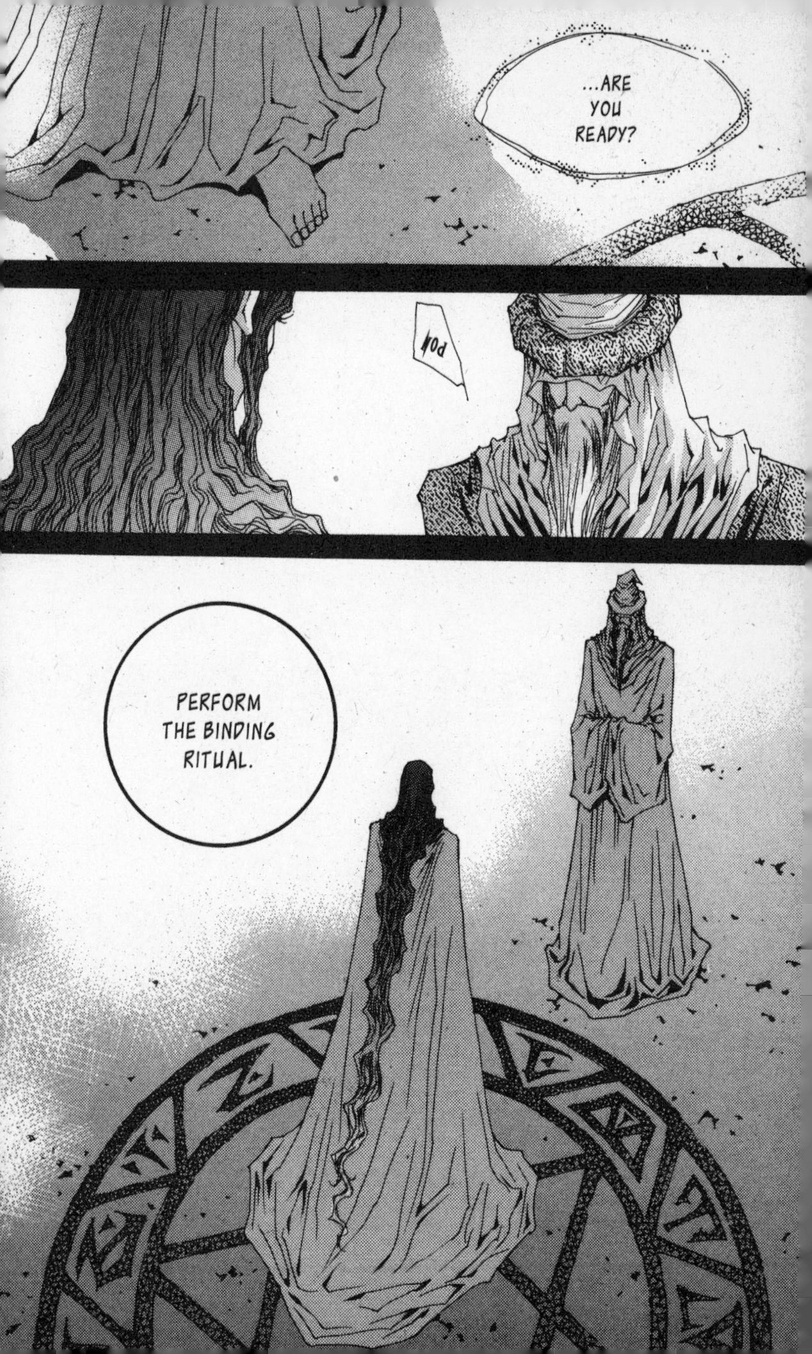
...ARE YOU READY?
nod
PERFORM THE BINDING RITUAL.

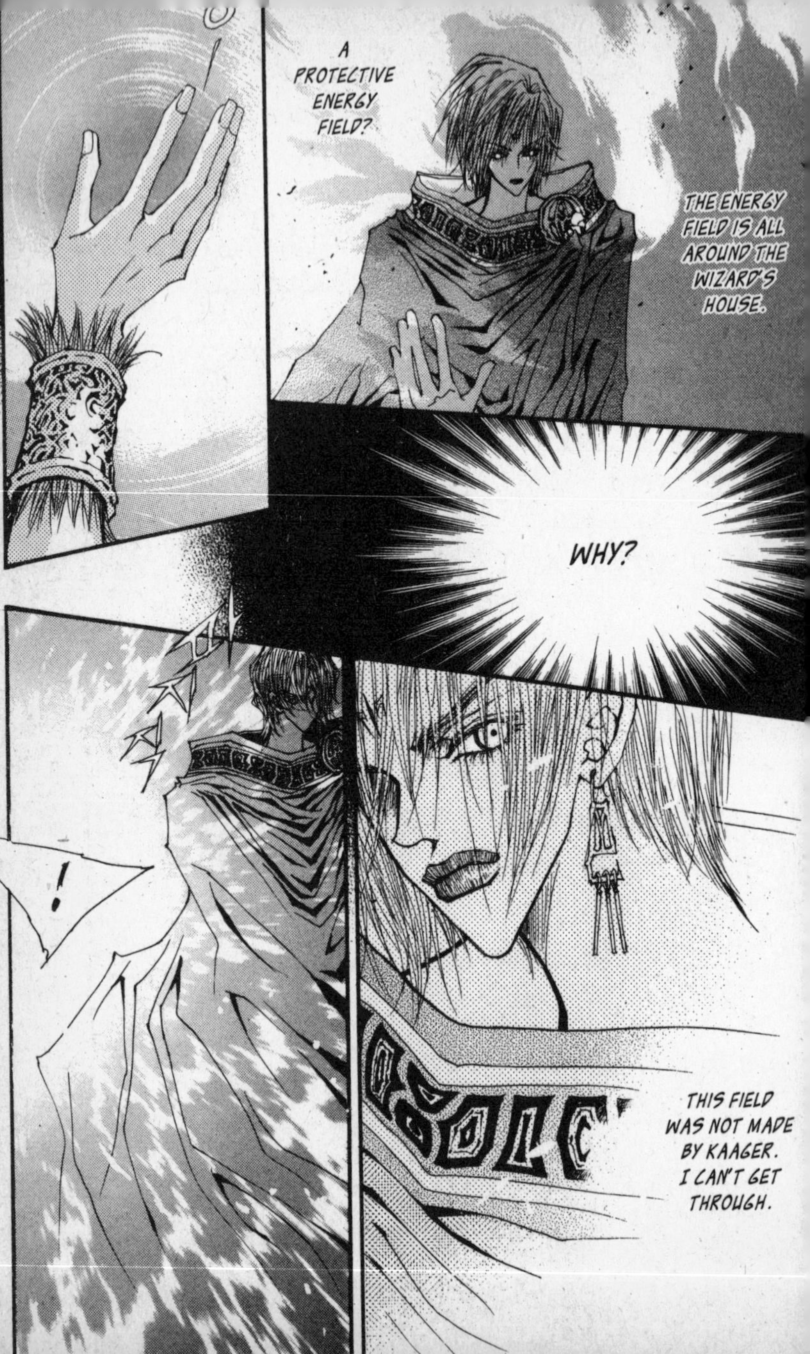
A PROTECTIVE ENERGY FIELD?
THE ENERGY FIELD IS ALL AROUND THE WIZARD'S HOUSE.
WHY?
!
THIS FIELD WAS NOT MADE BY KAAGER. I CAN'T GET THROUGH.

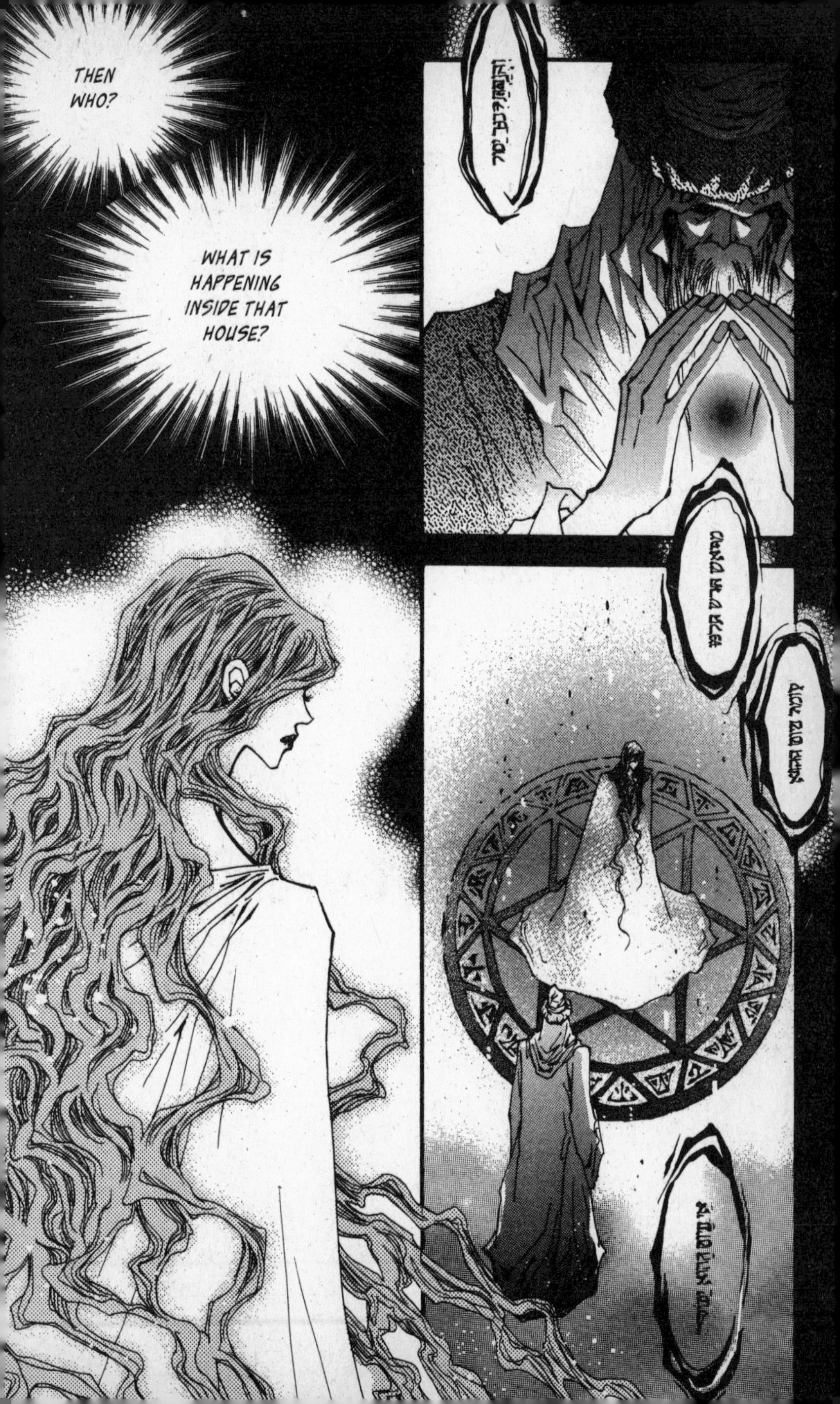
THEN WHO?
WHAT IS HAPPENING INSIDE THAT HOUSE?

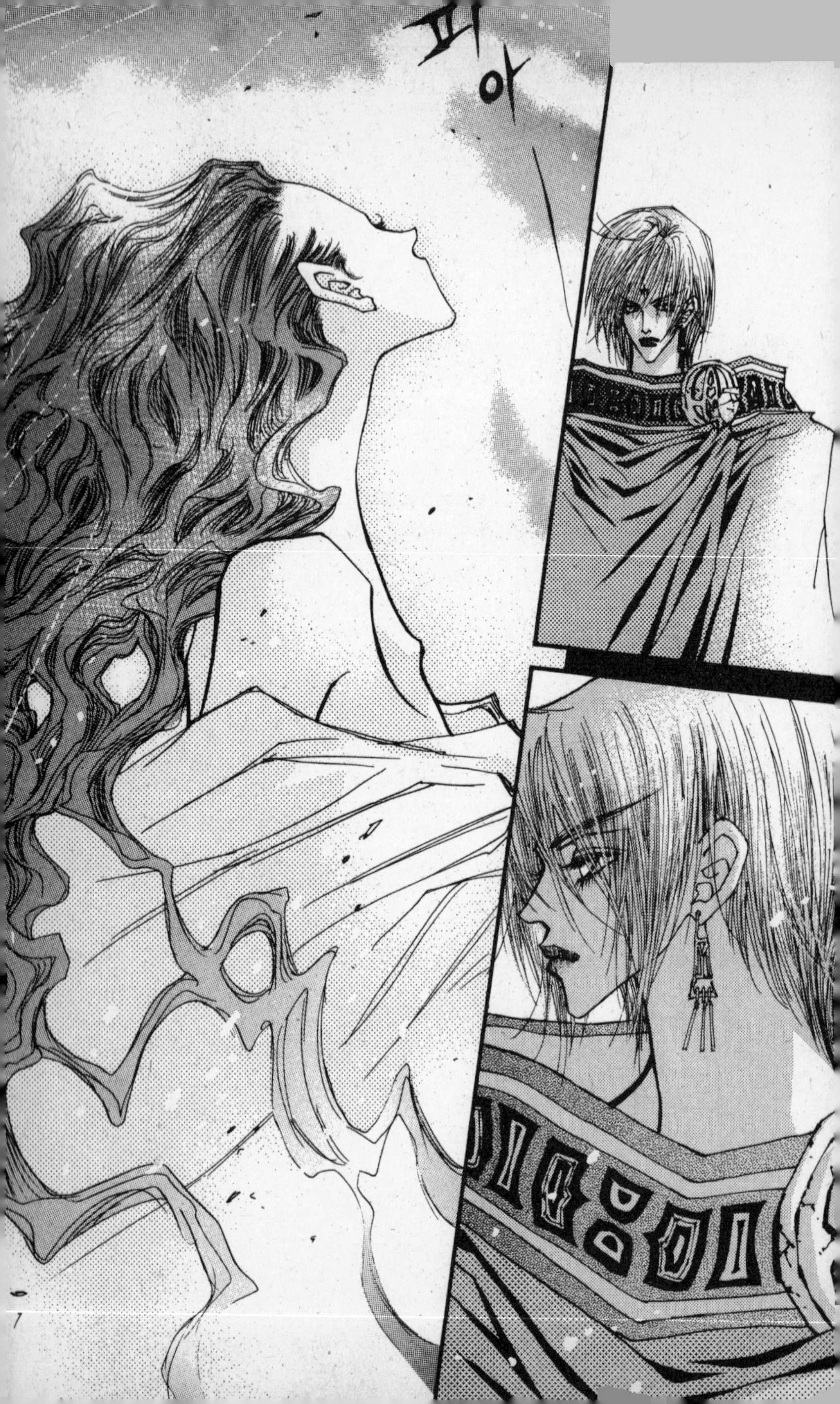
파아

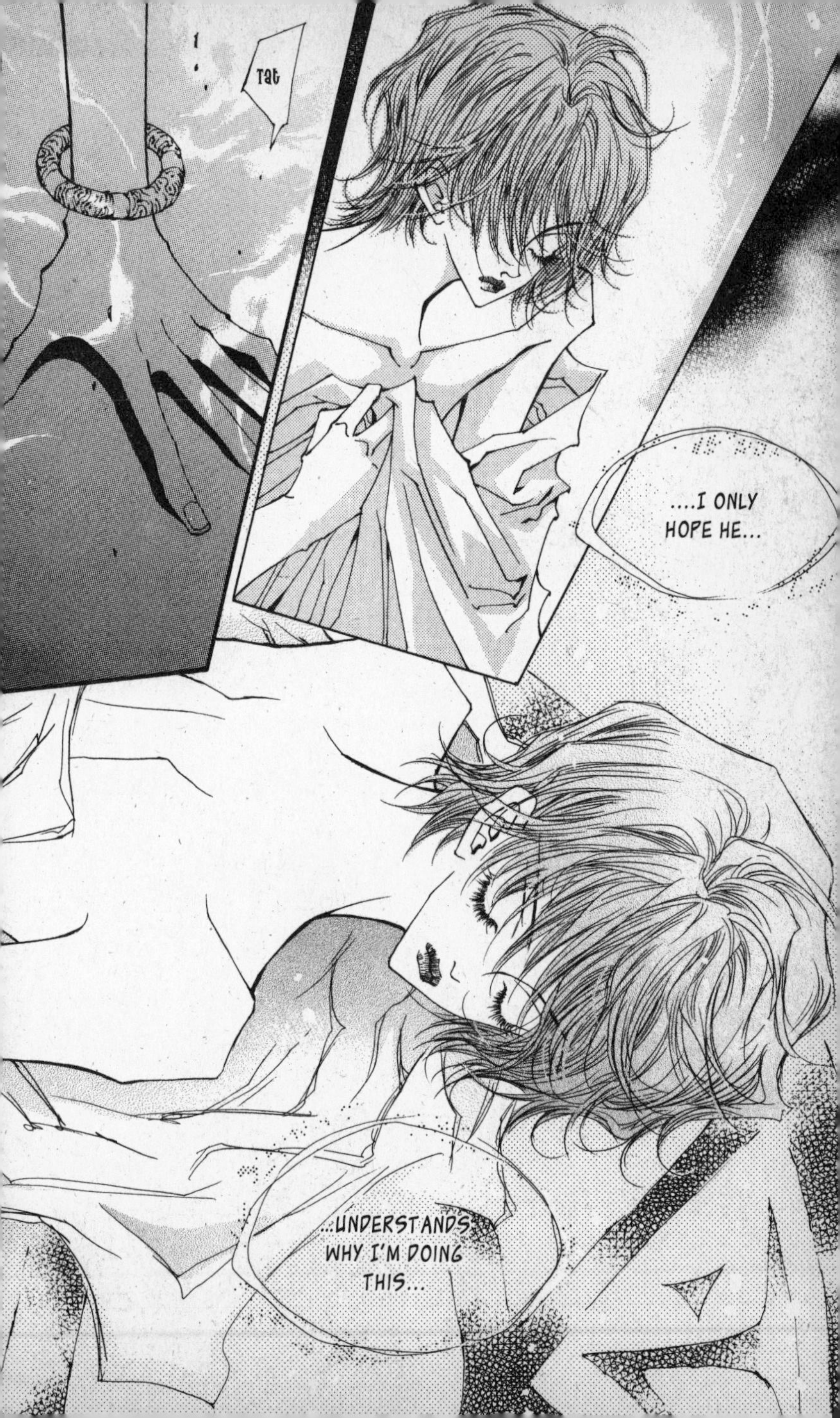
Tat
....I ONLY HOPE HE...
...UNDERSTANDS WHY I'M DOING THIS...

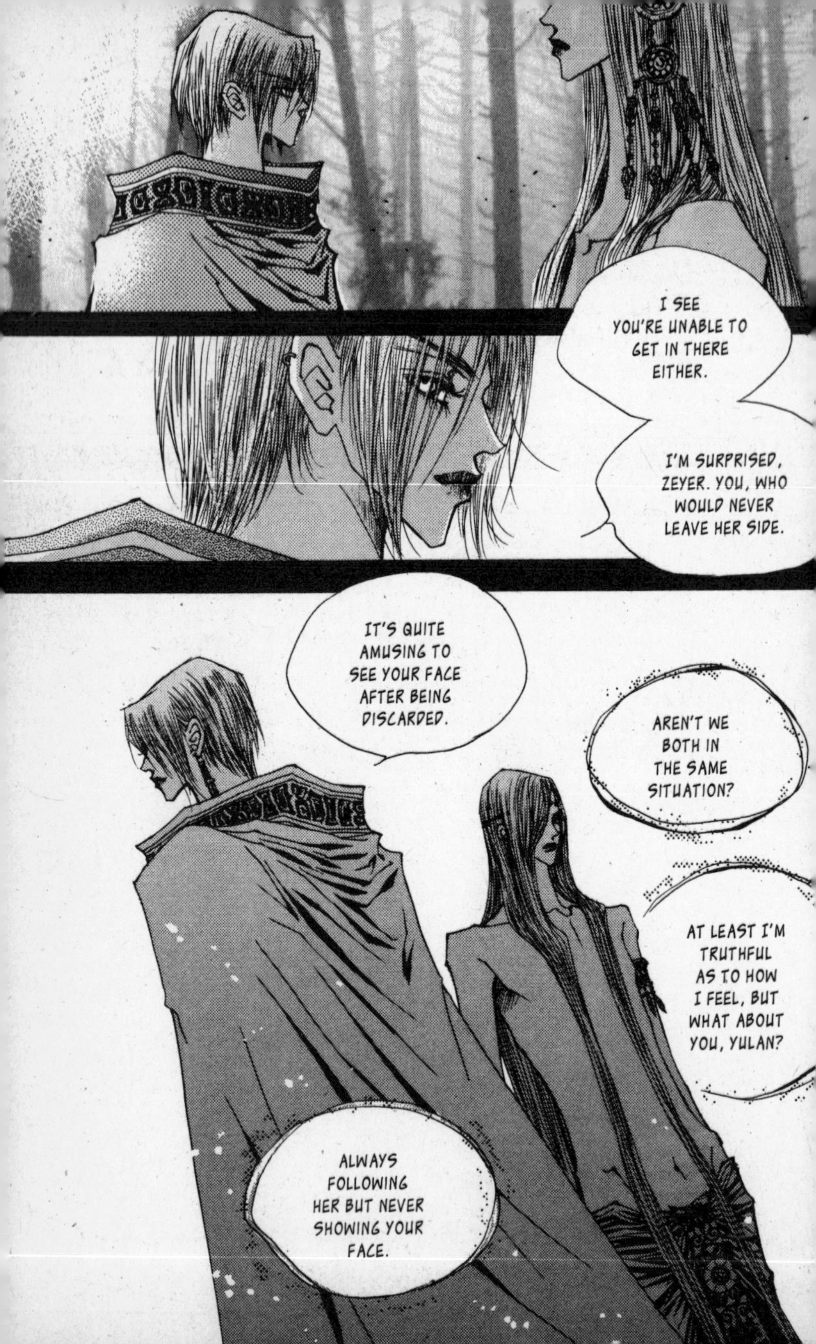
I SEE YOU'RE UNABLE TO GET IN THERE EITHER.
I'M SURPRISED, ZEYER. YOU, WHO WOULD NEVER LEAVE HER SIDE.
IT'S QUITE AMUSING TO SEE YOUR FACE AFTER BEING DISCARDED.
AREN'T WE BOTH IN THE SAME SITUATION?
AT LEAST I'M TRUTHFUL AS TO HOW I FEEL, BUT WHAT ABOUT YOU, YULAN?
ALWAYS FOLLOWING HER BUT NEVER SHOWING YOUR FACE.

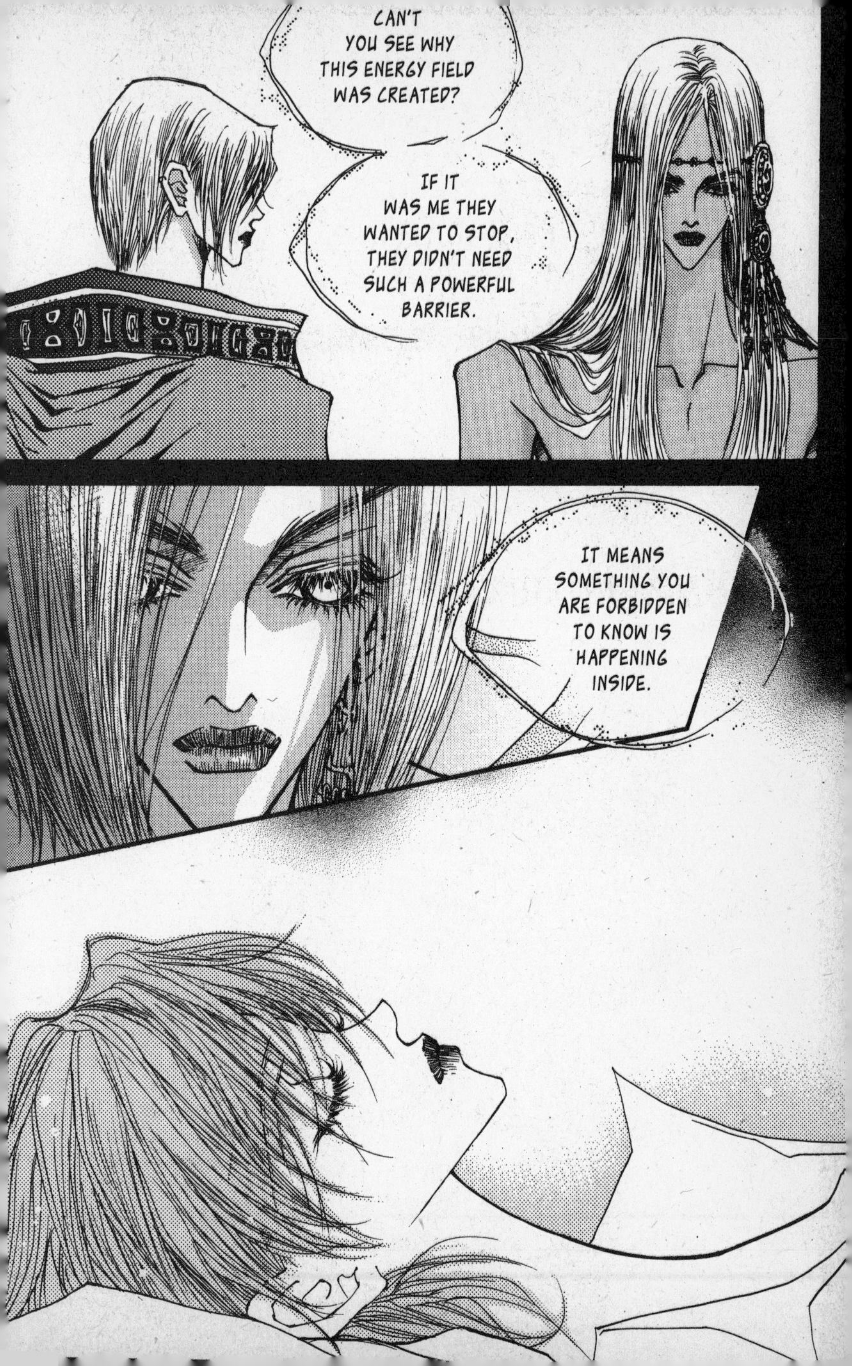
CAN'T YOU SEE WHY THIS ENERGY FIELD WAS CREATED?
IF IT WAS ME THEY WANTED TO STOP, THEY DIDN'T NEED SUCH A POWERFUL BARRIER.
IT MEANS SOMETHING YOU ARE FORBIDDEN TO KNOW IS HAPPENING INSIDE.

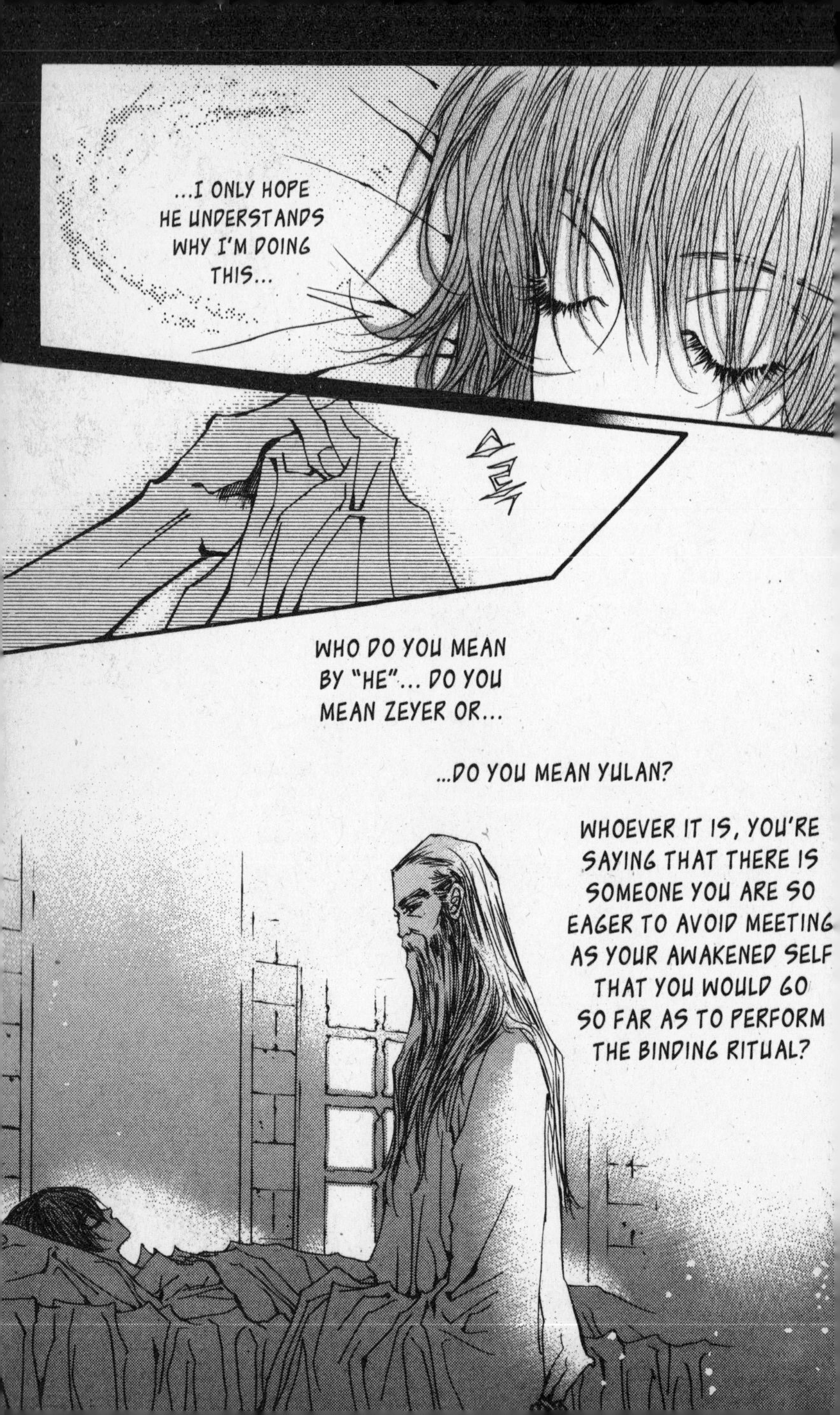
...I ONLY HOPE HE UNDERSTANDS WHY I'M DOING THIS...
WHO DO YOU MEAN BY "HE"... DO YOU MEAN ZEYER OR...
...DO YOU MEAN YULAN?
WHOEVER IT IS, YOU'RE SAYING THAT THERE IS SOMEONE YOU ARE SO EAGER TO AVOID MEETING AS YOUR AWAKENED SELF THAT YOU WOULD GO SO FAR AS TO PERFORM THE BINDING RITUAL?

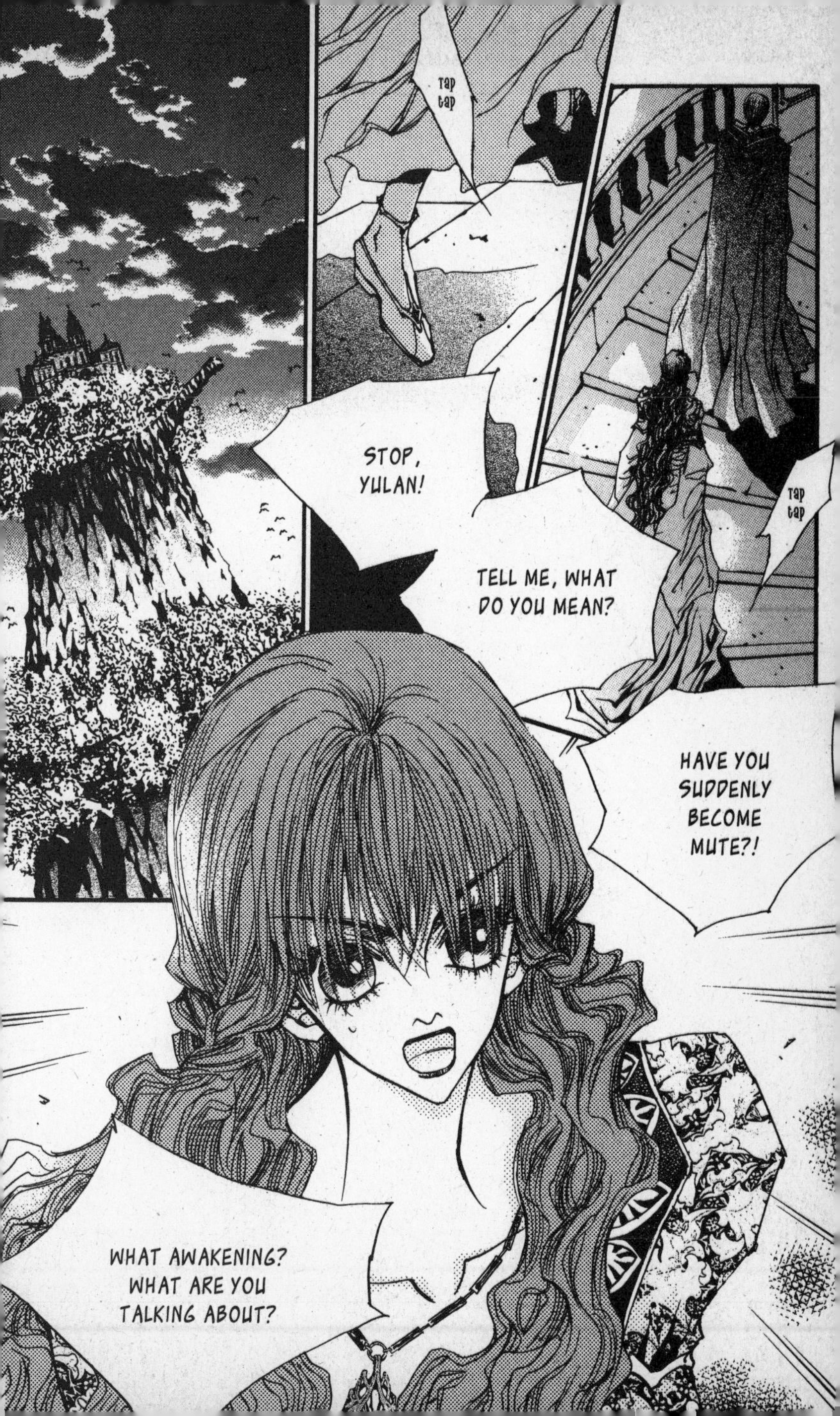
Tap tap
Tap tap
STOP, YULAN!
TELL ME, WHAT DO YOU MEAN?
HAVE YOU SUDDENLY BECOME MUTE?!
WHAT AWAKENING? WHAT ARE YOU TALKING ABOUT?

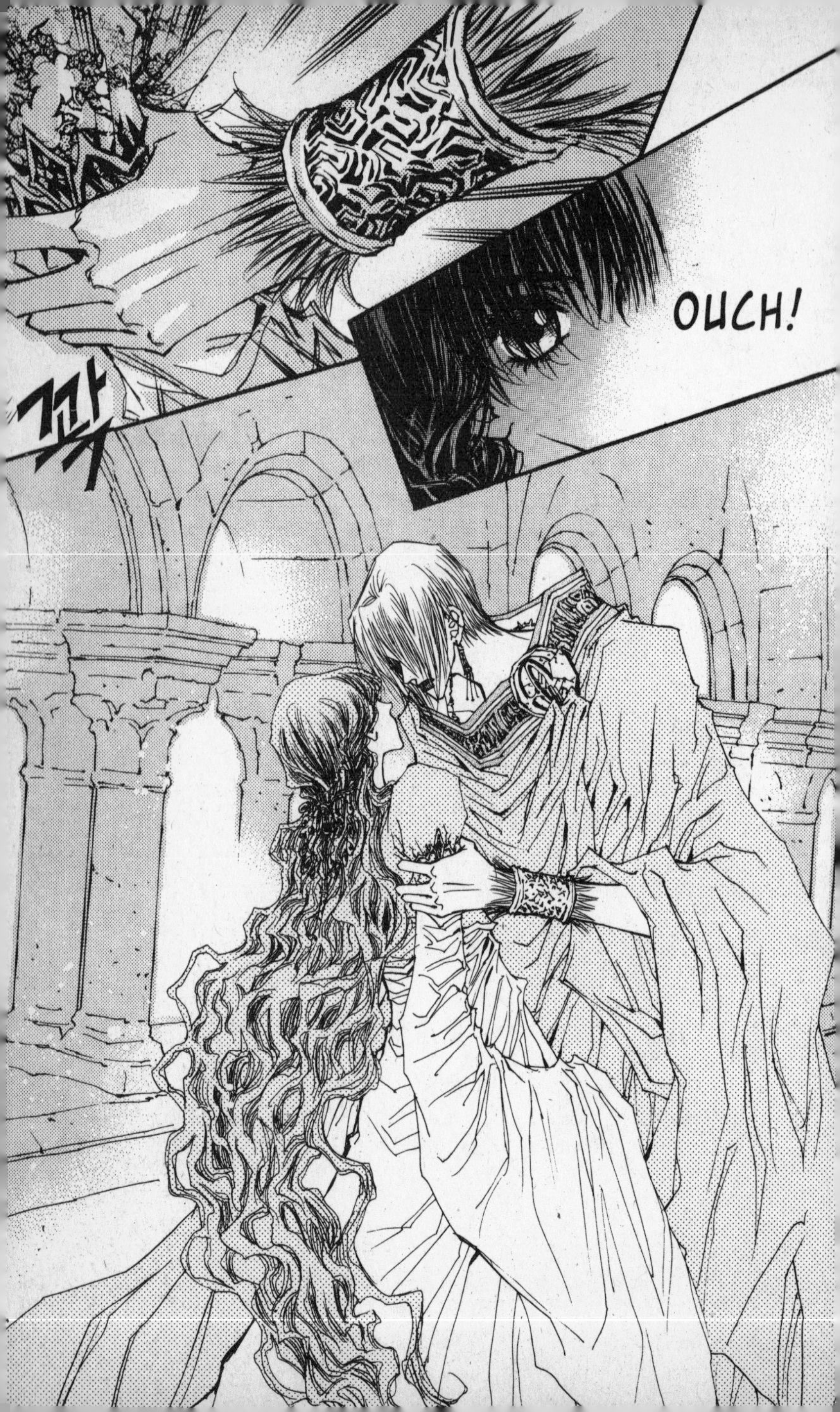
OUCH!

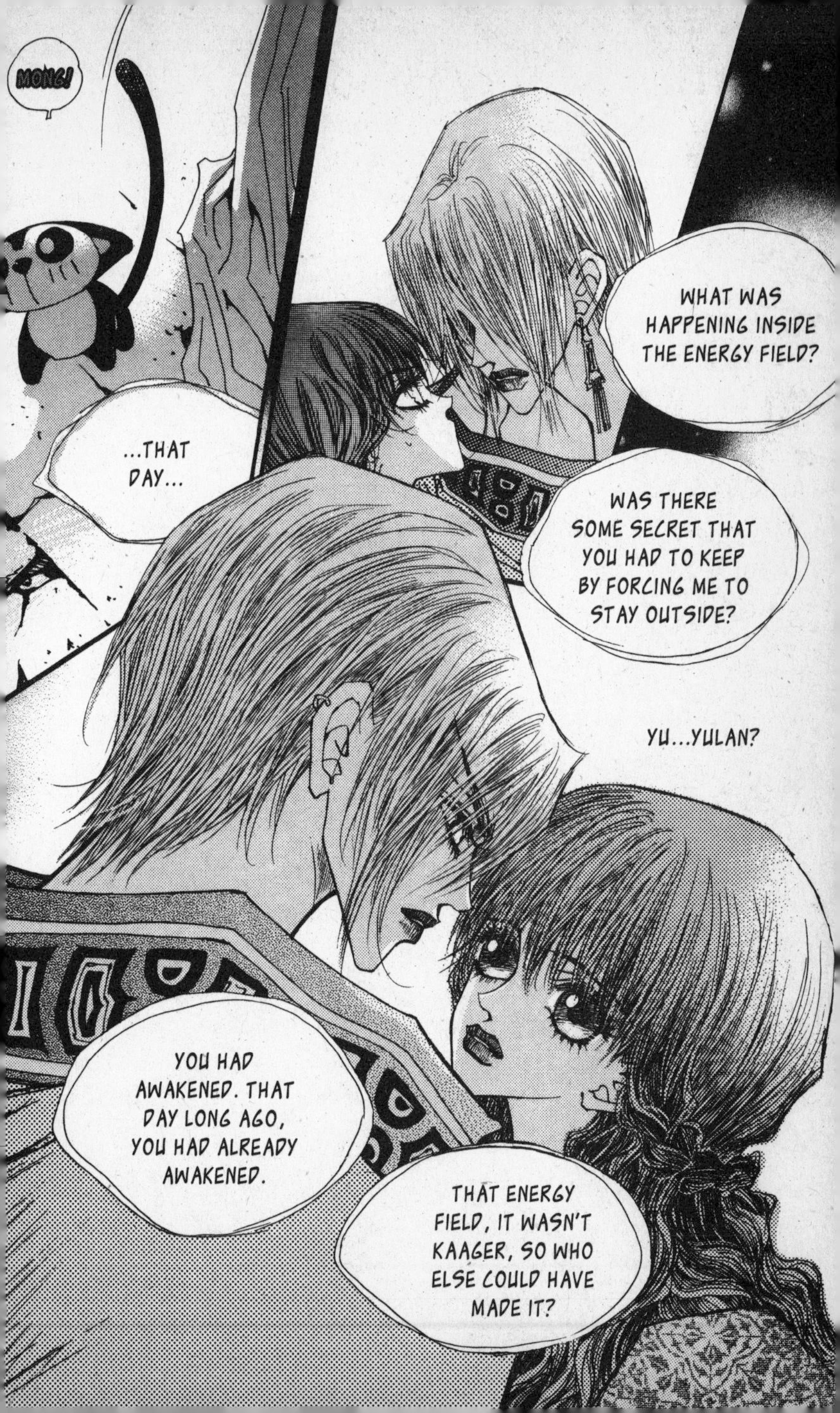
MONG!
...THAT DAY...
WHAT WAS HAPPENING INSIDE THE ENERGY FIELD?
WAS THERE SOME SECRET THAT YOU HAD TO KEEP BY FORCING ME TO STAY OUTSIDE?
YU...YULAN?
YOU HAD AWAKENED. THAT DAY LONG AGO, YOU HAD ALREADY AWAKENED.
THAT ENERGY FIELD, IT WASN'T KAAGER, SO WHO ELSE COULD HAVE MADE IT?

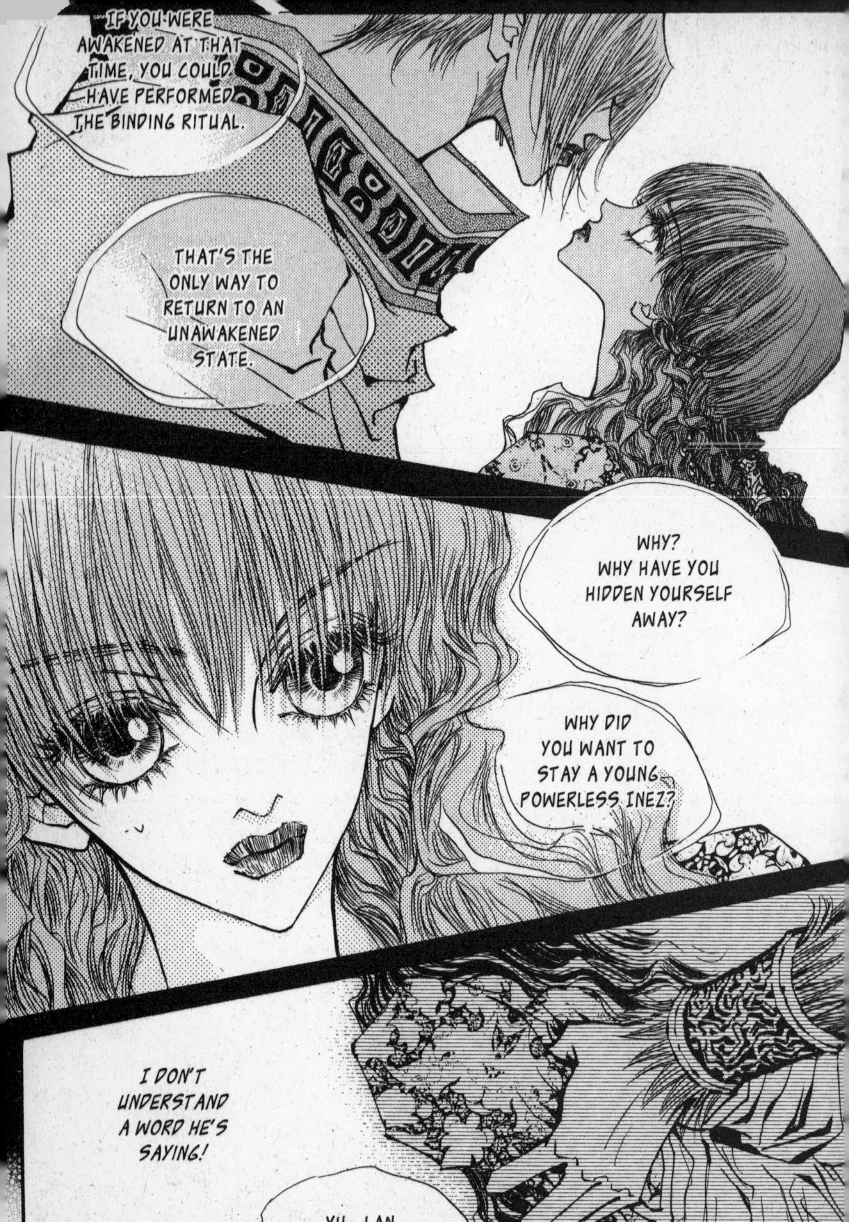
IF YOU WERE AWAKENED AT THAT TIME, YOU COULD HAVE PERFORMED THE BINDING RITUAL.
THAT'S THE ONLY WAY TO RETURN TO AN UNAWAKENED STATE.
WHY? WHY HAVE YOU HIDDEN YOURSELF AWAY?
WHY DID YOU WANT TO STAY A YOUNG POWERLESS INEZ?
I DON'T UNDERSTAND A WORD HE'S SAYING!
YU...LAN... IT HURTS...

YULAN?

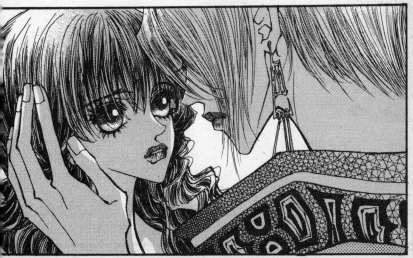

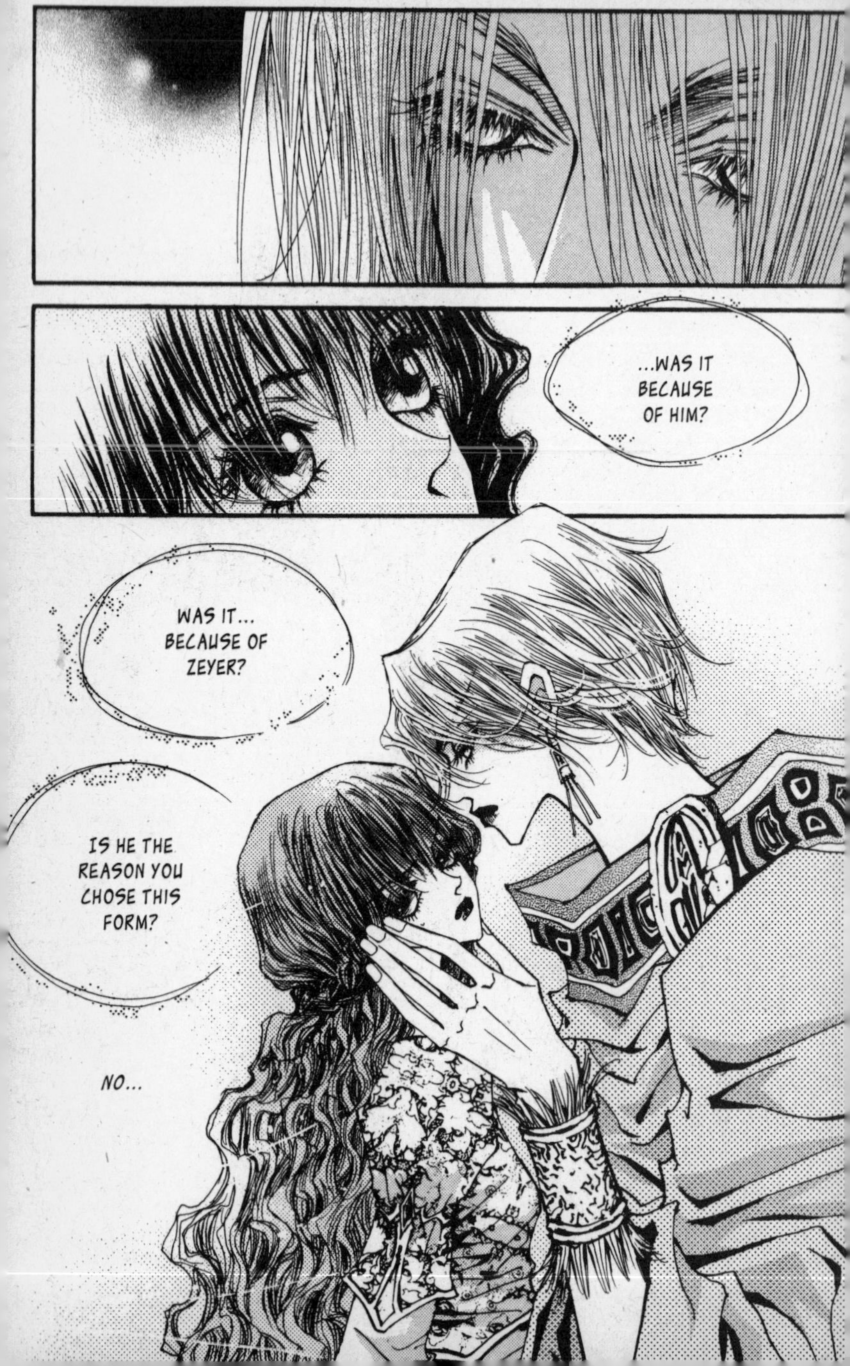
...WAS IT BECAUSE OF HIM?
WAS IT... BECAUSE OF ZEYER?
IS HE THE REASON YOU CHOSE THIS FORM?
NO...

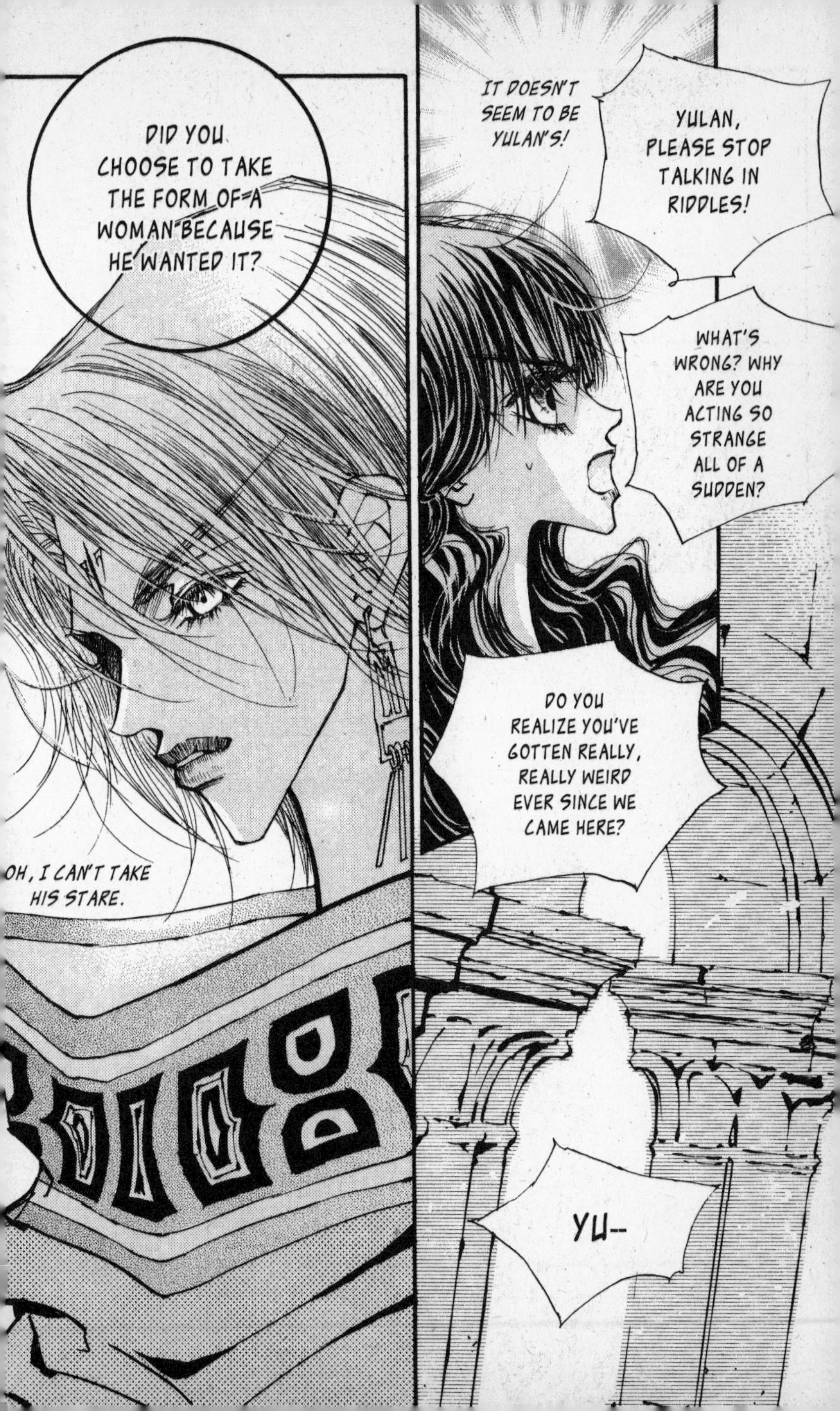
DID YOU CHOOSE TO TAKE THE FORM OF A WOMAN BECAUSE HE WANTED IT?
OH, I CAN'T TAKE HIS STARE.
IT DOESN'T SEEM TO BE YULAN'S!
YULAN, PLEASE STOP TALKING IN RIDDLES!
WHAT'S WRONG? WHY ARE YOU ACTING SO STRANGE ALL OF A SUDDEN?
DO YOU REALIZE YOU'VE GOTTEN REALLY, REALLY WEIRD EVER SINCE WE CAME HERE?
YU--

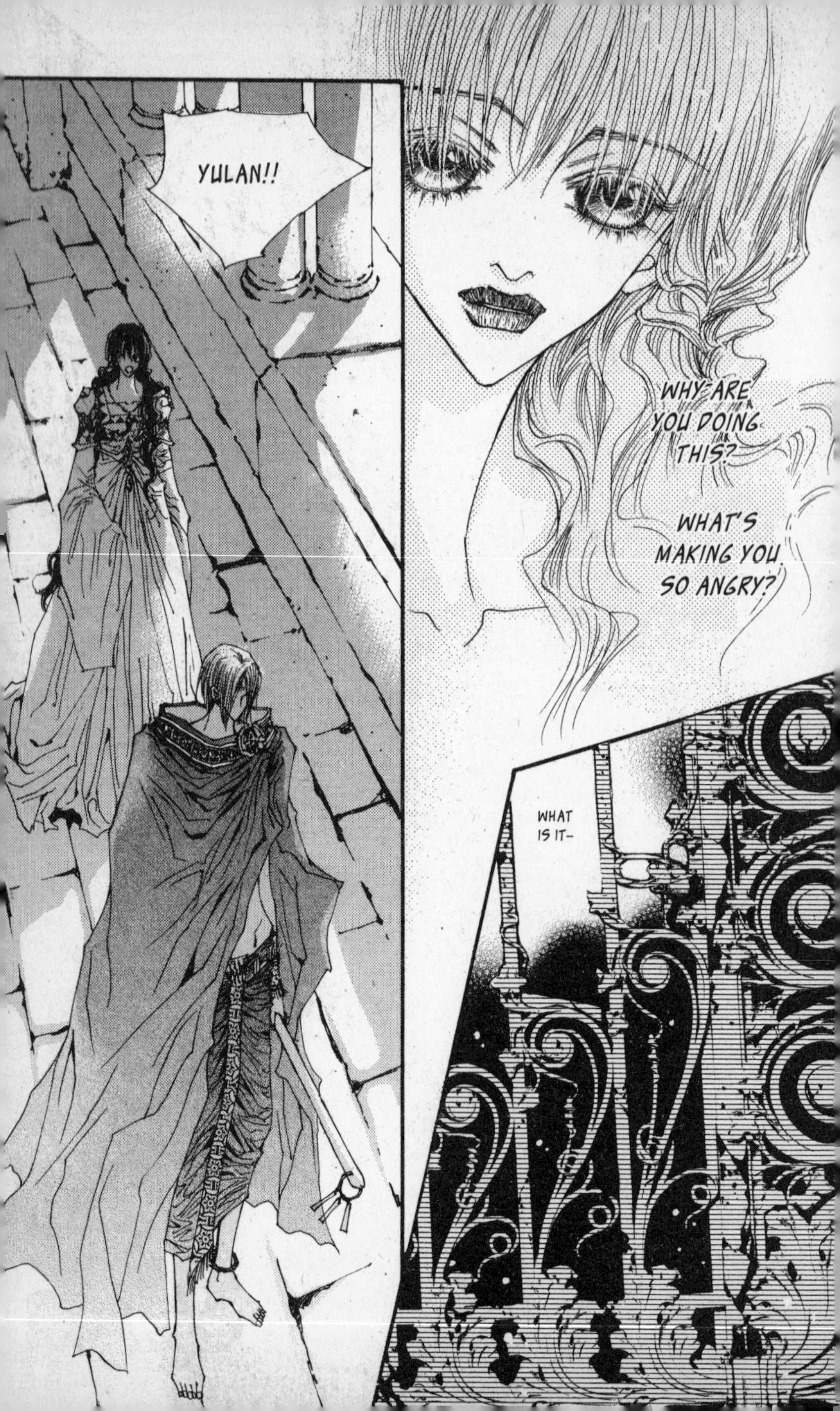
YULAN!!
WHY ARE YOU DOING THIS?
WHAT'S MAKING YOU SO ANGRY?
WHAT IS IT-

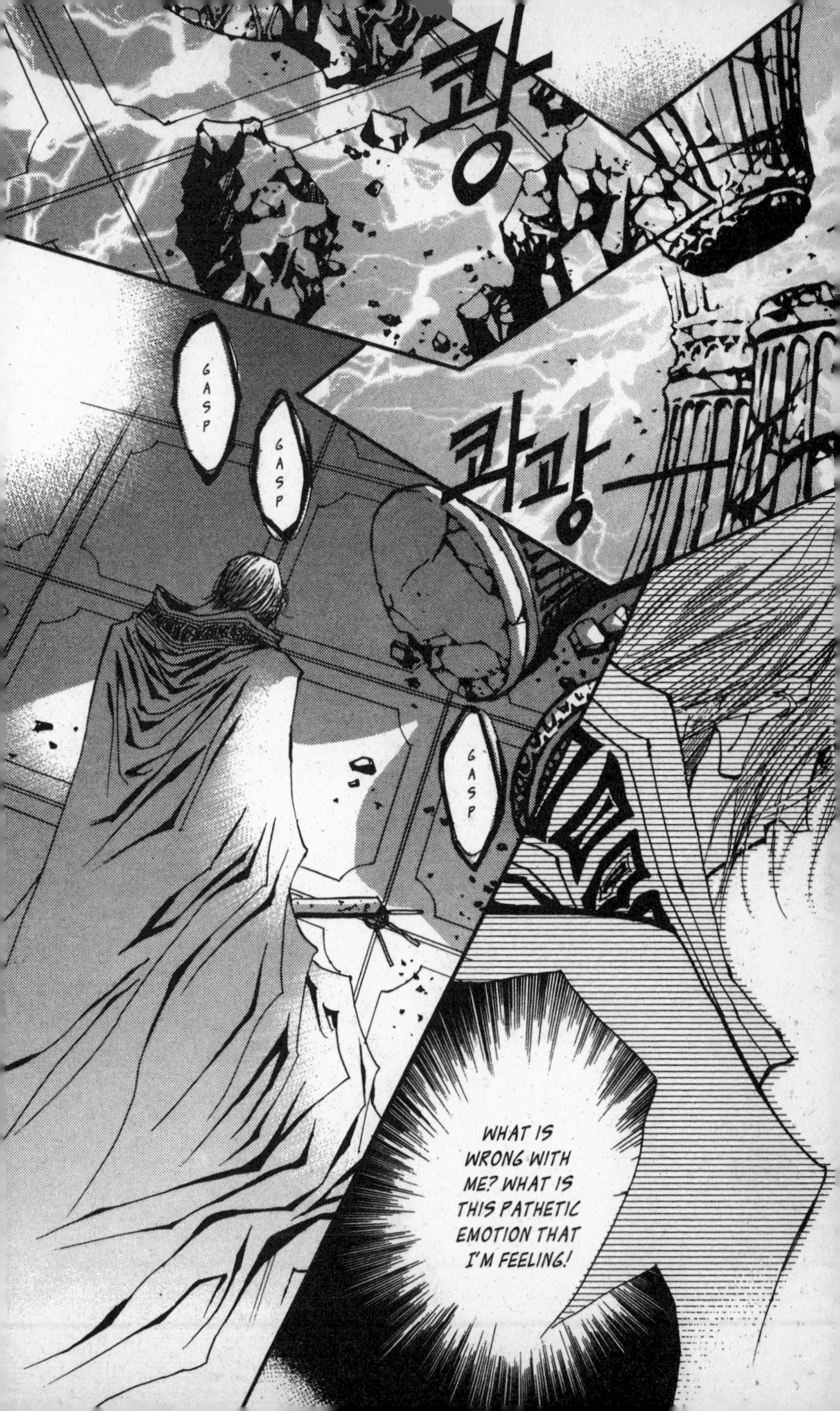

광
콰광—
GASP
GASP
GASP
WHAT IS WRONG WITH ME? WHAT IS THIS PATHETIC EMOTION THAT I'M FEELING!

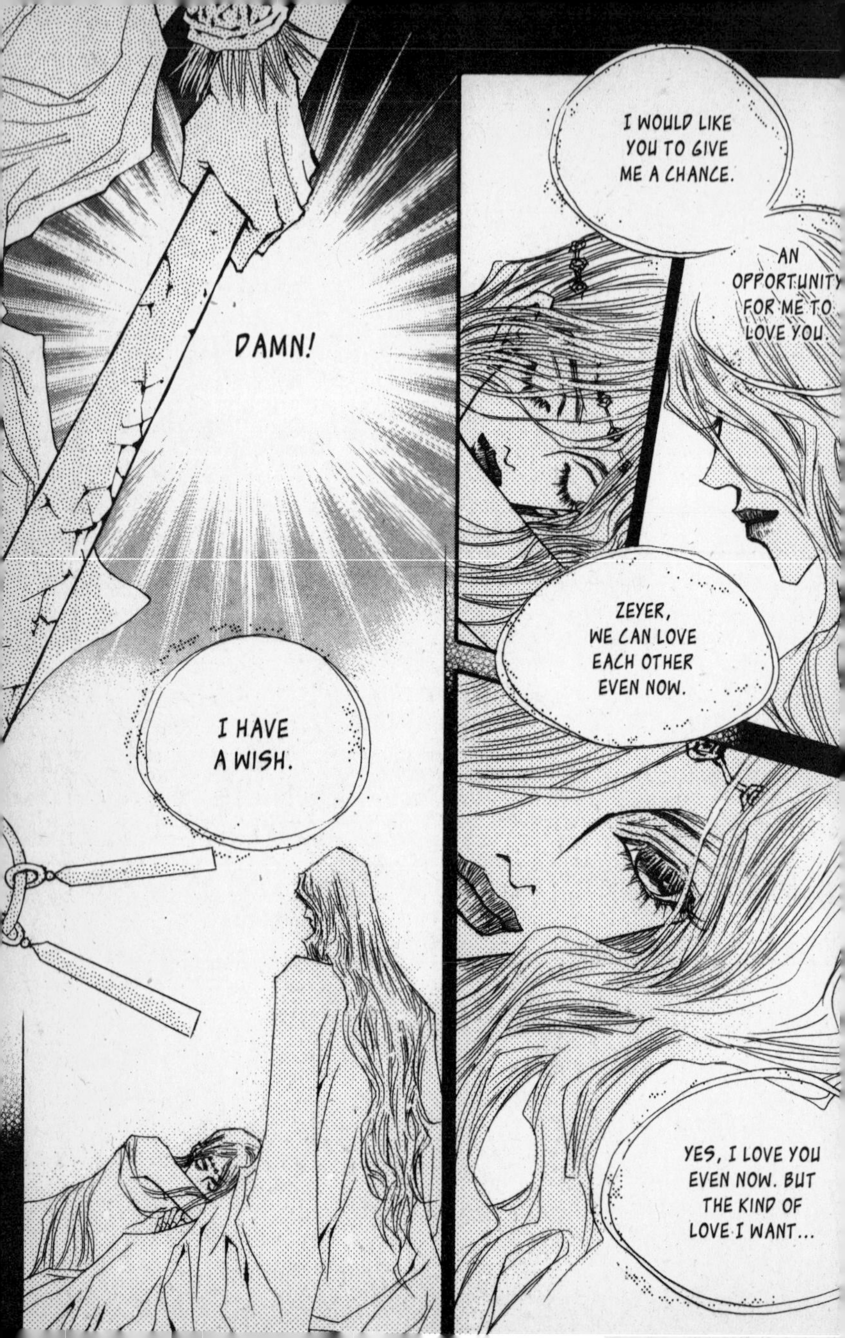
DAMN!
I HAVE A WISH.
I WOULD LIKE YOU TO GIVE ME A CHANCE.
AN OPPORTUNITY FOR ME TO LOVE YOU.
ZEYER, WE CAN LOVE EACH OTHER EVEN NOW.
YES, I LOVE YOU EVEN NOW. BUT THE KIND OF LOVE I WANT...

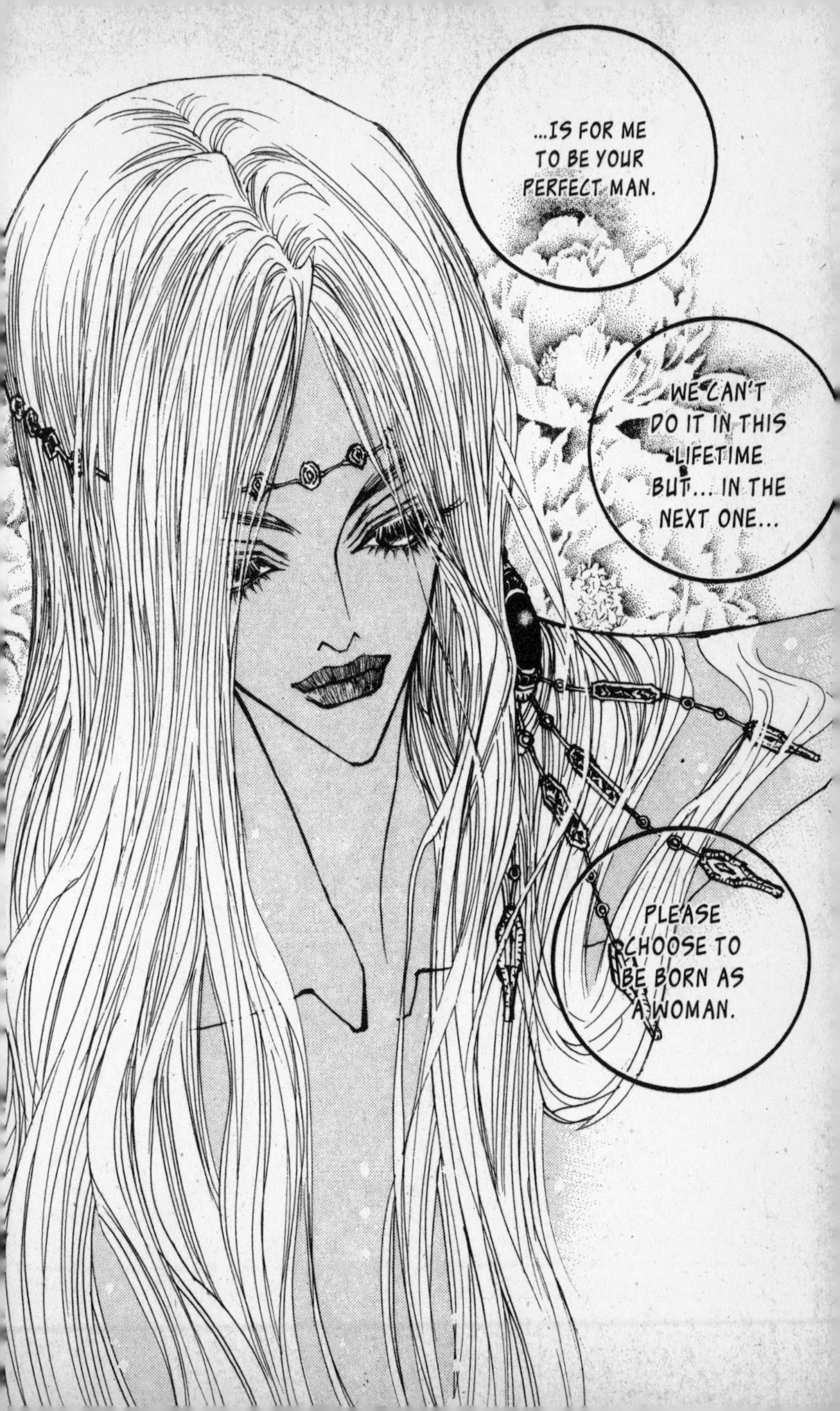
...IS FOR ME TO BE YOUR PERFECT MAN.
WE CAN'T DO IT IN THIS LIFETIME BUT... IN THE NEXT ONE...
PLEASE CHOOSE TO BE BORN AS A WOMAN.

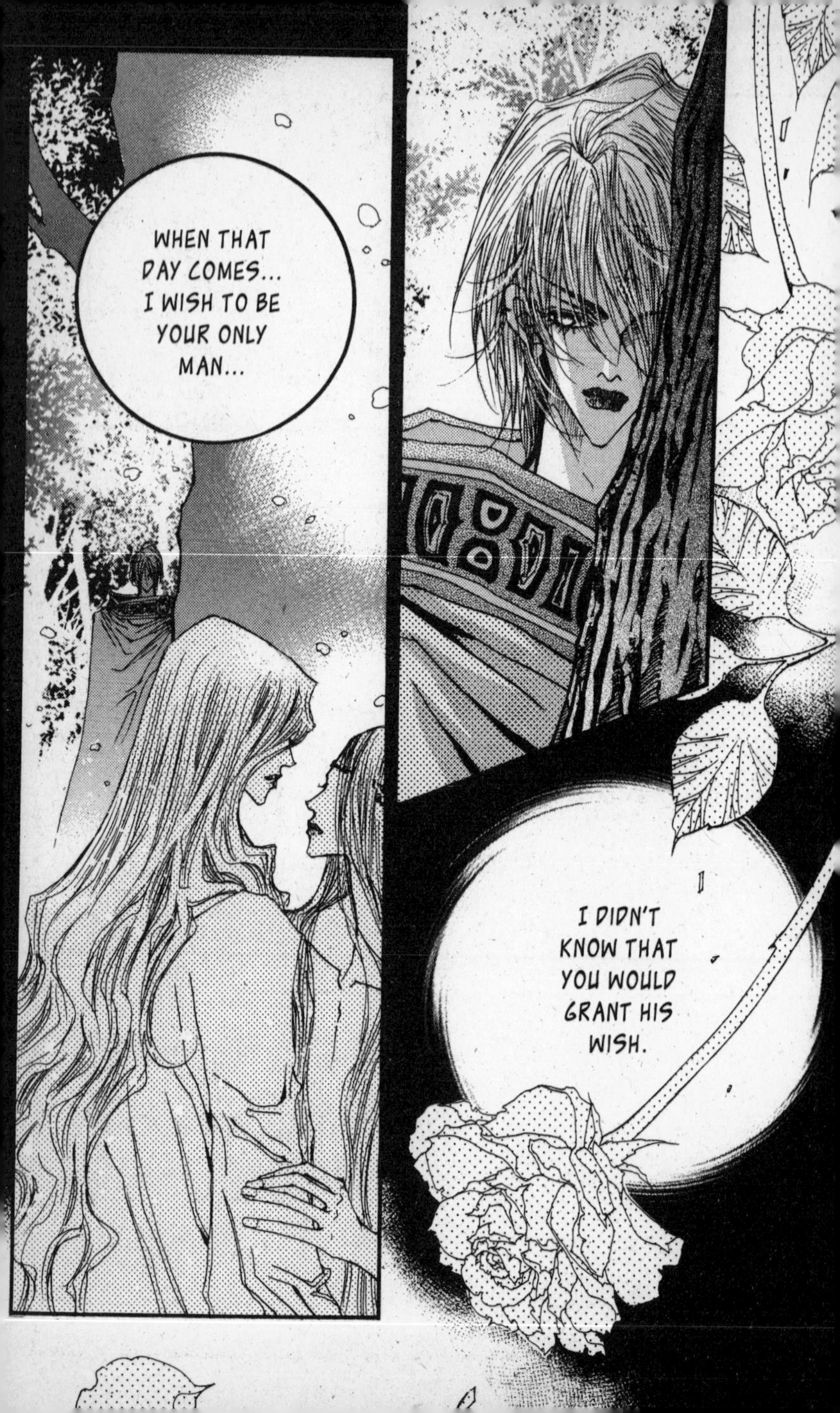
WHEN THAT DAY COMES... I WISH TO BE YOUR ONLY MAN...
I DIDN'T KNOW THAT YOU WOULD GRANT HIS WISH.

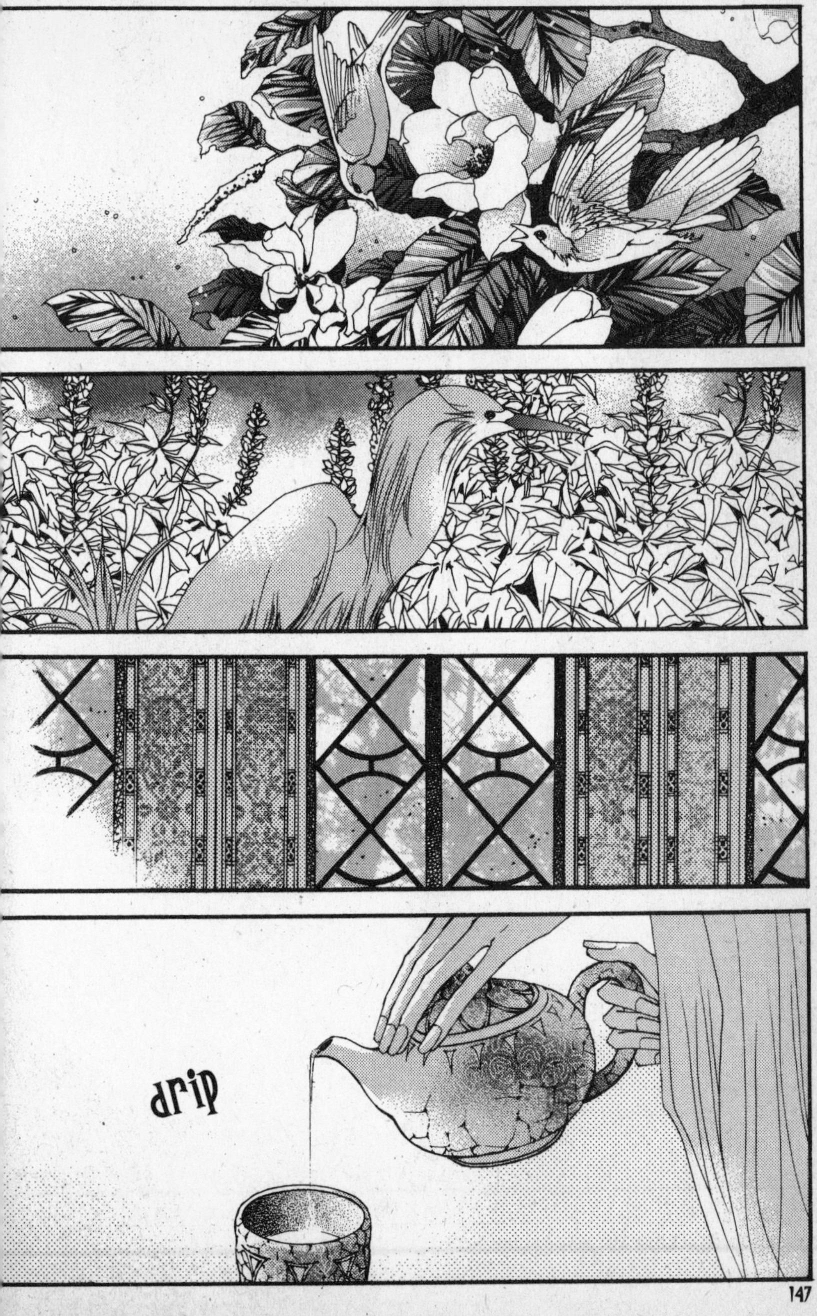
drip

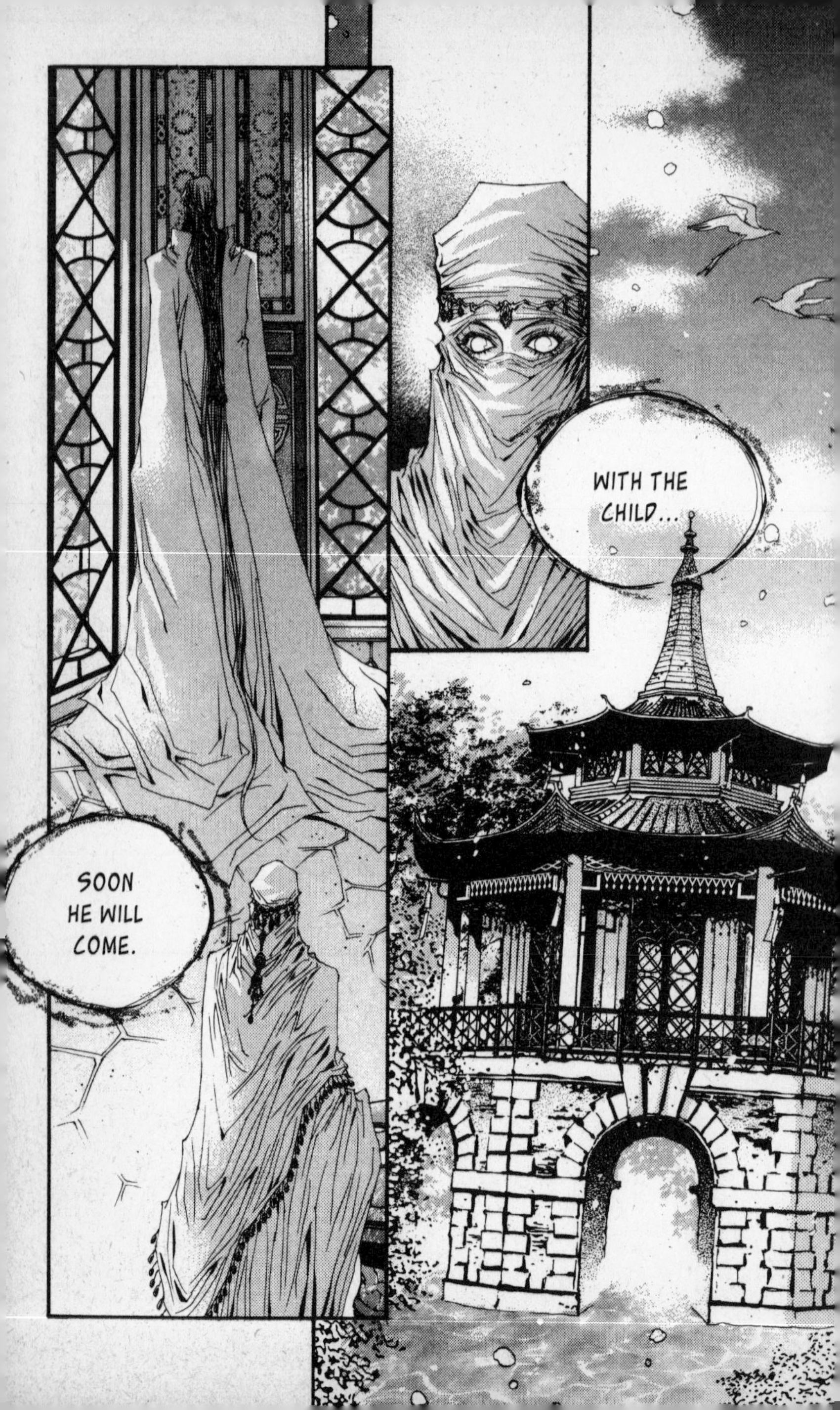
SOON HE WILL COME.
WITH THE CHILD...

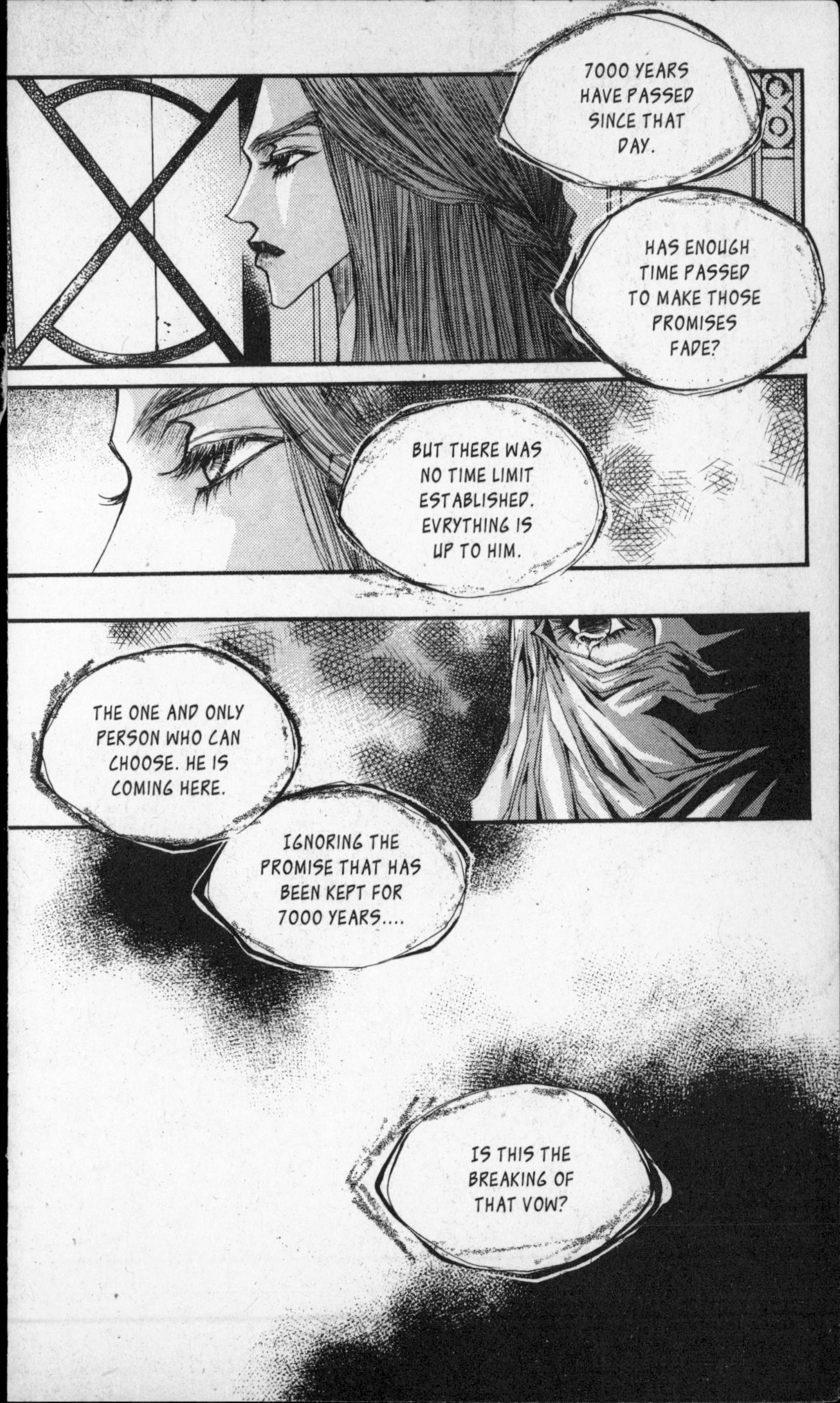
7000 YEARS HAVE PASSED SINCE THAT DAY.
HAS ENOUGH TIME PASSED TO MAKE THOSE PROMISES FADE?
BUT THERE WAS NO TIME LIMIT ESTABLISHED. EVRYTHING IS UP TO HIM.
THE ONE AND ONLY PERSON WHO CAN CHOOSE. HE IS COMING HERE.
IGNORING THE PROMISE THAT HAS BEEN KEPT FOR 7000 YEARS....
IS THIS THE BREAKING OF THAT VOW?

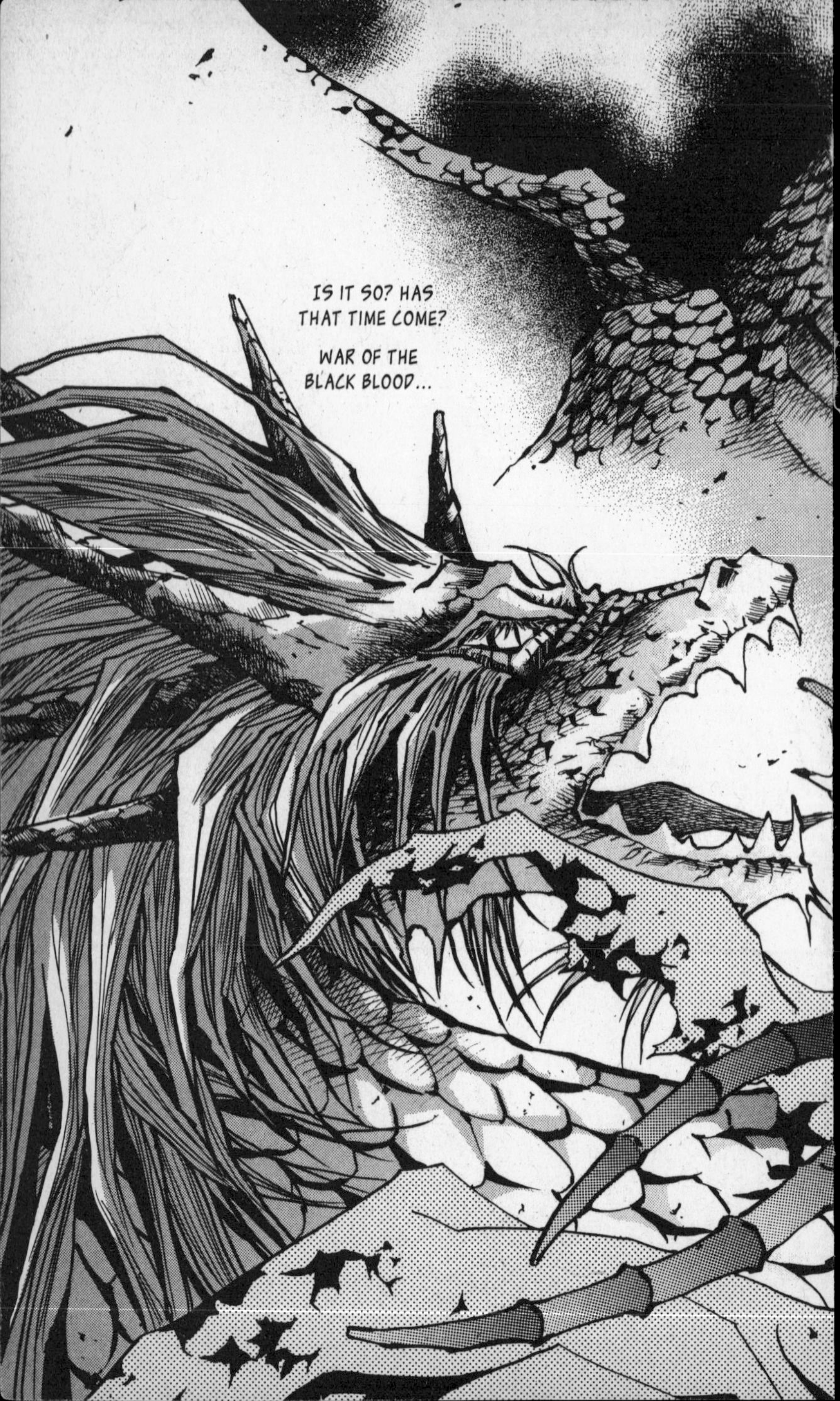
IS IT SO? HAS THAT TIME COME?
WAR OF THE BLACK BLOOD...

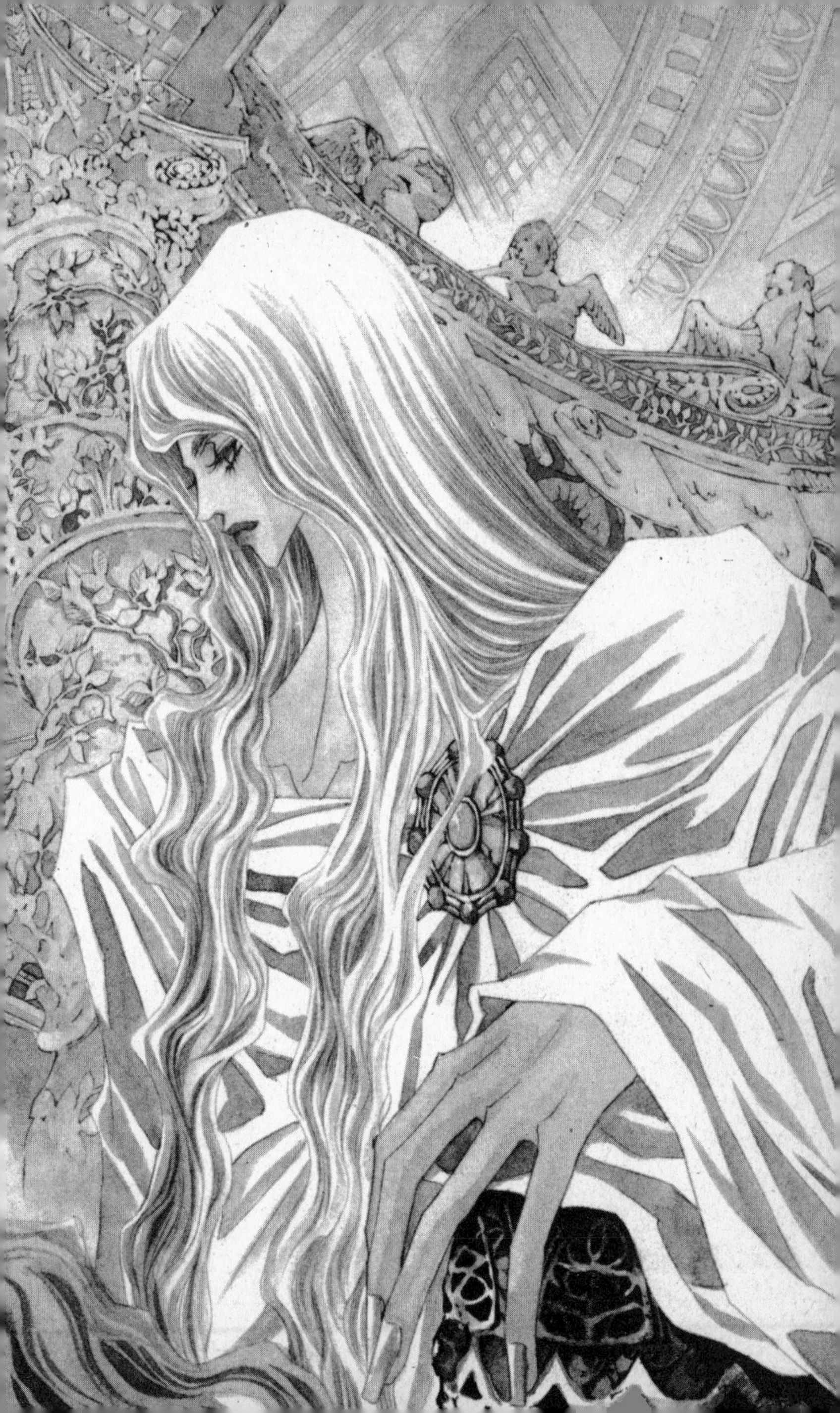

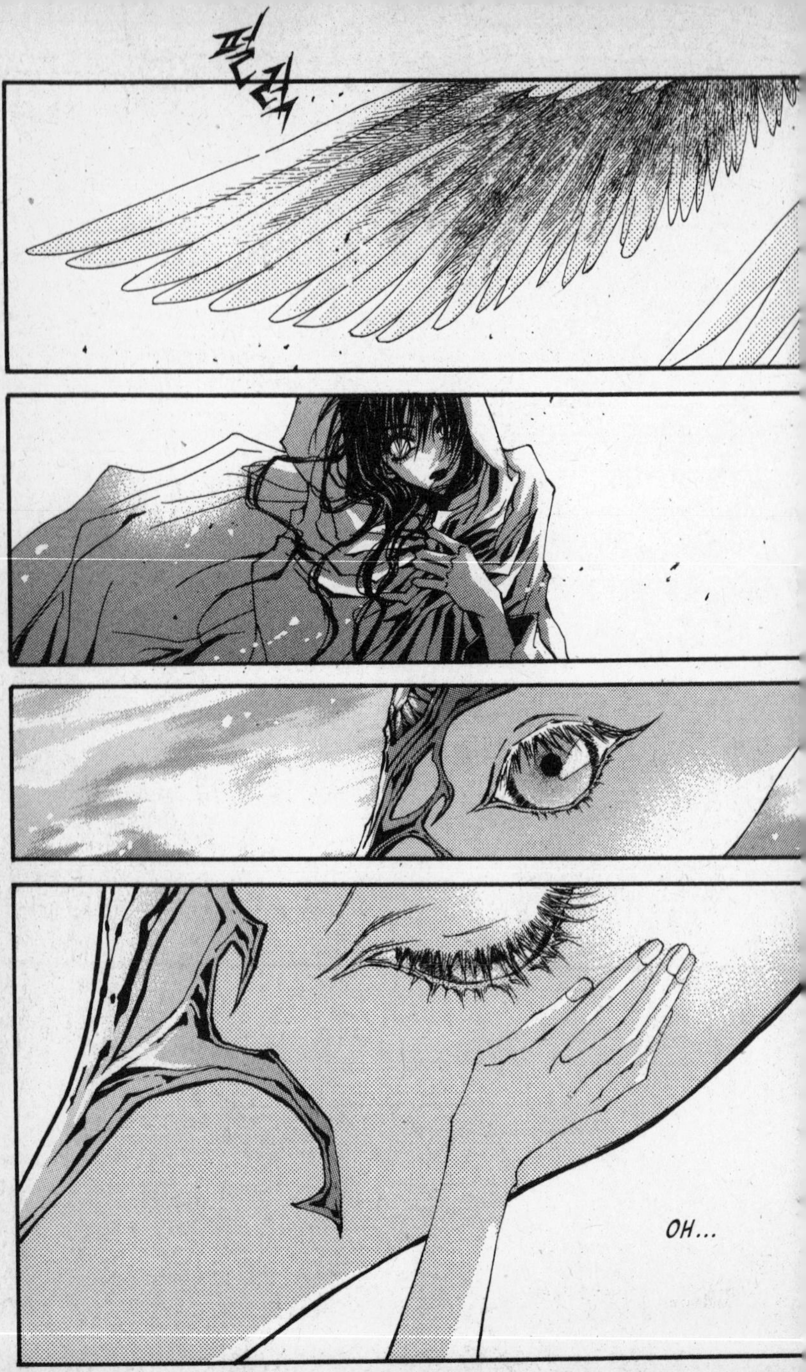

펄럭
OH...

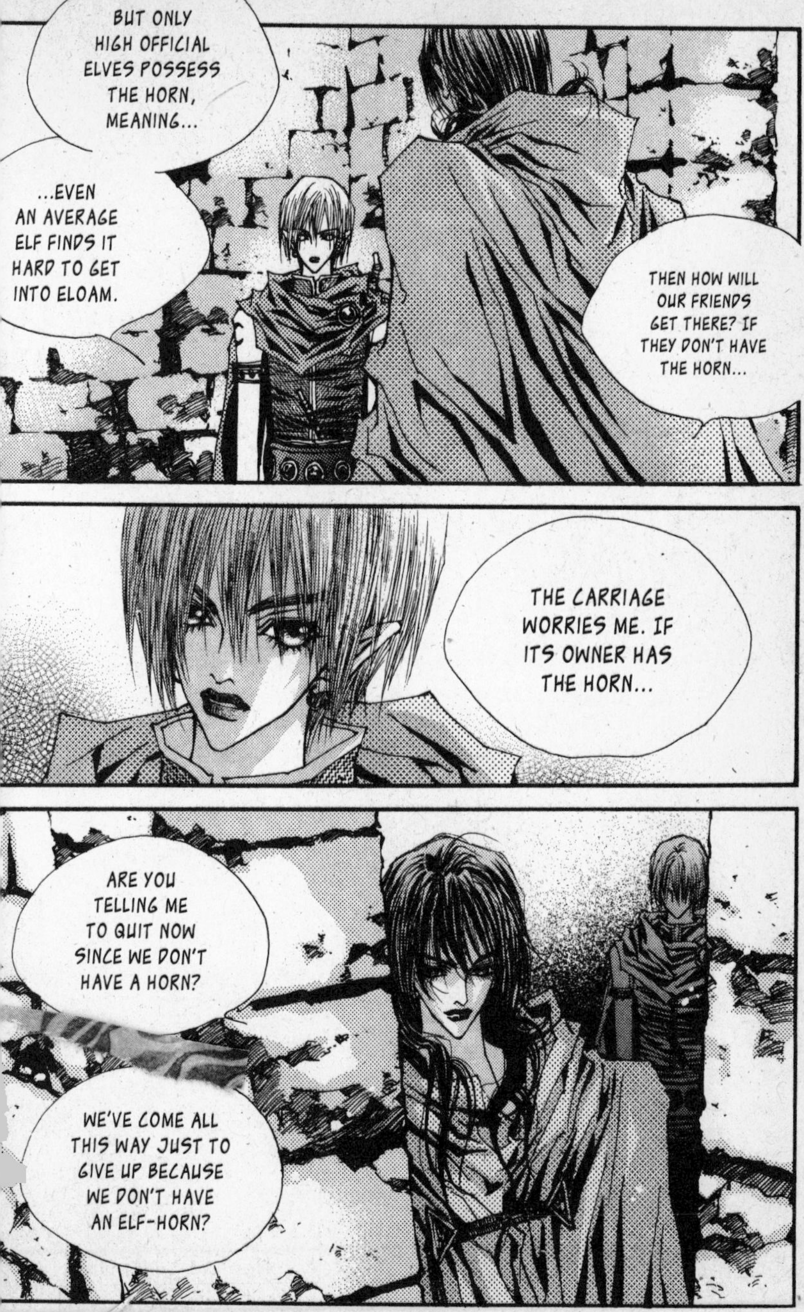
BUT ONLY HIGH OFFICIAL ELVES POSSESS THE HORN, MEANING...
...EVEN AN AVERAGE ELF FINDS IT HARD TO GET INTO ELOAM.
THEN HOW WILL OUR FRIENDS GET THERE? IF THEY DON'T HAVE THE HORN...
THE CARRIAGE WORRIES ME. IF ITS OWNER HAS THE HORN...
ARE YOU TELLING ME TO QUIT NOW SINCE WE DON'T HAVE A HORN?
WE'VE COME ALL THIS WAY JUST TO GIVE UP BECAUSE WE DON'T HAVE AN ELF-HORN?

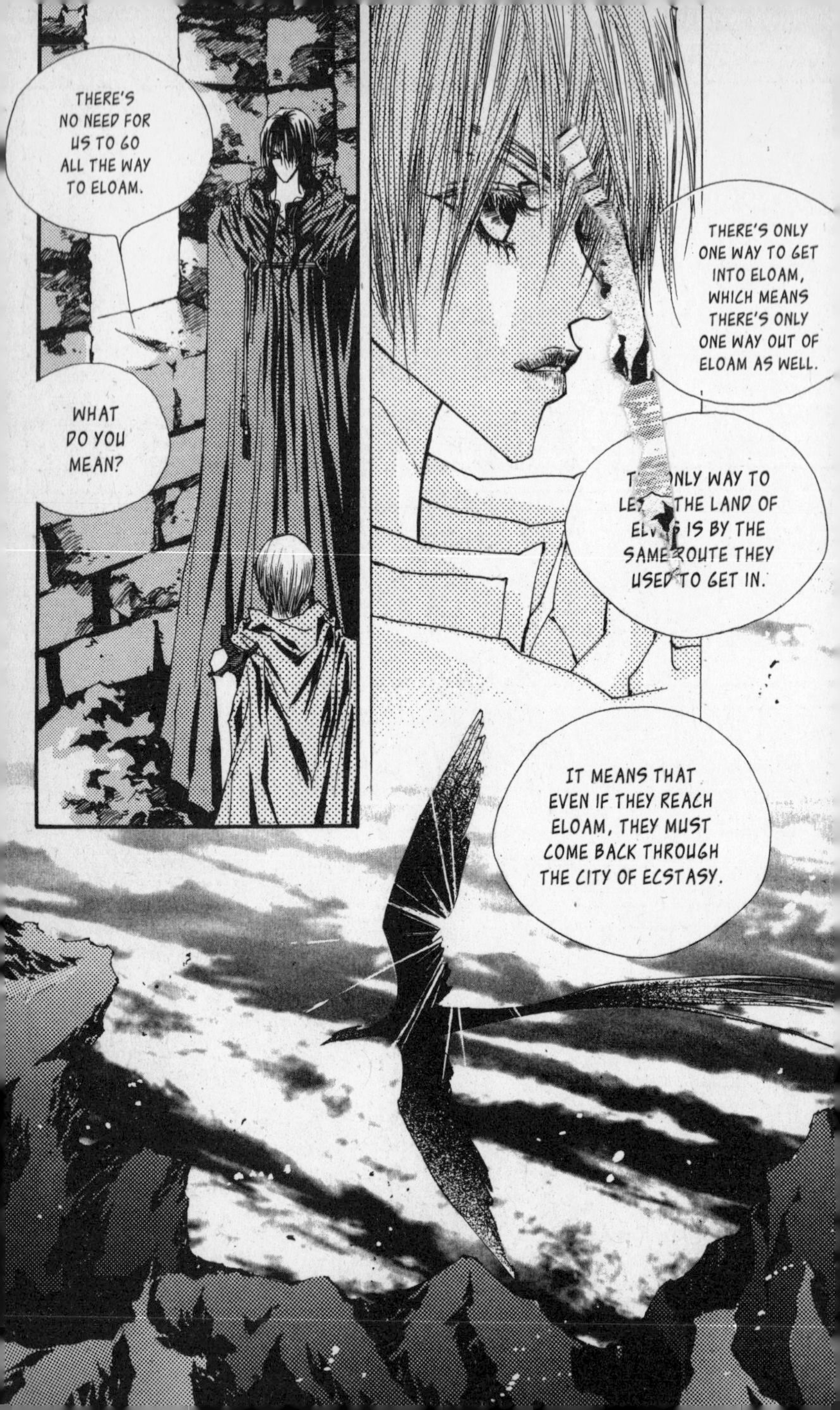
THERE'S NO NEED FOR US TO GO ALL THE WAY TO ELOAM.
WHAT DO YOU MEAN?
THERE'S ONLY ONE WAY TO GET INTO ELOAM, WHICH MEANS THERE'S ONLY ONE WAY OUT OF ELOAM AS WELL.
T ONLY WAY TO LE THE LAND OF EL IS BY THE SAME ROUTE THEY USED TO GET IN.
IT MEANS THAT EVEN IF THEY REACH ELOAM, THEY MUST COME BACK THROUGH THE CITY OF ECSTASY.

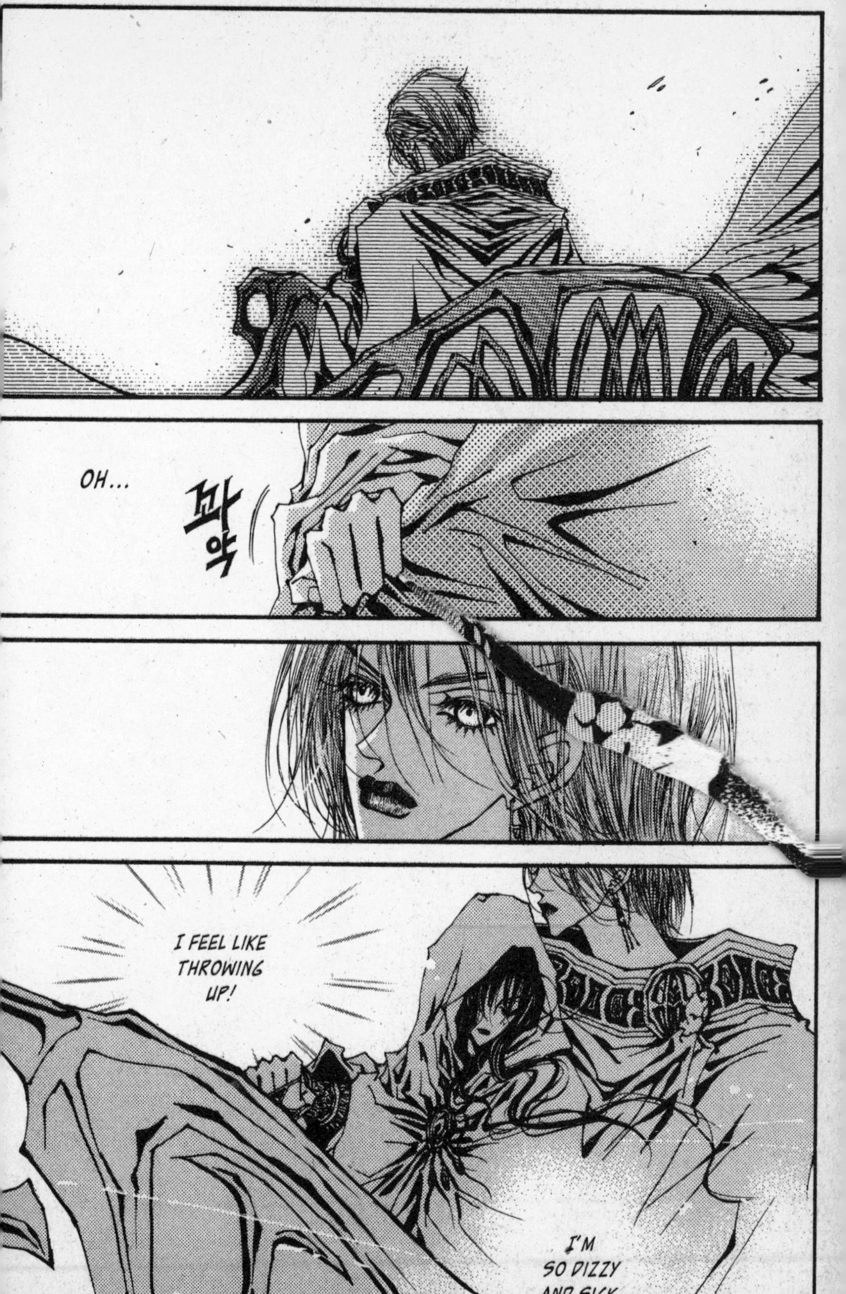
OH...
꽈악
I FEEL LIKE THROWING UP!
I'M SO DIZZY AND SICK.

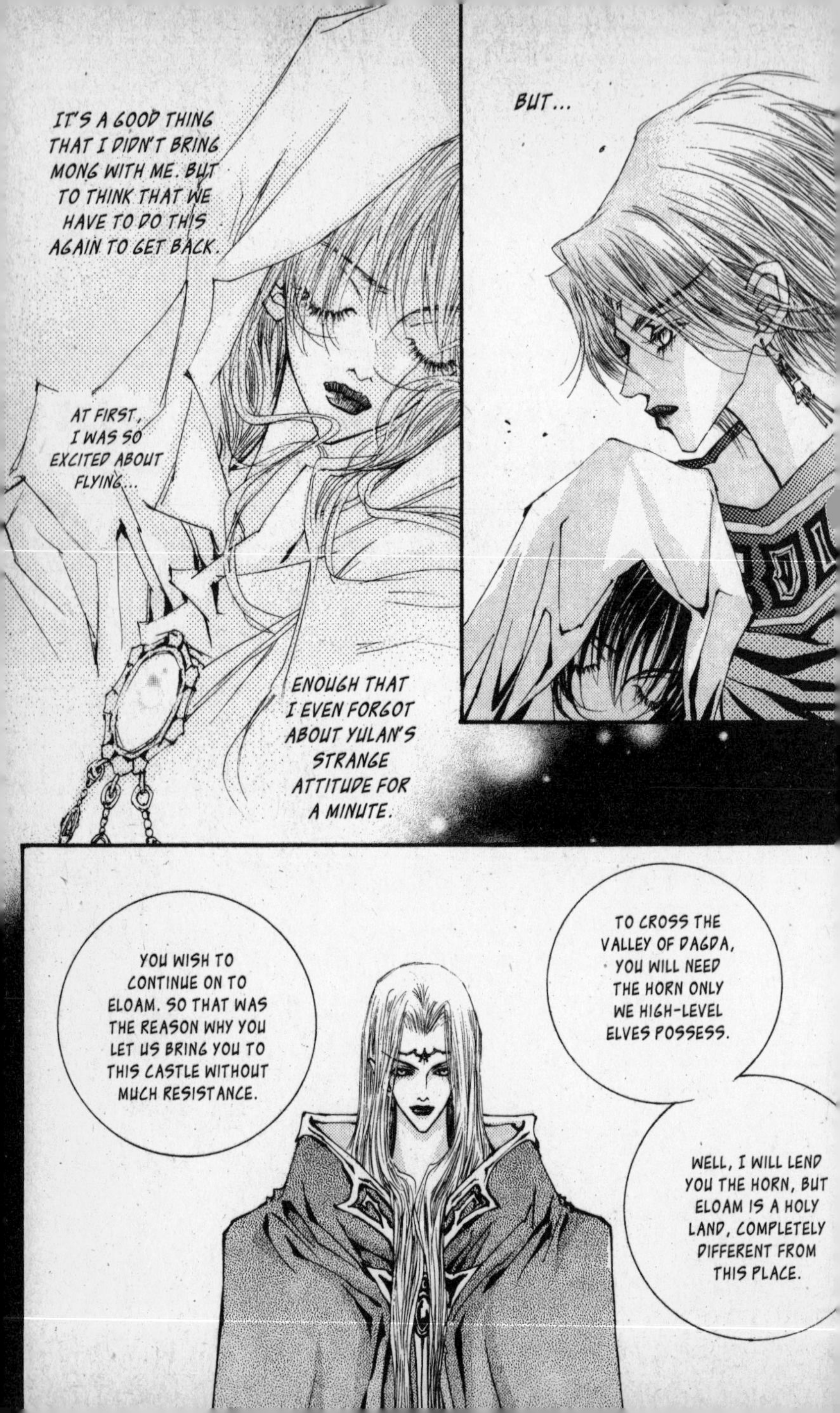
IT'S A GOOD THING THAT I DIDN'T BRING MONG WITH ME. BUT TO THINK THAT WE HAVE TO DO THIS AGAIN TO GET BACK.
AT FIRST, I WAS SO EXCITED ABOUT FLYING...
ENOUGH THAT I EVEN FORGOT ABOUT YULAN'S STRANGE ATTITUDE FOR A MINUTE.
BUT...
YOU WISH TO CONTINUE ON TO ELOAM. SO THAT WAS THE REASON WHY YOU LET US BRING YOU TO THIS CASTLE WITHOUT MUCH RESISTANCE.
TO CROSS THE VALLEY OF DAGDA, YOU WILL NEED THE HORN ONLY WE HIGH-LEVEL ELVES POSSESS.
WELL, I WILL LEND YOU THE HORN, BUT ELOAM IS A HOLY LAND, COMPLETELY DIFFERENT FROM THIS PLACE.

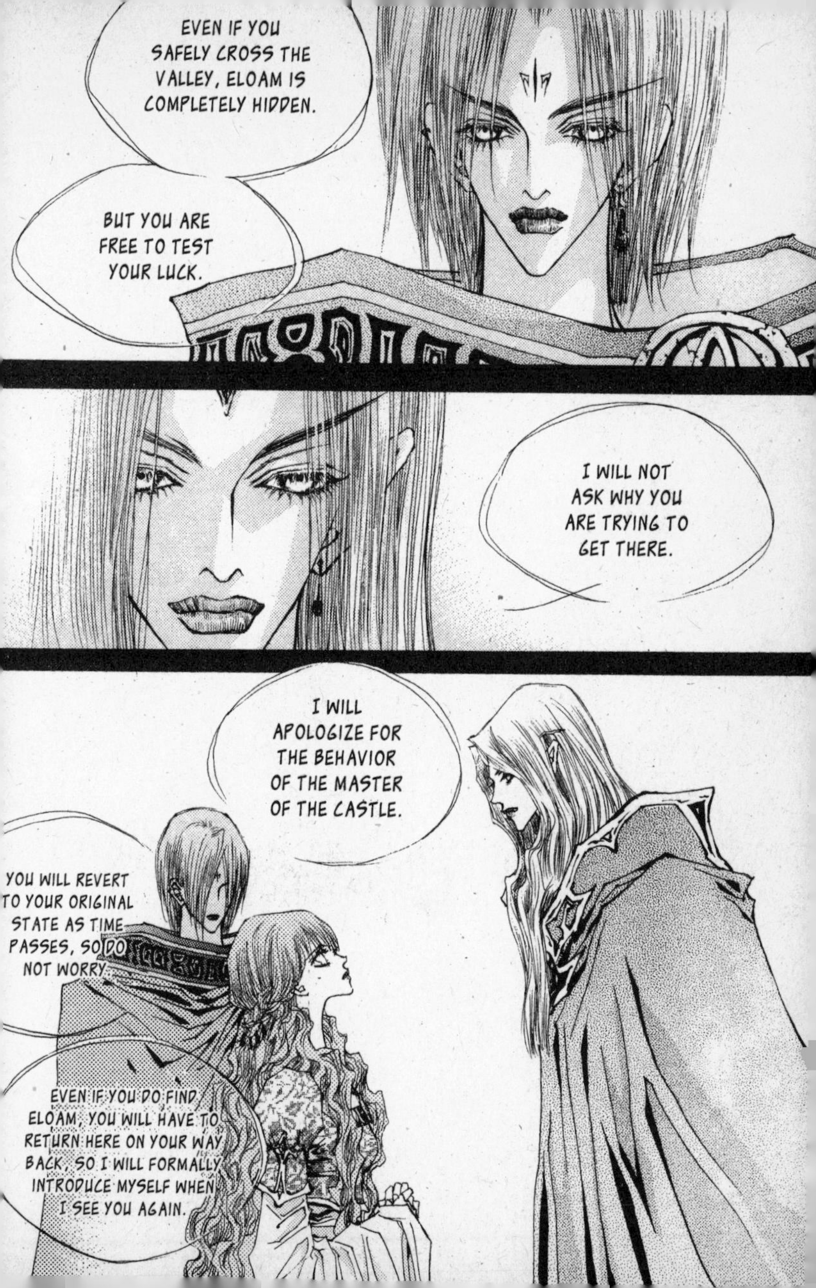
EVEN IF YOU SAFELY CROSS THE VALLEY, ELOAM IS COMPLETELY HIDDEN.
BUT YOU ARE FREE TO TEST YOUR LUCK.
I WILL NOT ASK WHY YOU ARE TRYING TO GET THERE.
I WILL APOLOGIZE FOR THE BEHAVIOR OF THE MASTER OF THE CASTLE.
YOU WILL REVERT TO YOUR ORIGINAL STATE AS TIME PASSES, SO DO NOT WORRY.
EVEN IF YOU DO FIND ELOAM, YOU WILL HAVE TO RETURN HERE ON YOUR WAY BACK, SO I WILL FORMALLY INTRODUCE MYSELF WHEN I SEE YOU AGAIN.

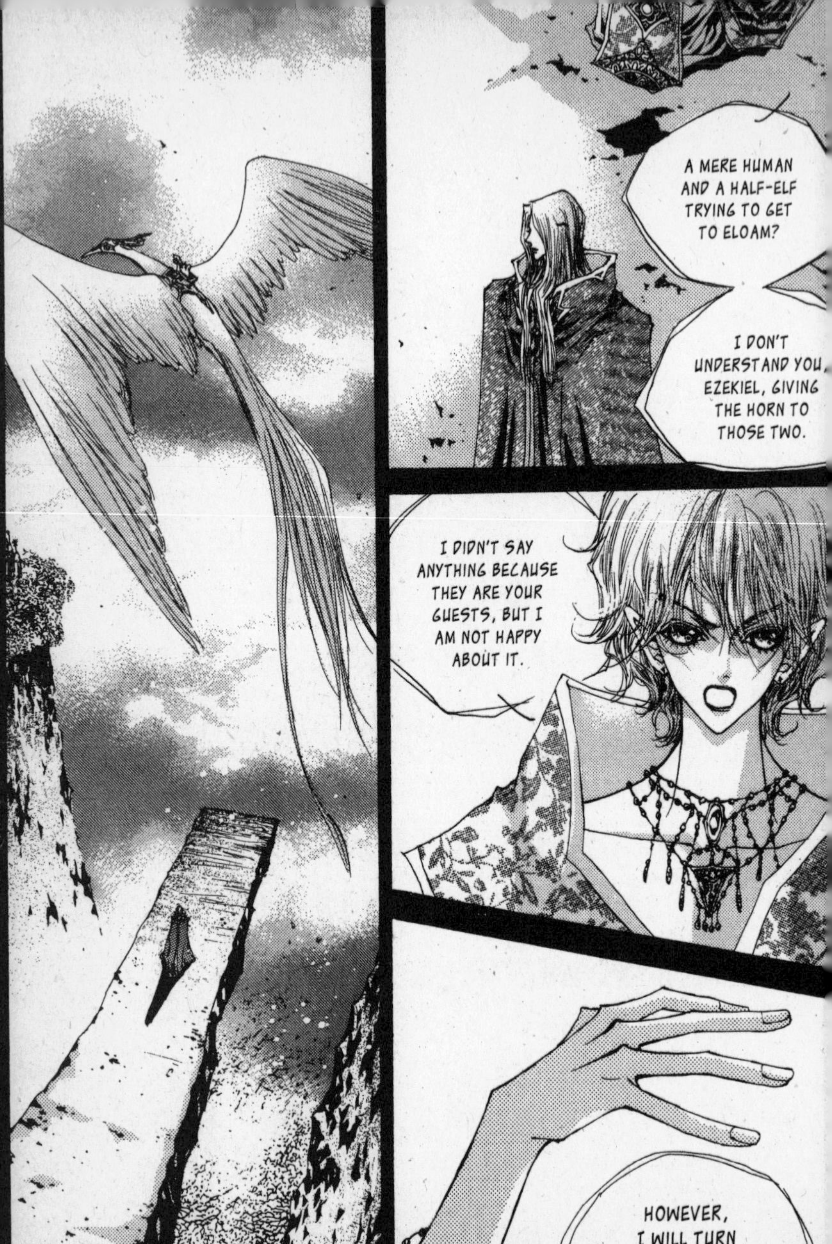
A MERE HUMAN AND A HALF-ELF TRYING TO GET TO ELOAM?
I DON'T UNDERSTAND YOU, EZEKIEL, GIVING THE HORN TO THOSE TWO.
I DIDN'T SAY ANYTHING BECAUSE THEY ARE YOUR GUESTS, BUT I AM NOT HAPPY ABOUT IT.
HOWEVER, I WILL TURN A BLIND EYE

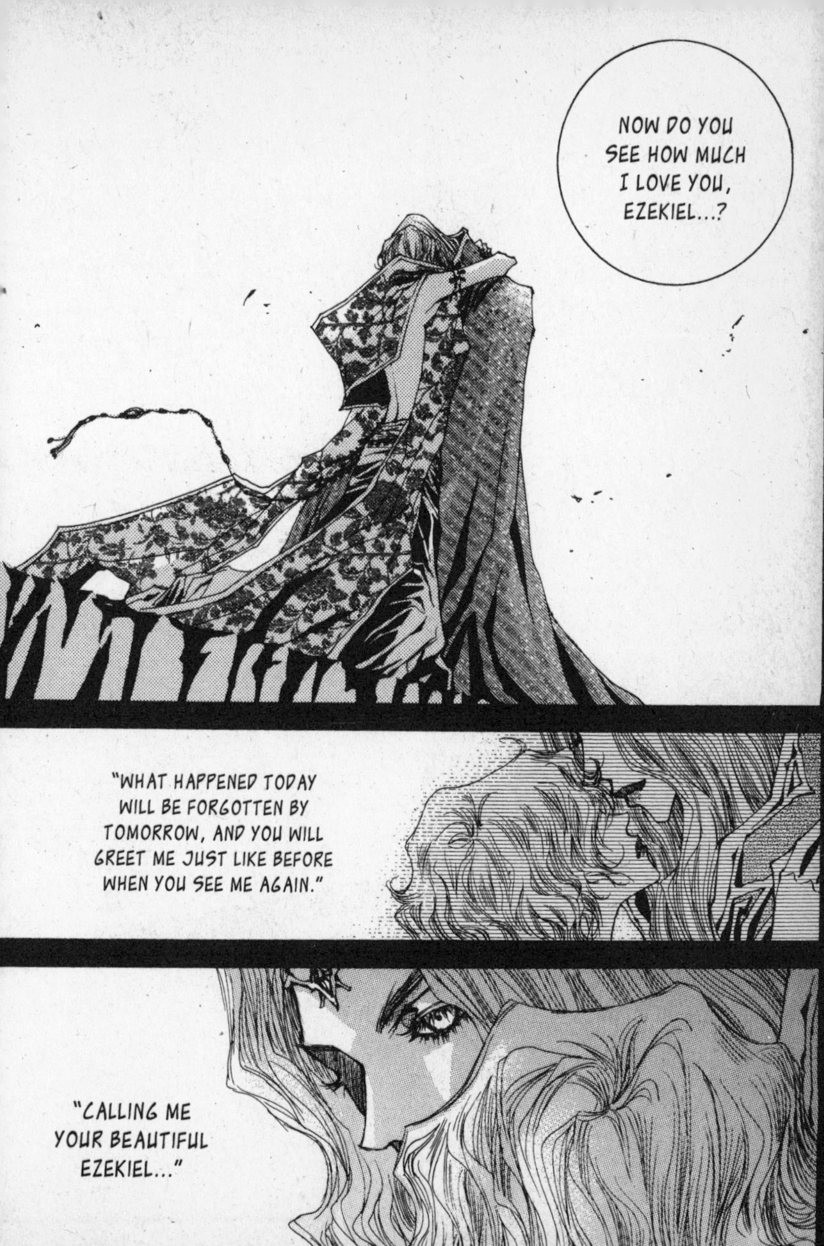
NOW DO YOU SEE HOW MUCH I LOVE YOU, EZEKIEL...?
"WHAT HAPPENED TODAY WILL BE FORGOTTEN BY TOMORROW, AND YOU WILL GREET ME JUST LIKE BEFORE WHEN YOU SEE ME AGAIN."
"CALLING ME YOUR BEAUTIFUL EZEKIEL..."

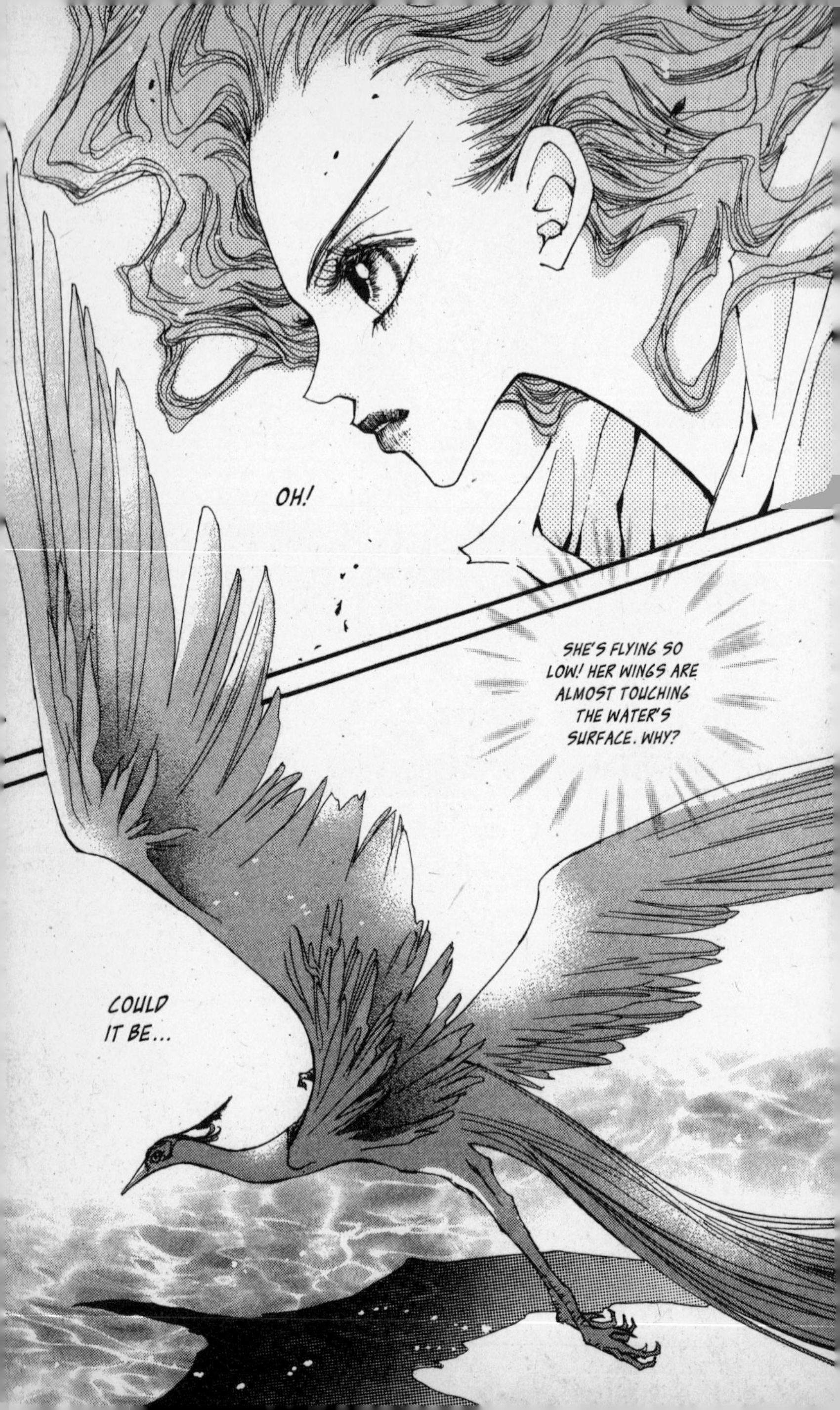
OH!
SHE'S FLYING SO LOW! HER WINGS ARE ALMOST TOUCHING THE WATER'S SURFACE. WHY?
COULD IT BE...

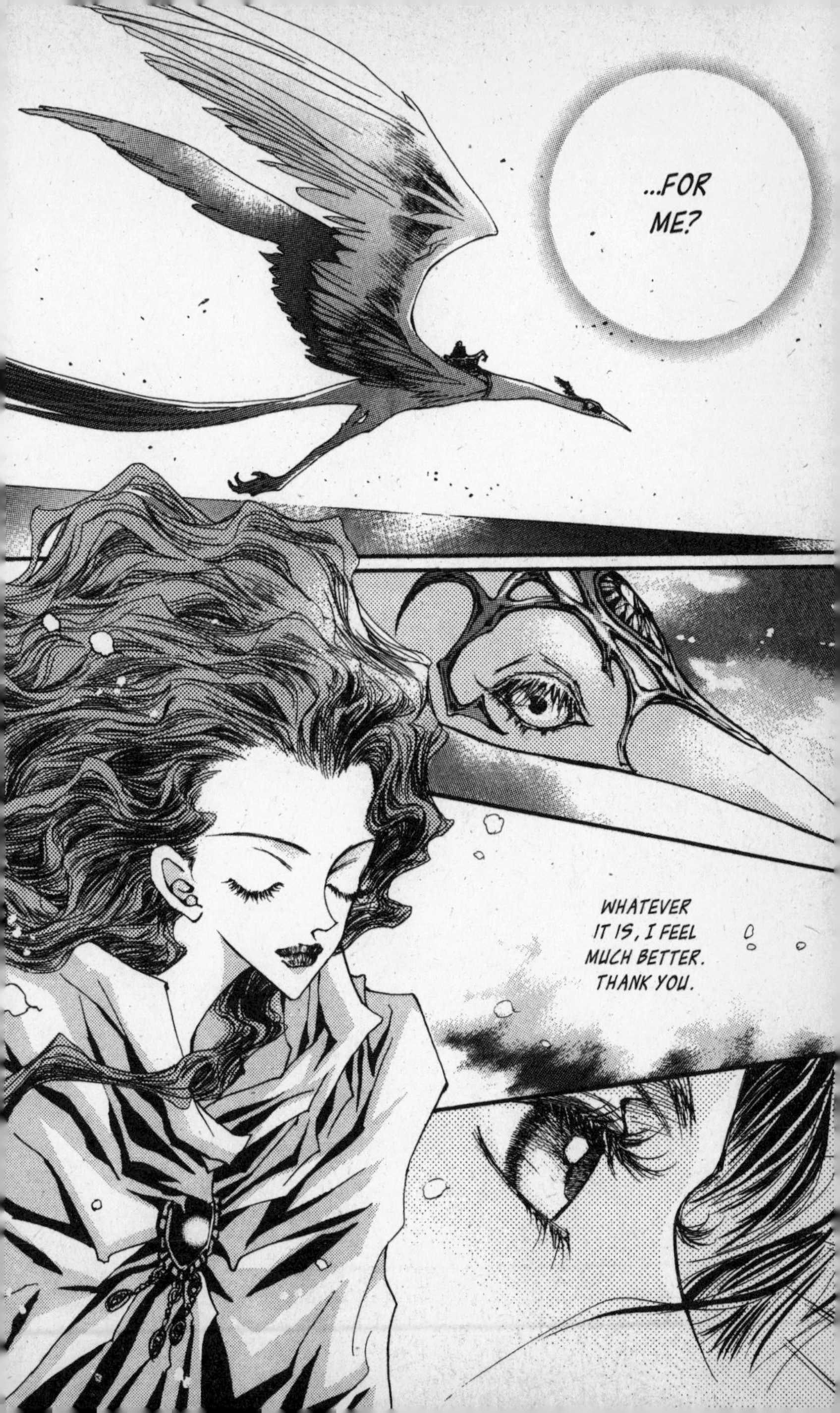
...FOR ME?
WHATEVER IT IS, I FEEL MUCH BETTER. THANK YOU.

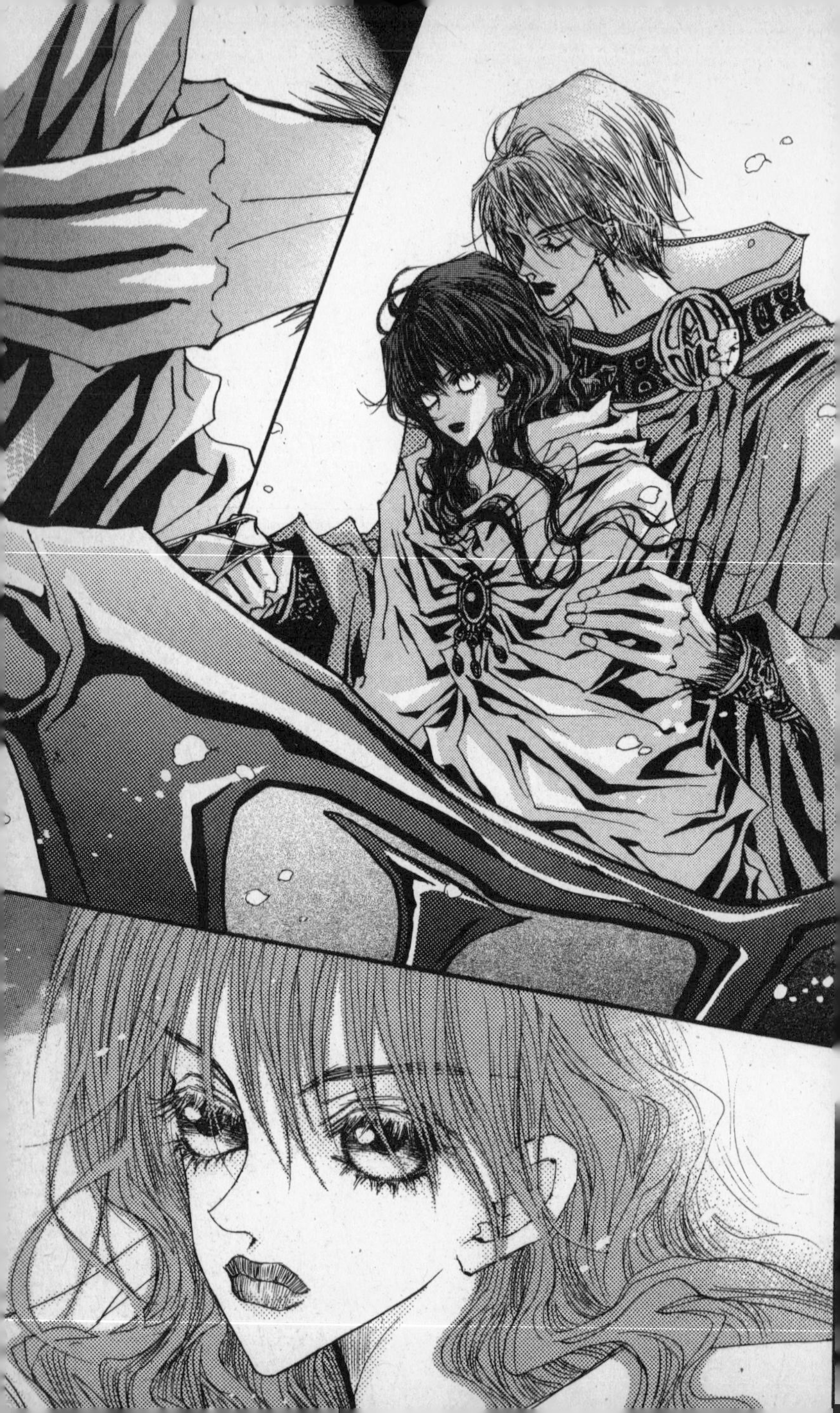

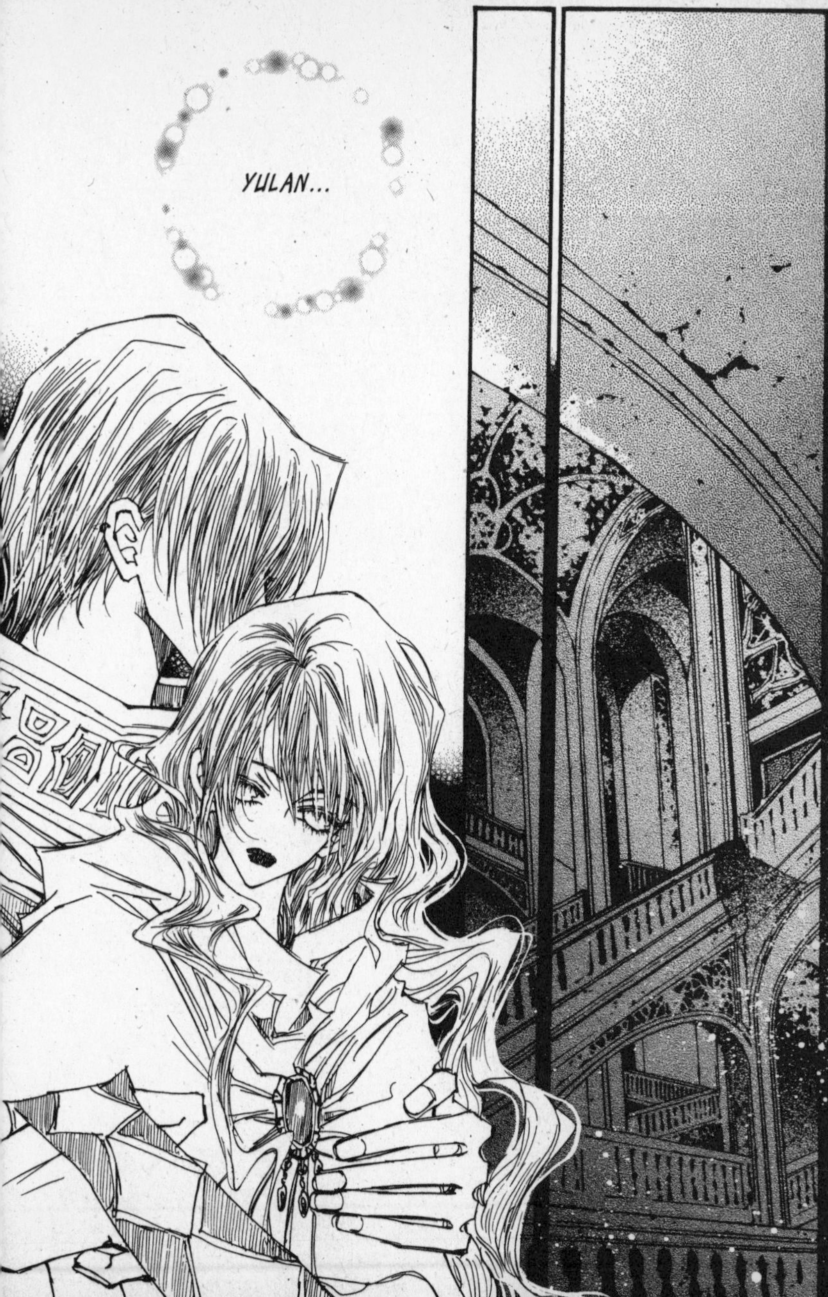
YULAN...

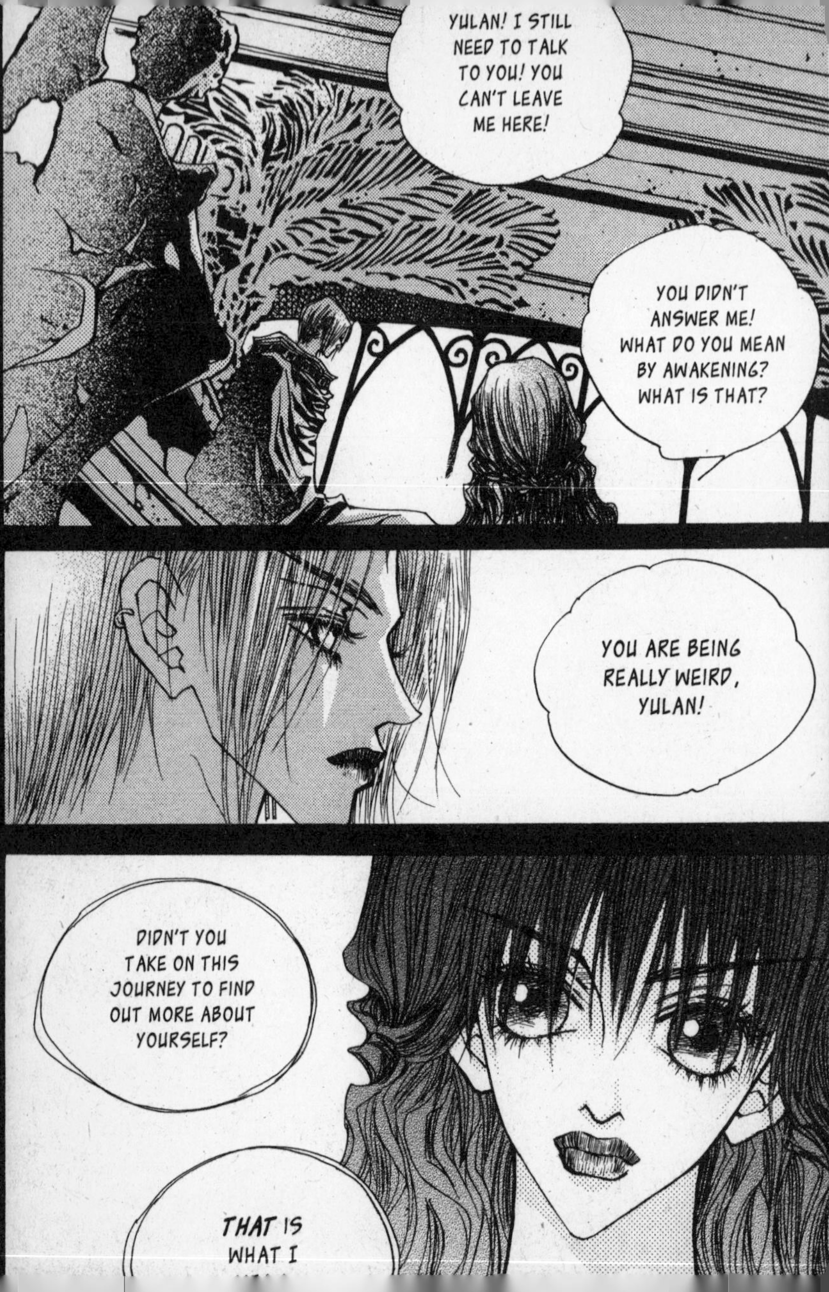
YULAN! I STILL NEED TO TALK TO YOU! YOU CAN'T LEAVE ME HERE!
YOU DIDN'T ANSWER ME! WHAT DO YOU MEAN BY AWAKENING? WHAT IS THAT?
YOU ARE BEING REALLY WEIRD, YULAN!
DIDN'T YOU TAKE ON THIS JOURNEY TO FIND OUT MORE ABOUT YOURSELF?
THAT IS WHAT I

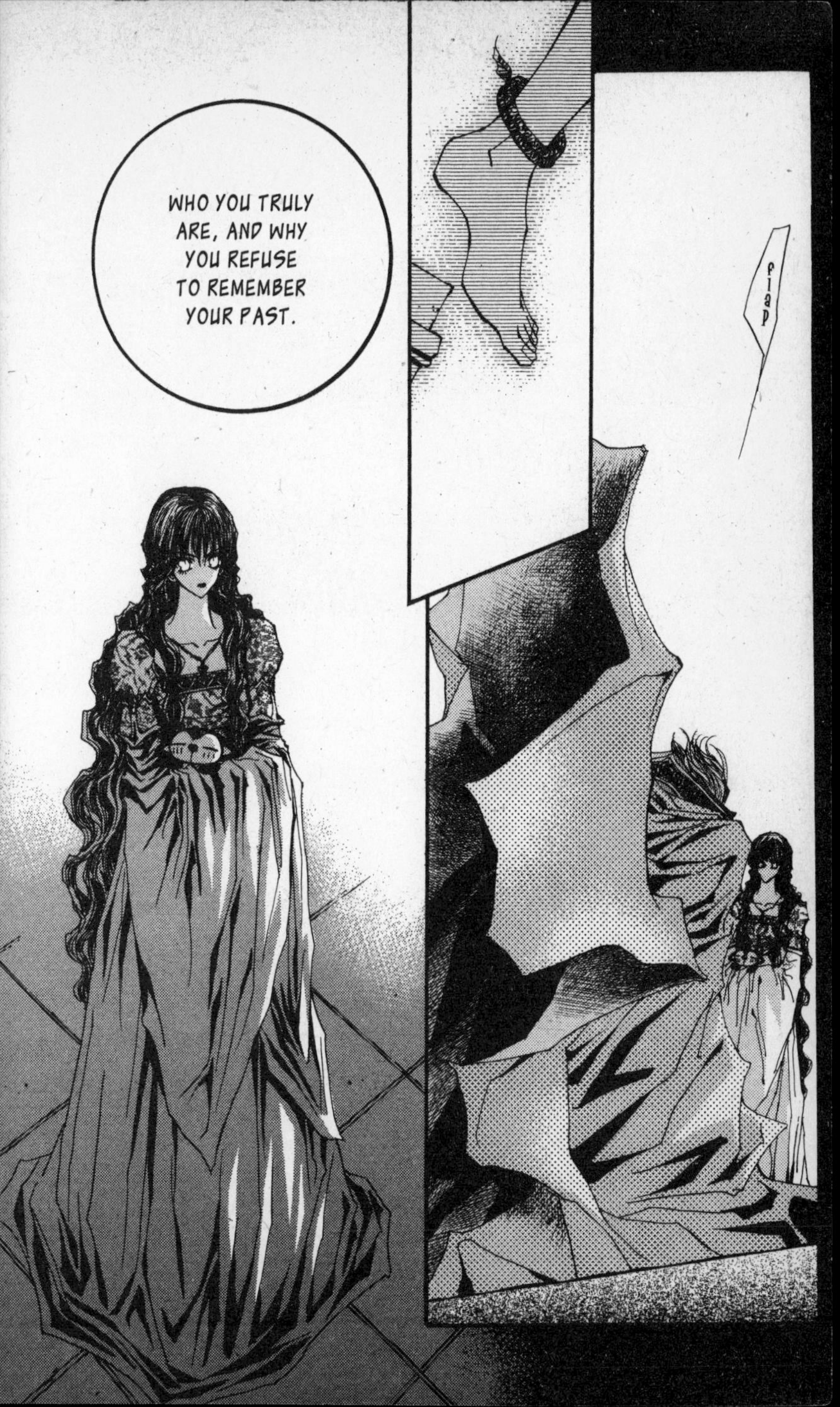
WHO YOU TRULY ARE, AND WHY YOU REFUSE TO REMEMBER YOUR PAST.
flap

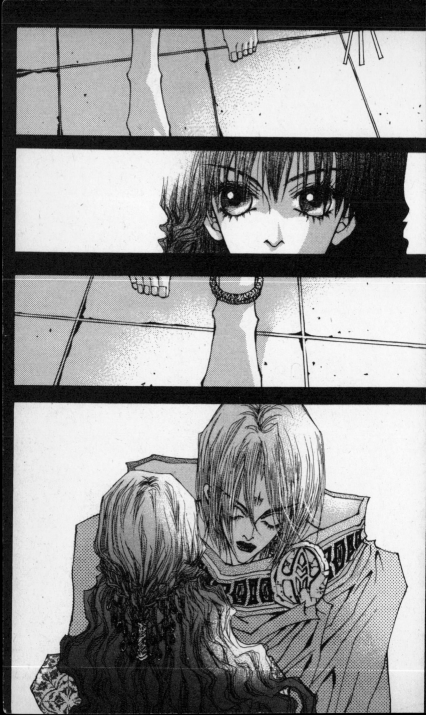

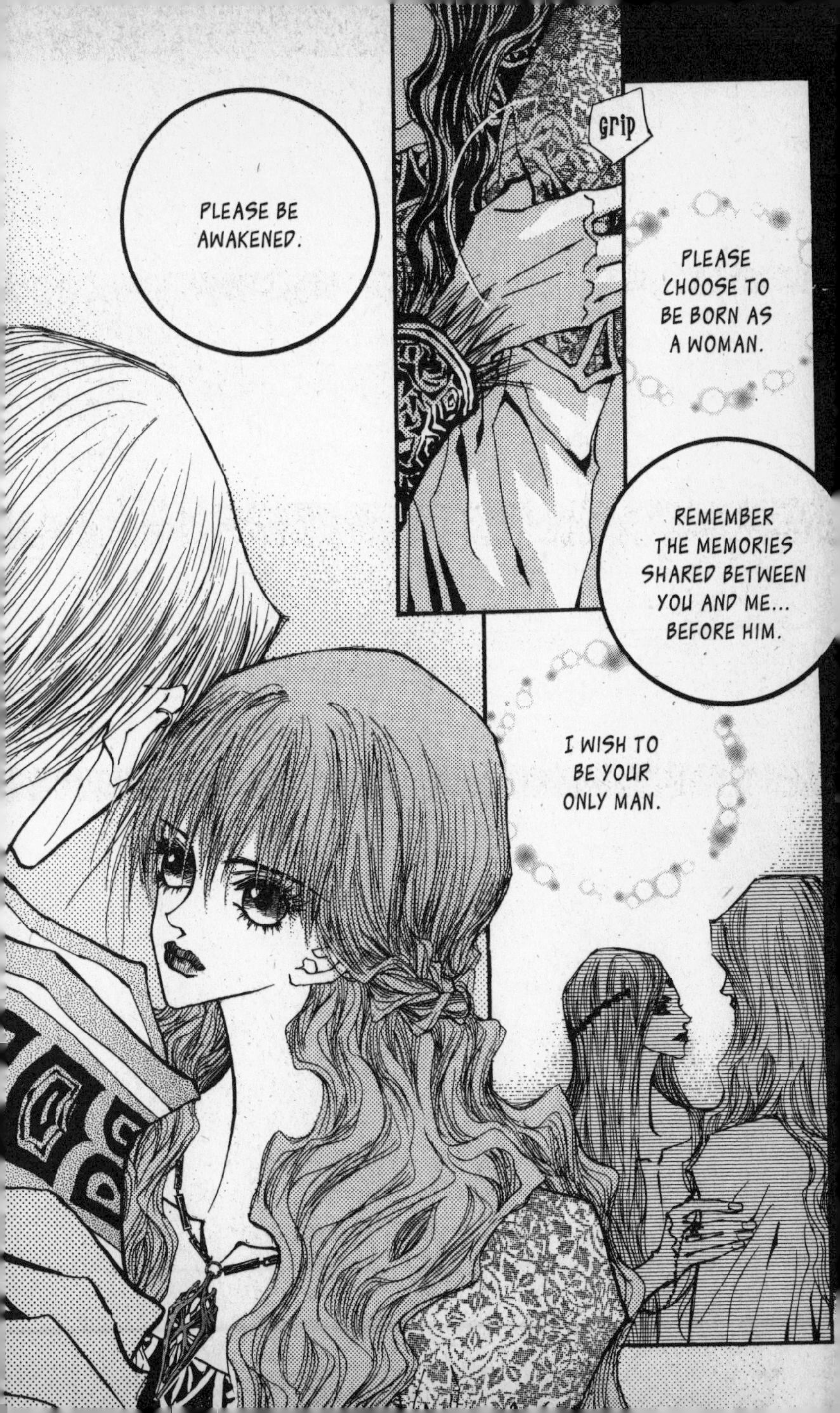
PLEASE BE AWAKENED.
Grip
PLEASE CHOOSE TO BE BORN AS A WOMAN.
REMEMBER THE MEMORIES SHARED BETWEEN YOU AND ME... BEFORE HIM.
I WISH TO BE YOUR ONLY MAN.

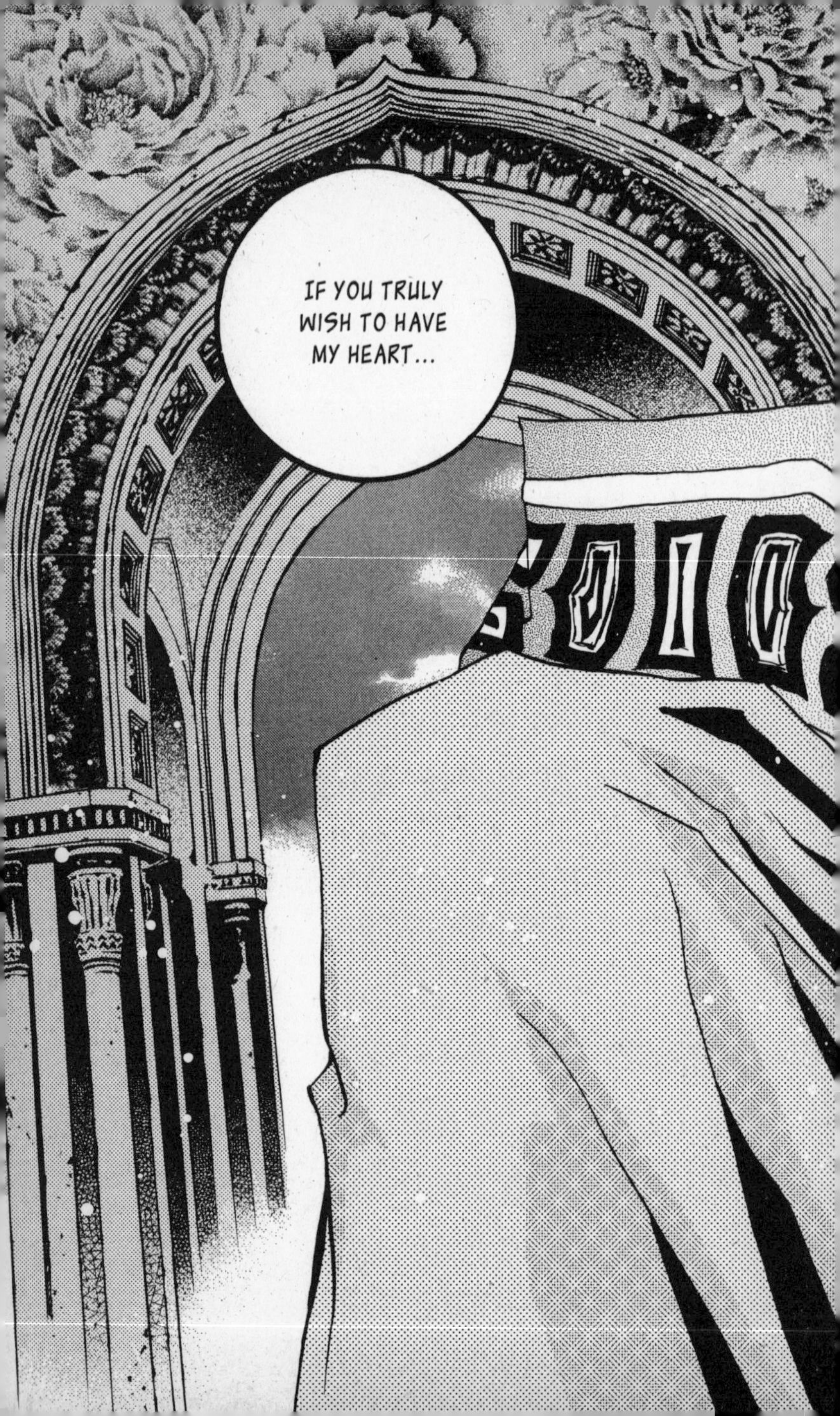
IF YOU TRULY WISH TO HAVE MY HEART...

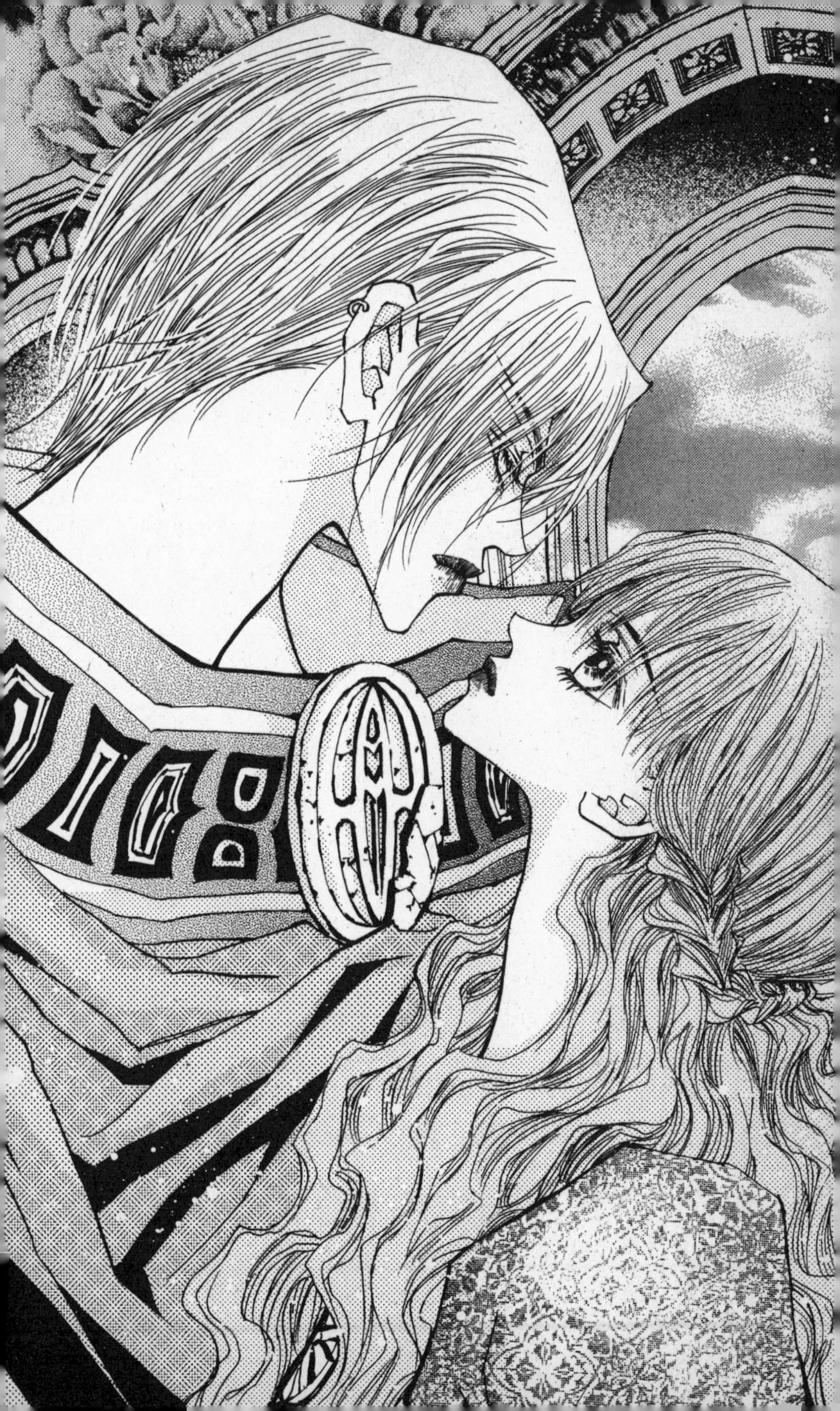

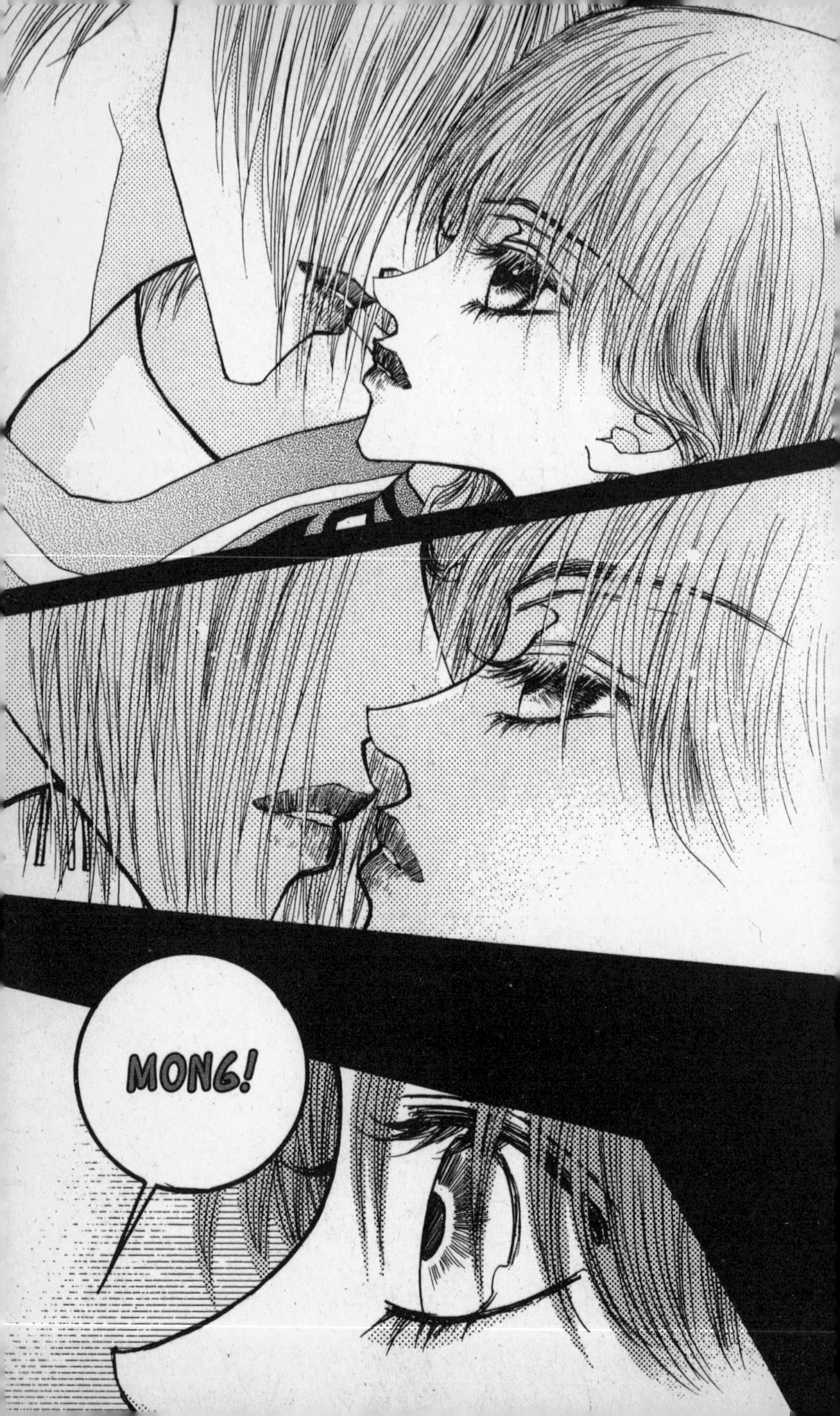
MONG!

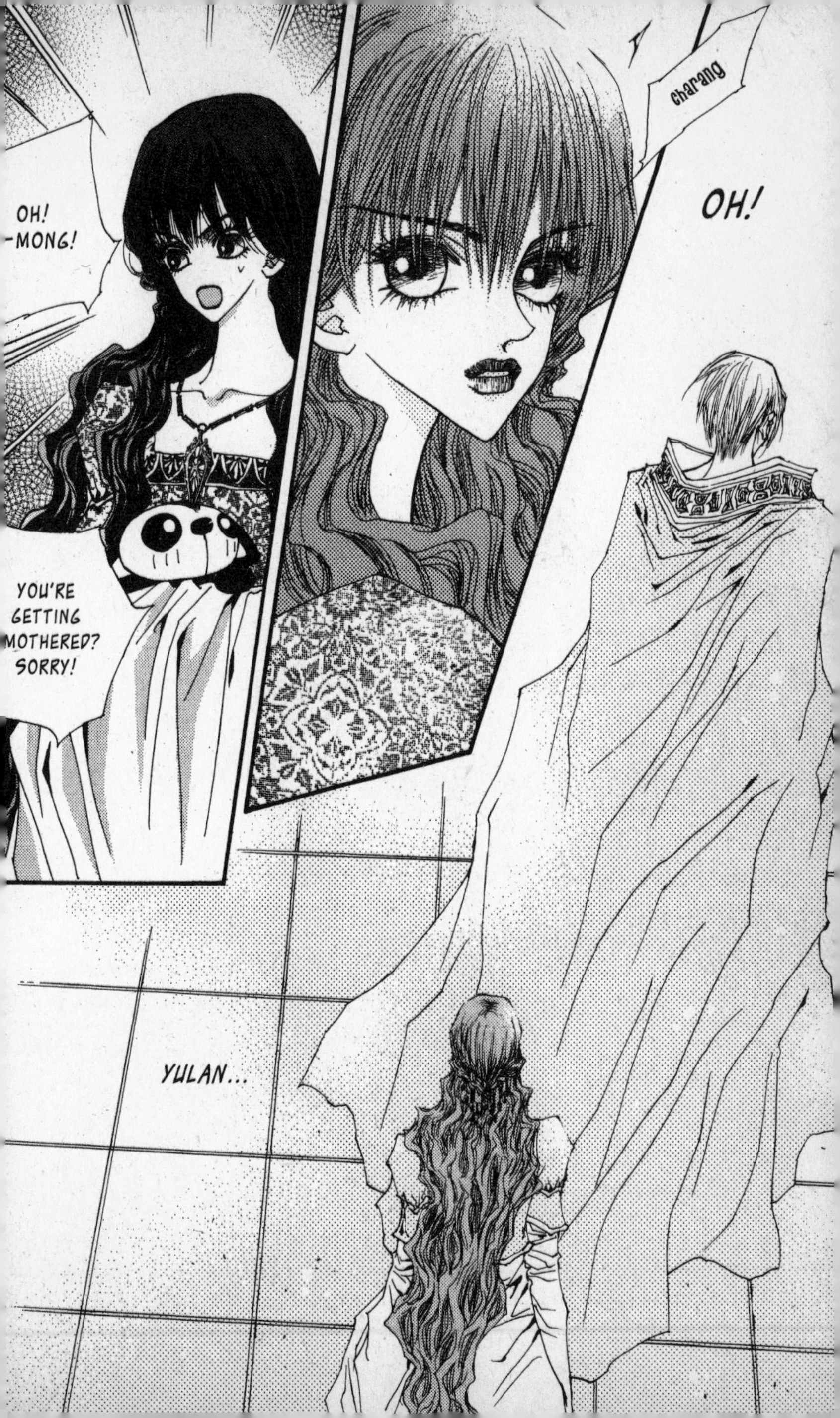

OH!
-MONG!
YOU'RE GETTING MOTHERED? SORRY!
charang
OH!
YULAN...

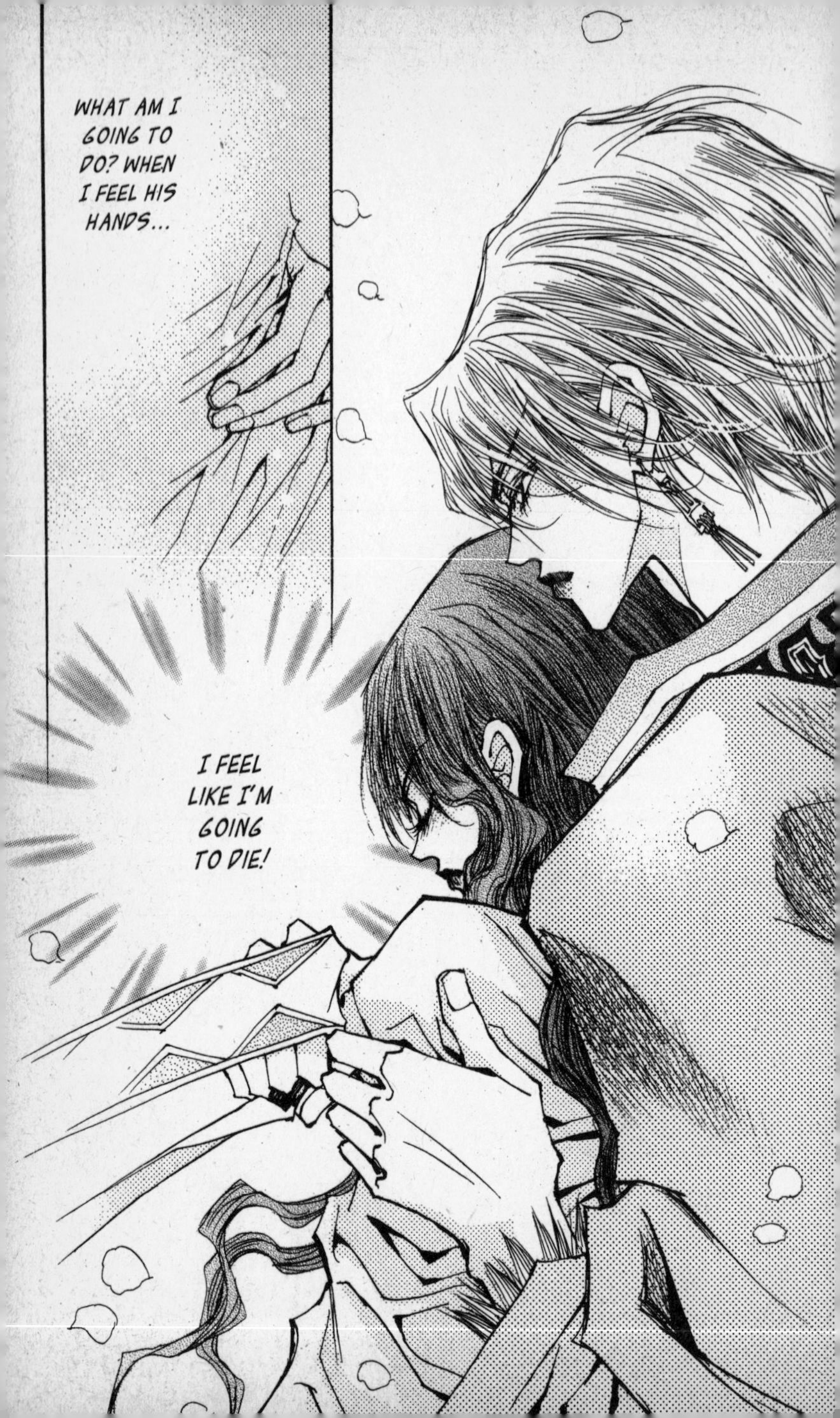
WHAT AM I GOING TO DO? WHEN I FEEL HIS HANDS...
I FEEL LIKE I'M GOING TO DIE!

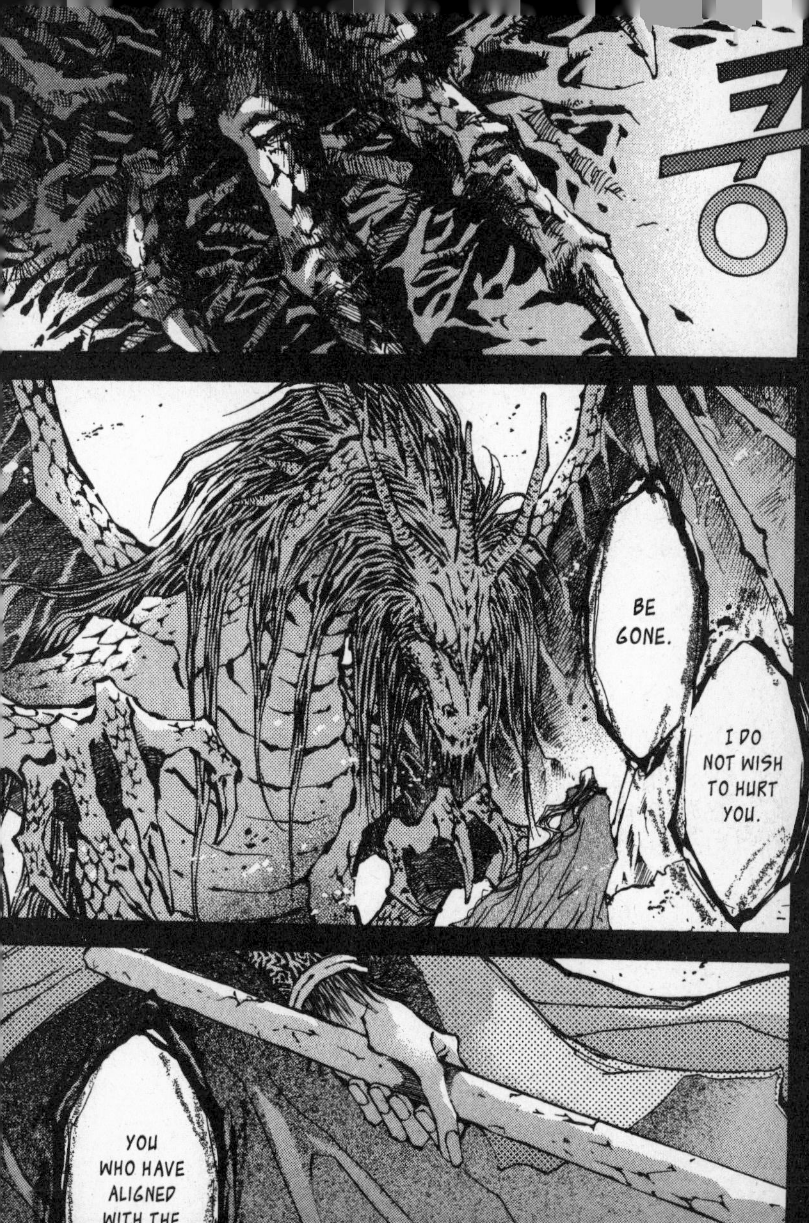
BE GONE.
I DO NOT WISH TO HURT YOU.
YOU WHO HAVE ALIGNED WITH THE HUMANS.

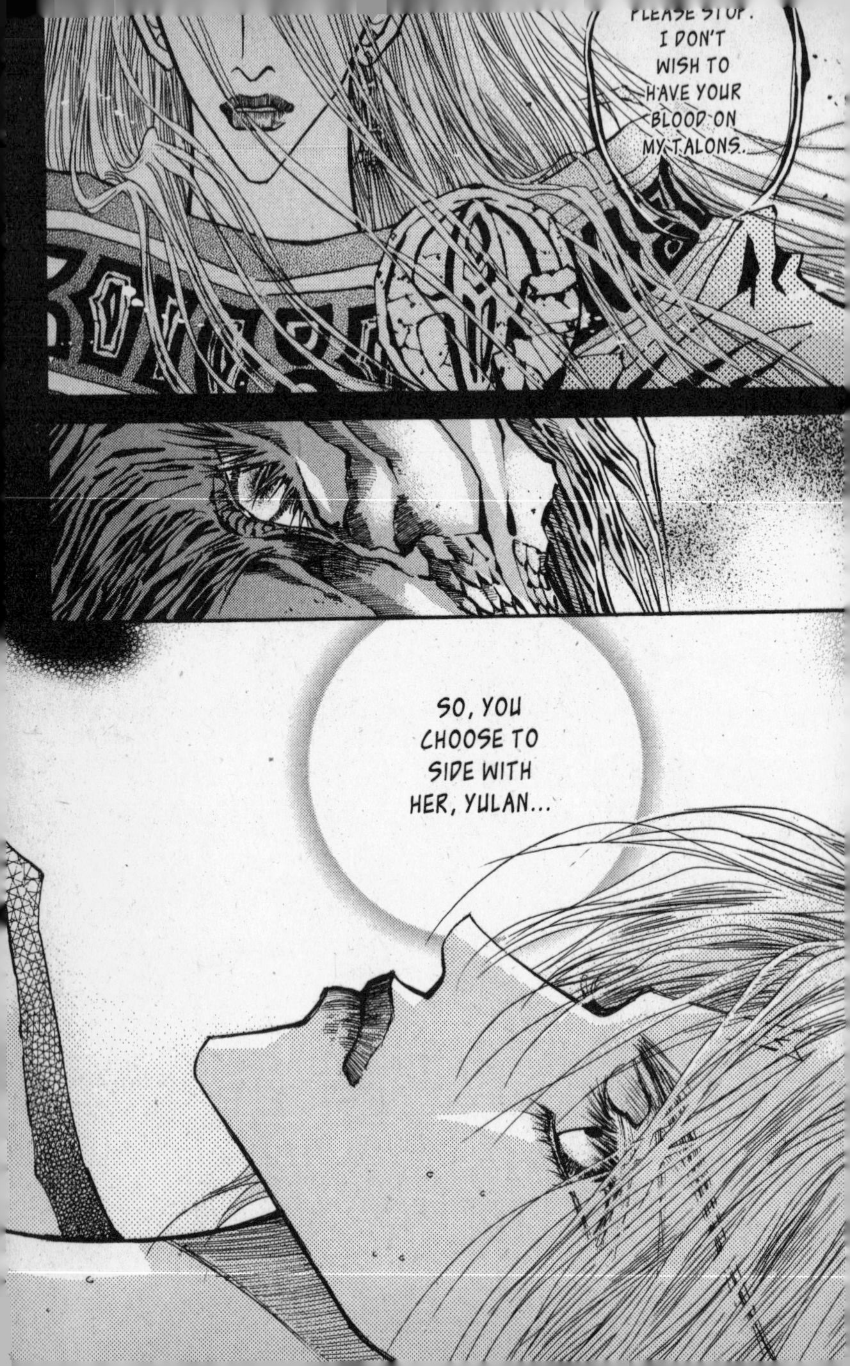
PLEASE STOP. I DON'T WISH TO HAVE YOUR BLOOD ON MY TALONS.
SO, YOU CHOOSE TO SIDE WITH HER, YULAN...

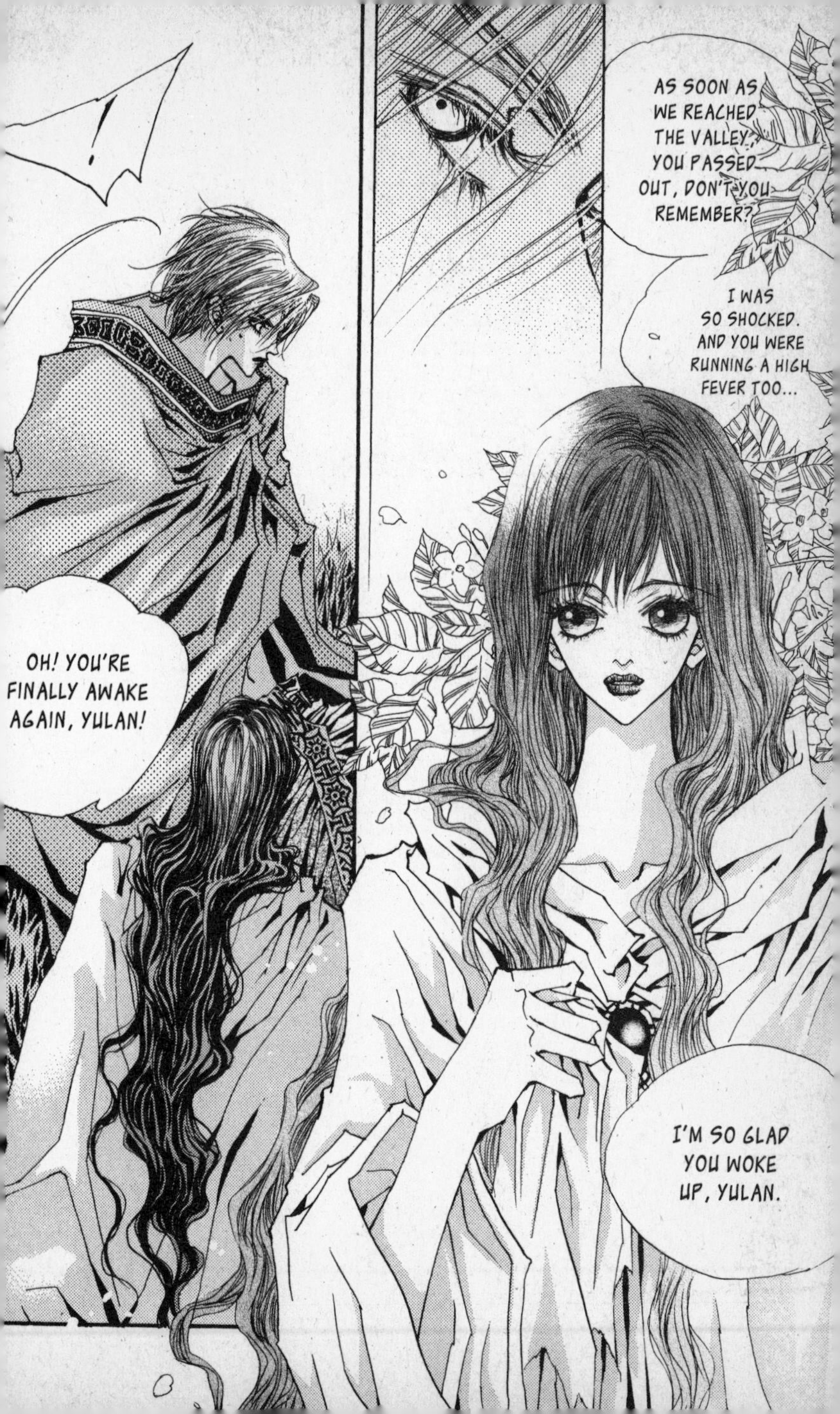
!
OH! YOU'RE FINALLY AWAKE AGAIN, YULAN!
AS SOON AS WE REACHED THE VALLEY, YOU PASSED OUT, DON'T YOU REMEMBER?
I WAS SO SHOCKED. AND YOU WERE RUNNING A HIGH FEVER TOO...
I'M SO GLAD YOU WOKE UP, YULAN.

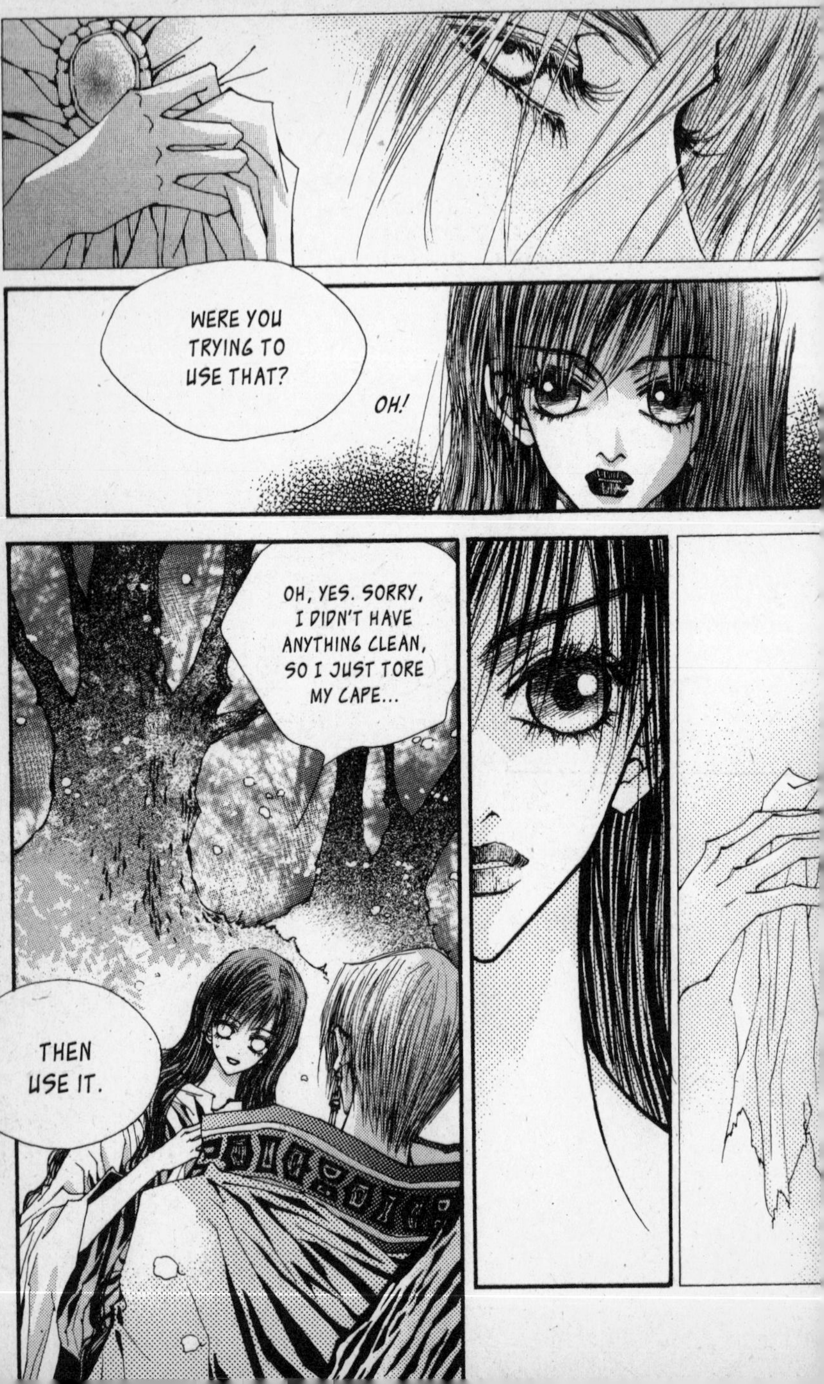
WERE YOU TRYING TO USE THAT?
OH!
OH, YES. SORRY, I DIDN'T HAVE ANYTHING CLEAN, SO I JUST TORE MY CAPE...
THEN USE IT.

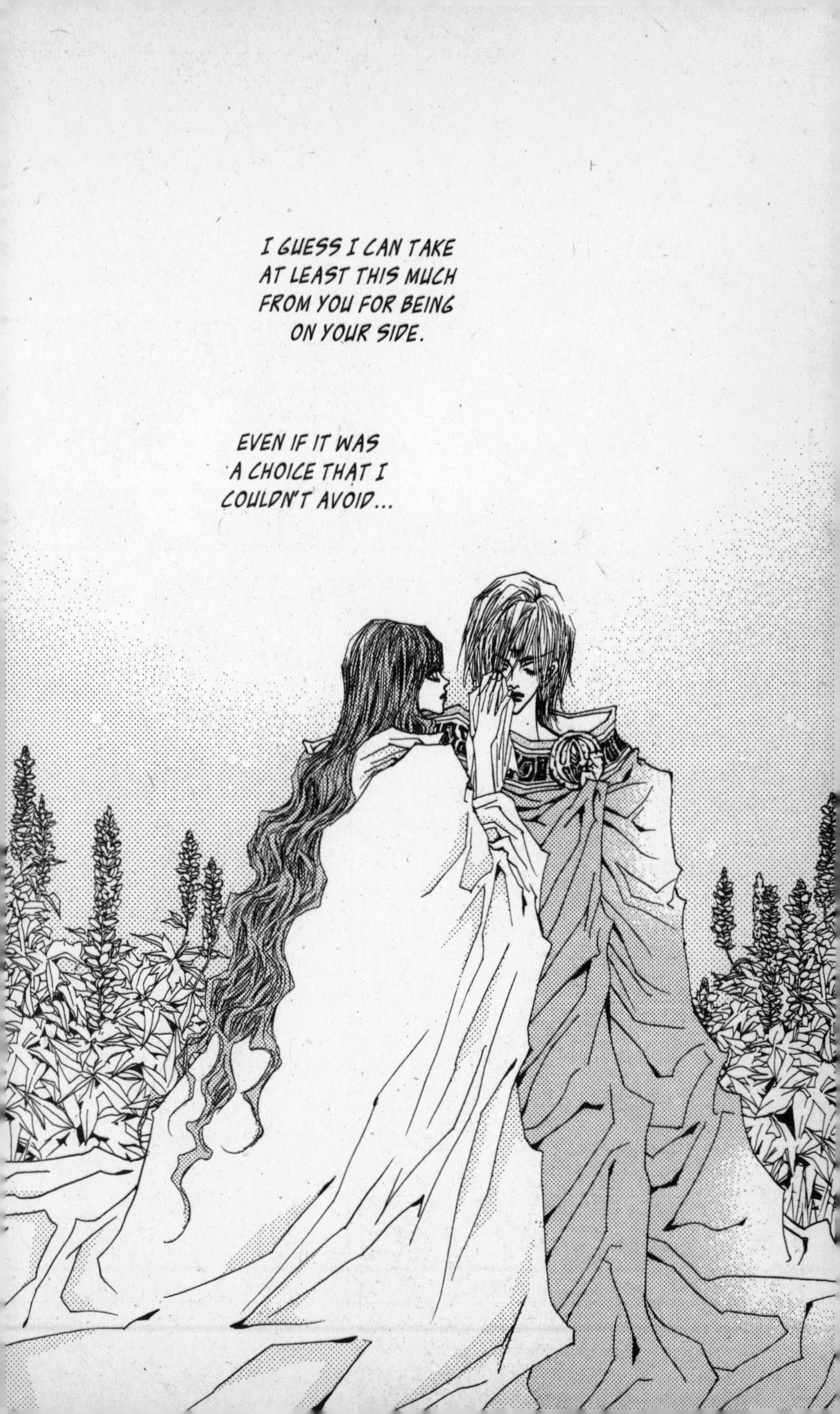
I GUESS I CAN TAKE AT LEAST THIS MUCH FROM YOU FOR BEING ON YOUR SIDE.
EVEN IF IT WAS A CHOICE THAT I COULDN'T AVOID...

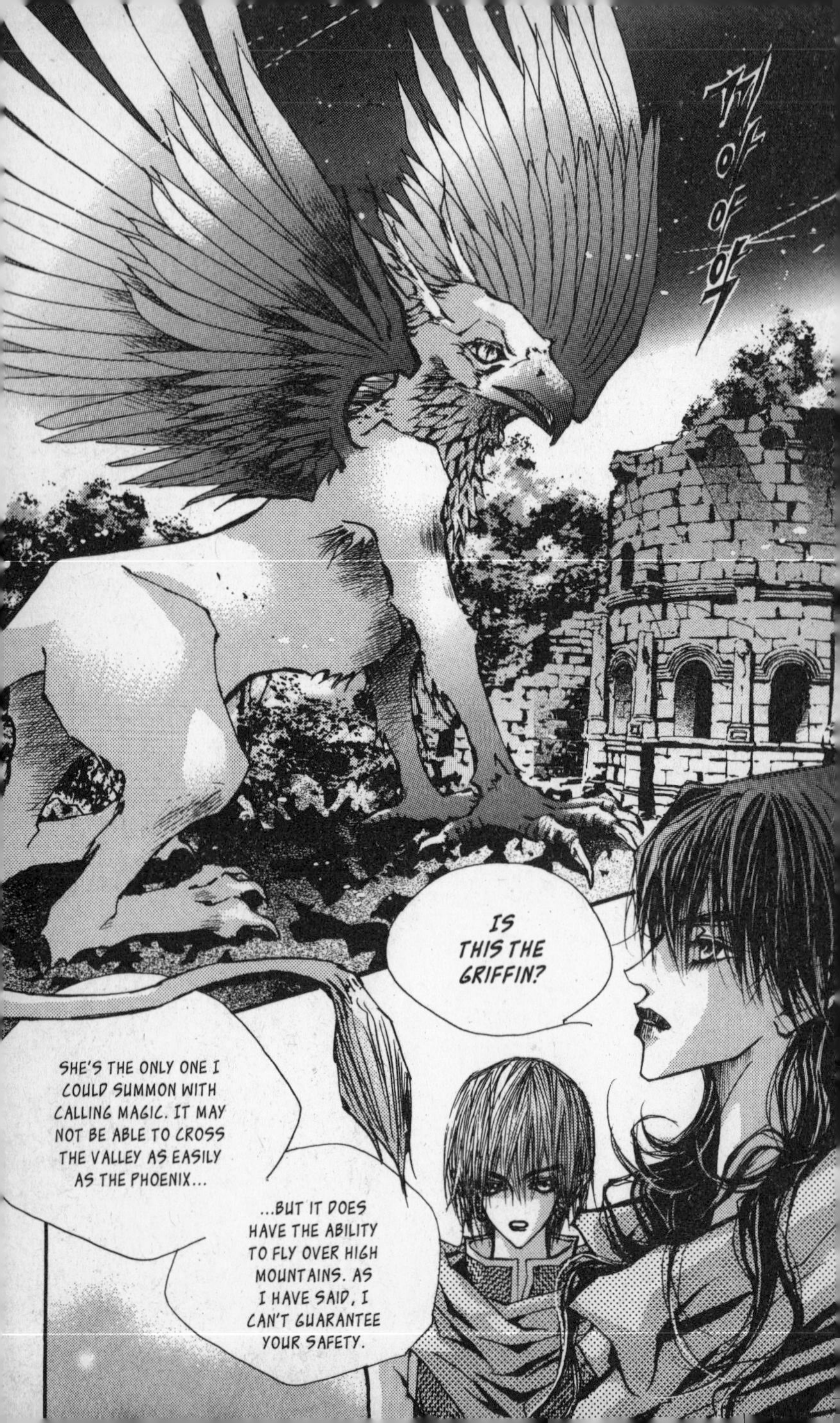
IS THIS THE GRIFFIN?
SHE'S THE ONLY ONE I COULD SUMMON WITH CALLING MAGIC. IT MAY NOT BE ABLE TO CROSS THE VALLEY AS EASILY AS THE PHOENIX...
...BUT IT DOES HAVE THE ABILITY TO FLY OVER HIGH MOUNTAINS. AS I HAVE SAID, I CAN'T GUARANTEE YOUR SAFETY.

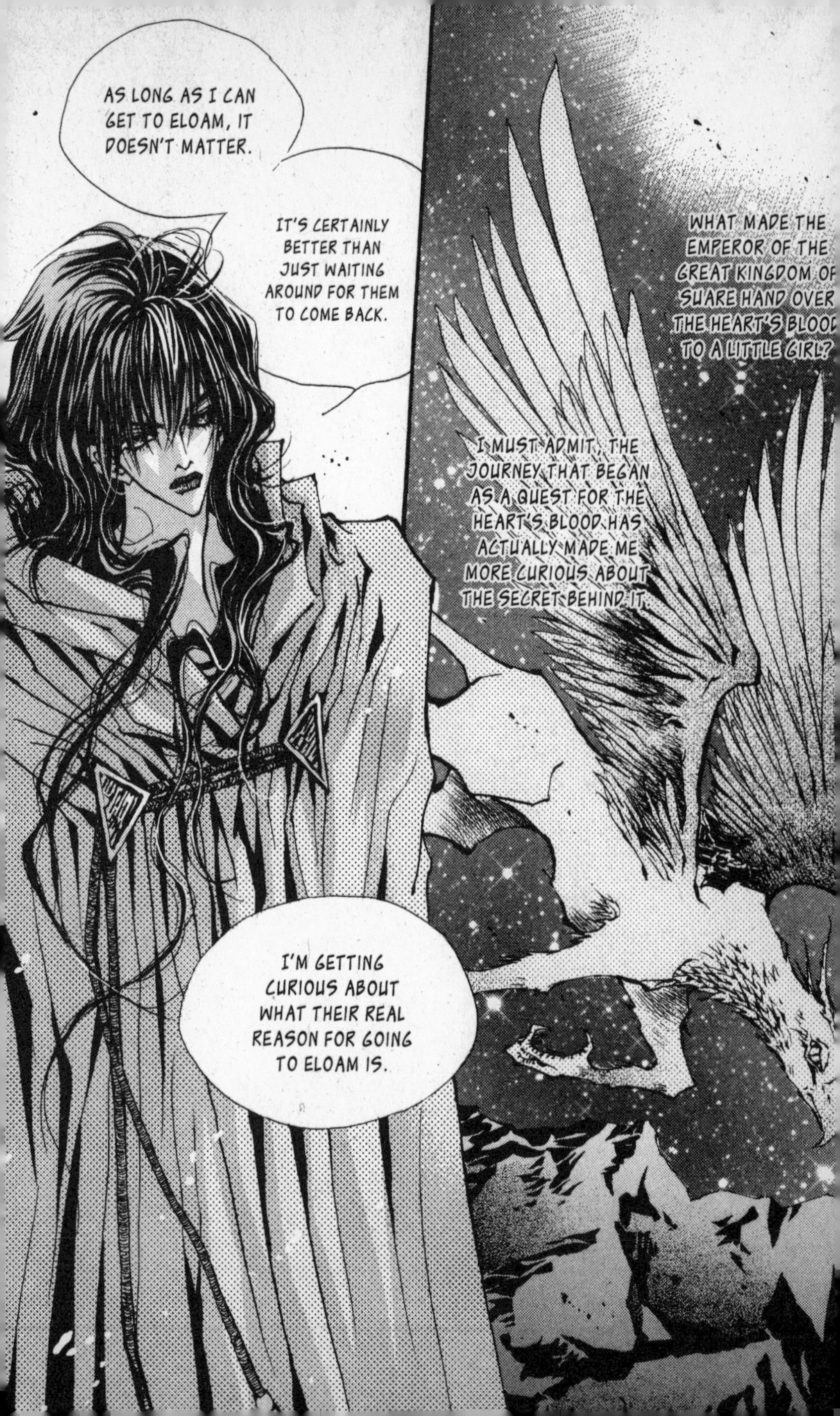
AS LONG AS I CAN GET TO ELOAM, IT DOESN'T MATTER.
IT'S CERTAINLY BETTER THAN JUST WAITING AROUND FOR THEM TO COME BACK.
I'M GETTING CURIOUS ABOUT WHAT THEIR REAL REASON FOR GOING TO ELOAM IS.
WHAT MADE THE EMPEROR OF THE GREAT KINGDOM OF SUARE HAND OVER THE HEART'S BLOOD TO A LITTLE GIRL?
I MUST ADMIT, THE JOURNEY THAT BEGAN AS A QUEST FOR THE HEART'S BLOOD HAS ACTUALLY MADE ME MORE CURIOUS ABOUT THE SECRET BEHIND IT.

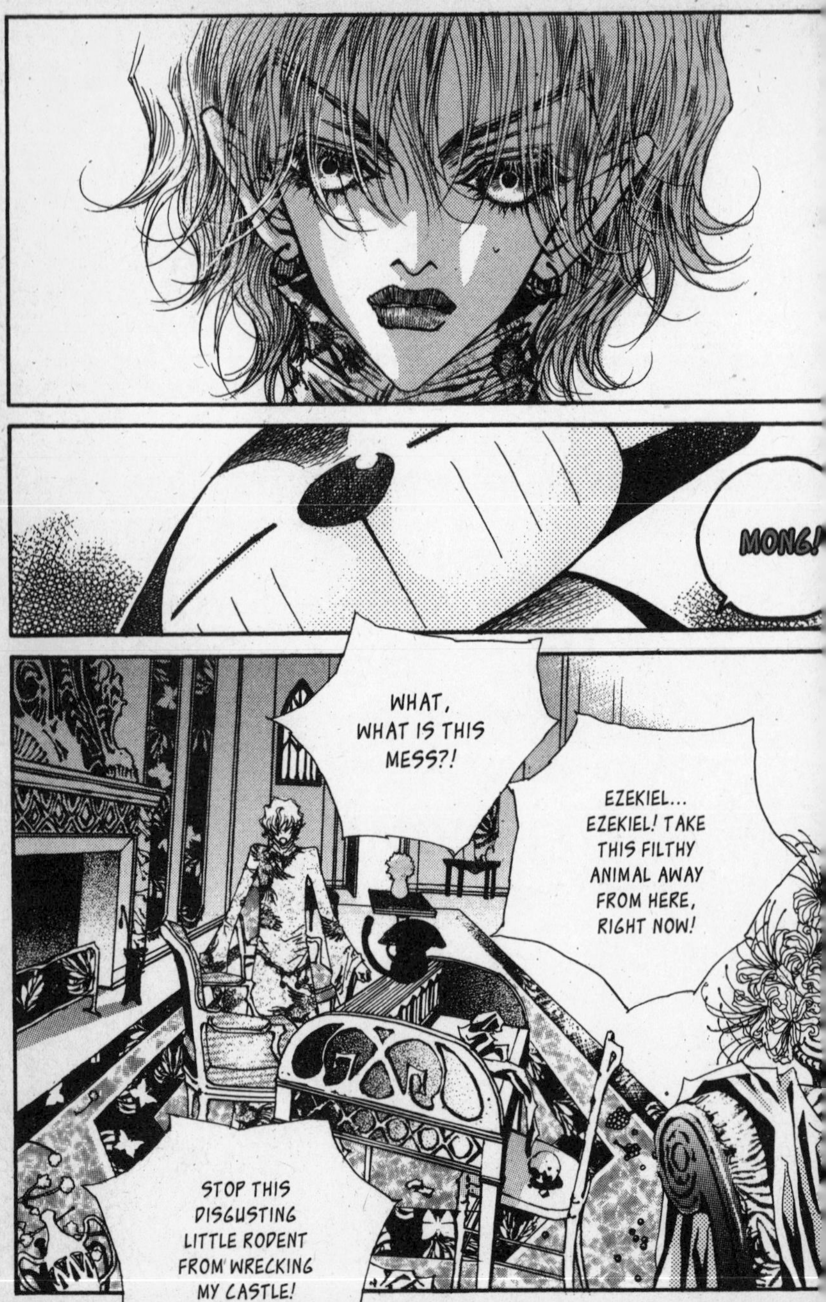
MONG!
WHAT, WHAT IS THIS MESS?!
EZEKIEL... EZEKIEL! TAKE THIS FILTHY ANIMAL AWAY FROM HERE, RIGHT NOW!
STOP THIS DISGUSTING LITTLE RODENT FROM WRECKING MY CASTLE!

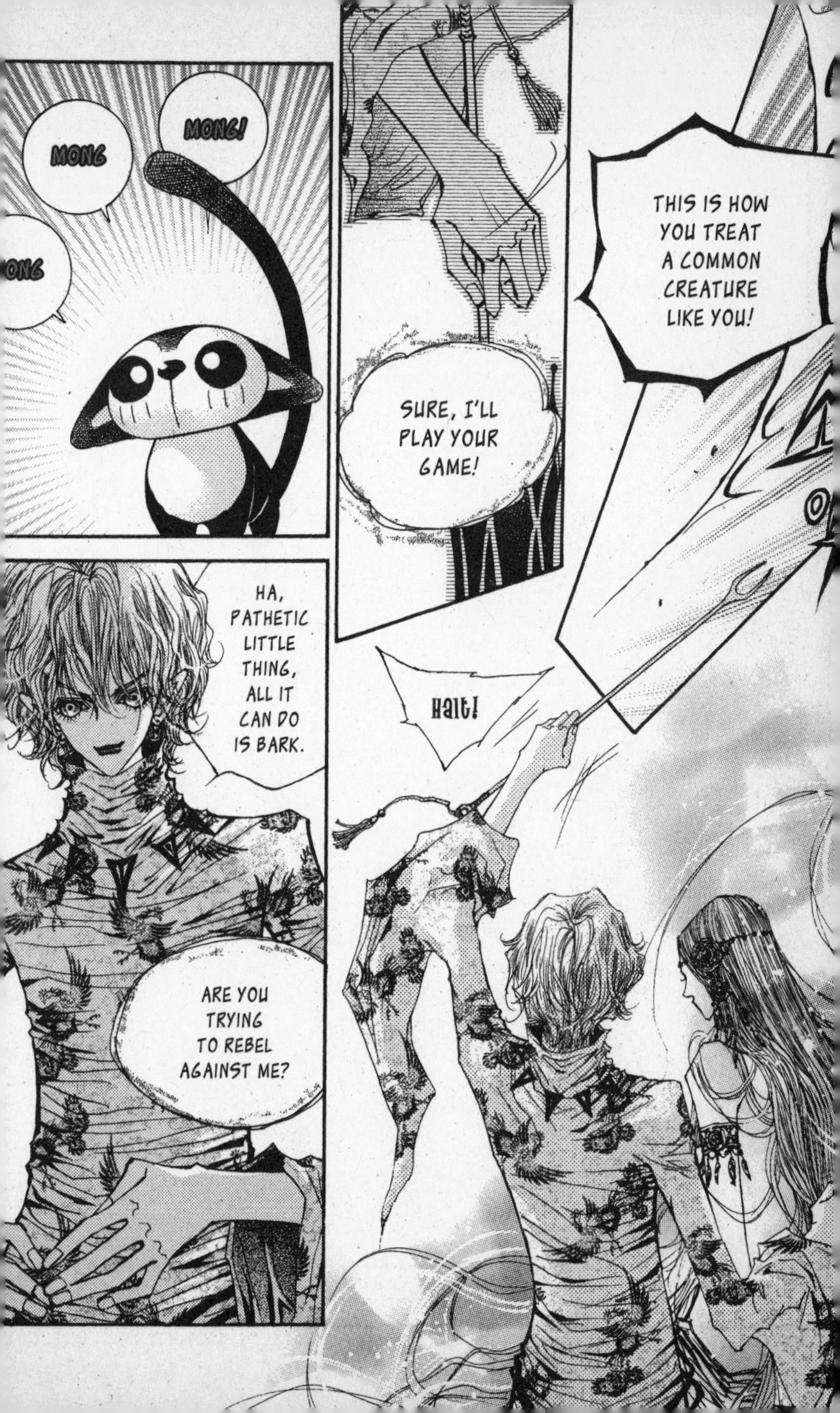
MONG
MONG!
ONG
SURE, I'LL PLAY YOUR GAME!
THIS IS HOW YOU TREAT A COMMON CREATURE LIKE YOU!
HA, PATHETIC LITTLE THING, ALL IT CAN DO IS BARK.
ARE YOU TRYING TO REBEL AGAINST ME?
Halt!

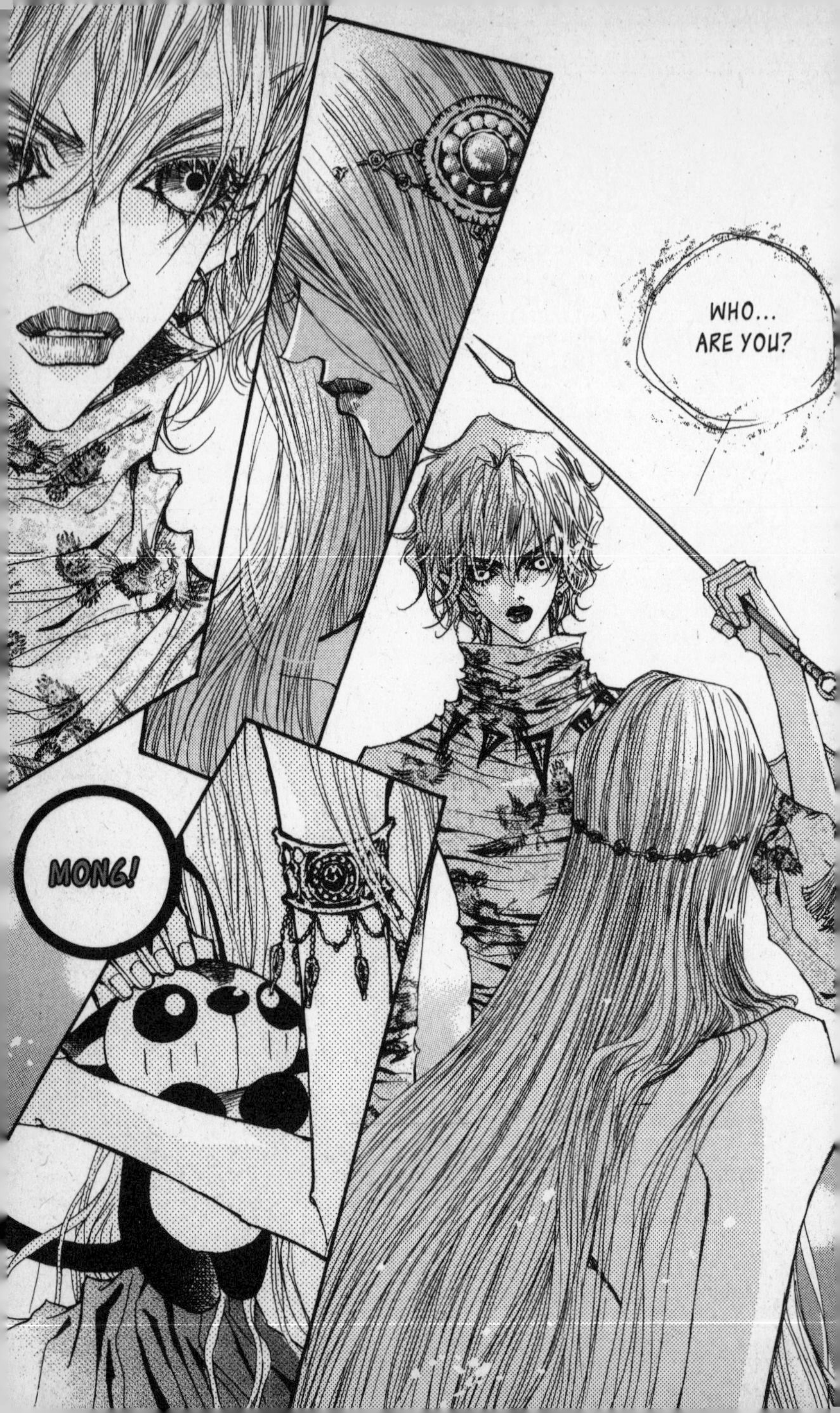
MONG!
WHO... ARE YOU?

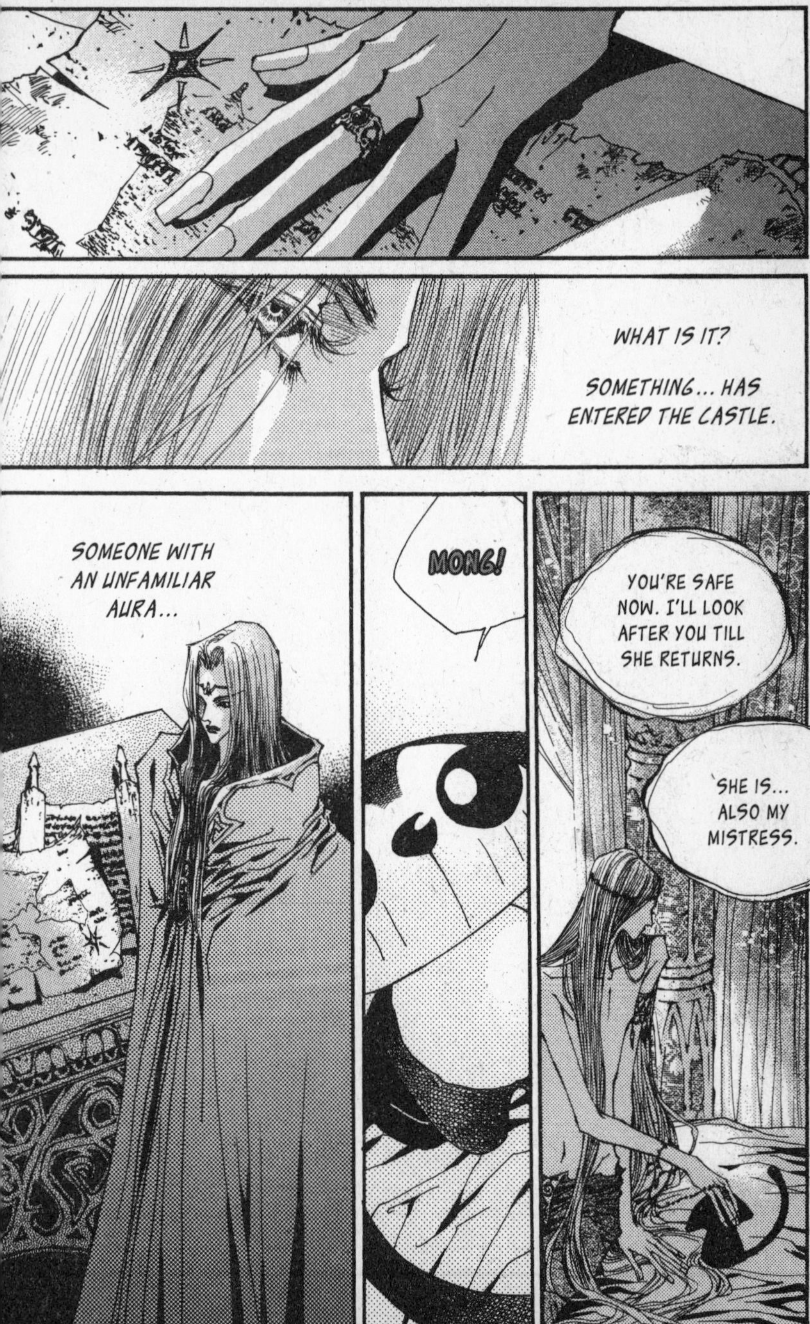
WHAT IS IT?
SOMETHING... HAS ENTERED THE CASTLE.
SOMEONE WITH AN UNFAMILIAR AURA...
MONG!
YOU'RE SAFE NOW. I'LL LOOK AFTER YOU TILL SHE RETURNS.
SHE IS... ALSO MY MISTRESS.

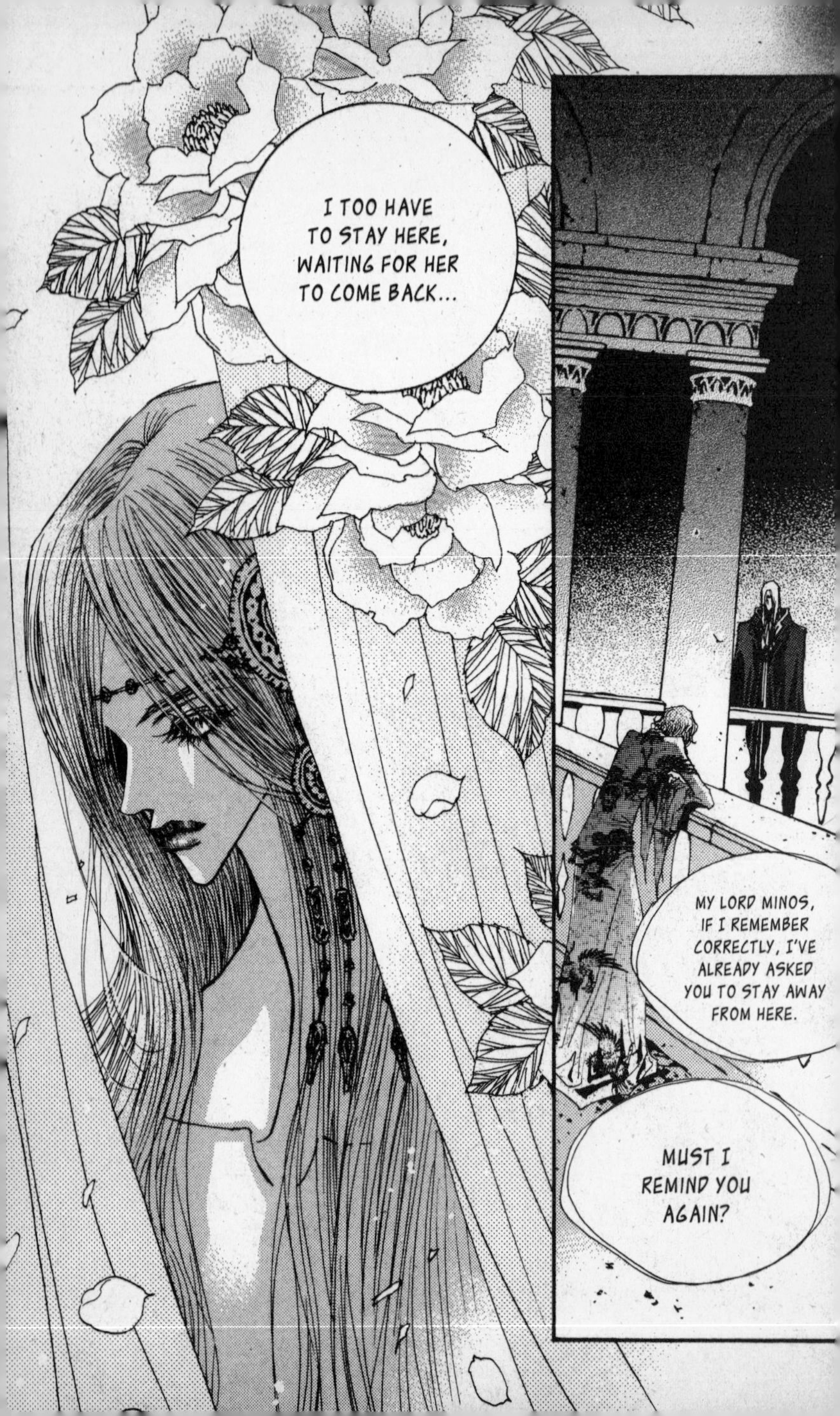
I TOO HAVE TO STAY HERE, WAITING FOR HER TO COME BACK...
MY LORD MINOS, IF I REMEMBER CORRECTLY, I'VE ALREADY ASKED YOU TO STAY AWAY FROM HERE.
MUST I REMIND YOU AGAIN?

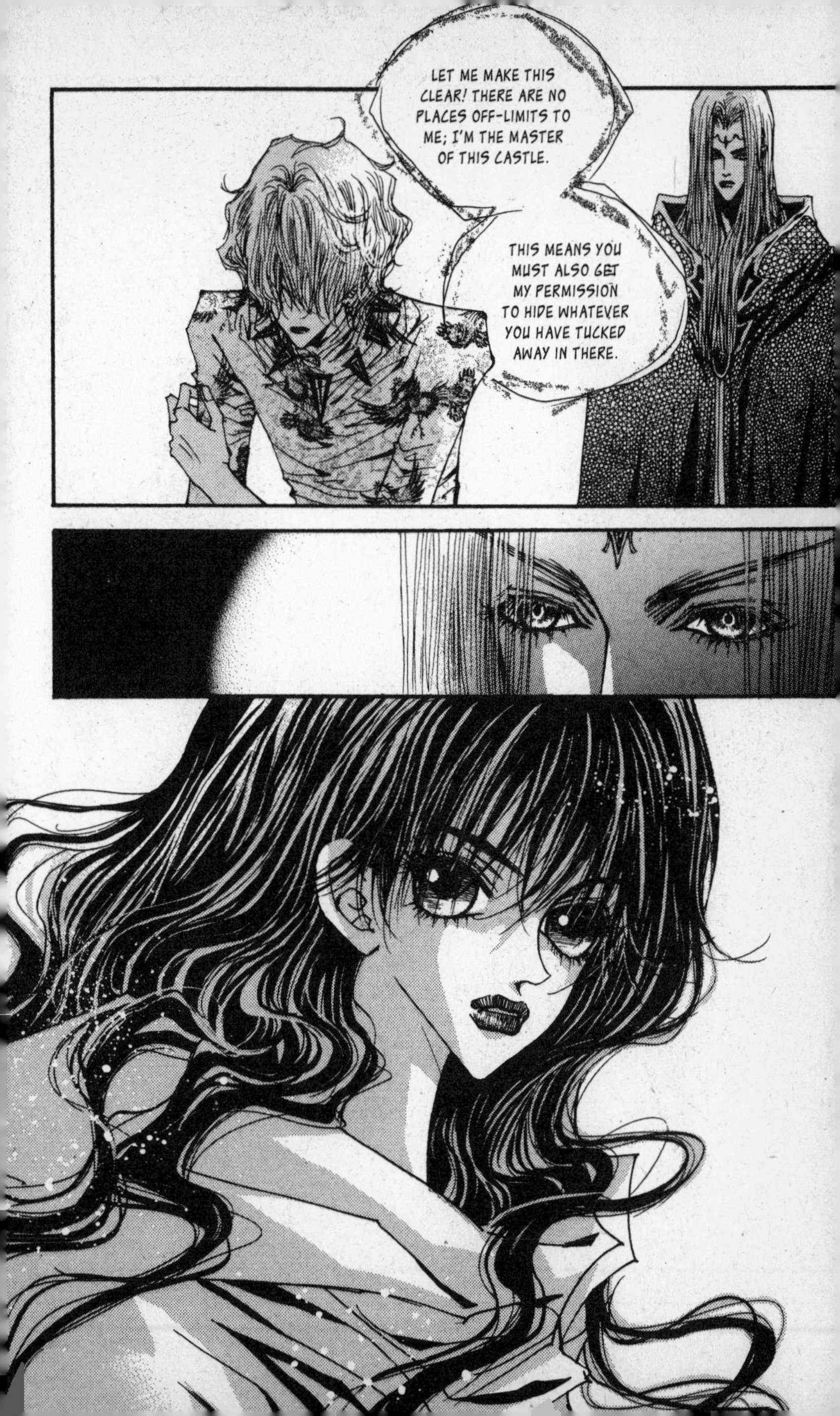
LET ME MAKE THIS CLEAR! THERE ARE NO PLACES OFF-LIMITS TO ME; I'M THE MASTER OF THIS CASTLE.
THIS MEANS YOU MUST ALSO GET MY PERMISSION TO HIDE WHATEVER YOU HAVE TUCKED AWAY IN THERE.

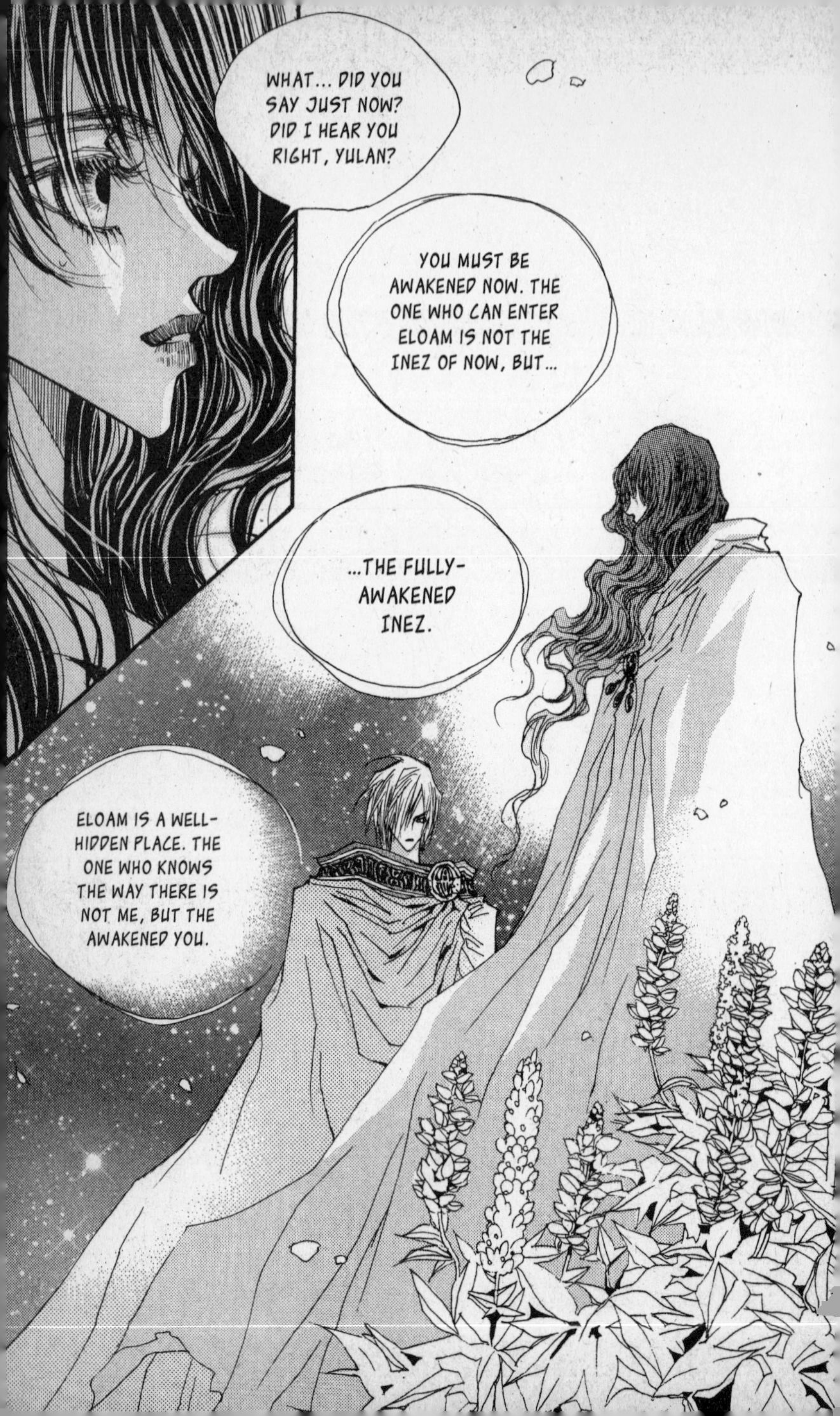
WHAT... DID YOU SAY JUST NOW? DID I HEAR YOU RIGHT, YULAN?
YOU MUST BE AWAKENED NOW. THE ONE WHO CAN ENTER ELOAM IS NOT THE INEZ OF NOW, BUT...
...THE FULLY-AWAKENED INEZ.
ELOAM IS A WELL-HIDDEN PLACE. THE ONE WHO KNOWS THE WAY THERE IS NOT ME, BUT THE AWAKENED YOU.

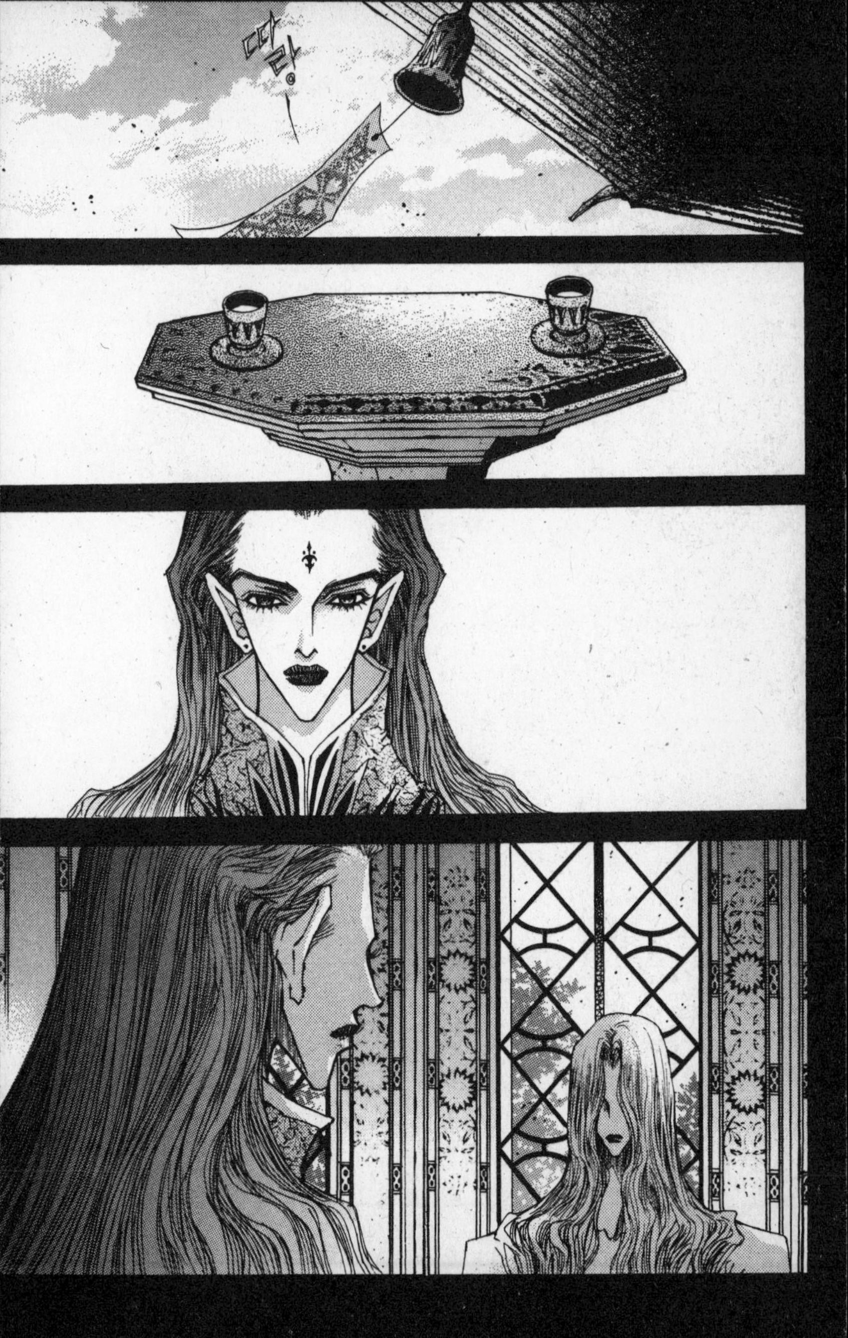
따랑-

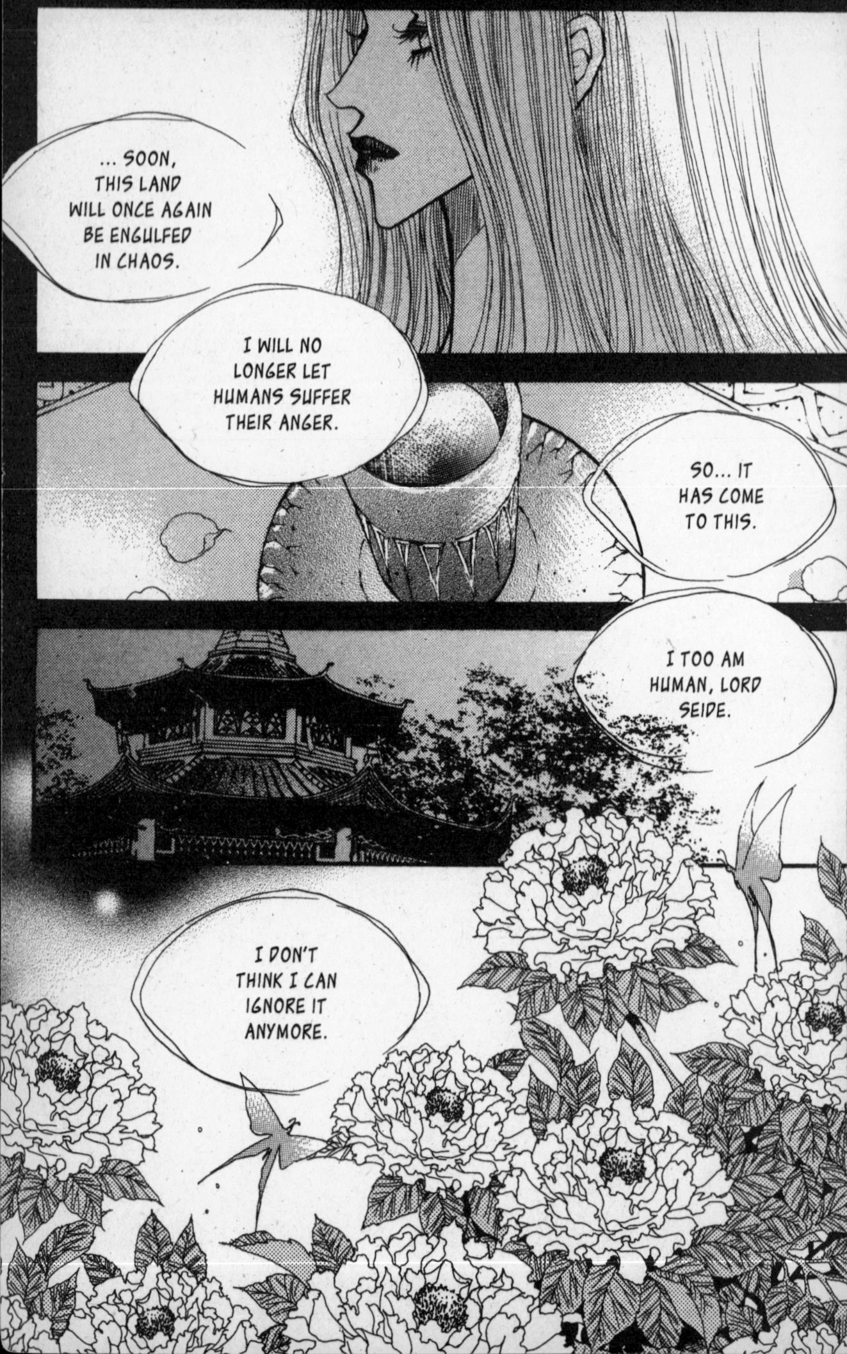
... SOON, THIS LAND WILL ONCE AGAIN BE ENGULFED IN CHAOS.
I WILL NO LONGER LET HUMANS SUFFER THEIR ANGER.
SO... IT HAS COME TO THIS.
I TOO AM HUMAN, LORD SEIDE.
I DON'T THINK I CAN IGNORE IT ANYMORE.

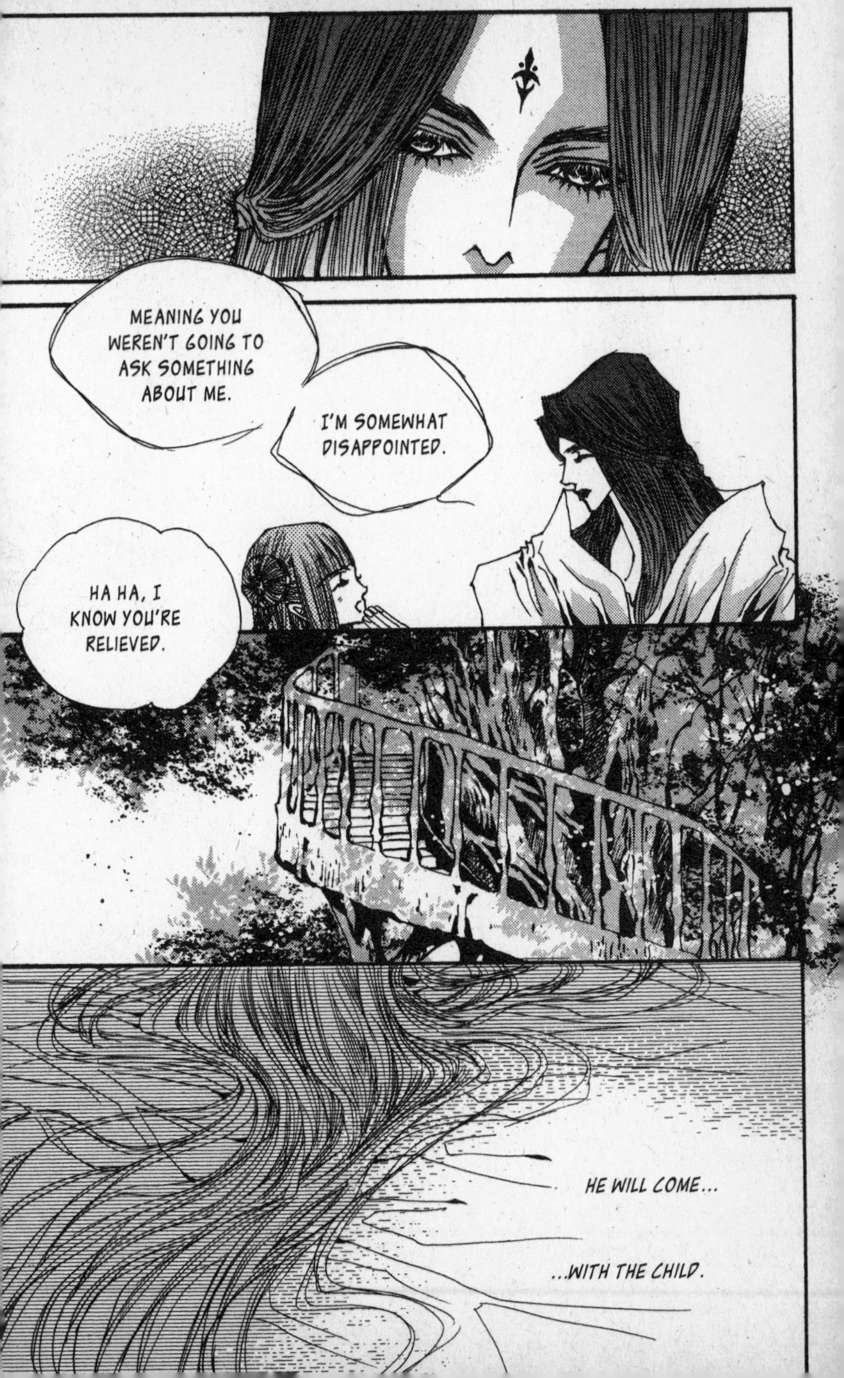
MEANING YOU WEREN'T GOING TO ASK SOMETHING ABOUT ME.
I'M SOMEWHAT DISAPPOINTED.
HA HA, I KNOW YOU'RE RELIEVED.
HE WILL COME...
...WITH THE CHILD.

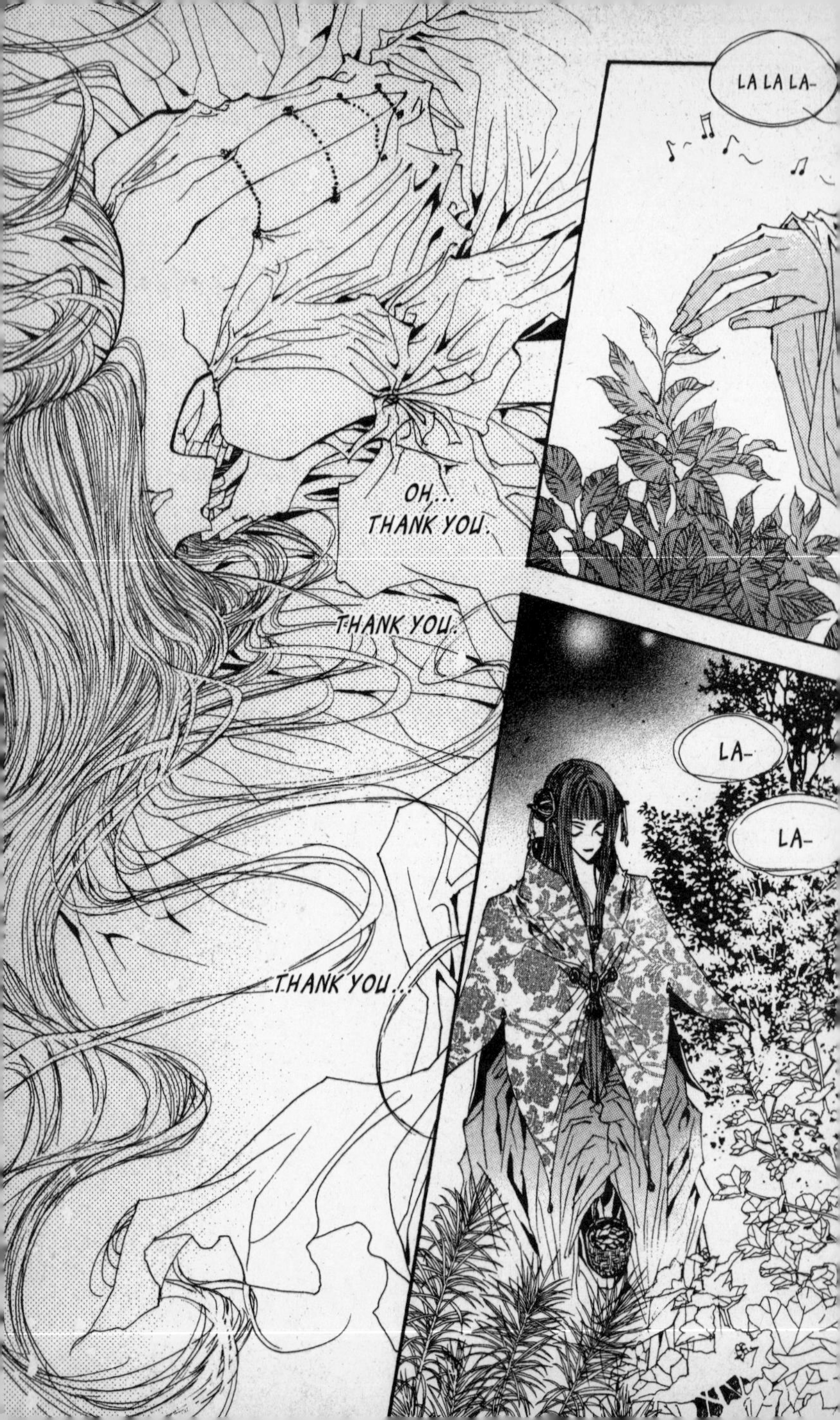
OH,...
THANK YOU.
THANK YOU.
THANK YOU...
LA LA LA-
LA-
LA-

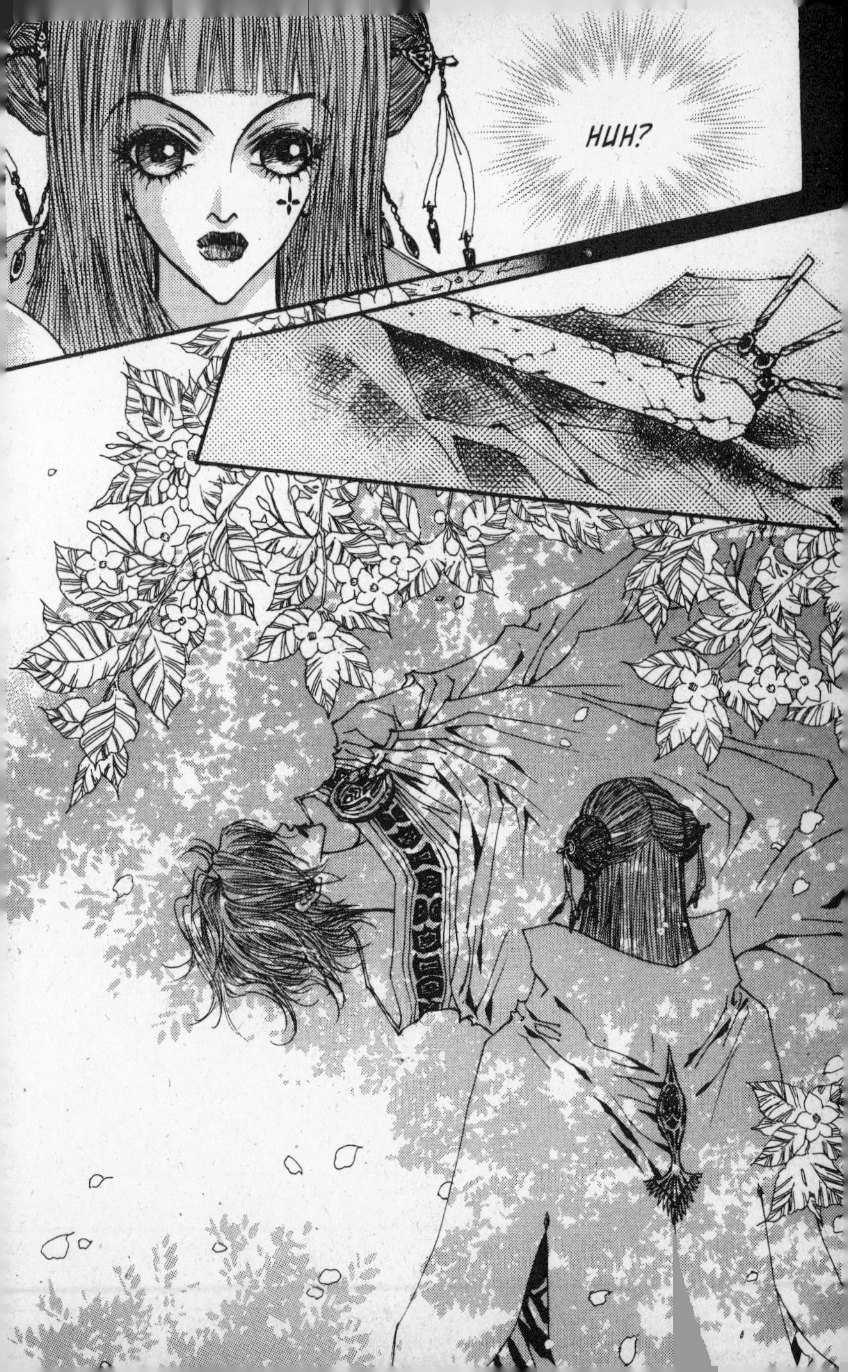
HUH?

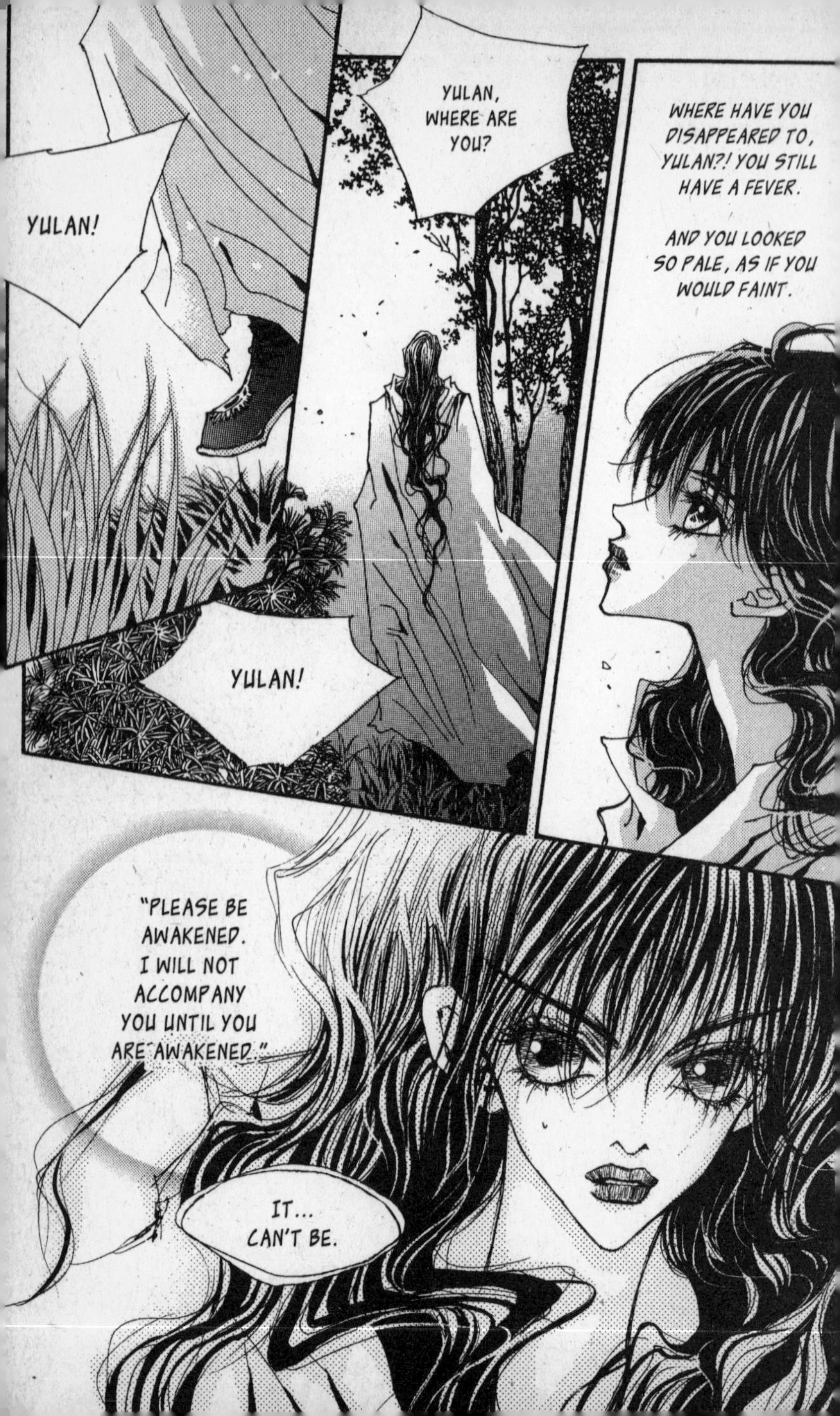
YULAN!
YULAN, WHERE ARE YOU?
YULAN!
WHERE HAVE YOU DISAPPEARED TO, YULAN?! YOU STILL HAVE A FEVER.
AND YOU LOOKED SO PALE, AS IF YOU WOULD FAINT.
"PLEASE BE AWAKENED. I WILL NOT ACCOMPANY YOU UNTIL YOU ARE AWAKENED."
IT... CAN'T BE.

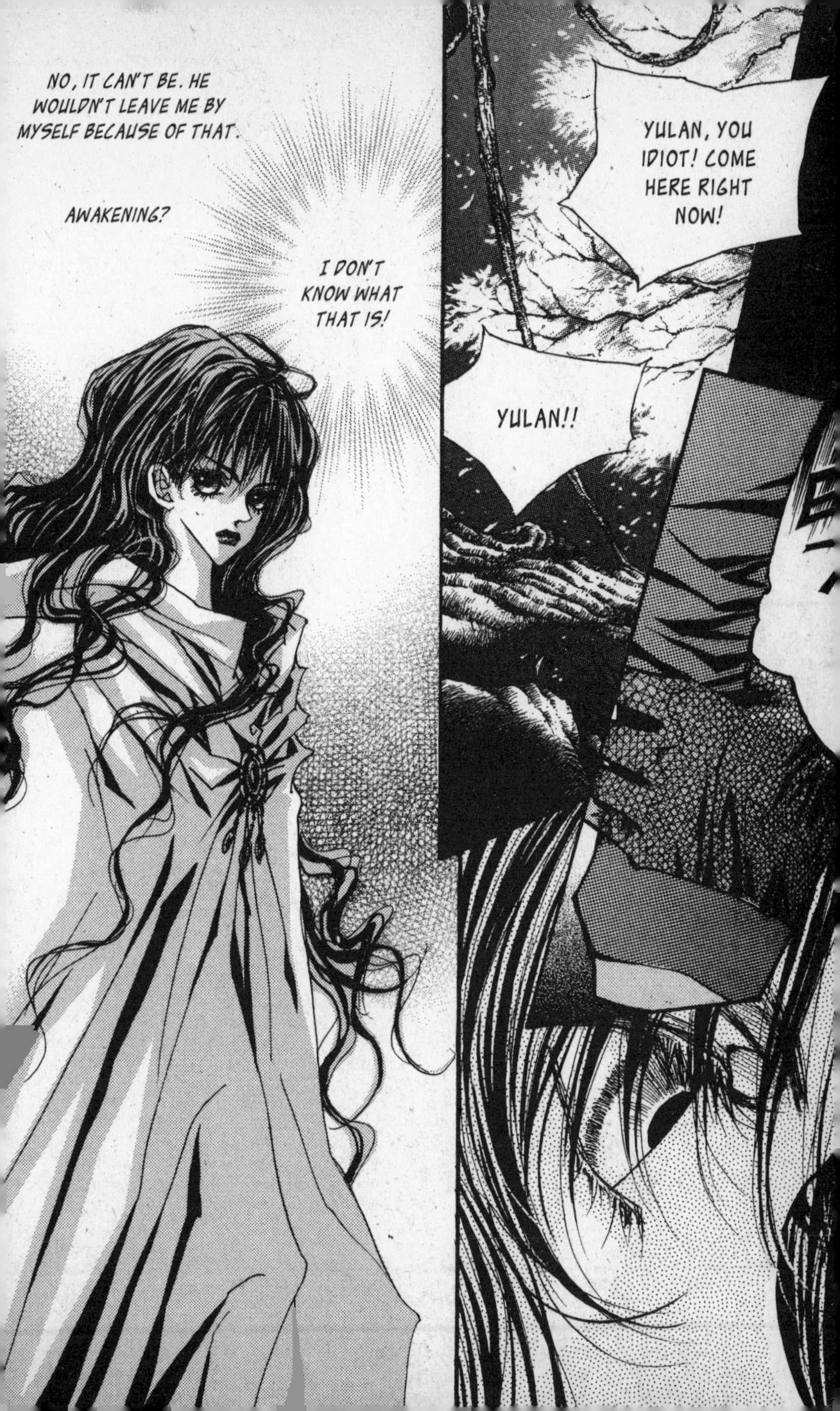
NO, IT CAN'T BE. HE WOULDN'T LEAVE ME BY MYSELF BECAUSE OF THAT.
AWAKENING?
I DON'T KNOW WHAT THAT IS!
YULAN, YOU IDIOT! COME HERE RIGHT NOW!
YULAN!!

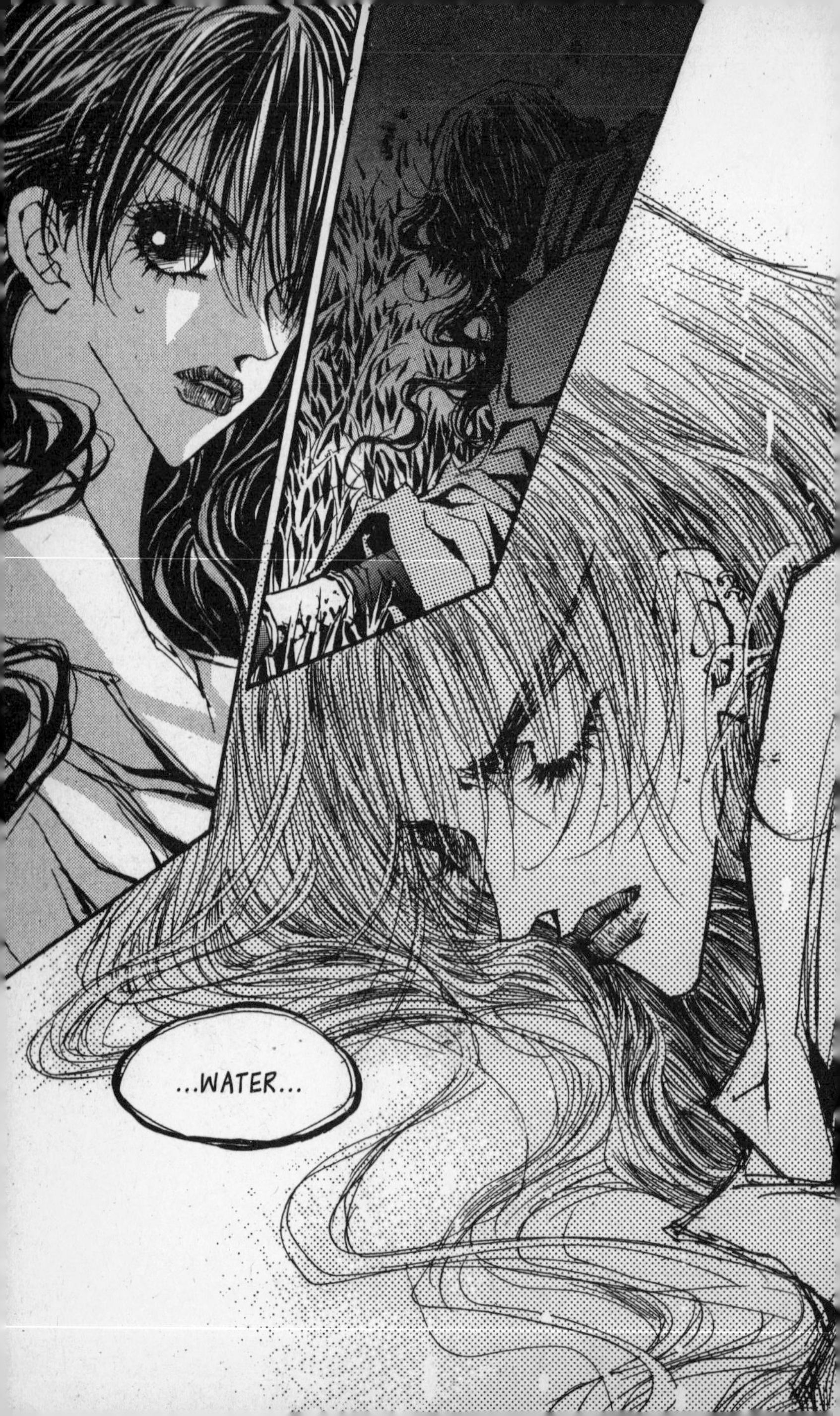
...WATER...